Authorized Self-Study Guide

Implementing Cisco Unified Communications Manager, Part 1 (CIPT1)

Dennis Hartmann, CCIE No.15651

Cisco Press

800 East 96th Street
Indianapolis, IN 46240 USA

Implementing Cisco Unified Communications Manager, Part 1 (CIPT1)

Dennis Hartmann

Copyright © 2008 Cisco Systems, Inc.

Published by:
Cisco Press
800 East 96th Street
Indianapolis, IN 46240 USA

Printed in the United States of America

First Printing May 2008

Library of Congress Cataloging-in-Publication Data:
Hartmann, Dennis.

 Cisco Unified Communications IP Telephony, part 1 (CIPT1 v6.0) /

Dennis Hartmann.

   p. cm.

 ISBN-13: 978-1-58705-483-9 (hardcover)

 ISBN-10: 1-58705-483-3 (hardcover)

 1. Internet telephony--Examinations--Study guides. I. Title.

 TK5105.8865.H38 2008

 621.385--dc22

2008014863

ISBN-13: 978-1-58705-483-9

ISBN-10: 1-58705-483-3

Warning and Disclaimer

Trademark Acknowledgments

Corporate and Government Sales

The publisher offers excellent discounts on this book when ordered in quantity for bulk purchases or special sales, which may include electronic versions or custom covers and content particular to your business, training goals, marketing focus, and branding interests. For more information, please contact: **U.S. Corporate and Government Sales**
1-800-382-3419   corpsales@pearsontechgroup.com

For sales outside the United States, please contact: **International Sales**   international@pearsoned.com

The Cisco Press self-study book series is as described, intended for self-study. It has not been designed for use in a classroom environment. Only Cisco Learning Partners displaying the following logos are authorized providers of Cisco curriculum. If you are using this book within the classroom of a training company that does not carry one of these logos, then you are not preparing with a Cisco trained and authorized provider. For information on Cisco Learning Partners please visit:www.cisco.com/go/authorizedtraining. To provide Cisco with any information about what you may believe is unauthorized use of Cisco trademarks or copyrighted training material, please visit: http://www.cisco.com/logo/infringement.html.

Feedback Information

At Cisco Press, our goal is to create in-depth technical books of the highest quality and value. Each book is crafted with care and precision, undergoing rigorous development that involves the unique expertise of members from the professional technical community.

Readers' feedback is a natural continuation of this process. If you have any comments regarding how we could improve the quality of this book, or otherwise alter it to better suit your needs, you can contact us through e-mail at feedback@ciscopress.com. Please make sure to include the book title and ISBN in your message.

We greatly appreciate your assistance.

Publisher: Paul Boger

Associate Publisher: Dave Dusthimer

Cisco Representative: Anthony Wolfenden

Cisco Press Program Manager: Jeff Brady

Executive Editor: Brett Bartow

Managing Editor: Patrick Kanouse

Development Editor: Kimberley Debus

Project Editor: Mandie Frank

Copy Editor: Keith Cline

Technical Editors: Manny Richardson, Michael Valentine

Editorial Assistant: Vanessa Evans

Designer: Louisa Adair

Composition: Octal Publishing, Inc.

Indexer: Tim Wright

Proofreader: Karen A. Gill

Americas Headquarters
Cisco Systems, Inc.
170 West Tasman Drive
San Jose, CA 95134-1706
USA
www.cisco.com
Tel: 408 526-4000
800 553-NETS (6387)
Fax: 408 527-0883

Asia Pacific Headquarters
Cisco Systems, Inc.
168 Robinson Road
#28-01 Capital Tower
Singapore 068912
www.cisco.com
Tel: +65 6317 7777
Fax: +65 6317 7799

Europe Headquarters
Cisco Systems International BV
Haarlerbergpark
Haarlerbergweg 13-19
1101 CH Amsterdam
The Netherlands
www-europe.cisco.com
Tel: +31 0 800 020 0791
Fax: +31 0 20 357 1100

Cisco has more than 200 offices worldwide. Addresses, phone numbers, and fax numbers are listed on the Cisco Website at **www.cisco.com/go/offices.**

About the Author

Dennis J. Hartmann, CCIE No. 15651, is a Unified Communications consultant. Dennis is also a lead instructor at Global Knowledge. Dennis was first exposed to CallManager during the CallManager 2.0 time frame when Cisco acquired Selsius. Dennis has various certifications, including the Cisco CCVP, CCSI, CCNP, CCIP, and the Microsoft MCSE. Dennis has worked for various Fortune 500 companies, including AT&T, Sprint, Merrill Lynch, KPMG, and Cabletron Systems. Dennis lives with his wife and children in Hopewell Junction, New York.

About the Technical Reviewers

Manny Richardson, CCIE No. 6056, is a Voice and Routing and Switching CCIE. He is a design and implementation engineer consultant with MARTA and the City of Atlanta in Atlanta, Georgia. He is also an instructor with more than 5 years of worldwide teaching experience. He has worked in the field of networking for 12 years, with the last 3 years primarily focused on Cisco Voice.

Mike Valentine has been in the IT field for 12 years, focusing on network design and implementation. He is currently a Cisco trainer with Skyline Advanced Technology Services and specializes in Cisco Unified Communications instruction and CCNA and CCNP courses. His accessible, humorous, and effective teaching style has demystified Cisco for hundreds of students since he began teaching in 2002. Mike has a bachelor of arts degree from the University of British Columbia, and he currently holds the MCSE: Security, CCDA, CCNP, CCVP, CTP, Convergence+, and CEH certifications. In addition to the popular *Exam Cram 2: CCNA* book, Mike has contributed to and served as technical editor for the Cisco Press titles *CCNP ONT Official Exam Certification Guide* and *CCNA Flashcards*, and he is currently on the courseware development team for the new Cisco UCAD (Unified Communications Architecture and Design) course.

Dedications

This book is dedicated to Missy, Dennis, and Johnny. I love you!

Acknowledgments

Thanks to my family and friends who have helped me over the years.

Thanks to everyone at Global Knowledge for providing me the opportunity to share my knowledge and experiences with my students.

I want to thank Brett Bartow, Chris Cleveland, Kimberley Debus, and the entire Cisco Press team involved in making this book a success. Thank You!

This Book Is Safari Enabled

The Safari® Enabled icon on the cover of your favorite technology book means the book is available through Safari Bookshelf. When you buy this book, you get free access to the online edition for 45 days.

Safari Bookshelf is an electronic reference library that lets you easily search thousands of technical books, find code samples, download chapters, and access technical information whenever and wherever you need it.

To gain 45-day Safari Enabled access to this book:

- Go to http://www.informit.com/onlineedition.
- Complete the brief registration form.
- Enter the coupon code 9XFX-8LSE-SHKM-B6E5-WTRZ.

If you have difficulty registering on Safari Bookshelf or accessing the online edition, please e-mail customer-service@safaribooksonline.com.

Contents at a Glance

Contents

Icons Used in This Book

 Cisco Unified Communications Manager

 Cisco Unified Communications Manager Express

 Cisco Unity Express

 ATA

 Contact Center

 Cisco Unity Server

 Router

 Voice-Enabled Router

 SRST-Enabled Router

 Multilayer Switch

 Switch

 Voice-Enabled Switch

 Local Director

 Content Engine

 Cisco Directory Server

 Wireless Access Point

 Access Server

 PBX Switch

 Server

 Mobile Access Phone

 IP Phone

 Phone Polycom

 Camera PC/Video

 Analog Phone

 Cell Phone

 3rd Party IP Phone

 PC

 Relational Database

 Firewall

 Ethernet Connection

 Serial Line Connection

 Network Cloud

Command Syntax Conventions

The conventions used to present command syntax in this book are the same conventions used in the IOS Command Reference. The Command Reference describes these conventions as follows:

- **Boldface** indicates commands and keywords that are entered literally as shown. In actual configuration examples and output (not general command syntax), boldface indicates commands that are manually input by the user (such as a **show** command).

- *Italic* indicates arguments for which you supply actual values.

- Vertical bars (|) separate alternative, mutually exclusive elements.

- Square brackets ([ ]) indicate an optional element.

- Braces ({ }) indicate a required choice.

- Braces within brackets ([{ }]) indicate a required choice within an optional element.

Foreword

Cisco Certification Self-Study guides are excellent self-study resources for networking professionals to maintain and increase internetworking skills and to prepare for Cisco Career Certification exams. Cisco Career Certifications are recognized worldwide and provide valuable, measurable rewards to networking professionals and their employers.

Cisco Press exam certification guides and preparation materials offer exceptional and flexible access to the knowledge and information required to stay current in your field of expertise or to gain new skills. Whether used to increase internetworking skills or as a supplement to a formal certification preparation course, these materials offer networking professionals the information and knowledge required to perform on-the-job tasks proficiently.

Developed in conjunction with the Cisco certifications and training team, Cisco Press books are the only self-study books authorized by Cisco. They offer students a series of exam practice tools and resource materials to help ensure that learners fully grasp the concepts and information presented.

Additional authorized Cisco instructor-led courses, e-learning, labs, and simulations are available exclusively from Cisco Learning Solutions Partners worldwide. To learn more, visit http://www.cisco.com/go/training.

I hope you will find this guide to be an essential part of your exam preparation and professional development and a valuable addition to your personal library.

Drew Rosen
Manager, Learning & Development
Learning@Cisco
December 2007

Introduction

Professional certifications have been an important part of the computing industry for many years and will continue to become more important. Many reasons exist for these certifications, but the most popularly cited reason is that of credibility. All other considerations held equal, the certified employee/consultant/job candidate is considered more valuable than one who is not.

Goals and Methods

The most important aspect of this book is to provide knowledge and skills in unified communications deploying the Cisco Unified Communications Manager (CUCM) product. Another goal of this book is to assist in the Cisco IP Telephony (CIPT) exam, which is part of the Cisco Certified Voice Professional (CCVP) certification. The methods used in this book are designed to help in both your job and the CCVP CIPT exam. This book provides many questions at the end of each chapter to reinforce the chapter content. Additional test preparation software from companies such as SelfTest Software (http://www.selftestsoftware.com) will give you even more test preparation questions to prepare you for exam success.

One key methodology used in this book is to help you discover the exam topics that you need to review in more depth, to help you fully understand and remember those details, and to help you prove to yourself that you have retained your knowledge of those topics. This book does not try to help you pass by memorization it helps you truly learn and understand the topics. The CIPT exam is one of the foundation topics in the CCVP certification, and the knowledge contained within this book is vitally important to consider yourself a truly skilled Unified Communications (UC) engineer. The book will help you pass the CIPT exam by using the following methods:

- Helping you discover which test topics you have not mastered

- Providing explanations and information to fill in your knowledge gaps

- Providing practice exercises on the topics and the testing process via test questions at the end of each chapter

Who Should Read This Book?

This book is designed to be both a general CUCM book and a certification preparation book. This book is intended to provide you with the knowledge required to pass the CCVP CIPT exam.

Why should you want to pass the CCVP CIPT exam? The CIPT test is one of the milestones toward getting CCVP certification. The CCVP could mean a raise, promotion, new job, challenge, success, or recognition; ultimately, however, you get to say what it means to you. Certifications demonstrate that you are serious about continuing the learning process and professional development. In technology, it is impossible to remain at the same level as the technology all around you advances. Engineers must continuously retrain themselves; otherwise, they will find themselves with outdated commodity-based skill sets.

Strategies for Exam Preparation

The strategy you use for exam preparation might differ from strategies used by others based on skills, knowledge, experience, and finding the recipe that works best for you. If you have attended the CIPT course, you might take a different approach than someone who learned Cisco Unified Communications Manager on the job. Regardless of the strategy you use or the background you have, this book is designed to help you understand the material so that you can pass the exam.

How This Book Is Organized

The book covers the following topics:

- **Chapter 1, "Cisco Unified Communications Manager Architecture,"** discusses the Architecture and all the components involved. CUCM hardware requirements, operating system, database, signaling, licensing, and database replication are discussed.

- **Chapter 2, "Deployment Models,"** covers the deployment models in which CUCM can be used. This chapter introduces the technologies required for the different UC models. The advantages and disadvantages of each deployment model are considered.

- **Chapter 3, "Installation and Upgrade,"** discusses the installation and upgrade options of CUCM.

- **Chapter 4, "Administration,"** covers the various CUCM administration user interfaces.

- **Chapter 5, "Initial Configuration Settings,"** examines the network configuration, Network Time Protocol (NTP), and DHCP configuration options of CUCM. The chapter also covers frequently adjusted CUCM enterprise and service parameters.

- **Chapter 6, "Managing User Accounts,"** examines user account configuration in CUCM administration, the Bulk Administration tool (BAT), and the Lightweight Directory Access Protocol (LDAP).

- **Chapter 7, "Endpoints,"** covers the various Cisco Unified IP Phones and the features that they support. Third-party Session Initiation Protocol (SIP) endpoint support is covered, in addition to the Cisco IP Phone boot cycle and registration process.

- **Chapter 8, "Cisco Catalyst Switches,"** covers the power and voice VLAN requirements of the Cisco IP Phone. The Catalyst switch configurations are examined for both Native IOS and CatOS switches. The Cisco and IEEE power specifications are also covered.

- **Chapter 9, "CUCM Configuration,"** examines the configuration options and procedure for inserting an IP phone into the CUCM database. The chapter also covers the hardening of the Cisco IP Phone to mitigate security risks.

- **Chapter 10, "Configuring Voice Gateways,"** discusses the configuration of Media Gateway Control Protocol (MGCP) gateways in both CUCM administration and Cisco IOS.

- **Chapter 11, "Call Routing Components,"** covers the fundamentals of call routing and a public switched telephone network (PSTN) dial plan. Digit analysis and path selection are achieved through the use of the router pattern, route list, and route group CUCM configuration elements.

- **Chapter 12, "Digit Manipulation,"** covers the process of digit manipulation through calling and called-party transformation masks, translation patterns, prefixing digits, and digit discard instructions (DDI).

- **Chapter 13, "Calling Privileges,"** covers the process of class of service through the use of partitions and calling search spaces. The chapter also covers time-of-day routing through the use of time periods and time schedules.

- **Chapter 14, "Call Coverage,"** covers the topic of call-coverage paths through the use of a hunt pilot, hunt list, and line groups. Call-hunting flow is discussed via the various distribution algorithms supported in CUCM.

- **Chapter 15, "Media Resources,"** discusses the media resources supported in and through CUCM. The media resource topics include music on hold (MOH), conference bridges, annunciators, transcoders, and media termination points. Media resource allocation is discussed through the application of CUCM Media Resource Manager (MRM), media resource group list, and media resource groups.

- **Chapter 16, "User Features,"** covers various CUCM features, including do not disturb, call park, directed call park, call pickup, hold reversion, intercom, call back, barge, privacy, and IP phone features.

- **Chapter 17, "Presence-Enabled Speed Dials and Lists,"** covers presence theory and configuration through the use of presence groups, presence speed dials, and presence calling search spaces.

- **Chapter 18, "Voice-Mail System Integration,"** covers the process of integrating Cisco Unity voice mail with Cisco Unified Communications Manager. Topics include voice-mail profiles, voice-mail ports, message waiting indicators, voice-mail call flow, Cisco TAPI service providers (TSP), and voice-mail subscriber creation.

- **Chapter 19, "Cisco Unified Video Advantage,"** covers the Cisco Unified Video Advantage camera, software, and video-streaming fundamentals. Topics include the CUCM configuration of video-enabled IP phones, including call admission control (CAC) video requirements.

- **Appendix A, "Answers to Chapter Review Questions"**

CHAPTER 1

Cisco Unified Communications Manager Architecture

A Cisco Unified Communications deployment relies on Cisco Unified Communications Manager (CUCM) (formerly known as Cisco Unified CallManager) for its call-processing and call-routing functions. Understanding the role that CUCM plays in a converged network from a system, software, and hardware perspective is necessary for successfully installing and configuring CUCM.

This lesson introduces and describes the role, architecture, hardware and software requirements, and the licensing model of the CUCM.

Chapter Objectives

Upon completing this chapter, you will have an understanding of the CUCM architecture and be able to meet the following objectives:

■ Describe the components of a Cisco Unified Communications solution and each component's functionality.

■ Describe the architecture and role of CUCM.

■ Describe the hardware requirements for CUCM.

■ Describe the characteristics of the CUCM operating system.

■ Describe the characteristics of the CUCM database and how it provides redundancy.

■ Describe the licensing model of CUCM.

■ Describe how to calculate, verify, and add license units to CUCM.

CUCM Overview

Cisco Unified Communications (UC) is an IP-based communications system integrating voice, video, data, and mobility products and applications. It enables more effective, secure communications and can transform the way in which we communicate. UC represents a communications paradigm shift like that of the invention of the telegraph. UC removes the geographic barriers of effective communications through the use of voice, video, and data integration. Business can be conducted with a fluidity that progresses and evolves with you. Information has been at our fingertips for a long time, but UC enables the sharing of this information to create knowledge and value.

Cisco UC is part of an integrated solution that includes network infrastructure, security, mobility, network management products, lifecycle services, flexible deployment and outsourced management options, end-user and partner financing packages, and third-party communication applications.

Cisco UC can drastically change the bottom line of business by creating more effective communications without losing the personal nature of a face-to-face conversation. More effective communication leads to reduced time to market and nimble transformation of business processes through collaboration.

Cisco UC Solution Components

The Cisco UC strategy encompasses voice, video, and data traffic within a single network infrastructure. Cisco UC equipment is capable of managing all three traffic types and interfacing with all standards-based network protocols.

Cisco IP Communications represents a new way of delivering UC functionality to enterprise customers. Instead of delivering a collection of disjointed products with individual release dates, testing methodology, and documentation, Cisco UC is a coordinated release of an *integrated* set of products that are tested, documented, and supported *as a system*.

Figure 1-1 illustrates the four standard layers of the Cisco UC voice infrastructure model and the components that make up the layers.

Figure 1-1 *Cisco Unified Communications Solution Components*

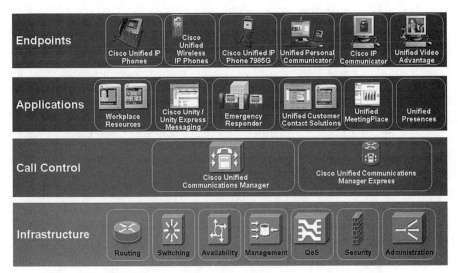

The components of the standard layers are as follows:

- **Infrastructure layer**: The infrastructure consists of routers, switches, and voice gateways. The infrastructure layer carries data, voice, and video between all network devices and applications. This layer also provides high availability, management, quality of service (QoS), and network security.

- **Call control layer**: The call control layer provides for call processing, device control, and administration of the dial plan and features.

  Call control can be provided by a CUCM, CUCM Express, or CUCM Business Edition (CMBE). This book focuses on the CUCM product, which is almost identical to the Cisco Unified CMBE. Call processing is physically independent from the infrastructure layer. For example, a CUCM, Cisco Unified CMBE, or CUCM Express in San Jose can process call control for a device physically located in Chicago.

■ **Applications layer**: Applications are independent from call-control functions and the physical voice-processing infrastructure. Applications, including those listed here, are integrated through IP, which allows the applications to reside anywhere within the network:

— Voice mail, integrated messaging, and unified messaging applications are provided through Cisco Unity, Cisco Unity Express, or Cisco Unity Connections products.

— Contact centers of various sizes can be built with Cisco Unified Contact Center and Cisco Unified Contact Center Express.

— Cisco Unified MeetingPlace and MeetingPlace Express are medium- to large-scale conferencing servers that support video integration. The MeetingPlace product integrates lecture-style conferences with scalable collaboration and control tools. Cisco Unified MeetingPlace Express is positioned to the small to medium-sized enterprises. MeetingPlace Express is the successor of the Cisco Conference Connection server.

— Cisco Emergency Responder (ER) enhances the existing emergency functionality offered by CUCM. Cisco ER provides physical location updates for mobile devices to guarantee that emergency calls to the public safety answering point (PSAP) are properly routed to the PSAP in charge of emergency calls for that site. Cisco ER identifies the caller location and maps all calls from that physical location to an emergency line identification number (ELIN) through the use of standard automatic number identification (ANI)/caller identification (CLID). The ELIN is registered with the PSAP as an Emergency Response Location (ERL). Deploying this capability helps ensure more effective compliance with legal or regulatory obligations, thereby reducing the life and liability risks related to emergency calls.

— The Cisco Unified Presence server collects information about the availability and communications capabilities of a user and provides this information to watchers of the user as a status indication. The status information includes the user's communications device availability. For example, the user might be available via phone, video, web collaboration, or video-conferencing.

— Standard protocol interfaces, including Telephony Application Programming Interface (TAPI), Java Telephony Application Programming Interface (JTAPI), Simple Object Access Protocol (SOAP), Q.SIG, H.323, Media Gateway Control Protocol (MGCP), and Session Initiation Protocol (SIP) are available to support third-party applications.

■ **Endpoints layer**: The endpoints layer brings applications to the user, whether the end device is a Cisco IP Phone, a PC using a software-based phone, or a communications client or video terminal. Cisco UC provides multiprotocol support for Skinny Client Control Protocol (SCCP), H.323, MGCP, and SIP.

Cisco UC Network

The Cisco UC system delivers fully integrated communications, converging voice, video, and data over a single network infrastructure using standards-based protocols. The Cisco UC system delivers unparalleled performance and capabilities to address current and emerging communications needs in the enterprise environment, as illustrated by the network topology in Figure 1-2.

Figure 1-2 *Cisco UC Network*

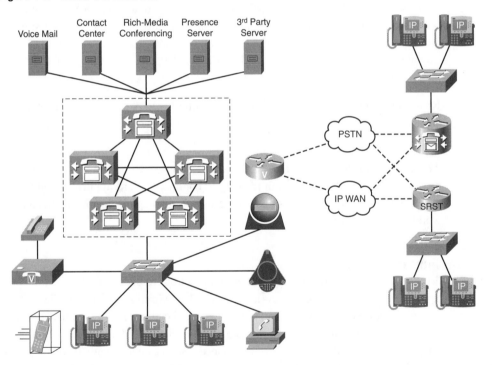

The Cisco UC product suite is designed to optimize functionality, reduce configuration and maintenance requirements, and provide interoperability with a variety of other applications. It provides this capability while maintaining high availability, QoS, and security.

The Cisco UC system integrates the following major communications technologies:

- **IP telephony**: IP telephony refers to technology that transmits voice communications over a network using IP standards. Cisco UC includes a wide array of hardware and software products such as call-processing agents, IP phones, voice-messaging systems, video devices, conferencing, and many other applications.

- **Customer contact center**: Cisco Unified Contact Center products are a combination of strategy and architecture to revolutionize call center environments. Cisco Unified Contact Center promotes efficient and effective customer communications across large networks by enabling organizations to draw from a broader range of resources to service customers. These resources include access to a large pool of agents and multiple channels of communication and customer self-help tools.

- **Video telephony**: The Cisco Unified Video Advantage products enable real-time video communications and collaboration using the same IP network and call-processing agent as Cisco UC. Cisco Unified Video Advantage does not require special end-user training. Video calling with Cisco Unified Video Advantage is as easy as dialing a phone number.

- **Rich-media conferencing**: Cisco Unified MeetingPlace creates a virtual meeting environment with an integrated set of IP-based tools for voice, video, and web conferencing.

- **Third-party applications**: Cisco works with leading-edge companies to provide the broadest selection of innovative third-party IP communications applications and products focused on critical business needs such as messaging, customer care, and workforce optimization.

CUCM Functions

CUCM extends enterprise telephony features and functions to packet telephony network devices. These packet telephony network devices include Cisco IP Phones, media-processing devices, VoIP gateways, and multimedia applications. Additional data, voice, and video services, such as converged messaging, multimedia conferencing, collaborative contact centers, and interactive multimedia response systems, interact with the IP telephony solution through the CUCM application programming interface (API).

CUCM provides these functions:

- **Call processing**: Call processing refers to the complete process of originating, routing, and terminating calls, including any billing and statistical collection processes.

■ **Signaling and device control**: CUCM sets up all the signaling connections between call endpoints and directs devices such as phones, gateways, and conference bridges to establish and tear down streaming connections. Signaling is also referred to as call control and call setup/call teardown.

■ **Dial plan administration**: The dial plan is a set of configurable lists that CUCM uses to perform call routing. CUCM is responsible for digit analysis of all calls. CUCM enables users to create scalable dial plans.

■ **Phone feature administration**: CUCM extends services such as hold, transfer, forward, conference, speed dial, redial, call park, and many other features to IP phones and gateways.

■ **Directory services**: CUCM uses its own database to store user information. User authentication is performed locally or against an external directory. Directory synchronization allows for centralized user management. Directory synchronization allows CUCM to leverage users already configured in a corporate-wide directory. Microsoft Active Directory (2000 and 2003), Netscape 4.*x*, iPlanet 5.1, and Sun ONE 5.2 directory integrations are supported. The local CUCM database is a Lightweight Directory Access Protocol (LDAP)-compliant database (LDAPv3) component in the IBM Informix Database Server (IDS).

■ **Programming interface to external applications**: CUCM provides a programming interface to external applications such as Cisco IP SoftPhone, Cisco IP Communicator, Cisco Unified IP Interactive Voice Response (IP IVR), Cisco Personal Assistant, Cisco Unified Personal Communicator, and CUCM Attendant Console.

■ **Backup and restore tools**: CUCM provides a Disaster Recovery System (DRS) to back up and restore the CUCM configuration database. The DRS system also backs up call details records (CDR), call management records (CMR), and the CDR Analysis and Reporting (CAR) database.

Figure 1-3 shows IP phones that logically register with one of the CUCMs in the cluster. Multiple CUCM servers share one database, and the phone maintains an active connection to both the primary and backup CUCM server. The figure shows the phone's logical TCP/IP connections to the primary server.

Figure 1-3   *CUCM Functions*

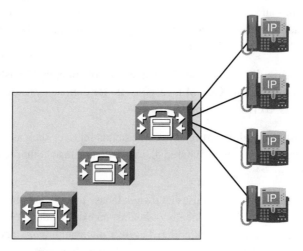

CUCM Signaling and Media Paths

CUCM uses SIP or SCCP to communicate with Cisco IP Phones for call setup and teardown and for supplementary service tasks.

After a call has been set up, media exchange occurs directly between the Cisco IP Phones across the IP network, using the Real-Time Transport Protocol (RTP) to carry the audio. CUCM is not involved in a call after the call has been set up. If the CUCM server were unplugged during the duration of the call, users would not notice unless they attempted to use a feature on the phone. CUCM is involved only in call setup, teardown, and features. If the CUCM server that set up the call were down during a conversation, end users would see a message indicating "CM Down, Features Disabled" on the LCD screen of the IP phone.

Example: Basic IP Telephony Call

Figure 1-4 illustrates a user at phone A placing a call to phone B.

At the beginning of a call, a user at IP phone A picks up the handset, and a message is sent to CUCM letting CUCM know that the device has gone off-hook. CUCM responds to this stimulus by replying with a message that tells the device to play the dial tone file that is stored in the flash memory of the phone. The user at phone A hears the dial tone and begins dialing the phone number of phone B. SCCP phones send their digits to CUCM as they are pressed (digit by digit), whereas SIP phones send their dialed digits in one message (enbloc signaling) by default. SIP phones have options that allow them to behave similarly to SCCP phones (Keypad Markup Language [KPML] and dial rules). CUCM performs digit analysis against the dialed digits. If a match is found, CUCM routes the call per its configuration. If CUCM does not find a match, a reorder tone is sent to the calling party.

Figure 1-4 *CUCM Signaling and Media Paths*

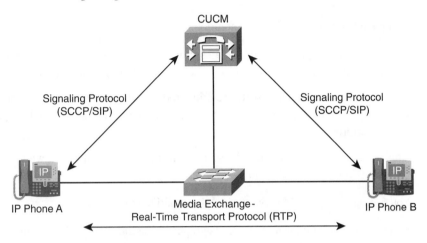

CUCM signals the calling party to initiate ringback, so the user at phone A will hear the ringback tone. CUCM also signals the call to the destination phone, which plays the ringdown tone. Additional information is provided to the phones to indicate the calling and called party name and number. (Phone A will show the destination device name and number, and phone B will show the calling party name and number.)

When the user at phone B accepts the call, CUCM sends a message to the devices letting them know the IPv4 socket (IPv4 address and port number) information in which they should communicate for the duration of the call. The RTP media path opens directly between the two phones.

The Cisco IP Phones require no further communication with CUCM until either phone invokes a feature, such as call transfer, call conferencing, or call termination.

CUCM Hardware, Software, and Clustering

CUCM Release 6.0 is a complete hardware and software solution that works as a network appliance. A network appliance is a closed system that supports only Cisco-authorized applications and utilities. Goals of the appliance model are to simplify the installation and upgrade of the system and to hide the underlying operating system. An appliance-based model makes it possible for an administrator to install, implement, and manage a CUCM server without requiring knowledge of or having access to the underlying operating system.

The CUCM appliance has these features:

■ Complete hardware and software solution.

   CUCM servers are preinstalled with all software that is required to operate, maintain, secure, and manage a server or cluster of servers (including Cisco Security Agent).

   CUCM is also provided as a software-only product, which may be installed on supported Cisco Media Convergence Servers (MCS) or Cisco-approved third-party server platforms.

■ Appliance operating system provides ease of installation and upgrade, while also providing security and reliability.

■ You can upgrade CUCM servers while they continue to process calls.

■ System administration is performed via graphical user interface (GUI), command-line interface (CLI), and through documented APIs for third-party access.

■ Outputs a variety of management parameters via a published interface to provide information to approved management applications, such as NetIQ Vivinet Manager, HP OpenView, and Integrated Research PROGNOSIS.

■ Appliance operates with or without keyboard, mouse, and monitor (also known as headed or headless). Third-party access is allowed via documented APIs only.

■ CUCM supports clustering of servers for the purpose of redundancy and load sharing. Database redundancy is provided by sharing a common database across multiple servers. Call-processing redundancy is achieved through the Call Manager Group setting, in which multiple servers are assigned to a device for the purposes of providing fault tolerance.

A CUCM cluster can have up to 20 servers in it. Only one publisher server is allowed in the cluster. The publisher houses the read/write copy of the database. Up to eight subscriber servers can be in the cluster, with the restriction that only four of the subscriber servers can perform active call processing. If more than four subscriber servers are used in a cluster, the additional servers are dedicated standby servers in case the active subscriber server is not available. The other 11 servers in the cluster can be responsible for various services, including TFTP and media resources (conferencing, music on hold, transcoding).

CUCM Cluster

Clustering allows the network to scale to several thousands of endpoints, provides redundancy in case of network or server failure, and provides a central point of administration. Figure 1-5 displays a Publisher database synchronizing database components to all the other servers in the cluster. The servers running the CCM.exe process are performing call processing, and the other servers are taking on special roles described in later chapters of this book. CUCM clustering creates scalability by segregating processes to other machines, which increases performance.

Figure 1-5   *CUCM Cluster*

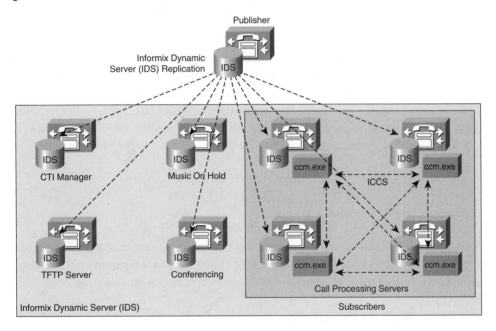

Device settings are stored in the IBM IDS database. The database is the repository for service parameters, features, device configurations, and dial plan configurations.

The database replicates nearly all configuration information in a hub-and-spoke topology (one publisher, many subscribers). CUCM nodes also use a second communication method to replicate runtime data using a mesh topology. (Every node updates every other node.) A mesh topology of information sharing provides dynamic registration and active call information that changes much more frequently than database changes. Real-time mesh replication is used to communicate newly registered phones, gateways, and digital signal processor (DSP) resources, guaranteeing optimum call routing.

Cisco 7800 Series Media Convergence Servers

Although it is possible for CUCM to run on most computers, Cisco supports CUCM running only on Cisco-approved hardware that they will support. The minimum hardware requirements for CUCM Release 6.0 are as follows:

- 2-GHz processor

- 2 GB RAM

- 72-GB hard disk

Minimum requirements for CUCM 6 are the same as for Cisco Unified CallManager Version 5, but only specific MCS models are approved.

The 7800 series servers are available in the –H or –I variants. –H stands for Hewlett-Packard, and –I stands for IBM server platforms. The 7825 server is a 19-inch or 23-inch rack-mountable server that provides a single SATA hard drive and one power supply. The 7835 server improves reliability and performance by including hot-swappable SCSI hard drives, hardware RAID 1 disc duplexing, and redundant power supplies. The 7845 improves reliability and performance by providing a second CPU and a backup fan assembly.

You can find the most detailed, current Cisco hardware specifications at http://www.cisco.com/en/US/products/hw/voiceapp/ps378/ prod_brochure0900aecd8062a4f9.html.

CUCM must be installed on a server that meets Cisco configuration standards. Cisco actively collaborates with two server hardware manufacturers to meet this requirement: Hewlett-Packard (HP) and IBM. You can find additional information at the following sites:

- **Cisco-approved IBM server solutions**: http://www.cisco.com/en/US/products/hw/ voiceapp/ps378/prod_brochure0900aecd80091615.html

- **Cisco-approved HP server solutions**: http://www.cisco.com/en/US/products/hw/ voiceapp/ps378/prod_brochure09186a0080107d79.html

Cisco UC Operating System

The CUCM operating system is based on Red Hat Linux. Operating system and application updates are provided by Cisco through patches that are digitally signed by Cisco. Unsupported software and applications (not digitally signed by Cisco) cannot be uploaded or installed into the system.

Root access to the file system is not permitted. The operating system has been hardened by disabling all unnecessary accounts and services. There is also no access to native operating system debug interfaces. Traces, alarms, and performance counters can be enabled and monitored through the CUCM GUI. Some files and directories are accessible through the Cisco CLI and GUI for maintenance purposes.

Remote-access support allows Cisco Technical Assistance Center (TAC) engineers to remotely access the CUCM server for a restricted time interval. Remote-access support can be enabled in CUCM serviceability tools.

The IBM IDS is the database for the Cisco UC applications. The IDS database installation and configuration is scripted into the CUCM installation DVDs. No UNIX or IBM IDS database knowledge is required to configure and operate CUCM.

Cisco Secure Agent is included with the appliance to provide protection against known and unknown attacks. Cisco Secure Agent is a host-based intrusion prevention system (HIPS).

A DHCP server is integrated into CUCM to provide IP telephony devices with their IP addressing requirements.

The Cisco UC operating system is also used for these Cisco UC applications:

■   Cisco Emergency Responder 2.0

■   Unity Connection 2.0

■   Cisco Unified Presence 6.0

Cisco UC Database

The data in the CUCM database is divided into two types, as described in the sections that follow.

Static Configuration Data

Static configuration data is created as part of the configuration of the CUCM cluster. Read/ write access to this data is provided for the publisher only. Subscribers provide only read-only access to this data. If the publisher becomes unavailable, the subscriber data can be used to process calls, but it cannot be modified. Database replication is unidirectional, from the publisher to the subscribers. Only CDRs and CMRs are replicated from the subscriber servers to the publisher. All other configuration information is downloaded from the publisher.

User-Facing Features

You have learned that the publisher is the only server with a read-write copy of the database, and all configuration changes should be made on the publisher. These changes are then replicated downstream to the subscribers. This model represents a single point of failure from the perspective of moves, adds, and changes (MAC). The problem is further exacerbated because the publisher was the only server in the cluster responsible for call-forwarding changes, extension mobility logins, and message-waiting indicators before CUCM 6.0.

CUCM 6.0 treats a portion of the database as dynamic configuration data. Read/write access to dynamic configuration data is provided on all servers, allowing certain information to be modified if the publisher server is unavailable. The dynamic information that can be changed during a publisher outage is known as user-facing features (UFF). UFF data is replicated from the subscriber servers where the change was initiated to all other subscriber servers in the CUCM cluster.

Examples of UFFs include the following:

- Call Forward All (CFA)

- Message Waiting Indication (MWI)

- Privacy, Enable/Disable

- Do Not Disturb, Enable/Disable (DND)

- Extension Mobility Login (EM)

- Hunt Group Login Status

- Monitor (future use)

- Device Mobility

- CTI CAPF Status (Computer Telephony Integration, Certificate Authority Proxy Function)

The services listed in Table 1-1 rely on the availability of the publisher server regardless of the version of CUCM used.

Table 1-1 *Publisher Server Required Services*

Component	Function
CCMAdmin	Provisions everything
CCMUser	Provisions user settings
BAT	Provisions everything initiated by the Bulk Administration tool
TAPS	Provisions everything initiated by the Tool for Auto-Registered Phone Support

Table 1-1 *Publisher Server Required Services (Continued)*

AXL	Provisions everything initiated by the AVVID XML Layer service
AXIS-SOAP	Enables and disables services through SOAP
CCM	Inserts phones (auto-registration only)
LDAP Sync	Updates end-user information
License Audit	Updates license tables

Database Access Control

Database access is secured using the embedded Red Hat, iptables dynamic firewall and a database security password.

The procedure to allow new subscribers to access the database on the publisher is as follows:

Step 1   Add the subscriber to the publisher database using CUCM Administration.

Step 2   During installation of the subscriber, enter the same database security password that was entered during installation of the publisher.

After this configuration, the following process occurs to replicate the database from the publisher to the newly added subscriber:

1.   The subscriber attempts to establish a connection to the publisher database using the database management channel.

2.   The publisher verifies the subscriber's authenticity and adds the subscriber's IP address to its dynamic firewall (iptables).

3.   The subscriber is allowed to access the publisher database.

4.   The database content is replicated from the publisher to the subscriber.

Figure 1-6 illustrates the iptables firewall allowing subscriber access to the publisher database.

You can find CUCM 6.0 TCP and UDP port usage information at http://www.cisco.com/en/US/docs/voice_ip_comm/cucm/port/6_0/60plrev1.pdf.

Figure 1-6 *Database Access Control*

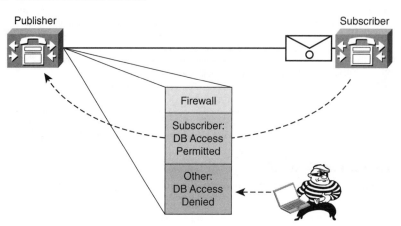

CUCM Licensing

Licensing is implemented in CUCM beginning with Release 5.0. Administration of license management is done through CUCM GUI administration, allowing accurate tracking of active device registrations compared to the license units that have been purchased. License enforcement occurs at the time of phone provisioning and CUCM service activation.

The publisher is the only licensing server. The licensing server is the logical component that keeps track of the licenses purchased and the licenses used. If the publisher fails, no new phones can register, and no configuration changes will be allowed. Existing phones will continue to operate during a publisher outage.

CUCM tracks the license compliance for devices, applications, and software as follows:

- **Device units licenses**: The maximum number of provisioned devices in the CUCM database will be tracked and enforced. Route points and CTI ports are not enforced.

- **Application licenses**: Application licenses are required for every call-processing server running the CallManager service. Application licenses are tied to the MAC address of the network interface card (NIC) of the server.

- **Software licenses**: Software licenses are tied to the major version of the software. Software licenses are required for upgrade to CUCM 6.

Licenses are created and distributed in accordance with the Cisco FlexLM process. Cisco product license registration is performed at http://www.cisco.com/go/license.

These two types of product IDs are available:

- **Cisco device license units**: Cisco device license units (DLU) are for Cisco devices only.

- **Third-party device license units**: Third-party DLUs can be converted to Cisco units, but not vice versa.

CUCM tracks the number of units required by each device, as shown in Figure 1-7. Each device type corresponds to a fixed number of units.

The number of DLUs consumed per device depends on the device type and capabilities of the phone.

The number of units required per device can be viewed from CUCM Administration. DLUs are perpetual and device independent. Figure 1-7 displays the number of DLUs consumed in CUCM 6.0 by some popular phones.

Figure 1-7 *Device License Units*

Phone License Feature

Type of Licensed Device	Units Consumed per Device
Analog Phone	0
CTI Port	0
Cisco 12 S	2
Cisco 12 SP	2
Cisco 12 SP+	2
Cisco 30 SP+	2
Cisco 30 VIP	2
Cisco 3951	3
Cisco 7902	1
Cisco 7905	2
Cisco 7906	2
Cisco 7910	2
Cisco 7911	3
Cisco 7912	3
Cisco 7920	4
Cisco 7921	4
Cisco 7931	4
Cisco 7935	3
Cisco 7936	3

Done

The main components of the license file are as follows:

- MAC address of the license server (publisher)

- Version (major release) of the CUCM software

- Number of node licenses (number of CUCM servers in cluster)

- Number of DLUs

License files are additive. (Multiple license files can be loaded.) The Cisco FlexLM process is used to obtain licenses, and integrity of license files is assured by a digital signature.

When upgrading from Cisco Unified CallManager 4.x, the number of DLUs required is calculated during the CUCM migration process, and an intermediate XML file containing these license counts is generated. The number of devices and servers that are in the database at the time of migration is the basis for the number of DLUs and node licenses in the interim license file. No additional phones may be added until the interim license file has been replaced by a real license file.

After upgrading to CUCM 6.0(1), use the **View File** option in the License File Upload window to view the intermediate XML file. Copy and paste the intermediate license file into the CUCM License Upgrade window on Cisco.com to obtain the actual license file. Upload the actual license file to the publisher (license server).

Existing device and node licenses from CUCM 5.x can be used in CUCM 6.x.

Example 1-1 shows an example license file.

Example 1-1   *Example License File*

```
INCREMENT PHONE_UNIT cisco 6.0 permanent uncounted \
VENDOR_STRING=<Count>1000</Count><OrigMacId>000BCD4EE59D</OrigMacId>
  <LicFileVersion>1.0</L icFileVersion> \
HOSTID=000bcd4ee59d NOTICE="<LicFileID>20050826140539162</LicFileID><LicLineID>2
  </LicLineID> \
<PAK></PAK>" SIGN="112D 17E4 A755 5EDC F616 0F2B B820 AA9C \
0313 A36F B317 F359 1E08 5E15 E524 1915 66EA BC9F A82B CBC8 \
4CAF 2930 017F D594 3E44 EBA3 04CD 01BF 38BA BF1B"
```

Significant fields are highlighted and described as follows:

- INCREMENT PHONE_UNIT Cisco 6.0 indicates a phone unit license file for Cisco Unified CM 6.0. There is no expiration date for this license, as indicated by the keyword *permanent*.

> **NOTE**   The INCREMENT type for CUCM node licenses is CCM_NODE cisco 6.0 permanent uncounted. The INCREMENT for software licenses is SW_FEATURE cisco 6.0 permanent uncounted.

- This license file includes 1000 license units.

- The MAC address of the license server is 000BCD4EE59D.

License File Request Process

Figure 1-8 displays the license file request process, which includes these steps:

1. The customer places an order for CUCM.

2. The manufacturing database scans the Product Authorization Key (PAK) and records it against the sales order.

3. The product (CD or paper claim certificate) is physically delivered to the customer.

4. The customer registers the product at http://www.cisco.com/go/license or a public web page and provides the MAC address of the publisher device that will become the license server.

5. The license fulfillment infrastructure validates the PAK, and the license key generator creates a license file.

6. The license file is delivered via e-mail to the customer. The e-mail also contains instructions on how to install the license file.

7. The customer installs the license file on the license server (publisher).

Figure 1-8   *License File Request Process*

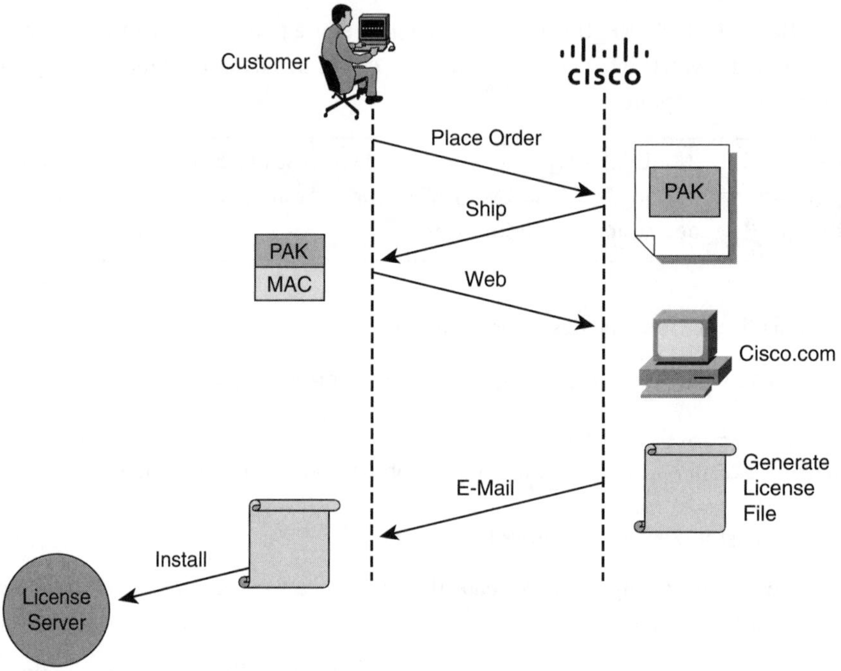

Obtaining Additional Licenses

The process of obtaining additional DLUs and node licenses is as follows:

1.   The customer places an order for the additional licenses for a license server (publisher MAC address has to be specified).

2.   When the order is received, Cisco.com generates a license file with the additional count and sends it to the customer.

3.   The new license file has to be uploaded to the license server and will be cumulative.

Consider this example. A CUCM server has an existing license file that contains 100 DLUs. Another 100 DLUs are purchased. The second license file that is generated will contain only 100 DLUs. When the new license file with 100 DLUs is uploaded to CUCM, the 100 DLUs from the first license file are added to the devices of the second license file, resulting in a total of 200 DLUs.

Licensing Components

The key licensing components of CUCM licensing are the license server and the license manager.

License Server

The license server service runs on the publisher in the CUCM cluster and is responsible for keeping track of the licenses purchased and consumed. The MAC address of the publisher is required to generate a license file.

License Manager

The license manager acts as a broker between CUCM applications that use licensing information and the license server. The license manager receives requests from the CUCM applications and forwards the requests to the license server. The license manager then responds back to the application after the request has been processed by the license server. The license manager acts a licensing proxy server.

An administration subsystem and alarm subsystem complete the functional diagram. Details of these two subsystems are as follows:

■ The administration subsystem provides the following capabilities:

—Keeps information about the license units required for each phone type. The customer can view this information using a GUI.

—Supports a GUI tool that calculates the required number of phone unit licenses. The customer inputs phone types and the number of phones of each type that the customer wants to purchase. The output is the total number of licenses that the customer needs for the given configuration.

—Supports a GUI tool that displays the total license capacity and the number of licenses in use and license file details. The tool can also report the number of available licenses.

■ The alarm subsystem generates alarms that are routed to event logs or sent to a management station as Simple Network Management Protocol (SNMP) traps to notify the administrator of the following conditions:

—**Overdraft**: Occurs when an overdraft condition exists. An overdraft condition occurs when more licenses are used than available but the amount of exceeding licenses is in an acceptable range. (5 percent overdraft is permitted.)

—**License server down**: Occurs when the License Manager cannot reach the license server.

—**Insufficient licenses**: Occurs when the license server detects the fact that there are not sufficient licenses to fulfill the request and raises an alarm to notify the administrator.

Issues with the license file occur when there is a version mismatch between the license file and the CUCM (license file version mismatch alarm), or when the number of licenses in the license file is less than the number of phones provisioned (license file insufficient licenses alarm). Another cause of this condition is an invalid MAC address (for instance, after a NIC change).

Figure 1-9 is a functional diagram stepping through the process of a license request, as described in the list that follows:

1. A request for a certain number of DLUs is made by the admin subsystem because of an event (for example, phone registration).

2. The License Manager service on a CUCM subscriber forwards the request to the publisher server running the License Server service.

3. The License Server service receives the license request event and allocates the required number of DLUs required based on the type of device. If not enough license units are available to accommodate the request, a deny message is sent back to the license manager on the subscriber server. If resources are available, the license server grants the request and sends a grant message to the license manager on the subscriber server.

4. The License Manager service on the subscriber server receives the license grant or deny message and allows the phone to register.

5. If the license request was denied, the subscriber server generates an alarm in the alarm subsystem. The deny message will be available in the CUCM syslog server by default.

Figure 1-9 *Licensing Functional Diagram*

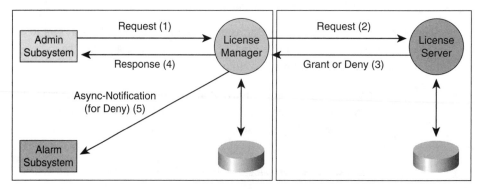

Calculating License Units

To calculate the number of phone licenses required, follow these steps:

Step 1 Choose **System > License > License Unit Calculator**. The License Unit Calculator window displays. The number of license units consumed per device and the current number of devices display as shown in Figure 1-10.

Step 2 In the Number of Devices column, enter the desired number of devices, corresponding to each node or phone.

Step 3 Click **Calculate**. The total number of CUCM node license units and DLUs required for specified configuration will display.

Figure 1-10 *License Unit Calculator*

CCM Node License Feature					
Type of Licensed Device	Units Consumed per Device	Current Number of Devices	Number of Units Consumed		Number of Devices
CCM Node	1	1	1		0
		Total CCM Node License Units Used:	1	Total CCM Node License Units Needed:	0

Phone License Feature					
Type of Licensed Device	Units Consumed per Device	Current Number of Devices	Number of Units Consumed		Number of Devices
Analog Phone	0	0	0		0
CTI Port	0	1	0		0
Cisco 12 S	2	0	0		0
Cisco 12 SP	2	0	0		0
Cisco 12 SP+	2	0	0		0
Cisco 30 SP+	2	0	0		0
Cisco 30 VIP	2	0	0		0

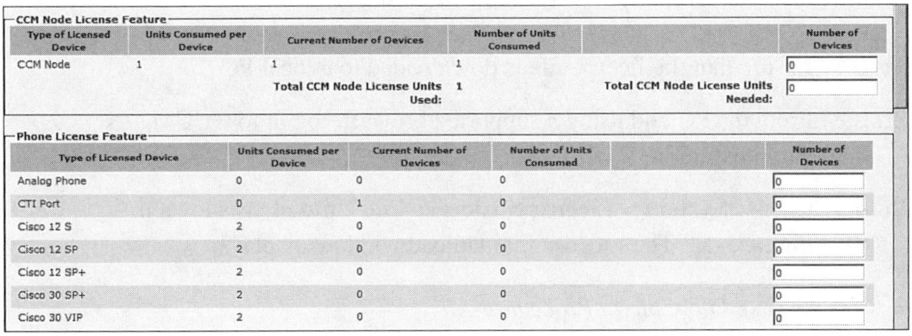

License Unit Reporting

License unit reports can be run to verify the number of licenses consumed and available for future expansion. Use the following procedure to generate a license unit report:

Step 1 Choose **System > License > License Unit Report**.

Step 2 The License Unit Report window displays as shown in Figure 1-11. This window displays the number of phone licenses and number of node licenses, in these categories:

- Units Authorized
- Units Used
- Units Remaining

Figure 1-11 *License Unit Report*

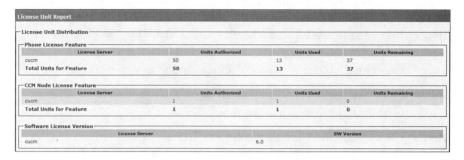

License files (CCMxxxxx.lic) are uploaded to the publisher (license server). To upload a license file to the publisher server, follow these steps:

Step 1   Ensure that the license file is downloaded to a local PC.

Step 2   From the PC and using a supported browser, log in to CUCM Administration.

Step 3   Choose **System > License > License File Upload**, as shown in Figure 1-12. The License File Upload window displays.

Figure 1-12 *License File Upload Procedure*

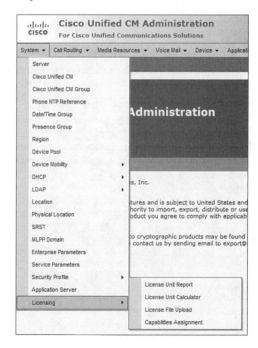

Step 4   In the window shown in Figure 1-13, click **Upload License File**.

Step 5   Click **Browse** to choose the license file from the local directory.

Step 6   Click **Upload**.

Figure 1-13   *License File Upload Procedure (continued)*

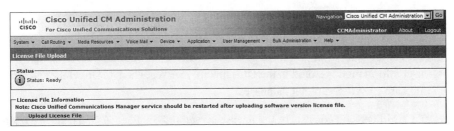

Step 7   After the upload process has completed, click the **Continue** prompt
when it appears. The content of the newly uploaded license file will
display.

Chapter Summary

The following list summarizes the key points that were discussed in this chapter:

■ Cisco Unified Communications (UC) is a community of components designed to
enable rapid, efficient communications. UC components include the following:

    —Endpoints

    —Application integration

    —Call control

    —Infrastructure

■ Cisco Unified Communications Manager (CUCM) is the call-routing component of
the Cisco UC ecosystem, providing call setup and teardown services to both voice
and video communications. CUCM provides a centralized command and control
topology to configuration management while leveraging the distributed nature of
IP communications.

■ CUCM is a software solution that is supported on various hardware configurations.
Media Convergence Servers (MCS) are Cisco-branded hardware solutions that run on
HP or IBM server platforms.

- CUCM Versions 5.0 and later use an appliance model where most administration is performed on a client pointing to the web services running on CUCM. The hardened operating system is based on the Red Hat Linux variant. There is no access to the Linux kernel, and this lack of access provides a high level of security to the Cisco UC platform. CUCM versions before 5.0 (4.x and earlier) used a Microsoft Windows-based operating system.

- CUCM database Versions 5.0 and later leverages the IBM Informix Dynamic Server (IDS) to store all configuration data, including the user database. Versions earlier than 5.0 use a Microsoft SQL server database for most configuration information, while user information is stored in the DC Directory server. The DC Directory and the IBM IDS are LDAP-compliant databases.

- CUCM licensing consists of the license server and the license manager. The license server component runs on the publisher server, whereas the license manager runs on every server.

Review Questions

Use the questions here to review what you learned in this chapter. The correct answers are found in Appendix A, "Answers to Chapter Review Questions."

1. Which layer of the Cisco Unified Communications components is responsible for delivering a dial tone?

   a. Endpoints

   b. Applications

   c. Call control

   d. Infrastructure

2. What is the name of the server in a CUCM cluster that maintains a read/write copy of the entire database?

   a. Member server

   b. Domain controller

   c. Subscriber

   d. Publisher

3. What protocol is responsible for transporting voice over IP?

   a. Skinny Client Control Protocol (SCCP)

   b. H.323

   c. Real-Time Transport Protocol (RTP)

   d. Real-Time Transport Control Protocol (RTCP)

   e. Media Gateway Control Protocol (MGCP)

   f. Skinny Gateway Control Protocol (SGCP)

4. How many call-processing agents can be active in a CUCM cluster?

   a. 20

   b. 4

   c. 8

   d. 9

   e. 2

5. How many call-processing agents can be in a CUCM cluster?

   a. 20

   b. 4

   c. 8

   d. 9

   e. 2

6. How many servers can be in a CUCM cluster?

   a. 20

   b. 4

   c. 8

   d. 9

   e. 2

7. Which CUCM server is the license manager component active on?

   a. Member server

   b. Domain controller

   c. Subscriber

   d. Publisher

   e. All servers

8. Which CUCM server is the license server component active on?

   a. Member server

   b. Domain controller

   c. Subscriber

   d. Publisher

   e. All servers

9. On which server in the CUCM cluster are license files loaded?

   a. Member server

   b. Domain controller

   c. Subscriber

   d. Publisher

   e. All servers

10. Which of the following features is *not* a user-facing feature (UFF)?

   a. Call Forward All (CFA)

   b. Message Waiting Indication (MWI)

   c. Attendant Console (Login/Logout)

   d. Privacy (Enable/Disable)

   e. Do Not Disturb (Enable/Disable) (DND)

   f. Extension Mobility (Login/Logout) (EM)

   g. Hunt Group Login Status

CHAPTER 2

Deployment Models

A solid understanding of the redundancy options and the recommended design and deployment practices of Cisco Unified Communications (UC) can provide availability at equal or higher levels to a traditional voice network.

This lesson introduces the Cisco Unified Communications Manager (CUCM) deployment models that provide a level of redundancy. The different redundancy models explored in this chapter can be applied to the deployment models that allow fault tolerance during network and device outages.

Chapter Objectives

Upon completing this chapter, you will understand the CUCM deployment and redundancy options and be able to meet the following objectives:

■ Identify the supported CUCM deployment options.

■ Describe the characteristics of a CUCM single-site deployment, and identify the reasons for choosing this deployment option.

■ Describe the characteristics of a CUCM multisite deployment with centralized call processing, and identify the reasons for choosing this deployment option.

■ Describe the characteristics of a CUCM multisite deployment with distributed call processing, and identify the reasons for choosing this deployment option.

■ Describe the characteristics of a CUCM multisite deployment with clustering over the WAN, and identify the reasons for choosing this deployment option.

■ Explain how call-processing redundancy is provided in a CUCM cluster, and identify the requirements for different redundancy scenarios.

CUCM: Single-Site Deployment

As illustrated in Figure 2-1, the Single-Site model for CUCM consists of a CUCM cluster located at a single site, or metropolitan-area network (MAN), with no telephony services provided over a WAN. All CUCM servers, applications, and digital signal processor (DSP) resources are located in the same physical location.

Figure 2-1 *Single-Site Model*

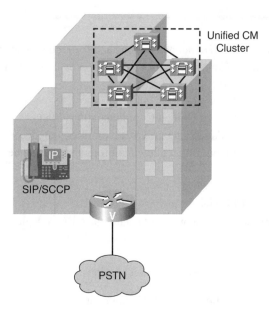

An enterprise would typically deploy the Single-Site model over a LAN or MAN, which carries the voice traffic within the site. In this model, calls beyond the LAN or MAN use the public switched telephone network (PSTN).

In a Single-Site deployment model, all CUCM servers, applications, and DSP resources are located in the same physical location.

The Single-Site model has the following design characteristics:

■ Maximum of 30,000 Skinny Client Control Protocol (SCCP) or Session Initiation Protocol (SIP) IP phones or SCCP video endpoints per cluster.

■ Maximum of 1100 H.323 devices (gateways, multipoint conference units [MCU], trunks, and clients) or Media Gateway Control Protocol (MGCP) gateways per CUCM cluster.

■ PSTN for all calls outside the site.

■ DSP resources for conferencing, transcoding, and media termination points (MTP) are located at the single site.

■ H.323 clients, H.323 MCUs - Cisco Unified Videoconferencing 3500 series, and H.323/H.320 gateways that must register with a Cisco IOS Gatekeeper (Cisco IOS Release 12.3(8)T or later). CUCM then uses an H.225 trunk or gatekeeper-controlled trunk to register with the gatekeeper. The gatekeeper provides call-routing and bandwidth management services for the H.323 devices registered to it (including CUCM). Multiple Cisco IOS Gatekeepers may be used to provide redundancy.

■ MCU resources are required for multipoint videoconferencing. Depending on conferencing requirements, these resources may be either SCCP or H.323 or both.

Follow these guidelines and best practices when implementing the Single-Site model:

■ Provide a highly available, fault-tolerant infrastructure based on a common infrastructure philosophy. A sound infrastructure is essential for easier migration to Cisco UC, integration with applications such as video streaming and videoconferencing, and expansion of your Cisco UC deployment across the WAN or to multiple CUCM clusters.

■ Know the calling patterns for your enterprise. Use the Single-Site model if most of the calls from your enterprise are within the same site or to PSTN users outside your enterprise.

■ Use G.711 codecs for all endpoints. This practice eliminates the consumption of DSP resources for transcoding. Those resources can be allocated to other functions such as conferencing and MTPs.

■ Use MGCP gateways for the PSTN if you do not require H.323 functionality. This practice simplifies the dial plan configuration. H.323 might be required to support specific functionality such as support for nonfacility-associated signaling (NFAS) or caller identification (CLID) on FXO analog gateways. CLID is supported on all T1-based MGCP gateways.

■ Implement a network infrastructure for high availability, in-line power for IP phones, quality of service (QoS) mechanisms, and security.

Multisite WAN with Centralized Call Processing

The Multisite WAN with Centralized Call Processing model consists of a centralized CUCM cluster that provides services for many sites and uses the IP WAN to transport IP telephony traffic between the sites.

The IP WAN also carries call-control signaling between the CUCM cluster at the central site and the IP phones at the remote sites.

Figure 2-2 illustrates a typical centralized call-processing deployment, with a CUCM cluster at the central site and an IP WAN with QoS enabled to connect all the sites. The remote sites rely on the centralized CUCM cluster to handle their call processing. In addition, applications such as voice mail and interactive voice response (IVR) systems are typically centralized to reduce the overall costs of administration and maintenance.

The Cisco Unified Survivable Remote Site Telephony (SRST) feature available in Cisco IOS gateways provides call-processing services to remote IP phones during WAN outage. When the IP WAN is down, the IP phones at the remote branch office can register to the SRST router. The SRST router can process calls between registered IP phones and can send calls to other sites through the PSTN. The phone-registration process is explained in further detail in Chapter 7, "Endpoints."

Deterioration of the quality of established calls can occur when WAN links are oversubscribed with voice traffic. To limit the number of calls between the sites, use call admission control (CAC). CUCM has no concept of limited bandwidth without the configuration of CAC. CUCM "believes" that bandwidth is infinite.

Centralized Call Processing models can take advantage of automated alternate routing (AAR) features. AAR allows CUCM to dynamically reroute a call over the PSTN if the call is denied because of CAC.

Figure 2-2 *Multisite WAN with Centralized Call Processing*

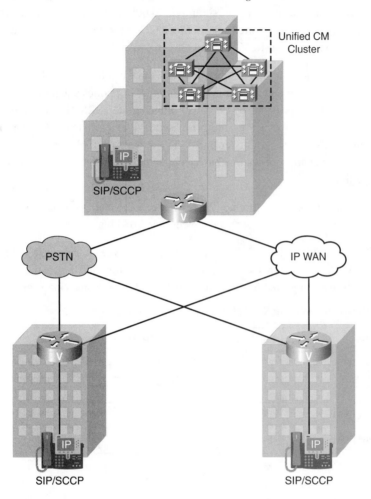

When implementing the Multisite WAN model with centralized call processing, consider the following guidelines:

■ Maximum of 1000 locations per CUCM cluster.

■ Maximum of 1100 H.323 devices (gateways, MCUs, trunks, and clients) or 1100 MGCP gateways per CUCM cluster.

■ Delay between CUCM and remote locations minimized to reduce voice cut-through delays.

- Locations mechanism in CUCM used to provide CAC into and out of remote branches. The locations can support a maximum of 30,000 IP phones per cluster when CUCM runs on the largest supported server. Since CUCM Release 5, you can use Resource Reservation Protocol (RSVP)-based CAC between locations.

- CUCM does not limit the number of devices that can be deployed at a remote branch, but best practice mandates deploying a number of phones equal to the IP phones at a capability that is provided by the SRST branch router. SRST limits remote branches to a maximum of 720 SCCP or 480 SIP Cisco IP Phones and 960 directory numbers during WAN outage or failover to SRST. The number of phones and lines (directory numbers) that are supported is based on the hardware and IOS version used at the branch.

- Minimum of 768 kb/s or greater WAN link speeds. Video is *not* recommended on WAN connections that operate at speeds lower than 768 kb/s.

- CAC is provided by CUCM locations for calls between sites controlled by the same CUCM cluster, and by the Cisco IOS Gatekeeper for calls between CUCM clusters. AAR is also supported for both intracluster and intercluster video calls.

Table 2-1   *Survivable Remote Site Telephony Hardware Requirements*

Cisco Router	Maximum Cisco Unified IP Phones
1751-V/1761-V	24
1760	24
261xXM/262xXM	36
2650XM/2651XM	48
2691	72
2801	24
2811	36
2821	48
2851	96
3725	144
3825	336
3845	720
6500 CMM	480

Multisite WAN with centralized call processing saves PSTN costs for intersite calls by using the IP WAN rather than the PSTN. IP WAN can also be used to bypass toll charges by routing calls through remote-site gateways, closer to the PSTN number dialed. This practice is known as tail-end hop-off (TEHO). TEHO is disallowed in some countries, and local regulations should be verified before implementing TEHO.

This deployment model maximizes the utilization of available bandwidth by allowing voice traffic to share the IP WAN with other types of traffic. Voice quality is ensured by deploying QoS and CAC.

Cisco Unified Extension Mobility can be used within the CUCM cluster, which allows roaming users to use their directory number at remote phones as if they were at their home phone.

When using the Multisite WAN with Centralized Call Processing deployment model, CUCM administration is centralized and therefore simpler compared to a Multisite with Distributed Call Processing model where multiple clusters have to be separately administered.

Multisite Deployment with Distributed Call Processing

As illustrated in Figure 2-3, the model for a multisite WAN deployment with distributed call processing consists of multiple independent sites, each with its own CUCM cluster, connected to an IP WAN that carries voice traffic between the distributed sites.

CUCM, applications, and DSP resources may be located at each site. The IP WAN carries signaling traffic only for intersite calls; signaling traffic for calls within a site remains local to the site. This way, the amount of signaling traffic between sites is reduced compared to a Centralized Call Processing model.

With the use of gatekeepers, a Distributed Call Processing model can scale to hundreds of sites. It also provides transparent use of the PSTN in the event that the IP WAN is unavailable.

Figure 2-3   *Multisite WAN with Distributed Call Processing*

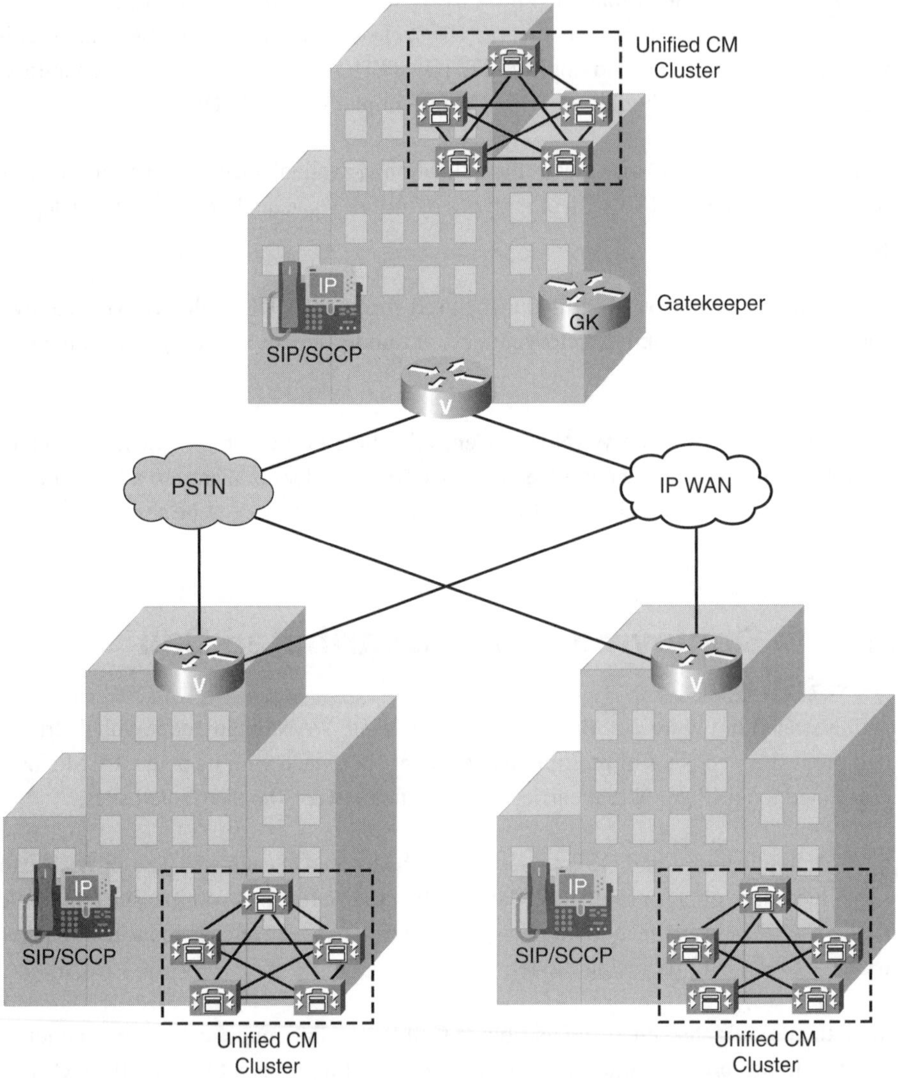

The Multisite with Distributed Call Processing model has the following design characteristics:

■   Maximum of 30,000 SCCP or SIP IP phones or SCCP video endpoints per cluster.

■   Maximum of 1100 MGCP gateways or H.323 devices (gateways, MCUs, trunks, and clients) per CUCM cluster.

- PSTN for all external calls.

- DSP resources for conferencing, transcoding, and MTP.

- Voice mail, unified messaging, and Cisco Unified Presence components.

- Capability to integrate with legacy PBX and voice-mail systems.

- H.323 clients, MCUs, and H.323/H.320 gateways that require a gatekeeper to place calls must register with a Cisco IOS Gatekeeper (Cisco IOS Release 12.3(8)T or later). CUCM then uses an H.323 trunk to integrate with the gatekeeper and provide call-routing and bandwidth management services for the H.323 devices registered to it. Multiple Cisco IOS Gatekeepers may be used to provide redundancy. Cisco IOS Gatekeepers may also be used to provide call-routing and bandwidth management between the distributed CUCM clusters. In most situations, Cisco recommends that each CUCM cluster have its own set of endpoint gatekeepers and that a separate set of gatekeepers be used to manage the intercluster calls. It is possible in some circumstances to use the same set of gatekeepers for both functions, depending on the size of the network, the complexity of the dial plan, and so forth.

- MCU resources are required in each cluster for multipoint videoconferencing. Depending on conferencing requirements, these resources may be either SCCP or H.323 or both, and they may all be located at the regional sites or may be distributed to the remote sites of each cluster if local conferencing resources are required.

- H.323/H.320 video gateways are needed to communicate with H.320 videoconferencing devices on the public ISDN network. All these gateways may be located at the regional sites, or they may be distributed to the remote sites of each cluster if local ISDN access is required.

- High-bandwidth audio (for example, G.711, G.722, or Cisco Wideband Audio) between devices in the same site, but low-bandwidth audio (for example, G.729 or G.728) between devices in different sites.

- High-bandwidth video (for example, 384 kb/s or greater) between devices in the same site, but low-bandwidth video (for example, 128 kb/s) between devices at different sites. The Cisco Unified Video Advantage wideband codec, operating at 7 Mb/s, is recommended only for calls between devices at the same site. Note that the Cisco VT Camera wideband video codec is not supported over intercluster trunks.

Benefits

The Multisite WAN with Distributed Call Processing model provides the following benefits:

- PSTN call cost savings when using the IP WAN for calls between sites.

- Use of the IP WAN to bypass toll charges by routing calls through remote-site gateways, closer to the PSTN number dialed (TEHO).

- Maximum utilization of available bandwidth by allowing voice traffic to share the IP WAN with other types of traffic.

- No loss of functionality during IP WAN failure because there is a call-processing agent at each site.

- Scalability to hundreds of sites.

- Gatekeeper networks can scale to hundreds of sites, and the design is limited only by the WAN topology.

Best Practices

A multisite WAN deployment with distributed call processing has many of the same require-ments as a single-site or a multisite WAN deployment with centralized call processing. Follow the best practices from these other models in addition to the ones listed here for the Distributed Call Processing model.

Among the key elements of this Multisite WAN model are the SIP or gatekeeper proxy servers. They each provide dial plan resolution, with the gatekeeper also providing CAC. A gatekeeper is an H.323 device that provides CAC and E.164 dial plan resolution.

The following best practices apply to the use of a gatekeeper:

- Use a Cisco IOS Gatekeeper to provide CAC into and out of each site.

- To provide high availability of the gatekeeper, use Hot Standby Router Protocol (HSRP) gatekeeper pairs, gatekeeper clustering, and alternate gatekeeper support. In addition, use multiple gatekeepers to provide redundancy within the network.

- Size the platforms appropriately to ensure that performance and capacity requirements can be met.

■ Use only one type of audio codec on the WAN, because the H.323 specification does not allow for Layer 2, IP, User Data Protocol (UDP), or Real-Time Transport Protocol (RTP) header overhead in the bandwidth request. Using one type of codec on the WAN simplifies capacity planning by eliminating the need to overprovision the IP WAN to allow for the worst-case scenario.

Clustering over the IP WAN

Cisco supports CUCM clusters over a WAN. Characteristics include the following:

■ Applications and CUCM of the same cluster distributed over the IP WAN.

■ IP WAN carries intracluster server communication and signaling.

■ Limited number of sites:

  —Two to four sites for local failover (two CUCM servers per site)

  —Up to eight sites for remote failover across the IP WAN (one CUCM server per site)

The cluster design, as illustrated in Figure 2-4, is useful for customers who require more functionality than the limited feature set offered by SRST. This network design also allows remote offices to support more IP phones than SRST in the event that the connection to the primary CUCM is lost.

Figure 2-4 *Clustering over the IP WAN*

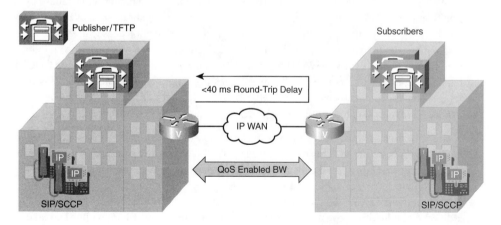

The design guidelines for clustering over the IP WAN are as follows:

■   Two CUCM servers in a cluster must have a maximum round-trip time (RTT) delay of 40 ms between them. Because of the strict 40-ms database replication requirement, this design can be used only between high-speed locations. The sites cannot be located on separate coasts of the United States, for example, because the speed of light is not capable of communicating between New York and California (propagation delay). In comparison to this strict RTT database requirement, high-quality voice guidelines dictate that one-way end-to-end delay should not exceed 150 ms.

■   For every 10,000 busy hour call attempts (BHCA) within the cluster, an additional 900 kb/s of WAN bandwidth for intracluster runtime communication must be supported. The BHCA represents the number of call attempts made during the busiest hour of the day.

■   Up to eight small sites are supported using the Remote Failover deployment model. Remote failover allows one server per location with a maximum of eight call-processing servers supported in a cluster. In the event of CUCM failure, IP phones register to another server over the WAN. SRST is not required in this deployment model. The remote failover design may require significant additional bandwidth, depending on the number of telephones at each location.

NOTE   In earlier versions of CUCM, subscriber servers in the cluster used the publisher's database for read/write access, and they used their local database for read access only when the publisher's database could not be reached.

With CUCM 6.x, subscriber servers in the cluster read their local database. Database modifications can occur in the local database (for special applications such as user-facing features). IBM Informix Dynamic Server (IDS) database replication is used to synchronize the databases on the various servers in the cluster. Therefore, when recovering from failure conditions such as the loss of WAN connectivity for an extended period of time, the CUCM databases must be synchronized with any changes that might have been made during the outage. This process happens automatically when database connectivity is restored and can take longer over low-bandwidth links.

In rare scenarios, manual reset or repair of the database replication between servers in the cluster might be required. This reset/repair is performed by using commands such as **utils dbreplication repair all** and **utils dbreplication reset all** at the command-line interface (CLI). Repair or reset of database replication using the CLI on remote subscribers over the WAN causes all CUCM databases in the cluster to be resynchronized, in which case additional bandwidth above 1.544 Mb/s might be required. Lower bandwidths can take longer for database replication repair or reset to complete.

Although there are stringent requirements, clustering over the IP WAN design offers these advantages:

- Single point of administration for users for all sites within the cluster

- Feature transparency

- Shared line appearances

- Extension mobility within the cluster

- Unified dial plan

The clustering over IP WAN design is useful for customers who want to combine the resiliency advantages of this model with the benefits provided by a local call-processing agent at each site. Intrasite signaling is kept local, and WAN failures will not result in loss of functionality. This network design also allows remote offices to support more Cisco IP Phones than SRST in the event of WAN failure.

These features make clustering across the IP WAN ideal as a disaster recovery plan for business-continuance sites or as a single solution for up to eight small or medium sites.

CUCM Call-Processing Redundancy

A CUCM cluster is a group of physical servers working as a single IP PBX system. With CUCM 6.0, a cluster may contain up to 20 servers, of which a maximum of 8 servers may run the Cisco CallManager service performing call processing in a cluster. Other servers can be used as TFTP servers or provide media resources such as software conference bridges or music on hold (MOH).

CUCM call-processing redundancy is implemented by grouping servers running the Cisco CallManager service into CUCM groups. A CM group is a prioritized list of one or more call-processing servers. Figure 2-5 shows this 1:1 redundancy design.

The following rules apply for the CM groups:

- Multiple CM groups can exist in the same cluster.

- Each call-processing server can be assigned to more than one CM group.

- Each device has to have a CM group assigned that will determine the primary and backup servers to which it can register.

Figure 2-5 *1:1 Redundancy Design*

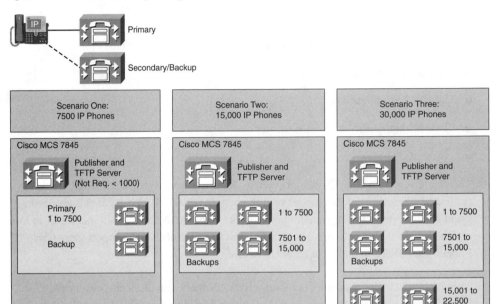

Cisco IP Phones register with their primary server. When idle, the Cisco IP Phones and CUCM exchange signaling application keepalives. In addition, Cisco IP Phones establish a TCP session with their secondary server and exchange TCP keepalives. When the connection to the primary server is lost (no keepalives received), the Cisco IP Phone registers to the secondary server. The Cisco IP Phone will continuously try to reestablish a connection with the primary server; if successful, the Cisco IP Phone will reregister with the primary server.

A 1:1 CUCM call-processing redundancy deployment design guarantees that Cisco IP Phone registrations will never overwhelm the backup servers. Multiple primary servers can fail concurrently, and the cluster would still be fully operational. The 1:1 design has an increased server count compared to other redundancy design models. This design is not the most cost-effective, but it offers the highest level of fault tolerance.

Each cluster must also provide a TFTP service. The TFTP service is responsible for delivering IP phone configuration and firmware files to telephones, along with streamed media files, such as MOH and ring files; therefore, the server running the TFTP service can experience a considerable network and processor load. Depending on the number of devices that a server is supporting, you can run the TFTP service on a dedicated server, on the database publisher server, or on any other server in the cluster.

In this example, a Cisco 7845 Media Convergence Server (MCS) is used as the dedicated database publisher and TFTP server. In addition, there are two call-processing servers supporting a maximum of 7500 Cisco IP Phones (on the Cisco 7845 MCS platform). One of these two servers is the primary server, and the other is a dedicated backup server. The function of the database publisher and the TFTP server can be provided by the primary or secondary call-processing server in a smaller IP telephony deployment (fewer than 1250 IP phones with the MCS 7845). In this case, only two servers are needed in total.

When you increase the number of IP phones, you must increase the number of CUCM servers that are required to support the telephones. Some network engineers may consider the 1:1 redundancy design excessive, because a well-designed network is unlikely to lose more than one primary server at a time. With the low possibility of server loss and the increased server cost, many network engineers choose to use a 2:1 redundancy design, as shown in Figure 2-6.

Figure 2-6 *2:1 Redundancy Design*

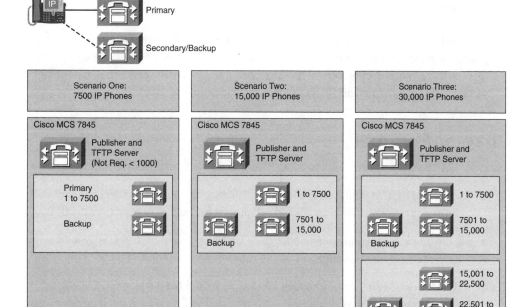

Although the 2:1 redundancy design offers some redundancy, there is the risk of over-whelming the backup server if multiple primary servers fail. In addition, upgrading the CUCM servers can cause a temporary loss of service because rebooting the CUCM servers is required after the upgrade is complete.

Network engineers use this 2:1 redundancy model in most IP telephony deployments because of the reduced server costs. If a Cisco MCS 7845 is used (shown in the figure), that server is equipped with redundant, hot-swappable power supplies and hard drives. It is unlikely that multiple primary servers will fail at the same time, which makes the 2:1 redundancy model an attractive option for most businesses.

Cisco recommends dedicating a TFTP server in any cluster that exceeds 1250 phones. In a large cluster, Cisco recommends dedicating two servers to TFTP functionality.

As shown in the first scenario, when using no more than 7500 IP phones, there is no saving in the 2:1 redundancy design compared to the 1:1 redundancy design (simply because there is only a single primary server).

In the second scenario of Figure 2-6 with up to 15,000 IP phones, there are 2 primary servers (each serving 7500 IP phones) and 1 secondary server. As long as only one primary server fails, the backup server can take over. If both primary servers fail, the backup server could serve only half of the IP phones.

The third scenario in Figure 2-6 illustrates a deployment with 30,000 IP phones. Four primary servers are required to facilitate this number of IP phones. For each pair of primary servers, there is one backup server. As long as no more than two servers fail, the backup servers can take over, and all IP phones will operate normally.

Chapter Summary

The following list summarizes the key points that were discussed in this chapter:

- Supported CUCM deployment models are single-site, multisite with centralized call processing, multisite with distributed call processing, and clustering over the IP WAN.

- In the Single-Site deployment model, the CUCM, applications, and DSP resources are at the same physical location; all offsite calls are handled by the PSTN.

- The Multisite with Centralized Call Processing model has a single CUCM cluster; applications and DSP resources can be centralized or distributed; the IP WAN carries call-control signaling traffic even for calls within a remote site.

- The Multisite with Distributed Call Processing model has multiple independent sites, each with a CUCM cluster; the IP WAN carries traffic only for intersite calls.

- Clustering over the WAN provides centralized administration, a unified dial plan, feature extension to all offices, and support for more remote phones during failover, but it places strict delay and bandwidth requirements on the WAN.

- Clusters provide redundancy. A 1:1 redundancy design offers the highest availability but requires most resources and is not as cost-effective as 1:2 redundancy.

Review Questions

Use the questions here to review what you learned in this chapter. The correct answers are found in Appendix A, "Answers to Chapter Review Questions."

1. What is the maximum number of phones per CUCM cluster?

    a. 10,000

    b. 7,500

    c. 30,000

    d. 20,000

2. How is call admission control handled in the Centralized Call Processing model?

    a. QoS

    b. H.323 gateway

    c. H.323 gatekeeper

    d. CUCM locations

    e. CUCM regions

3. What technology is used in the Centralized Call Processing model to reroute a call to a remote destination if there is not enough bandwidth to accommodate the call?

    a. Automated alternate routing

    b. Call admission control

    c. Quality of service

    d. Intercluster trunks

4. What technology is used to bypass toll charges by routing calls through remote-site gateways, closer to the PSTN number dialed?

   a. Automated alternate routing

   b. Tail-end hop-off

   c. Extension mobility

   d. Call admission control

5. Which call-processing model allows extension mobility between sites?

   a. Single-Site model

   b. Centralized model

   c. Distributed model

   d. Clustering over the WAN model

6. Gatekeepers are used within which call-processing model?

   a. Single-Site model

   b. Centralized model

   c. Distributed model

   d. Clustering over the WAN model

7. What is the maximum round-trip time requirement between CallManager servers in the Clustering over the WAN model?

   a. 20 ms

   b. 150 ms

   c. 40 ms

   d. 300 ms

8. What is the minimum amount of bandwidth that must be dedicated to database replication in the Clustering over the WAN model?

   a. 900 kb/s

   b. 1.544 Mb/s

   c. 80 kb/s

   d. 2.048 Mb/s

9. How many servers are required to accommodate 7500 phones using the 7845 server in the 2:1 redundancy model?

    a.   1

    b.   2

    c.   3

    d.   4

CHAPTER 3

Installation and Upgrade

Installing or upgrading software is a fundamental task that you need to perform to support the deployment of CUCM Release 6.0. This lesson covers the CUCM Release 6.0 installation framework, installation requirements, and the procedures to perform an installation or an upgrade.

Chapter Objectives

Upon completing this chapter, you will be able to describe the CUCM Release 6.0 installation framework, installation and upgrade procedures, and hardware requirements, and you will be able to meet the following objectives:

- Identify the CUCM installation and upgrade options.

- Describe how to perform a new installation of CUCM.

- Describe how to perform an upgrade during a new installation of CUCM.

- Describe how to upgrade to CUCM 6.0 from Version 4.

- Describe how to upgrade from CUCM 5.0 or later.

CUCM Installation and Upgrade Overview

CUCM can be upgraded from the various previous releases of Windows Server-based CUCM or appliance-based CUCM.

Cisco CallManager Releases 3.x and earlier for Windows Server have to be upgraded to Release 4.1(3) or later before upgrade to 6.0(1) is possible.

Appliance-based CUCM releases earlier than 5.1(1) have to be upgraded to Release 5.1(1) before upgrade to 6.0(1) is possible.

Figure 3-1 displays the various upgrade path options available for CUCM 6.0(1).

Figure 3-1   *CUCM Upgrade Paths*

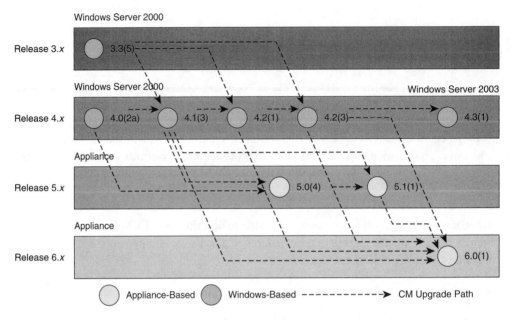

CUCM Installation and Upgrade Options

Of the four installation options, only the first three options are available when booting from the DVD. These options are available when CUCM has been chosen in the Product Deployment Selection screen.

Upgrade from 5.1 does not require booting from the installation DVD, but it is presented here as one of the upgrade options.

CUCM 6.0(x) uses an installation framework similar to CUCM Release 5.x. The installation process allows performing a basic installation, upgrading to a newer service release during the installation, and upgrading from CUCM 4.1(3) or later to CUCM 6.0(1).

The sections that follow describe how the installation and upgrade options work.

Basic Install

This option represents the basic installation and does not use imported data. This type of installation generally starts by booting a system from an installation DVD or powering up a new system from the factory (with preinstalled software).

Upgrade During Install

This option performs a basic installation on a system and allows the system to be upgraded to a specific service release patch level before the completion of the basic installation. This option performs a basic installation before prompting the installer for additional upgrade information.

> **NOTE** Ensure that the patches are available on DVD or SFTP/FTP during this installation option.

Windows Upgrade

This option upgrades a Windows-based CUCM system to an appliance-based system and migrates data from an existing Windows Server-based CUCM system. This installation method can be done on the same machine or a different machine from the Windows Server-based CUCM machine. The Windows migration file can be saved to a variety of locations, including a remote hard drive or tape system. The CUCM then uploads the file from one of these locations during the upgrade process.

> **NOTE** During upgrade from a Windows-based release, new software licenses and configuration files generated with the Data Migration Assistant tool (DMA) are required.

5.x or Later Upgrade

If you are upgrading from CUCM Release 5.x, the upgrade filename has the following format:

cisco-ipt-k9-patch$X.X.X.X$-X.tar.gz.sgn

Where $X.X.X.X$-X represents the release and build number. An upgrade from 5.x or later is performed from the Cisco Unified Operating System Administration.

> **CAUTION** Installation on an existing server formats the hard drive. All existing data on the drive is lost.

Upgrade Methods

The first method is a full installation from scratch where the customer inserts a DVD and loads the operating system and CUCM Release 6.0 application. This method is primarily for customers who have an existing Media Convergence Server (MCS) or when users purchase servers from a Cisco-approved third-party vendor.

The second method is a factory preinstallation in which the customer orders an MCS platform, and the operating system and CUCM Release 6.0 application are preloaded to the server at the factory and then shipped to the customer. This method is primarily for customers who order a new MCS platform. A preinstallation without configuration can also be done from the installation DVD by selecting Skip during the Platform Installation wizard prompt. In this case, only the software is installed, but no configuration is applied. When the server is booted the next time, the Configuration wizard starts automatically (like on a factory preinstalled system).

Installation Disc

The installation disc enables you to install the operating system and CUCM from the same DVD. The installation disc performs a hardware check to verify hardware requirements for the release. If any unsupported component is found, an applicable error message displays, and the installation halts.

The disc can be used for full installation or for recovery if you have a backup of the data.

A separate recovery disc is available for use for system recovery if you want to recover the operating system and application files without a backup of the data.

Cisco Unity Connection and Cisco Unified Communications Manager Business Edition (CMBE) can also be installed from the same DVD; select the product that you want to install. This lesson describes only the installation and upgrade of CUCM.

NOTE   Only the products that are supported on your server appear in the list.

Hardware Configuration

Hardware configuration is integrated with the Cisco Unified Communications (UC) installation process. The hardware configuration includes the following:

- A check for correct hardware configuration, supported platforms, and minimum hardware requirements

- Configuration of the correct BIOS and RAID settings on the supported platforms

Basic Installation (Installation DVD)

This topic describes the process for performing a basic installation of the operating system and CUCM Release 6.0 application on the publisher. CUCM Release 6.0 has to be installed on the publisher before installing it on any subscriber nodes.

To select the Basic installation option, choose **No** in both the Apply Additional Release window and the Import Windows Data window.

Important Configuration Information

During the installation process, the installation prompts for various required information based on the installation engineer's answers to the installation prompts. Table 3-1 lists important configuration information requested during CUCM setup.

Table 3-1 *Installation Configuration Information*

Field	Description	Usage
Administrator ID	This field specifies the name that you want to assign to this account.	Ensure that the name is unique; it can contain lowercase, alphanumeric characters, hyphens, and underscores. It must start with a lowercase alphanumeric character. For this mandatory field, you should record it for use when logging in to the CLI or into Cisco Unified Communications Operating System Administration.
Administrator Password	This field specifies the password that you use for logging in to the CLI on the platform and for logging in to Cisco Unified Communications Operating System Administration.	Ensure that the password is at least six characters long; it can contain alphanumeric characters, hyphens, and underscores. For this mandatory field, you should record it for use when logging in to the CLI or into Cisco Unified Communications Operating System Administration.
DHCP	Dynamic Host Configuration Protocol.	Choose Yes if you want to use DHCP to automatically configure the network settings on your server. If you choose No, you must enter a hostname, IP address, IP mask, and gateway.
DNS Enabled	A DNS server represents a device that resolves a hostname into an IP address or an IP address into a hostname.	If you do not have a DNS server, choose No. When DNS is not enabled, you should enter only IP addresses (not hostnames) for all network devices in your Cisco UC network. If you have a DNS server, Cisco recommends that you choose Yes to enable DNS. Disabling DNS limits the system ability to resolve some domain names.

continues

Table 3-1   *Installation Configuration Information (Continued)*

Field	Description	Usage
DNS Primary	The server contacts this DNS server first when it attempts to resolve hostnames.	Enter the IP address of the DNS server that you want to specify as the primary DNS server. Enter the IP address in dotted-decimal format as *ddd.ddd.ddd.ddd*, where *ddd* can have a value between 0 and 255 (except 0.0.0.0). Consider this field mandatory if DNS is set to Yes.
DNS Secondary	When a primary DNS server fails, the server attempts to connect to the secondary DNS server.	In this optional field, enter the IP address of the secondary DNS. Enter the IP address in dotted-decimal format as *ddd.ddd.ddd.ddd*, where *ddd* can have a value between 0 and 255 (except 0.0.0.0).
Domain	This field represents the name of the domain in which this machine is located.	Consider this field mandatory if DNS is set to Yes.
First Cisco Unified Communications Manager Node	This field specifies the first CUCM node that contains the database. Subsequent nodes connect to the first node to access database content. The first node also synchronizes with an external Network Time Protocol server and provides time to the other nodes.	Choose Yes if you are configuring the first CUCM node in the cluster.
Hostname	A hostname represents an alias that is assigned to an IP address to identify it.	Enter a hostname that is unique to your network. The hostname can consist of up to 64 characters and can contain alphanumeric characters and hyphens. If DHCP is set to No, consider this field mandatory.

Table 3-1   *Installation Configuration Information (Continued)*

Field	Description	Usage
IP Address	This field specifies the IP address of this machine. It uniquely identifies the server on this network. Ensure that another machine in this network does not use this IP address.	Enter the IP address in the form *ddd.ddd.ddd.ddd*, where *ddd* can have a value between 0 and 255 (except 0.0.0.0). If DHCP is set to No, consider this field mandatory.
IP Mask	This field specifies the IP subnet mask of this machine. The subnet mask, together with the IP address, defines the network address and the host address.	Enter the IP mask in the form *ddd.ddd.ddd.ddd*, where *ddd* can have a value between 0 and 255 (except 0.0.0.0). A valid mask should have contiguous 1 bits on the left side and contiguous 0 bits on the right. For example, a valid mask follows: 255.255.240.0 (11111111.11111111.11110000.00000000) An invalid mask follows: 255.255.240.240 (11111111.11111111.11110000.11110000)
NIC Speed	This field specifies the speed of the server network interface card in megabits per second.	The possible speeds include 10 or 100.
NIC Duplex	This field specifies the duplex setting of the server network interface card.	The possible settings include Half and Full.
NTP Server	This field identifies the NTP servers with which you want to synchronize.	Enter the hostname or IP address of one or more NTP servers. Note that you can add additional NTP servers or make changes to the NTP server list at a later time.
NTP Server Enable	When enabled, this server acts as an NTP server and provides time updates to the subsequent nodes in the cluster.	Choose Yes if you want to enable this machine to be an NTP server. This option is available only on the first node in a cluster.

continues

Table 3-1 *Installation Configuration Information (Continued)*

Field	Description	Usage
Security Password	Servers in the cluster use the security password to communicate with one another. You are asked to enter the same security password for each subsequent node in the cluster.	Enter the security password. Enter the same password in the Confirm Password field. The password must contain at least six alphanumeric characters. It can contain hyphens and underscores, but it must start with an alphanumeric character. All nodes in the cluster must have the same password.
Set Hardware Clock	This field specifies the date and local time for the machine. Note that if you set the hardware clock manually, the node does not use an external NTP server for time synchronization.	Choose Yes if you want to set the date and local time for the time zone that you choose. Enter the hours based on a 24-hour format. Note that if you configure an external NTP server, the hardware clock gets set automatically.
SMTP	This field specifies the name of the SMTP host that is used for outbound e-mail.	Enter the hostname or dotted-decimal IP address for the SMTP server. For a host, it can contain alphanumeric characters, hyphens, or periods. For a hostname, it must start with an alphanumeric character. You must fill in this field if you plan to use electronic notification. If not, you can leave it blank.
Subnet IP Address	By entering a subnet address, you can specify a range of IP addresses that will be granted access to query this NTP server.	Enter an IP subnet that will be granted access to the NTP server During installation, you can enter only two subnets.
Subnet Mask	This field specifies the subnet mask for the subnet address.	Enter the subnet mask for the IP subnet.
Time Zone	This field specifies the local time zone and offset from Greenwich mean time.	Choose Yes if you want to change the time zone. Choose the time zone that most closely matches the location of your machine.

Installation Procedures for Basic Install

Installation starts the same way for all three installation options: Insert the installation disc in the DVD drive and reboot the server. The DVD Found window displays after the server completes the boot sequence.

Figure 3-2 provides a flowchart displaying the various steps involved in installing CUCM from a DVD.

Figure 3-2 *Basic Installation Flow (DVD Installation)*

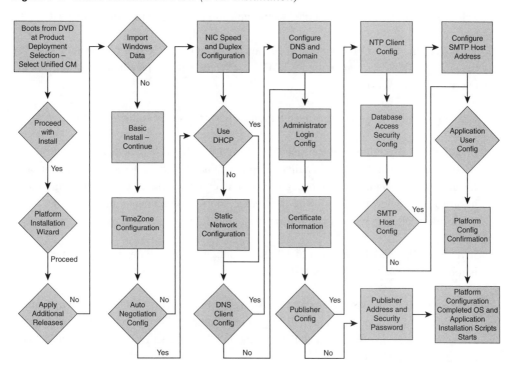

The DVD prompts the installer to perform a media check. To perform the media check, choose **Yes**. To skip the media check, choose **No**. If **Yes** was chosen, the installation process performs a media check of the image on the DVD to ensure that the image is error free before installation. If the disk is okay, the installation continues.

A hardware check is then performed to determine whether the correct hardware is installed, and then the RAID and BIOS settings are configured.

After the hardware checks are complete, the Product Deployment Selection window displays. In the Product Deployment Selection window, you can choose from the following options:

- Cisco Unified Communications Manager

- Cisco Unity Connection

- Cisco Unified Communications Manager Business Edition (includes CUCM and Cisco Unity Connection)

Select the first option (Cisco Unified Communication Manager) to install only CUCM.

The Overwrite Hard Drive window then indicates the current software version on your hard drive and the version on the DVD. Choose No to halt the installation. Choose Yes to overwrite the hard drive.

Next, choose the desired type of installation by performing the following steps.

In both the Apply Additional Release window and the Import Windows Data window, choose **No** to select the Basic installation option. When you click **Continue**, the Platform Installation wizard guides you through the installation process and gathers the required information. Review this window to familiarize yourself with navigating within the Platform Installation wizard, and follow these guidelines:

If you click Proceed, the Product Installation Configuration window displays immediately before any software is copied or installed.

If you click Skip, the software is first transferred to the hard drive, and the system shuts down. At the next boot, the system displays the Installation Configuration window. This is the same state as on a factory-installed system, in which the software is preloaded but no configuration has been done.

When the preloaded system boots, the Configuration dialog is completely skipped if a Universal Serial Bus (USB) drive with a configuration file that includes all configuration parameters is found. Such a configuration file can be prepared using the Answer File Generator, as covered in the following section.

Basic Installation (Preinstalled)

After you boot the system, the Preexisting Installation Configuration window displays. If preexisting configuration information generated by the Answer File Generator and stored on a floppy disc or a USB key exists, you must insert the disc or the USB key and then click **Continue**. In this case, the Installation wizard reads the configuration information from the

USB key. If no configuration file on a USB key is provided, the Installation wizard prompts for configuration data. Figure 3-3 shows this install process.

Figure 3-3 *Basic Installation Flow (Preinstalled)*

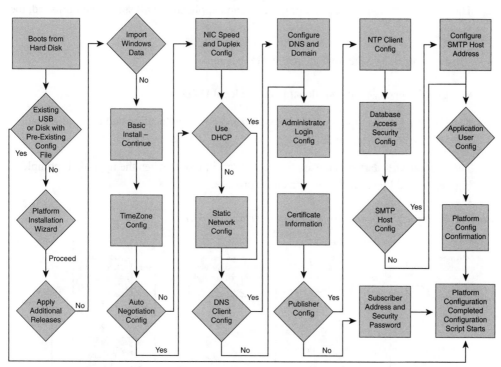

The only difference to a basic installation executed from the installation DVD is the ability to skip over the configuration portion by providing a configuration file on a USB key.

The Answer File Generator is a web-based tool available at Cisco.com that provides the answer file based on the form entries that the user has filled out. The Answer File Generator was located at http://www.cisco.com/web/cuc_afg/index.html at the time of this writing. A Cisco.com search for "Answer File Generator" will provide a link to the current version of the tool.

Upgrade During Install

Service releases, engineering special updates, and security updates may be installed during Basic installation. To install, make sure the additional release is downloaded and prepared on a DVD or FTP/SFTP server before starting the installation. Click **Yes** in the Apply Additional Release window.

The installation starts when the server is booted from the installation DVD. Verify the checksum for the DVD, and click **Overwrite Hard Disk**.

In the Platform Installation wizard, click **Yes** in the Apply Additional Releases window. Then the installation of the operating system and application will start; when finished, the system reboots.

After reboot, choose the upgrade retrieval mechanism:

■   **Local**: Specify path and filename on the local DVD.

■   **FTP/SFTP**: Configure network settings and enter the location and login information for the remote file server.

The upgrade will start, and the appliance server will reboot when the upgrade is complete. Figure 3-4 and Figure 3-5 show the entire process.

Figure 3-4   *Upgrade During Installation Flowchart (1 of 2)*

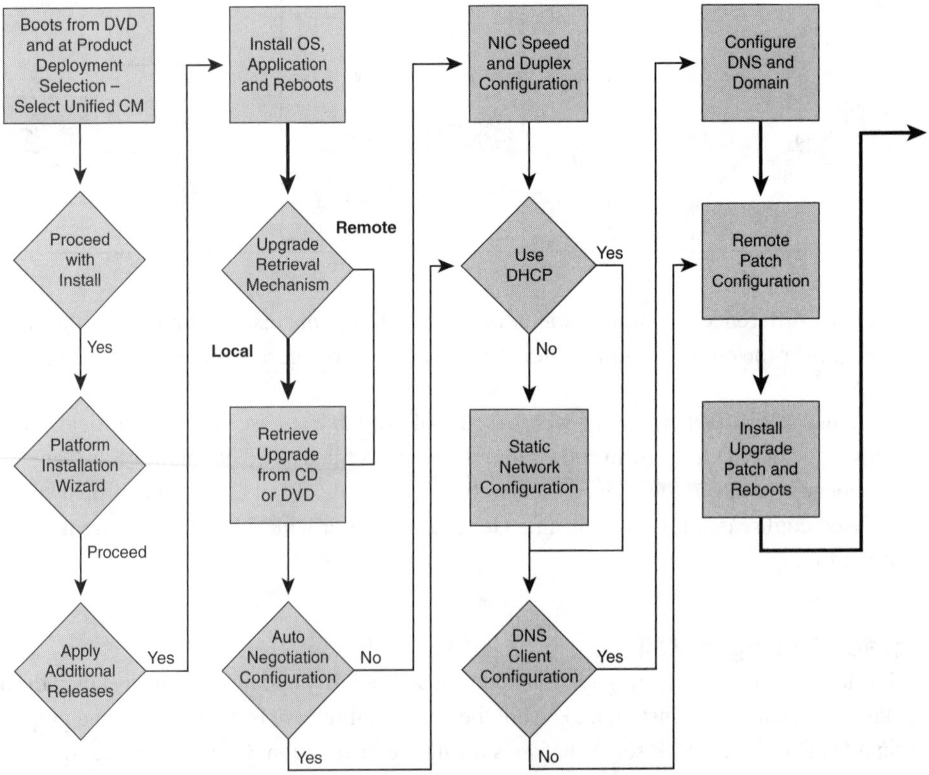

Figure 3-5 *Upgrade During Installation Flowchart (2 of 2)*

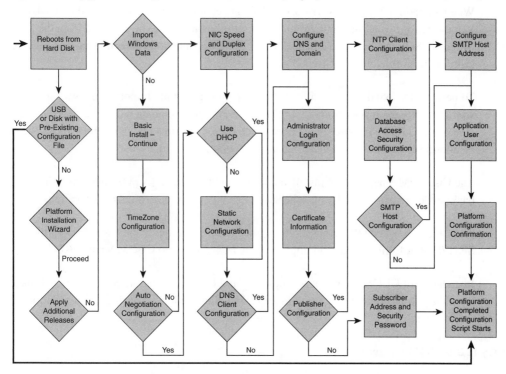

Table 3-2 outlines the information required to configure the remote path, which includes the location and login information necessary for CUCM to access patches to the product via the file transfer mechanism specified.

Table 3-2 *Remote Path Information Description*

Field	Description
Remote Server Name or IP	IP address of the FTP/TFTP server. If using a hostname, ensure that the DNS is configured and that the hostname can be resolved to a valid IP address.
Patch Directory	Specifies the directory path for the patch.
Remote Login ID	Login ID for the FTP or SFTP servers.
Remote Password	Remote passwords for the FTP or SFTP server.
SFTP	Specifies the filename for the patch.

Windows Upgrade

When upgrading from Windows-based CUCM (Version 4.x) to the appliance-based CUCM Version 5.x or 6.x, all the configuration and runtime data has to be exported from the Microsoft SQL database and transformed to the new format of the Informix database. These tasks are performed by the Cisco DMA tool.

To perform the Windows upgrade installation, click **Yes** in the Import Windows Data window. After the installation of CUCM 6, the configuration data will be retrieved from tape or an FTP/SFTP source. This installation option requires that you run DMA on the Windows-based CUCM 4.x version before the upgrade installation.

The Cisco DMA needs to be installed and run on the CUCM 4.x publisher server. The backup file created by DMA must be saved to a tape drive or to a network location.

The CUCM 6.0(1) publisher installation procedure then retrieves the DMA backup file via SFTP/FTP or from the tape and migrates CUCM 4.x data into CUCM Version 6.0(1).

Installation of CUCM subscribers follows the publisher installation. Subscribers pull data from the publisher database; therefore, no DMA files are loaded during the installation of a subscriber.

Figure 3-6 *DMA Overview*

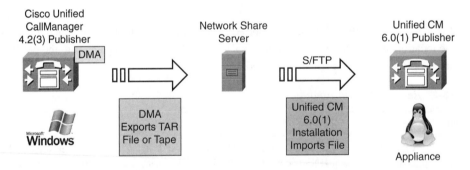

Caveats to keep in mind when using the DMA include the following:

- Customized music on hold (MOH) files have to be backed up manually to be reinstalled on all CUCM servers after upgrade to 6.0(1).

- Special phone load files and background images stored on the TFTP server will also be lost; these files have to be backed up and can be uploaded to the newly installed TFTP server after upgrade.

- Files on CUCM subscriber servers will not be backed up, because the DMA only runs on the publisher server.

- The default user ID for the CUCM administrator needs to be set during the CUCM 6.0(1) installation; a default user ID of CCMAdministrator is no longer mandatory.

- All usernames are migrated, but the passwords and PINs are reset to a default defined during installation. After the upgrade, users can change their passwords and PINs on the CCMUser web pages.

CUCM 5.x and 6.x Upgrades

Updates from appliance-based CUCM versions (5.x) are performed from the CUCM Operating System Administration web page.

> **NOTE** CUCM Version 5.0 requires an upgrade to CUCM Version 5.1(1) before it can be upgraded to CUCM Version 6.

The system does not have to be rebooted, because the current operating system and application are not overwritten by the new version. Instead, they are installed to a second (inactive) partition.

The upgrade procedure includes the following steps:

Step 1 Back up the existing CUCM 5.x or 6.x system using the CUCM Disaster Recovery System (DRS).

Step 2 Ensure that the SFTP/FTP server is available to perform the upgrade remotely or that the upgrade image is available on the DVD to perform the upgrade locally.

Step 3 Log in to the Cisco Unified Operating System Administration page and start the upgrade.

Step 4 CUCM upgrades can be done without affecting call processing, and the server can be rebooted later during a service window after the upgrade.

Step 5 Install the updated license file (required when upgrading from 5.x to 6.0).

Dual Partitions

Since Release 5.x, CUCM supports dual partitions, which simplify software updates:

- Each partition keeps one version of the CUCM software and databases.

- Operation continues during upgrades.

- Upgrade installs to the inactive partition.

- During reboot, versions (active and inactive partitions) can be swapped. The previously active partition becomes inactive and retains "old" software and databases until the next upgrade. Any changes made to the active partition are not replicated to the inactive partition. All changes made since the upgrade are lost when reverting.

- If versions are switched again before the next upgrade, you revert to the previous version (downgrade).

An upgraded system always maintains two versions of software (does not apply to upgrade from 4.x).

Chapter Summary

The following list summarizes the key points that were discussed in this chapter:

- Direct upgrades from Versions 3.x, 4.0(2), and 5.0(1) to 6.x are not supported.

- CUCM Basic installation can be performed from a bootable DVD or factory preinstalled systems.

- Using the Upgrade During Install option saves time when applying service release updates.

- The CUCM administrator user ID can be freely chosen. The account CCMAdministrator is no longer mandatory.

- Upgrades from Version 5.x to 6.x can be done via a Cisco Unified Operating System Administration software upgrade.

Review Questions

Use the questions here to review what you learned in this chapter. The correct answers are found in Appendix A, "Answers to Chapter Review Questions."

1. Which version of CallManager cannot be upgraded directly to CUCM 6.0(1)?

   a. 4.1(3)

   b. 5.0(1)

   c. 5.0(4)

   d. 5.1(1)

2. The installation of CUCM from the Product Deployment Selection window may include which products? (Choose three.)

   a. CUCM

   b. Cisco Unified Unity

   c. Cisco Unified CMBE

   d. Cisco Unity Connection

3. Patches are available from which mechanisms? (Choose three.)

   a. DVD

   b. TFTP

   c. FTP

   d. SFTP

Administration

CUCM provides several GUIs and a command-line interface (CLI) to administer the CUCM OS and application. This chapter describes the available CUCM administration and user interfaces.

Chapter Objectives

Upon completing this lesson, you will be able to describe the purpose and basic functionality of all CUCM administrative and user interfaces, be able to access and navigate between them, and be able to meet the following objectives:

- Describe CUCM administration and user interface options.

- Describe how to access the CUCM User Options web interface and what features it provides.

- Describe how to access the CUCM Administration web interface and what features it provides.

- Describe how to access the CUCM Serviceability web interface and what features it provides.

- Describe how to access the CUCM Disaster Recovery System web interface and what features it provides.

- Describe how to access the CUCM Operating System Administration web interface and what features it provides.

- Describe how to access the CUCM CLI and what features it provides.

CUCM User Interface Options

CUCM 5.x and 6.x operate on an appliance model where access to the system is possible only through CUCM GUIs and the CUCM CLI. The available interfaces are shown in Figure 4-1 and described in Table 4-1.

Figure 4-1   *CUCM Interface Options*

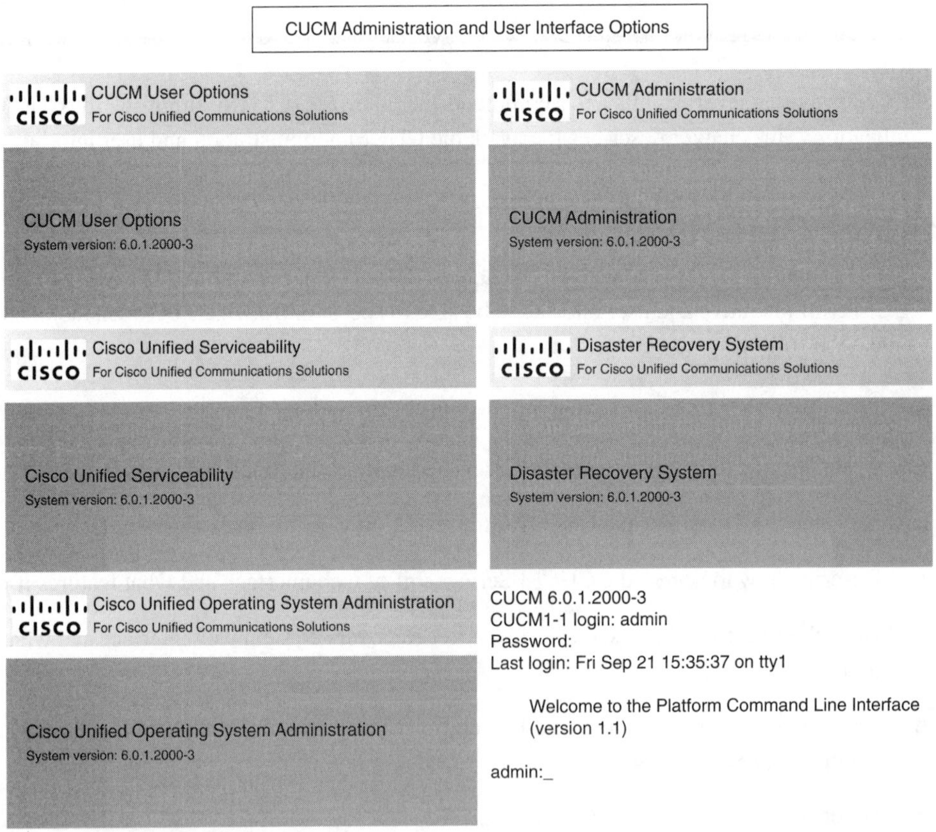

Table 4-1   *Publisher Server Required Services*

Interface Option	Description
CUCM User Options	Allows end users to customize their own IP phone settings, configuration, and features
CUCM Administration	Allows CUCM administrators to configure call routing, voice mail, devices, applications, end users, and so on

Table 4-1 *Publisher Server Required Services (Continued)*

Interface Option	Description
Cisco Unified Serviceability	Allows CUCM administrators to control feature and network services, configure alarms and trace information, and so on
Disaster Recovery System	Allows platform administrators to perform CUCM backup and restore tasks
Cisco Unified Operating System - Administration	Allows platform administrators to manage the CUCM operating system
Administration CLI	Allows platform administrators to manage the CUCM operating system via a CLI

CUCM User Options Interface

CUCM has functionality that allows end-user accounts to be configured and associated with one or more IP phones, and enables end users to configure personal features for their IP phones. The configurable features include the following:

■ Call Forwarding.

■ Speed Dial Numbers.

■ End users can configure speed dial buttons on each IP phone. Speed dial buttons configured via the phone button template on the IP phone are limited by the number of buttons on the IP phone. The User Options web interface also allows the end user to configure up to 99 abbreviated dialing soft keys.

■ Subscribe to IP Phone Services.

■ Most Cisco IP Phone models can be used to access Extensible Markup Language (XML)-based web applications end users can freely subscribe to.

■ Configure Personal Address Book and Fast Dials.

■ Change Message Waiting Lamp Policy.

■ Change User Locale (Phone Language), Password, and PIN.

Users with permission to access the web interface may do so via the following URL: https://*<ip-address>*/ccmuser. Users must use the username and password that has been provided by the CUCM administrator. Figure 4-2 shows the CCMUser login page.

Figure 4-2   *CUCM User Options Interface*

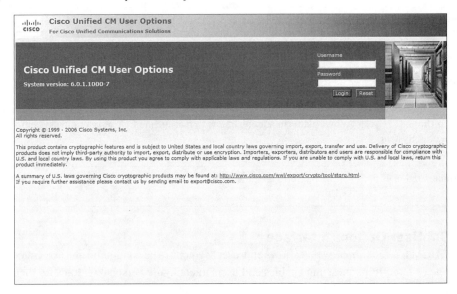

Once logged in, the end user will see the web page displayed in Figure 4-3.

Figure 4-3   *CUCM User Options Menus*

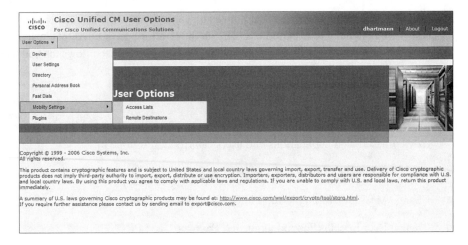

CUCM Administration Interface

The CUCM Administration web interface provides the following functions:

- System configuration, including CUCM groups, presence groups, device mobility groups, device pools, regions, locations, phone security profile, and so on

- Call-routing configuration, including dial rules, route patterns, call hunting, time-of-day routing, partitioning and CSS, intercom, call park, call pickup, and so on

- Media resource configuration, including conference bridges, transcoders, music on hold (MOH), media termination points (MTP), and so on

- Voice-mail configuration

- Device configuration, including gateways, gatekeepers, trunks, IP phones, and so on

- Application configuration, including manager - assistant, attendant console, and so on

- User management, including end users, application users, groups, and role configuration

When accessing the CUCM Administration web interface, shown in Figure 4-4, the CUCM administrator must log in with the CCMAdministrator username and password. The initial Communications Manager administrator account is created during installation. Additional CM administrator accounts can be created from the CUCM Administration web interface by assigning the appropriate user group to the user. This is covered in a later chapter with multilevel administration (MLA). The CUCM Administration page is available at https:// <ip-address>/ccmadmin.

Figure 4-4 *Administrator Web Interface*

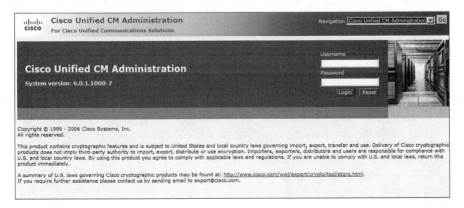

Figure 4-5 illustrates the main configuration menu options that are available from the CUCM Administration configuration page.

Figure 4-5   *Administrator Configuration Menus*

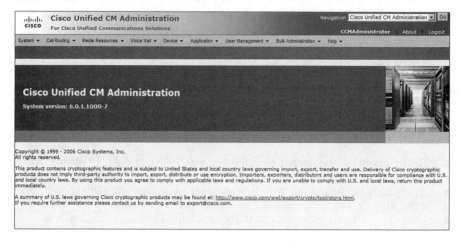

Cisco Unified Serviceability Interface

The Cisco Unified Serviceability web interface provides the following functions:

- Configure alarms, logs, and traces (for monitoring and troubleshooting CUCM).

- Configure call details records (CDR) disk storage and external billing servers. CUCM can create CDRs and call management records (CMR), providing detailed information about call activities and voice quality. Using CUCM Serviceability, an administrator can limit the disk space used for these records and configure CUCM to copy or move these files containing CDRs and CMRs to external billing servers using the Secure File Transfer Protocol (SFTP).

- Activate, deactivate, start, stop, and restart network and feature services.

- Configure Simple Network Management Protocol (SNMP) settings.

- Configure serviceability reports. Serviceability reports are automatically created every night and allow system analysis based on monitored objects. CUCM administrators can obtain the generated reports from the CUCM Serviceability web pages.

The CUCM Serviceability web interface is accessible via the Navigation drop-down menu on any of the GUI web interfaces except the user web interface. Figure 4-6 shows the Navigation menu.

Figure 4-6 *Navigation Menu*

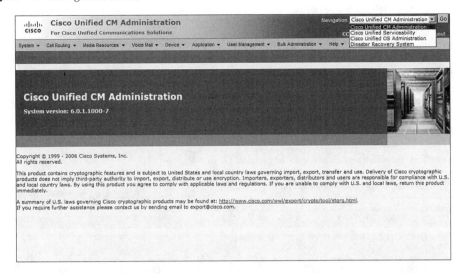

The CUCM Serviceability menu is also accessible directly via the following URL: https://
<ip-address>/ccmservice. Figure 4-7 shows the CUCM Serviceability login page. The
CUCM Administrator user has access to the Serviceability menu.

Figure 4-7 *Cisco Unified Serviceability Login*

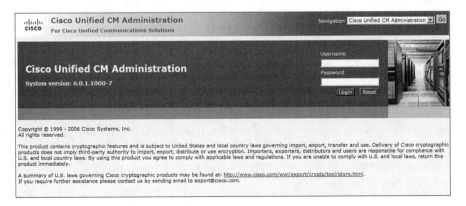

Figure 4-8 shows the CUCM Serviceability menu options.

Disaster Recovery System

The CUCM Disaster Recovery System web interface provides the following functions:

- Write backups to a physical tape drive or remote SFTP server

- Support full cluster backups

- Support ad hoc backup and restore jobs

- Support scheduled backups

Figure 4-8   *Cisco Unified Serviceability Menu Options*

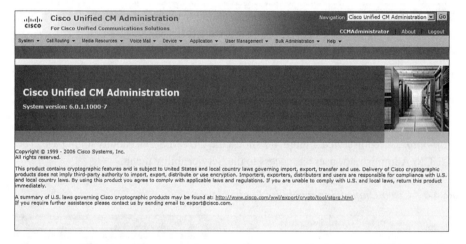

The CUCM Disaster Recovery System web interface can be accessed only by a platform administrator. The initial platform administrator account is created during installation of the CUCM product. During the installation of CUCM, the installer must configure a username and password for both the CallManager administration and the operating system administration. Security best practices mandate these accounts use a different username, but the username of the platform and operating system administrators can be the same. Additional platform administrator accounts can be created only from the CUCM CLI using the **set account** command.

The CUCM Disaster Recovery System web page is accessible via the Navigation drop-down menu shown in Figure 4-6 or via https://*<ip-address>*/drf. Figure 4-9 shows the Disaster Recovery System login page.

Figure 4-9 *Disaster Recovery System Login Page*

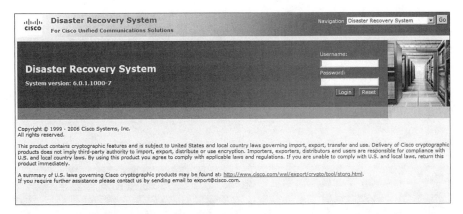

Figure 4-10 shows the Disaster Recovery System menu.

Figure 4-10 *Disaster Recovery System Menu Page*

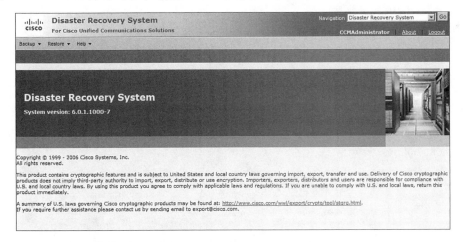

Operating System Administration

The CUCM Operating System Administration web interface allows platform administrators to configure and manage the CUCM operating system. Examples of operating system administration tasks include the following:

- Check software and hardware status

- Upgrade system software and install or upgrade options

- View or update IP addresses

- Manage Network Time Protocol (NTP) servers

- Manage server security, including IPsec configuration and certificates
- Ping other network devices
- Manage remote support (Technical Assistance Center, TAC) accounts

The Operating System Administration web page is accessible via the Navigation drop-down menu or directly at https://*<ip-address>*/cmplatform. Figure 4-11 shows the Operating System Administration web page.

Figure 4-11 *Operating System Login Page*

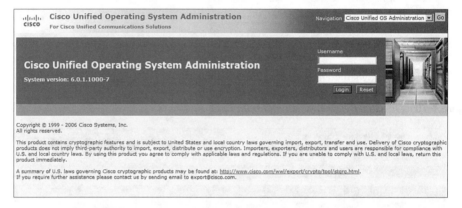

The platform administrator username is required for access to the Operating System Administration page. Figure 4-12 shows the Operating System Administration page menu options.

Figure 4-12 *Operating System Menu Page*

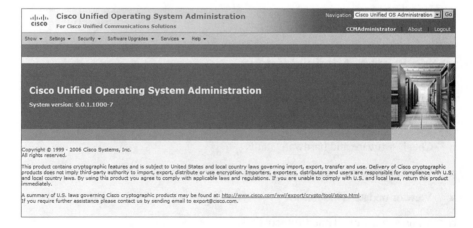

Command-Line Interface

The CUCM CLI provides similar features to platform administrators that they can find in the CUCM OS and CUCM DRS GUI and includes some additional functions:

■ Display platform information, such as product version, CPU, memory, disk usage, platform hardware, serial number, and so on

■ Display network, process, and load information

■ Configure additional platform administrator accounts

■ Change platform administrator account password and security passwords

■ Perform disaster recovery tasks

■ Use tools such as ping, traceroute, and packet capture

■ Change network configuration settings

■ Start, stop, and restart services

■ Perform system restarts, shutdowns, and switch versions

When accessing the CUCM CLI, the platform administrator has to log in with a username and password. The CLI is accessible via the physical Media Convergence Server (MCS) platform or over the network via a Secure Shell (SSH) client. Telnet is not supported on CUCM because Telnet does not provide transport security.

When using the CUCM CLI, you can use **?** to see the available commands or command options. In the first example shown in Figure 4-13, the **?** was used at the root access level; therefore, all top-level commands displayed. In the second example, the command **show ?** was entered; therefore, all available **show** commands displayed. Finally, all utility commands (**utils**) displayed because the **utils ?** command was entered.

Figure 4-13   *Command-Line Interface Navigation*

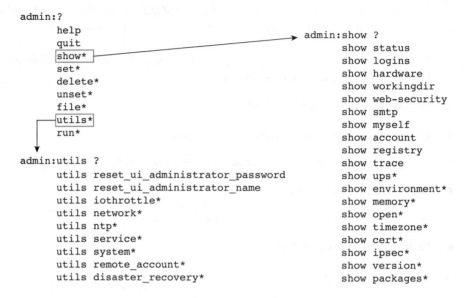

Chapter Summary

The following list summarizes the key points that were discussed in this chapter:

- The User Options web interface allows end users to customize their own IP phone settings, configuration, and features.

- The Administration web interface allows CUCM administrators to provision the system and configure call routing, voice e-mail, devices, applications, end users, and so on.

- The Serviceability web interface enables CUCM administrators to control the feature and network services and to configure alarms, traces, and so on.

- The Disaster Recovery web interface enables CUCM platform administrators to perform or schedule CUCM backup and restore tasks.

- The Operating System Administration web interface enables CUCM platform administrators to manage the CUCM operating system.

- The Administration CLI allows CUCM platform administrators to manage the CUCM operating system and perform backup and restore tasks from a command-line interface.

Review Questions

Use the questions here to review what you learned in this chapter. The correct answers are found in Appendix A, "Answers to Chapter Review Questions."

1. Which of the following is not one of the CUCM management interfaces?

   a. CUCM Operating System Administration

   b. CUCM Administrator

   c. CUCM Serviceability

   d. CUCM Control Panel

2. From what URL can you back up and restore the CUCM database?

   a. https://*ip-address*/ccmadmin

   b. https://*ip-address*/drs

   c. https://*ip-address*/drf

   d. https://*ip-address*/ccmuser

   e. https://*ip-address*/cmplatform

   f. https://*ip-address*/ccmservice

3. What URL is used for CUCM administration?

   a. https://*ip-address*/ccmadmin

   b. https://*ip-address*/drs

   c. https://*ip-address*/drf

   d. https://*ip-address*/ccmuser

   e. https://*ip-address*/cmplatform

   f. https://*ip-address*/ccmservice

4. What URL is used to configure the IP address of CUCM?

   a. https://*ip-address*/ccmadmin

   b. https://*ip-address*/drs

   c. https://*ip-address*/drf

   d. https://*ip-address*/ccmuser

   e. https://*ip-address*/cmplatform

   f. https://*ip-address*/ccmservice

5.   What URL is used to stop, start, and restart services in CUCM?

a.   https://*ip-address*/ccmadmin

b.   https://*ip-address*/drs

c.   https://*ip-address*/drf

d.   https://*ip-address*/ccmuser

e.   https://*ip-address*/cmplatform

f.   https://*ip-address*/ccmservice

6.   What is the mechanism available to move between different administrative interfaces in CUCM?

a.   The Navigation menu

b.   The Navigator menu

c.   The Hyperlink menu

d.   The Task Bar menu

7.   Which of the following user interfaces is used to administer dial plans on CUCM?

a.   Disaster Recovery System

b.   CUCM User Options

c.   CUCM Serviceability

d.   CUCM Administration

8.   Which of the following user interfaces is used to set speed dials on CUCM? (Choose two.)

a.   Disaster Recovery System

b.   CUCM User Options

c.   CUCM Serviceability

d.   CUCM Administration

9.   Which of the following user interfaces is used to configure alarms on CUCM?

a.   Disaster Recovery System

b.   CUCM User Options

c.   CUCM Serviceability

d.   CUCM Administration

CHAPTER 5

Initial Configuration Settings

CUCM configuration includes basic settings plus specific settings that depend on the features and services used. This lesson describes how basic settings on CUCM are configured to enable the system and prepare CUCM for endpoint deployment.

Chapter Objectives

Upon completing this lesson, you will be able to activate required CUCM services and settings to enable features and remove Domain Name System (DNS) reliance, and you will be able to meet the following objectives:

- Identify elements used for general, initial configuration.

- Identify network configuration options of CUCM.

- Identify the reasons for using Network Time Protocol (NTP) servers and enabling DHCP services in CUCM.

- Describe the reliance on DNS by IP phones when server names are used rather than server IP addresses.

- Describe the difference between network and feature services and explain how they can be managed using the Cisco Unified Serviceability web interface.

- Describe the purpose of enterprise parameters and explain key parameters.

- Describe the purpose of service parameters and explain key parameters.

CUCM Initial Configuration

After you install CUCM, some initial configuration has to be done before starting to deploy endpoints. This initial configuration includes the items in Table 5-1.

Table 5-1 *Publisher Server Required Services*

Configuration Item	Description
Network settings	Basic network settings have already been configured during installation, but some of them should be revisited (use of external NTP and DNS servers), and network settings that are not configurable during installation (for example, enabling DHCP services on CUCM) have to be addressed before endpoint deployment.
Network and feature services	CUCM servers run network services (automatically activated) and feature services (activated by the administrator). After installation, network services should be checked, and desired feature services have to be activated.
Enterprise parameters	CUCM has cluster-wide configuration settings called enterprise parameters. After installation, enterprise parameter default values should be verified and modified if required.
Service parameters	CUCM services have configurable parameters that can usually be set per CUCM server. After installation and service activation, service parameter default values should be verified and modified if required.

Network Components

CUCM leverages various IP networking protocols and systems.

Network Time Protocol

Network Time Protocol (NTP) is a protocol for synchronizing the clocks of computer systems over IP networks through use of a hierarchical clock strata organization. A stratum level 1 timing source device is an extremely precise clock source using the rare earth element cesium. Cesium clocks used to be very expensive, but most service providers with large central offices now have local stratum level 1 clocks. Global positioning system (GPS) satellites provide a stratum level 1 clocking source that provides a cost-effective synchronization system.

Stratum level 1 clocks are distributed over networks to provide timing information to a large number of devices. A linear relationship exists between the number of nodes passed and the degradation of the timing quality.

Stratum level 2 timing sources are based on the rare earth element rubidium. Distribution of stratum 2 time information becomes inaccurate more quickly than stratum 1 information.

Stratum level 2 timing is not as accurate as stratum level 1, but the timing is accurate enough to time a large SONET node. SONET nodes are very high-speed networks that are used by service providers to transport time-division multiplexing (TDM) voice calls through networks operating at up to OC-192 speeds (almost 10 Gbp/s). T1 and T3 voice interfaces are provisioned from SONET nodes, such as the Cisco ONS 15454.

> **NOTE**   More information on SONET, optical networking, and the ONS 15454 is available in *Cisco Self-Study: Building Cisco Metro Optical Networks (METRO)*, by Dave Warren and Dennis Hartmann (Cisco Press, 2003).

Stratum level 3 timing sources are based on the rare earth element quartz, which has become affordable enough that it is built in to most off-the-shelf wristwatches. Stratum level 3 is accurate enough to time a SONET node, but it quickly loses accuracy when distributed to other nodes. Most T3 (44.736 Mb/s) controllers have built-in oscillators with a stratum level 3 timing source. T3 interfaces multiplex (28) individual T1 interfaces for a total of 672 voice channels.

CUCM has an option to use NTP to obtain time information from a time server. Only the CUCM publisher will communicate with one or more NTP servers. The timing that the publisher receives is synchronized to the subscriber servers. If an external NTP server is not used, CUCM can be manually configured with the date and time. The system time in most servers is a stratum level 4 timing source and should not be relied on to time a production network.

Dynamic Host Configuration Protocol

Dynamic Host Configuration Protocol (DHCP) is a protocol that allows IP endpoints to obtain their IP settings dynamically from a server. The most important settings include the IP address, subnet mask, default gateway, TFTP server (option 150), and DNS server. CUCM features a DHCP server that was designed to serve Cisco IP Phones only.

Trivial File Transfer Protocol

Trivial File Transfer Protocol (TFTP) is a simple file transfer protocol used by Cisco IP Phones to obtain configuration files and their software (binary image load). A CUCM server has to run the TFTP service on at least one server to be able to support Cisco IP Phones.

Domain Name System

Domain Name System (DNS) is a name-resolution protocol that allows IP applications to refer to other systems by logical names rather than IP addresses. A CUCM cluster can be configured to use either DNS or IP addresses.

NTP and DHCP Considerations

NTP can be configured during installation of the CUCM product. NTP can also be configured after the installation procedure using the CUCM Administration web pages.

It is extremely important that all network devices have accurate time information because the system time of CUCM is relevant in the following situations:

■ Cisco IP Phones display date and time information; this information is obtained from CUCM unless an NTP reference is assigned to the phone. NTP references can be configured in date/time groups in CUCM versions 5.*x* and later. The date/time group is then added to Cisco IP Phone devices.

■ Call details records (CDR) provide time-stamped call reporting, analysis, and billing information. Call management records (CMR) contain quality of service (QoS) information regarding the quality of phone calls, including the number of lost packets (per direction), average jitter (delay variation), and maximum jitter. CMRs are mapped to CDRs.

■ Alarms, log files, and trace files include time stamps with millisecond-level accuracy. One second of processing in a CUCM server can have hundreds of lines of trace output. Troubleshooting calls that involve multiple servers frequently require the correlation of alarm, event, and trace information available in different systems. Correlation of these records is possible only if all devices in the network have the same date and time information.

■ CUCM includes features that rely on date and time. These features include time-of-day routing, certificate-based security features, and remote support.

> **NOTE** *Cisco Unified Communications IP Telephony, Part 2* (Cisco Press, 2007) explains the operation of X.509v3 certificates, certificate trust lists, IPsec, transport layer security, and Secure Skinny Client Control Protocol (SCCPS).

Figure 5-1 displays a master reference clock from which the publisher server is synchronizing time. The publisher server redistributes the timing information to the subscriber servers.

Figure 5-1 *Network Time Protocol*

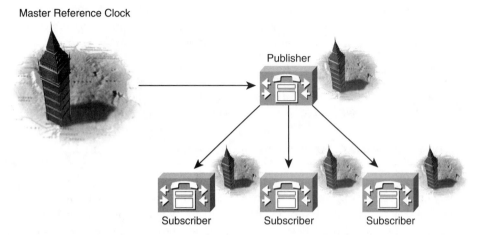

CUCM and all network devices should synchronize their time from a stratum level 1 NTP server. To modify NTP configurations in CUCM, navigate to **System > NTP Servers** from the CUCM Administration web pages, as shown in Figure 5-2. NTP servers can be added, deleted, or modified.

Figure 5-2 *Network Time Protocol Configuration*

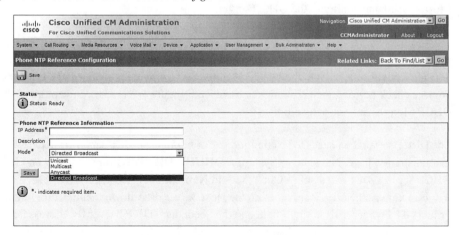

DHCP

The CUCM DHCP server is designed to serve IP phones in small deployments (maximum of 1000 devices). It provides a subset of the functionality that was provided by the Windows 2000 Server in CUCM versions earlier than CallManager 5.0.

> **NOTE**   Due to the CPU load impact, CUCM DHCP server must not be used in deployments larger than 1000 registered devices. The CPU load of the server can be monitored using the Real-Time Monitoring Tool (RTMT). If high CPU load is experienced, the DHCP service should be provided by other devices (DHCP server, switch, or router). RTMT is covered in *Cisco Unified Communications IP Telephony, Part 2.*

Only one DHCP server can be configured per CUCM cluster; no backup configuration is possible. The CUCM DHCP server can be configured with multiple subnets. DHCP relay must be enabled in remote subnets to allow the DHCP broadcast request packets to be forwarded to the DHCP server. Routers drop all broadcast packets by default, but the packets can be configured with DHCP relay by using the **ip helper-address** command.

To configure DHCP support on CUCM, follow these steps:

Step 1   Activate the DHCP Monitor Service.

Step 2   Add and configure the DHCP server.

Step 3   Configure the DHCP subnets.

Navigate to the Cisco Unified Serviceability web pages. From the Tools menu, choose **Service Activation**. Activate the DHCP Monitor Service by clicking the **DHCP Monitor Service** check box and then clicking the **Save** icon. Figure 5-3 is a screen capture of the DHCP Monitor Service activation.

The DHCP server then needs to be configured. Configure the DHCP server from the CUCM Administration page. Navigate to **System > DHCP > DHCP Server**. The Find and List DHCP Servers page will display. Click the **Add New** button. Choose the CUCM server that will be acting as the DHCP server from the Host Server drop-down menu. Configure the Primary TFTP Server IP Address field and the Secondary TFTP Server IP Address field. It is advisable to have two CUCM servers running the TFTP service for fault-tolerance purposes. Figure 5-4 shows the DHCP server configuration page options.

Figure 5-3 *Service Activation: DHCP Monitor Service*

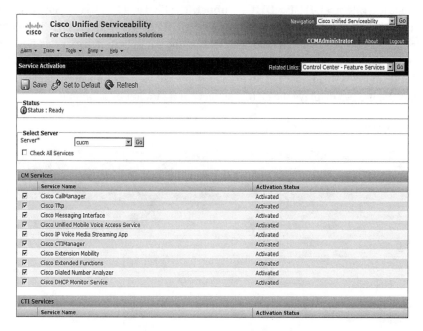

Figure 5-4 *DHCP Server Configuration*

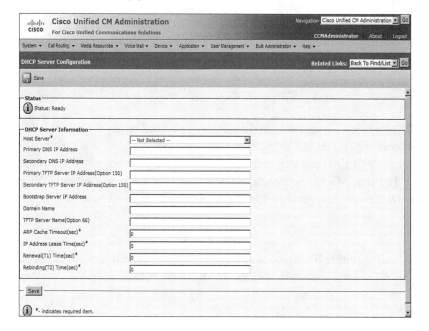

The DHCP subnet(s) needs to be configured from the CUCM Administration page. Navigate to **System > DHCP > DHCP Subnet**. The Find and List DHCP Subnets page will display. Click the **Add New** button. Choose the DHCP server from the DHCP Server drop-down menu. This is a required field. All fields in the configuration pages that have an asterisk (*) to the upper right of the configuration option are required fields. Specify the subnet IP address, IP address range, primary router IP address, subnet mask, and TFTP servers. Figure 5-5 displays the DHCP subnet configuration page options.

Figure 5-5 *DHCP Subnet Configuration*

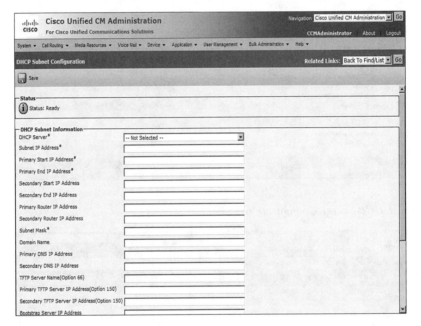

In CUCM releases earlier than 5.0, DHCP services could be provided by the Windows-based operating system of CUCM. If the Windows DHCP server was used and CUCM is upgraded to a CUCM release running the Linux operating system, all DHCP configuration is lost. The Data Migration Assistant (DMA) does not migrate Windows DHCP configuration. DHCP can configured on CUCM servers beginning with Release 5.0.

DNS

CUCM can use either IP addresses or names to refer to other IP devices in application settings. When names are used, they need to be resolved to IP addresses by DNS.

Both methods have some advantages:

- **Using IP addresses**: The system does not depend on a DNS server. This prevents loss of service when the DNS server cannot be reached. Clients, using DNS, query the server with a name lookup request and receive a reply in which the DNS server resolves the hostname record of the query to an IP address. Eliminating the requirement of a DNS server reduces the danger of DNS configuration errors, DNS outages, and the latency issues involved in sending a query and receiving a response using the DNS model. Troubleshooting is simplified when using IP addresses rather than DNS names because there is no need to perform name resolution.

- **Using DNS**: Management is simplified because logical names are easier to remember than IP addresses. If IP addresses change, there is no need to modify any of the application settings that rely on the existing IP address. When DNS is used, the applications point to a DNS name that does not change; the underlying IP address might change at any time with no consequence to the IP addresses that rely on the server. CUCM server addressing is sent to Cisco IP Phones in the CUCM group in the phone's XML configuration file. The addressing sent down to the IP phone can be based on IP addresses or names.

Because of the additional point of failure introduced using DNS, the Cisco best practices recommendation is to *not use* DNS with CUCM.

Table 5-2 summarizes the advantages and disadvantage of using DNS with CUCM.

Table 5-2 *IP Addressing and DNS Comparison*

IP Addressing Advantages	DNS Advantages
Does not require a DNS server	Simplifies management because of the use of names rather than numbers
Prevents the IP telephony network from failing if the IP phones lose connection to the DNS server	Enables easier IP address changes because of name-based IP paths
Decreases the amount of time required when a device attempts to contact the Unified CM server	Allows server to IP phone NAT
Simplifies troubleshooting	

Before the IP phone can communicate with CUCM, it has to resolve the name of the server. Signaling messages are then exchanged between the Cisco IP Phone and CUCM, as illustrated in Figure 5-6.

Figure 5-6 *Call Flow with DNS*

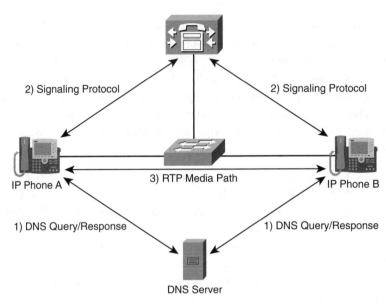

When DNS naming is not used in the CUCM cluster, there is no need to resolve the name of the CUCM to an IP address. The signaling between the IP phone and CUCM can be set up faster, and calls can be processed even if the DNS service is not available. CUCM will have higher availability and faster response times by removing any DNS reliance. Call flow without the use of DNS is illustrated in Figure 5-7.

Figure 5-7 *Call Flow Without DNS*

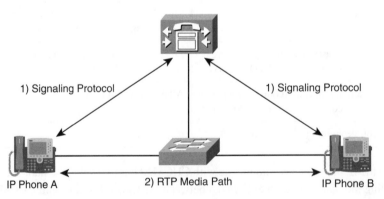

To change the system to operate without a DNS server, follow these steps:

Step 1   In CUCM Administration, go to **System > Server**.

Step 2   Click the **Find** button and select the first (next) available server from the list of CUCM servers.

Step 3   Change the server name to the IP address of the server and save the changes, as shown in Figure 5-8.

NOTE   Repeat Steps 2 and 3 for each server in the cluster.

Figure 5-8   *Server Configuration*

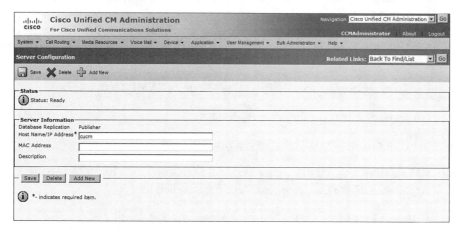

Network and Feature Services

A CUCM cluster can consist of up to 20 servers. Each server can fulfill different tasks, such as running a TFTP or DHCP server, being the database publisher, processing calls, providing media resources, and so on.

Depending on the usage of a server, different services have to be activated on the system. There are two types of services on CUCM servers:

■   **Network services**: Network services are automatically activated and are required for the operation of the server. Network services cannot be activated or deactivated by the administrator, but they can be stopped, started, or restarted from the Cisco Unified Serviceability web interface. Just choose **Control Center > Network Services**.

■ **Feature services**: Feature services can be selectively activated or deactivated per server to assign specific tasks or functions (call processing, TFTP, and so on) to a certain server. Feature services can be activated and deactivated by the administrator from the Cisco Unified Serviceability web interface (**Tools > Service Activation**). Feature services can be started, stopped, or restarted from the Cisco Unified Serviceability web interface (**Control Center > Feature Services**).

Network Services

Network services are the operating system services that CUCM relies on. Network services are summarized as follows:

■ **Performance and monitoring services**: Cisco CallManager Serviceability RTMT, Cisco RTMT Reporter

■ **Backup and restore services**: Cisco DRF Master, Cisco DRF Local System Services: Cisco CallManager Serviceability, Cisco CDP, Cisco Trace Collection Service

■ **Platform services**: Cisco Database, Cisco Tomcat, SNMP Master Agent

■ **DB services**: Cisco Database Layer Monitor

■ **SOAP services**: SOAP Real Time Service APIs and so on

■ **CM services**: Cisco CallManager Personal Directory, Cisco Extension Mobility Application, Cisco CallManager Cisco IP Phone Services

■ **CDR services**: Cisco CDR Repository Manager, CDR Agent

■ **Admin services**: Cisco CallManager Admin

Feature Services

Feature services are the CUCM-related services that run on top of the operating system and database. Feature services are summarized as follows:

■ **Database and admin services**: Cisco AXL Web Service, Cisco Bulk Provisioning Service, Cisco TAPS Service

- **Performance and monitoring services**: Cisco Serviceability Reporter, Cisco CallManager SNMP Service

- **CM services**: Cisco CallManager, Cisco TFTP, Cisco CTIManager, Cisco Extension Mobility

- **CTI services**: Cisco CallManager Attendant Console Server, Cisco IP Manager Assistant, Cisco WebDialer Web Service

- **CDR services**: Cisco SOAP, including CDRonDemand Service, Cisco CAR Scheduler, Cisco CAR Web Service

- **Security services**: Cisco CTL Provider, Cisco Certificate Proxy Function

- **Directory Services**: Cisco DirSync

- **Voice Quality Reporter Services**: Cisco Extended Functions

Service Activation

To activate or deactivate feature services for a server, follow these steps in the Cisco Unified Serviceability web interface:

Step 1   Go to **Tools > Service Activation**.

Step 2   Select the server where you want to activate or deactivate a service.

Step 3   Check or uncheck the check box for each service you want to modify, and save the changes.

Step 4   Use the Control Center to verify that the service has been started (**Tools > Control Center – Feature Services**).

Figure 5-9 illustrates the Service Activation configuration page in CUCM. The Related Links drop-down menus in the upper-right portion of the CUCM web pages hyperlink to different areas of CUCM configuration. Learning how to leverage the related links can increase the speed in which you can provision services in CUCM.

Control Center

The Control Center for feature services is used to start, stop, or restart services. It is also used to verify the current status and the activation status of feature services per server in the cluster.

Figure 5-9 *Service Activation*

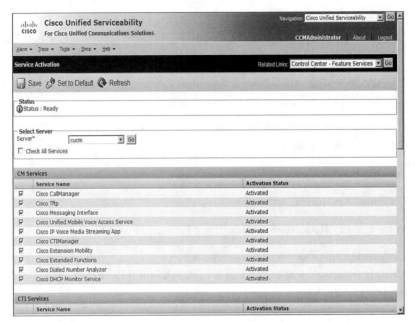

Figure 5-10 illustrates the process of viewing a service status and runtime. The figure also shows the process of selecting the radio button related to a particular service so that the service can be started, stopped, restarted, or refreshed.

Global Server Settings

Two types of settings parameters can be changed in CUCM globally across a server or globally across the cluster: enterprise parameters and service parameters.

Enterprise Parameters

Enterprise parameters are used to define cluster-wide system settings, and they apply to all devices and services in the cluster. After installation, enterprise parameter default values should be verified and modified if required before deploying endpoints. Some enterprise parameters will specify initial values of device defaults.

CAUTION   Only change enterprise parameters if you are fully aware of the impact of your modifications or if instructed to do so by Cisco Technical Assistance Center (TAC).

Figure 5-10 *Control Center*

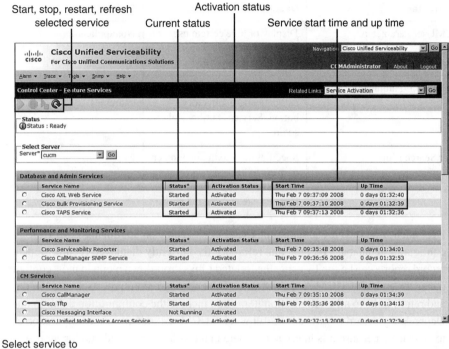

You can modify many enterprise parameters. Table 5-3 displays some frequently modified enterprise parameters.

Table 5-3 *Enterprise Parameters*

Parameter	Description	Default Value
Auto Registration Phone Protocol	Specifies the protocol that auto-registered phones should boot with during initialization	SCCP
Enable Dependency Records	Determines whether to display dependency records	False

continues

Table 5-3   *Enterprise Parameters (Continued)*

Parameter	Description	Default Value
CCMUser Parameters	Display or hide certain user-configurable settings from the CCMUser web page	Not applicable
Phone URL Parameters	URLs for IP phone authentication, Directory button, Services button, and so on	Hostnames rather than IP addresses
User Search Limit	Specifies the maximum number of users to be retrieved from a search in the Corporate Directory feature on the phone	64

Dependency records are a feature of CUCM that enable an administrator to view configuration database records that reference the currently displayed record. Dependency record reports can be run by using the Related Links drop-down menu in most configuration pages throughout CUCM Administration. Dependency record reports search the database and return links to all configuration items that include the configuration detail in question. Dependency record reports are useful when CUCM will not allow a configuration element to be deleted because it is in use somewhere in the system but should no longer be in use. Because dependency records could cause a CPU spike in the server platform, it is not recommended that they be run during high-usage periods.

To modify enterprise parameters, follow these steps in the CUCM Administration web interface:

Step 1   Navigate to **System > Enterprise Parameters**.

Step 2   Change the enterprise parameter values as desired and save the changes.

NOTE   To obtain additional information about specific enterprise parameters, click the **?** symbol in the upper-right corner of the screen. The same help system is available by clicking the hyperlink of the enterprise parameter name.

Figure 5-11 shows the procedure to hide configuration elements from the CCMUser configuration pages. A business might not want end users to be able to change the Call

Forward All options of their phone in the CCMUser configuration pages, but the option exists in the page by default. Using the enterprise parameter options shown in Figure 5-11, the administrator can choose to remove the hyperlink to Call Forward All in the CCMUser section of the Enterprise Parameters Configuration page. All default settings appear on the right side of the Enterprise Parameter Configurations page.

Figure 5-11   *Enterprise Parameter Configuration*

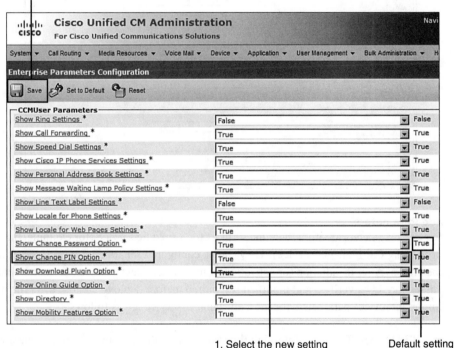

When you are removing DNS reliance, all hostnames within enterprise URL parameters have to be changed to IP addresses. Phone URL parameters change the website that the phone launches when the settings, services, or directories buttons are clicked on the Cisco IP Phone. The phone URL parameters are part of the enterprise parameters. Figure 5-12 shows the configuration of the phone URL parameters.

Figure 5-12 *Phone URL Parameters*

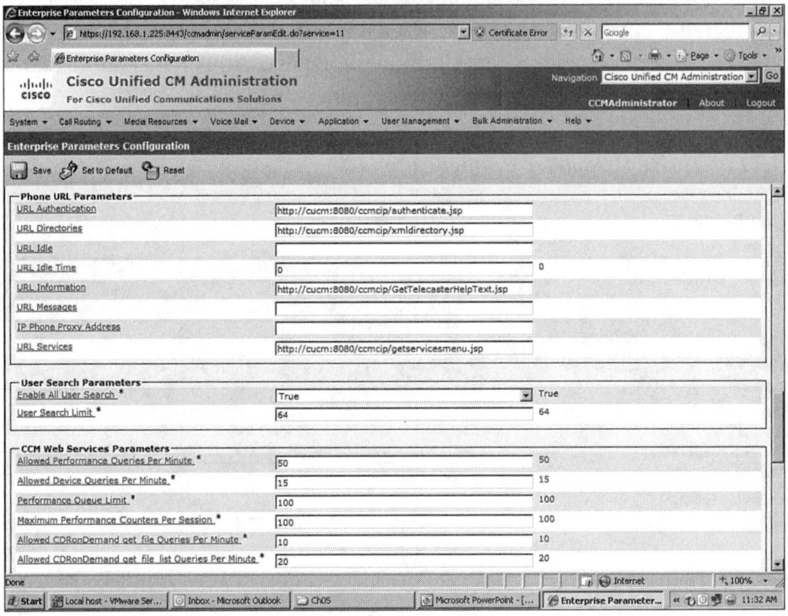

Service Parameters

Service parameters are used to define settings for a specific service (for example, the call-processing CallManager service). They can be configured separately for each server in the cluster. After installation (or activation of feature services), service parameter default values should be verified and modified if required, before deploying endpoints. The most important service parameters for the CallManager service are as follows:

■   **T302 timer**: The T.303 interdigit timeout specifies the interdigit timeout value used to route calls when there are multiple possible matches in the database. Multiple possible matches is a condition that will exist when variable-length numbers (international) or overlapping dial plans are being analyzed by CUCM. Reducing the default T.302 value will accelerate the call-routing decision of CUCM when users dial international phone numbers or a phone number that overlaps with another. The default T.302 timer is 15,000-ms (15 seconds). A value of 15 seconds is too long for most environments. Best practice is to reconfigure this timer to a value of 5000 ms (5 seconds). An example of an overlapping dial plan is extension 1500 and extension 15001. CUCM would not know whether it was done receiving digits if the digits of 1500 were received. The user might dial another 1, which would direct the call to a different extension. In this situation, CUCM waits for the T.302 timer to expire and then extends the call to extension 1500.

- **CDR and CMR**: CDRs are the basis for call reporting, accounting, and billing. The service parameters are used to enable CDRs and CMRs. CMRs report QoS information related to the phone call (lost packets, average jitter, maximum jitter, and so forth).

- **Cisco Unified Extension Mobility maximum login time**: After expiration of this timer, a user is logged out of Cisco Unified Extension Mobility.

- **Cisco Unified Attendant Console username**: Specifies the application username that is used by the Cisco Unified Attendant Console application when logging in to the CUCM Computer Telephony Integration (CTI) interface.

By default, not all service parameters display. To see the complete list of service parameters, click the **Advanced** button. The Change B-Channel Maintenance Status service parameter is an example of a CallManager service parameter that does not show by default. Table 5-4 includes some frequently modified service parameters. Hundreds of service parameters are available to CUCM, many of which you will never encounter. The best way to find one of the parameters listed in Table 5-4 is to use the Find function of your web browser to locate the option on the page.

Table 5-4 *Service Parameter Examples*

Parameter	Description	Default Value
CDR Enabled Flag	This parameter determines whether CDRs are generated.	False
Station Keepalive Interval	This parameter designates the interval between keepalive messages sent from Cisco IP Phones to the primary CUCM.	30 seconds
T302 Timer	This parameter specifies an interdigit timer for sending the setup acknowledgment message. When this timer expires, CUCM routes the dialed digits.	15 seconds
Automated Alternate Routing Enable	This parameter determines whether to use automated alternate routing when the system does not have enough bandwidth.	False
Change B-Channel Maintenance Status (click Advanced button first)	This parameter allows CUCM to change individual B channel maintenance status for PRI and CAS interfaces in real time for troubleshooting.	No default

To modify service parameters, follow these steps in the CUCM Administration web interface:

Step 1   Navigate to **System > Service Parameters**.

Step 2   Select the server and the service for which you want to change service parameters.

Step 3   Change the service parameter values as desired and save the changes.

Step 4   Click **Save**.

Steps 2 through 4 are illustrated in Figures 5-13 and 5-14.

Figure 5-13   *Service Parameters: Server and Service Selection*

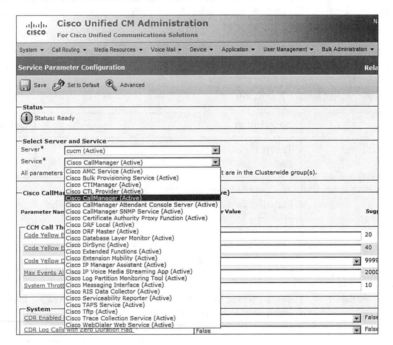

Figure 5-14   *Service Parameters: Configuration*

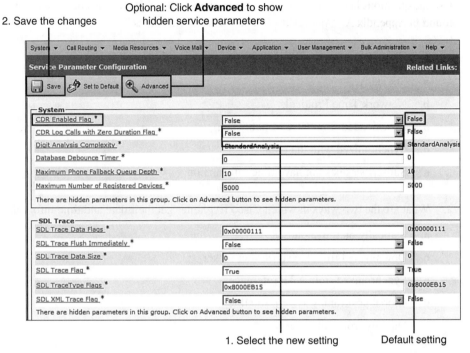

Chapter Summary

The following list summarizes the key points that were discussed in this chapter:

■   CUCM initial configuration includes network configuration, activation of feature services, and enterprise and service parameter configuration.

■   CUCM network configuration options include NTP configuration, DHCP server configuration, and using DNS versus IP addresses.

■   The CUCM DHCP service is designed to serve IP phones.

■   To avoid DNS reliance of IP phones, change hostnames to IP addresses.

■   Network services are automatically activated, whereas feature services are activated by the CUCM administrator.

■   Enterprise parameters are used to define cluster-wide system settings.

■   Service parameters are used to configure parameters of specific services.

Review Questions

Use the questions here to review what you learned in this chapter. The correct answers are found in Appendix A, "Answers to Chapter Review Questions."

1. How do subscriber servers get their time configuration?

    a. Statically.

    b. Network Time Protocol.

    c. Downloaded from CUCM publisher.

    d. Synchronized with the phone.

    e. Subscriber does not have time information.

2. What are the two ways in which Cisco IP Phones get their date and time information?

    a. Statically on the phone

    b. Downloaded from the subscriber server

    c. Synchronized from NTP reference

    d. Global positioning system satellite

    e. Directly from publisher

3. What tool enables you to install and remove a service from CUCM?

    a. Cisco Unified Serviceability

    b. Control Center

    c. Service Activation

    d. Add/Remove Programs

    e. Microsoft Service Console

4. What information does the DHCP option 150 provide?

    a. CUCM publisher IP address

    b. CUCM TFTP server IP address

    c. DHCP server IP address

    d. DNS server IP address

    e. XML service server

5. What default signaling protocol is used between CUCM and Cisco IP Phones?

   a. SIP

   b. SCCP

   c. RTP

   d. RTCP

   e. H.323

   f. MGCP

   g. Ethernet

6. Is the use of a DNS server in an IP telephony environment going to increase or decrease post dial delay?

   a. Increase

   b. Decrease

7. What tool enables you to start, stop, and restart CUCM services from CUCM?

   a. Cisco Unified Serviceability

   b. Control Center

   c. Service Activation

   d. Add/Remove Programs

   e. Microsoft Service Console

8. Which of the following is used to restart network service in CUCM?

   a. Cisco Unified Serviceability

   b. Control Center - Network Services

   c. Service Activation

   d. Control Center - Feature Services

   e. Add/Remove Programs

   f. Microsoft Service Console

9. In CUCM, where can you change the URLs that phone buttons access?

  a. Enterprise parameters

  b. Service parameters

  c. CUCM Serviceability

  d. CUCM Administration

10. Where can call details records and call management records be enabled?

  a. Enterprise parameters

  b. Service parameters

  c. CUCM Serviceability

  d. Cisco Real-Time Monitoring Tool

CHAPTER 6

Managing User Accounts

CUCM includes several features that are related to user accounts, including end-user features and administrative privileges. CUCM users can be managed using CUCM configuration tools or by integrating CUCM with a Lightweight Directory Access Protocol Version 3 (LDAPv3) directory. This lesson describes the types of user accounts used by CUCM and how they can be managed.

Chapter Objectives

Upon completing this lesson, you will be able to manage user accounts with CUCM and meet the following objectives:

- Identify the different user accounts in CUCM and explain how they are used.

- Describe how to add and delete users and how to assign privileges to them.

- Identify LDAPv3 synchronization characteristics and name the types of LDAPv3 support provided by CUCM

- Describe how LDAPv3 can be used for user provisioning and authentication.

CUCM User Accounts

Several CUCM features require user accounts for authentication purposes. These features include an administrative web page, user web pages, and the following applications:

- Cisco Unified Attendant Console

- Cisco Unified Extension Mobility

- Cisco Unified Manager Assistant (CUMA)

Cisco IP Phones can browse corporate and personal directories to find the directory number of a user. CUCM is provisioned with a user's first and last name to provide this directory-browsing functionality.

CUCM IP phone services can be configured to require a user login before providing access to the service. Users can authenticate with their username and password (alphanumeric) or PIN (numeric), depending on the needs of the application. CUCM sends authentication requests to an internal library called the Identity Management System (IMS) library, which is responsible for authenticating the user login credentials against the user database.

User Account Types

There are two types of user accounts in CUCM:

- **End users**: End users are associated with an individual and have an interactive login. End users can have administrative roles based on the user group role configuration.

- **Application users**: Application users are associated with applications such as Cisco Unified Attendant Console, Cisco Unified Contact Center Express (UCCX), or Cisco Unified Manager Assistant. The mentioned applications need to authenticate with CUCM, but application users do not have the ability to interactively log in. Application users are leveraged for internal process-level communications between applications.

Table 6-1 summarizes the differences between end users and application users.

Table 6-1 *User Account Types in CUCM*

End Users	Application Users
Associated with an individual	Associated with an application
Provide interactive logins	Provide noninteractive logins
User feature and system administration authorization	Application authorization
Included in phone directory	Not included in phone directory
Can be provisioned and authenticated using an external LDAPv3 directory server	Cannot use LDAPv3

The attributes associated with end users are separated into three categories, as follows:

- Personal and organizational settings:

    —*User ID*, first, middle, and last name

    —Manager user ID, department

    —Phone number, mail ID

■ Password

■ CUCM administration settings:

    —PIN, SIP digest credentials

    —User privileges (user groups and roles)

    —Associated PCs, controlled devices, and directory numbers

    —Application and feature parameters

User Privileges

CUCM allows for the assignment of user privileges to application users and end users.

Privileges that can be assigned to users include the following:

■ Access to administration and user web pages

■ Access to specific administrative functions

■ Access to application interfaces such as Computer Telephony Integration (CTI) and Simple Object Access Protocol (SOAP)

User privileges are configured using two configuration entities:

■ **User groups**: A collection of application users and end users with similar privilege levels

■ **Roles**: Resources for an application

    Each role refers to exactly one application, and each application has one or more resources. Access privileges are configured per application resource in the role configuration. Roles are assigned to user groups.

Figure 6-1 illustrates the access that four users have to two different applications. The needs of the four users are achieved through the assignment of two user groups.

User1 and User2 are assigned to Group1, which has two roles assigned to it for Application1. The privilege levels of Role1 and Role2 refer to the same application but provide different levels of access (privileges) to the resource. The overlapping configuration can be configured to give the highest or lowest overlapping privilege level.

User3 is assigned to both Group1 and Group2. Group1 and Group2 have role assignments of 1, 2, and 3. Role1 and Role2 both control different privilege levels to Application1 and Application2. It is best to avoid overlapping role privileges (Role1 and Role2) when possible.

User4 is assigned to Group2, which has privilege levels to Application1 and Application2, controlled through Role2 and Role3. User4 does not have overlapping privilege challenges.

Figure 6-1   *User Privilege Component Interaction*

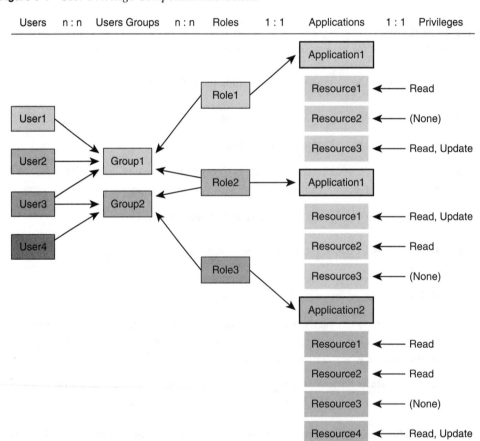

The goal of the configuration illustrated in Figure 6-2 is to create administrative groups that have read, write, and update access to the Communications Manager configuration web pages (CCMAdmin), and junior-level administrators who have read-only privileges to the CCMAdmin configuration web pages. The following text relates to the example illustrated in Figure 6-2.

CUCM has various Administration web pages associated with functions, such as the *Call Park web pages* (used to the configure call park feature), the *AAR Group web pages* (used to configure automated alternate routing), the *CallManager group web pages* (for CUCM configuration), and the *DRF Show Status page* (used to check the status of Disaster Recovery System backup or restore jobs).

CUCM has many default roles, called standard roles. Some of the standard roles are associated with CUCM Administration applications (CCMAdmin). There are many predefined roles in CUCM by default, but we explore two in this example. Two standard roles for CUCM Administration exist: Standard CCMAdmin Administration and Standard CCMAdmin Read-Only. Standard CCMAdmin Administration has all privileges of the CCMAdmin application set to Update, whereas Standard CCMAdmin Read-Only has CCMAdmin privileges set to Read-Only Access. Standard roles can be copied, renamed, and reconfigured to achieve the needs of the organization deploying CUCM.

CUCM has many default user groups, called standard user groups. Two examples of standard user groups are Standard CCM Super Users and Standard CCM Read-Only. User group Standard CCM Super Users is associated with role Standard CCMAdmin Administration, and user group Standard CCM Read-Only is associated with role Standard CCMAdmin Read-Only. This is illustrated in Figure 6-2.

To assign an end user full access to all configuration pages of CUCM Administration, you have to assign the end user just to the Standard CCM Super Users group. End users who should have read-only access to all configuration pages of CUCM Administration just have to be assigned to the Standard CCMAdmin Read-Only user group. The appropriate application privileges are configured in the default roles, and the default roles are assigned to the corresponding user groups.

The final step required to achieve the objective of Figure 6-2 is to assign the users John and Jane to the Standard CCM Super Users group and to assign Kim and Tom to the Standard CCM Read-Only user group.

Figure 6-2 *Roles and User Groups*

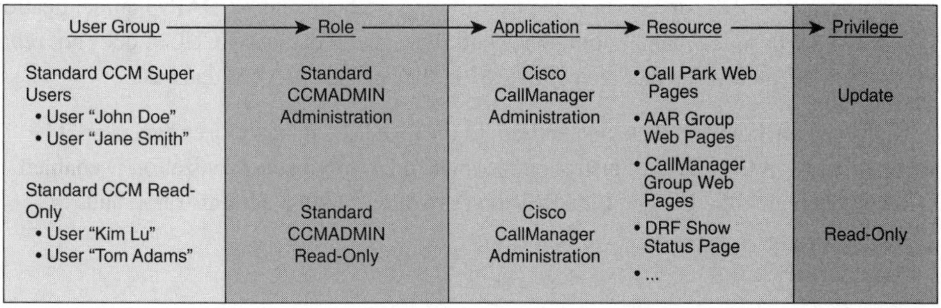

> **NOTE**   CUCM has numerous default user groups that cover the needs of most requirements. Examples of default user groups include the following:
>
> - CCM Super Users
>
> - Standard CCMAdmin Read-Only
>
> - Standard CAR Admin Users
>
> - Standard CCM Server Maintenance
>
> - Standard CCM Server Monitoring
>
> - Standard CCM Phone Administration
>
> - Standard CCM End User
>
> - Standard CCM Gateway Administration

User Management

User management options in CUCM include the following:

- **CUCM Administration**: Suitable for configuring a small number of users or doing single updates to the configuration of a user. CUCM administration of users is not scalable for large deployments of CUCM.

- **Bulk Administration tool (BAT)**: BAT is a tool that allows large insertions, updates, and deletions of users when LDAPv3 synchronization is not leveraged. Many learning institutions have frequent changes to the user database. BAT is an excellent tool for initial deployment or large updates to many configuration options, including the user database.

- **LDAPv3 integration**: LDAPv3 integration allows end users to be synchronized from a centralized database to CUCM. This option proves useful when all the end users already exist in an LDAPv3 database. LDAPv3 user synchronization is available only to end users. LDAPv3 authentication is another LDAPv3 feature that can be leveraged. LDAPv3 authentication passes any authentication requests through the CUCM server to the LDAPv3 server where the user login is authenticated. LDAPv3 authentication has the benefit of maintaining one central password database. CUCM does not replicate the passwords that are configured in the central LDAPv3 database.

LDAPv3 synchronization replicates data to the CUCM database. User data cannot be modified from CUCM administration tools when LDAPv3 synchronization is enabled. User data is modified on the LDAPv3 server by the LDAPv3 administrator, and resynchronization will occur at the next resynchronization interval. Depending on the resynchronization schedule, the resynchronization event might not occur for days or weeks. Manual synchronization can be performed at any time.

Passwords are not replicated to the CUCM database when LDAPv3 authentication is turned on. User passwords may exist in both CUCM and the LDAPv3 server if the user exists in both servers. It is recommended to combine LDAPv3 authentication with LDAPv3 synchronization to avoid inconsistencies in usernames and to eliminate the need for maintaining multiple usernames.

Table 6-2 summarizes the differences between the local CUCM database, LDAPv3 synchronization, and LDAPv3 authentication.

Table 6-2   *End-User Data Location*

	No LDAPv3 Integration	LDAPv3 Synchronization	LDAPv3 Authentication
User ID, First Name, Middle Name, Last Name, Manager User ID, Department, Phone Number, Mail ID	Local database	LDAPv3 (replicated to local database)	LDAPv3 (replicated to local database)
Password	Local database	Local database	LDAPv3
PIN, Digest Credentials, Groups, Roles, Associated PCs, Controlled Devices, Extension Mobility Profile, CAPF Presence Group, Mobility	Local database	Local database	Local database

Managing User Accounts

CUCM user management is performed from the Cisco Unified Communications Manager Administration User Management menu. The administrator must use an account with user management privileges. Any end-user account that has the user management privilege assigned can modify user accounts (including the CCMAdministrator).

The User Management menu includes options to configure application users, end users, roles, and user groups, as shown in Figure 6-3.

Figure 6-3 *User Management Menu*

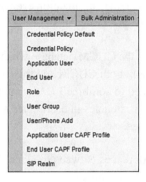

Figure 6-4 shows the Application User Configuration page. The most important settings are the user ID and the password. The user ID and password must match on the application server if the application user is configured for integration with another server. The application user could be associated with multiple devices (phones, CTI route points, and pilot points). Navigate to **User Management > Application User** from the CUCMAdministration to add an application user. Click the **Add New** button.

Figure 6-4 *Application User Configuration*

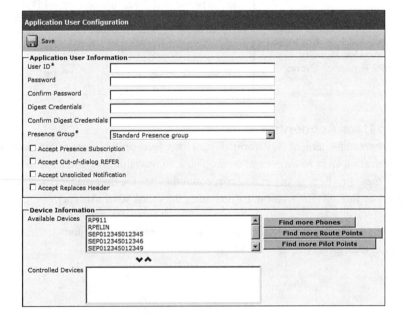

At the bottom of the Application User Configuration page, the application user can be added to user groups, as shown in Figure 6-5. The roles that are assigned to the user groups are listed in the Roles field under the Groups field.

Figure 6-5   *Application User Group Configuration*

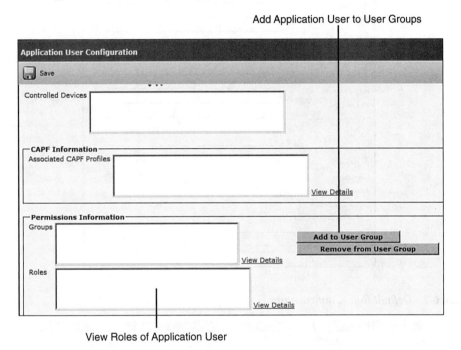

The End User Configuration page is similar to the Application User Configuration page. User ID, password, and group membership are the most important settings. Figure 6-6 displays the End User Configuration page in CUCM. Navigate to **User Management > End User** to add an end user in CUCM Administration. Click the **Add New** button.

Standard roles cannot be deleted or modified. Custom roles, however, can be created from scratch or by copying and then modifying a standard role. Figure 6-7 shows an abbreviated listing of CUCM roles. Navigate to **User Management > Role** to find an existing role configuration. Click the **Find** button to display all existing roles. Click **Find**.

Figure 6-6   *End User Configuration*

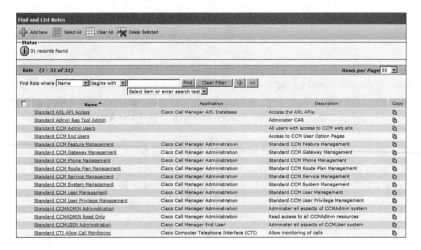

Figure 6-7   *Default Role Configuration*

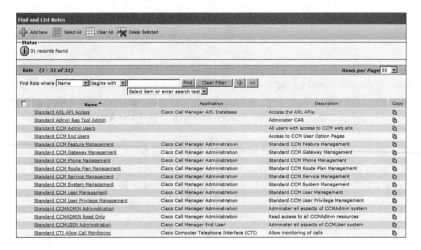

Figure 6-8 displays the Role Configuration page. When configuring a new role, you have to select an application on the configuration web page. The application resources will be displayed and read, or update privilege can be assigned to each. The Role Configuration pages are accessible via **User Management > Role** in CUCM Administration.

Figure 6-8 *Role Configuration Page*

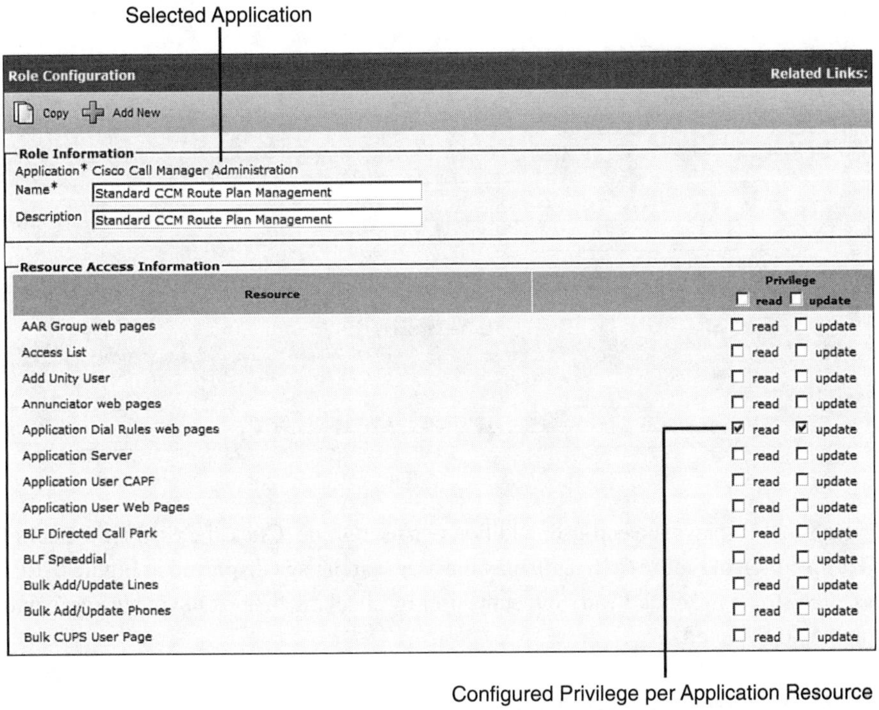

Selected Application

Configured Privilege per Application Resource

Standard user groups cannot be deleted or modified. Custom user groups can be created from scratch or by copying an existing user group. Figure 6-9 displays an abbreviated list of the default user groups. Navigate to **User Management > User Group** and click the **Find** button to display existing user groups. Click **Find**. Click a user group.

Figure 6-9 *Default User Groups*

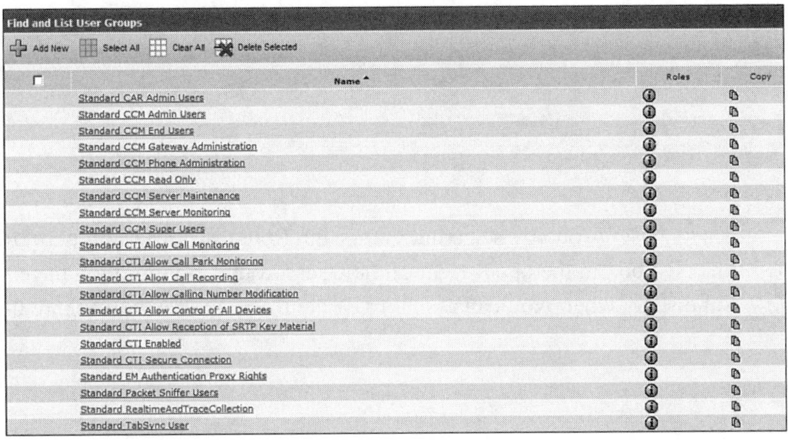

Figure 6-10 displays the User Group Configuration page in which users can be added to a user group. In this example, the Standard CCM Super Users Group was selected.

Figure 6-10   *User Group Configuration*

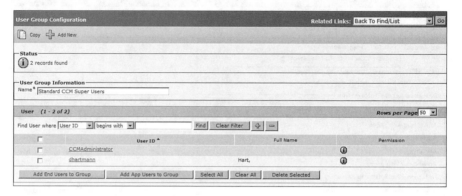

Figure 6-11 displays the end-user addition to a user group. Click the **Add End Users to Group** button of Figure 6-10 to display the user search page displayed in Figure 6-12. Enter a search string and click **Find**. Select the user by checking the box next to the user, and then click **Add Selected**.

Figure 6-11   *User Group Configuration*

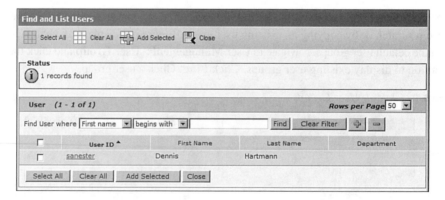

Assign roles to a user group by selecting the Assign Role to User Group item from the Related Links list box in the upper right of the User Group Configuration page. A new window will display where you can assign or delete roles, as shown in Figure 6-12.

Figure 6-12 *User Group Role Assignment*

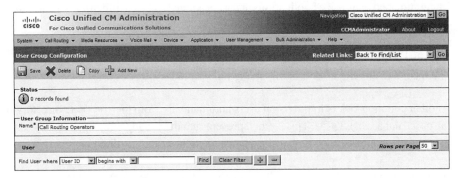

Click the **Add Role to Group** button. Select the roles that you would like to add, as shown in Figure 6-13, and then click the **Add Selected** button.

Figure 6-13 *User Group Role Assignment*

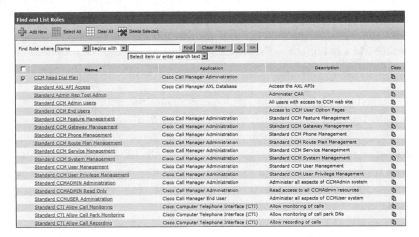

Lightweight Directory Access Protocol

LDAPv3 directories typically store data that does not change often, such as employee information and user privileges on the corporate network. The information is stored in a database that is optimized for a high number of read and search requests and occasional write and update requests.

LDAPv3 Integration

Integration between voice applications and a corporate LDAPv3 directory is a common task for many enterprise IT organizations.

LDAPv3 directory services are leveraged to enable user lookups from IP phones. Users can dial a contact directly after looking up the number in the directory.

Another common task is to provision users automatically from the corporate directory into the user database of CUCM. This method prevents having to add, remove, or modify core user information manually each time a change occurs in the corporate directory.

Authentication of end users and CUCM administrators using the corporate directory credentials is typically desired. LDAPv3 allows a single sign-in functionality to any applications integrated with the LDAPv3 server. Single sign-in greatly reduces the number of passwords that each user needs to maintain across different corporate applications.

Cisco Unified IP Phones access the LDAPv3 directory when the Directory button is pressed. The IP phone responds to the Directory button click by sending an HTTP directory lookup request to the Apache web server on CUCM. The response from CUCM contains Extensible Markup Language (XML) user information objects that the phone displays to the person using the phone.

Cisco Unified IP Phones perform user lookups against the embedded CUCM database by default. The directory lookup can be configured to allow the IP phones to access a corporate LDAPv3 directory. The phones would then send their HTTP user lookup requests to an external web server that operates as a proxy to the LDAPv3 server. The user lookup requests are translated into LDAPv3 queries against the corporate directory. The LDAPv3 response is then encapsulated in the appropriate XML objects and sent back to the phones via HTTP.

CUCM supports the following directories:

- Microsoft Active Directory (2000 and 2003)

- Netscape Directory Server 4.*x*

- iPlanet Directory Server 5.1

- Sun ONE Directory Server 5.2

CUCM supports two types of LDAPv3 integration, which can be enabled independently of each other:

- **LDAPv3 synchronization**: Allows user provisioning where personal and organizational data is managed in an LDAPv3 directory and replicated to the Cisco Unified CM IDS database.

- **LDAPv3 authentication**: Allows user authentication against an LDAPv3 directory. Passwords are managed in the central LDAPv3 server when LDAPv3 authentication is turned on.

> **NOTE**   Application users are not affected by LDAPv3 integration. They are always configured from CUCM Administration, and their data is always stored in the CUCM configuration database.

LDAPv3 Synchronization

The Cisco Directory Synchronization (DirSync) process is used to synchronize a number of user attributes. The process can be scheduled to run at different intervals or performed manually. Users are provisioned on the corporate directory and replicated to the CUCM LDAPv3 database when directory synchronization is used.

LDAPv3 synchronization disallows end-user additions or deletions from CUCM Administration. End users are added and deleted only in the LDAPv3 directory.

Users and their pertinent personal and organizational data are replicated from LDAPv3 to CUCM. Most replicated user parameters are read-only in CUCM Administration. User passwords and CUCM settings must be configured from CUCM Administration.

CUCM authenticates user credentials against a corporate LDAPv3 directory when using LDAPv3 authentication. End-user passwords are not stored in the CUCM database.

CUCM user data (associated devices, username, password, PIN, and so on) is stored in the CUCM database. To avoid duplication of effort in the management of user accounts, combine LDAPv3 authentication with LDAPv3 synchronization. LDAPv3 synchronization will force the user authentication request to be processed against the LDAPv3 server.

Synchronization Agreements

LDAPv3 synchronization is performed in one of the following ways:

■ Full synchronization is used with Microsoft Active Directory 2000 and 2003. All records are replicated from the LDAPv3 directory to the CUCM database. Full synchronization can cause considerable load in large deployments. Synchronization events should be carefully planned in large deployments.

■ Incremental synchronization is a method used with all supported directory servers other than Microsoft Active Directory. Only changes are propagated to the CUCM database with the incremental synchronization mechanism. The incremental synchronization method requires fewer resources than the full synchronization method.

Synchronization agreements are pointers to a domain or subdomain within an LDAPv3 structure. Synchronization agreements have to use the same synchronization method. Synchronization agreements between Microsoft Active Directory and other LDAPv3 servers on the same CUCM cluster are not supported.

One LDAPv3 username attribute (sAMAccountName, uid, mail, or telphoneNumber) has to be mapped to the User ID field of a user in CUCM. This identifier must be unique across all users.

Synchronization between a corporate LDAPv3 directory and CUCM eliminates the need to reconfigure users who already exist in the LDAPv3 directory.

Figure 6-14 illustrates the authentication of users against the CUCM database and user lookups from the Cisco IP Phone.

Table 6-3 shows the differences between end users and application users in the CUCM user database.

Table 6-3 *Directory Synchronization Parameters*

End Users	Application Users
Associated with a person	Associated with an application
Interactive logins	Noninteractive logins
User features and administrator logins	Application authorization
Included in user directory	Not included in user directory
Synchronized from LDAPv3 server	No LDAPv3 synchronization

Figure 6-14 *LDAPv3 Synchronization*

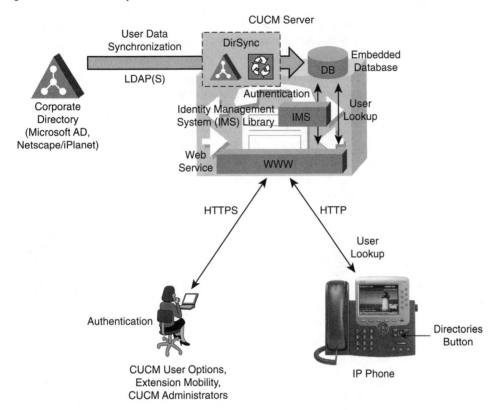

The **sn** attribute in the LDAPv3 server must be populated with data; otherwise, the record will not be imported. If the primary attribute used during import of end-user accounts matches any application user in the CUCM database, the user is skipped.

CUCM database fields provide a choice of directory attributes, but you can choose only a single mapping for each synchronization agreement.

Synchronization Search Base

A synchronization agreement specifies a search base. A search base is an area of the directory that is used for synchronization. The synchronization agreement specifies a position in the directory tree where CUCM begins its search. The search level has access to all levels lower in the tree, but not to higher levels in the tree.

Users should be organized in a structure in the LDAPv3 directory. The existing structure can be used to control the user groups that were imported. A single synchronization agreement can specify the root of the domain, and all users of the domain are synchronized. The search base does not normally point to the domain root.

In Figure 6-15, two synchronization agreements are represented. One synchronization agreement specifies User Search Base 1 and imports users jsmith, jdoe, and jbloggs. These users are in separate organizational unit (OU) containers under the Site 1 Users organizational unit. User Search Base 2 represents a second synchronization agreement and imports users jjones, bfoo, and tbrown. The CCMDirMgr account is not imported because it does not reside within one of the two specified user search bases.

Figure 6-15   *User Search Base*

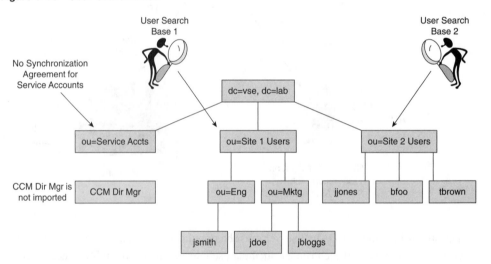

CUCM performs a bind to the LDAPv3 directory using the LDAPv3 Manager Distinguished Name in the LDAPv3 directory configuration. The account used for the LDAPv3 Manager Distinguished Name must be available in the LDAPv3 directory for CUCM to log in. It is recommended that you create a specific account with the permission to read all user objects within the subtree that was specified by the user search base.

It is possible to control the import of accounts by limiting read permissions of the LDAPv3 Manager Distinguished Name account. For example, if the account is restricted to have read access to ou=Eng but not to ou=Mktg, only the accounts located under the Eng OU will be synchronized.

Synchronization agreements can specify multiple directory servers for redundancy purposes.

Each synchronization agreement is configured with a synchronization start time and a period configured in hours, days, weeks, or months. A synchronization agreement can be configured to run only once.

The synchronization process is as follows:

1. At the beginning of the synchronization process, all existing CUCM end-user accounts are deactivated.

2. If there were any differences in the LDAPv3 server, LDAPv3 user accounts that exist in the CUCM user database are reactivated, and their settings are updated.

3. LDAPv3 user accounts that exist in LDAPv3 only are added to the CUCM database and activated.

4. Deactivated accounts are purged from the CUCM database after 24 hours.

Synchronization Best Practices

The account that CUCM uses to read the LDAPv3 directory should be configured in the following way:

■ Create a dedicated account used only for synchronization. Set LDAPv3 server permissions for this account to read all user objects located below the user search bases specified in the synchronization agreements.

■ The password of the account should be set to never expire.

Synchronization times should be configured during intervals when there are no office hours. All overhead and management processes are scheduled during off-hours to minimize the CPU load overhead incurred as a result of synchronization. Call-processing impact should be limited during business hours.

Different start times should be set to reduce the load on the servers when multiple synchronization agreements are configured.

Avoid a single point of failure by configuring at least two LDAPv3 servers, and use IP addresses rather than hostnames to eliminate DNS reliance.

The connection between the CUCM publisher server and the directory server can be secured by enabling Secure LDAPv3 (sLDAPv3) on CUCM and the LDAPv3 server. sLDAPv3 enables LDAPv3 to be sent over a Secure Sockets Layer (SSL) encryption at 128-bit-level encryption.

LDAPv3 Synchronization Configuration

The LDAPv3 synchronization configuration procedure includes the following steps:

Step 1   Add CUCM directory user and assign administrator access rights in the LDAPv3 directory (depends on LDAPv3 directory server).

Step 2   Activate the Cisco DirSync service.

Step 3   Configure the LDAPv3 system.

Step 4   Configure the LDAPv3 directory.

The synchronization is performed by a feature service called Cisco DirSync. DirSync has to be activated on the publisher server.

The Cisco DirSync service has some configurable service parameters that you can configure from the following CUCM Administration location: **System > Service Parameters**. Choose the Cisco DirSync service from the appropriate server. The service parameters include the maximum number of synchronization agreements, hosts (directory servers), and several timers.

Navigate to **System > LDAPv3 > LDAPv3 System** to configure the LDAPv3 server type (Microsoft Active Directory or other) and the LDAPv3 attribute that should be mapped to the CUCM user ID. Check the **Enable Synchronizing from LDAP Server** check box, as shown in Figure 6-16.

Figure 6-16   *LDAPv3 System Configuration*

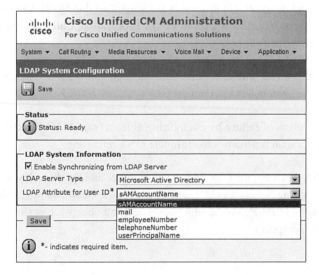

The LDAPv3 directory configuration is configured once per synchronization agreement (session). Navigate to **System > LDAPv3 > LDAPv3 Directory** and click **Add New** to add a new synchronization agreement. A warning will display indicating that all existing end users who are not found in the LDAPv3 directory will be deleted. The LDAPv3 directory will overwrite the CUCM user database. Figure 6-17 shows the LDAPv3 directory configuration.

Figure 6-17 *LDAPv3 Directory Configuration*

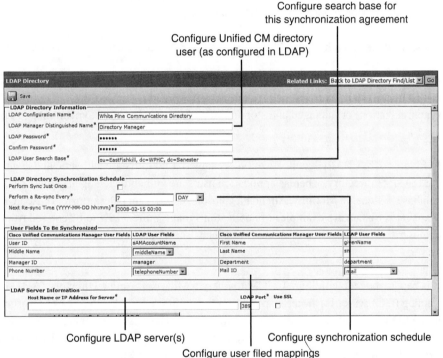

Navigate to **User Management > End User** and check the LDAPv3 sync status to verify LDAPv3 synchronization. Synchronized users are marked Active. Inactive users were configured in CUCM, but not in LDAPv3. Inactive users will be deleted after a 24-hour period. Microsoft refers to this 24-hour period as tombstoning. Tombstoning ensures that misconfigurations do not immediately impact users. Users can no longer be added or deleted from the CUCM database. Users can be synchronized only from the LDAPv3 server.

Click an active user to view that user's configuration page. Username, personal, and organizational settings cannot be modified; however, password, PIN, digest credentials, and PC association can be changed.

LDAPv3 Authentication

When LDAPv3 authentication is enabled, CUCM performs the following tasks:

■ End-user passwords are authenticated against the corporate directory.

■ End-user passwords are managed in LDAPv3, not in CUCM.

■ End-user passwords are stored only in LDAPv3.

Application users are still authenticated against the CUCM database. Application-user passwords are stored only in the CUCM database.

End-user PINs and other CUCM user settings are configured and stored in CUCM only.

Personal and organizational user settings such as phone number, manager, first, middle, and last name are either managed and stored in LDAPv3 and replicated to CUCM (LDAPv3 synchronization) or managed and stored in CUCM only. (LDAPv3 synchronization is not used.)

In Figure 6-18, LDAPv3 authentication is enabled. End users are authenticated against the LDAPv3 directory, whereas application users are authenticated against the CUCM database. Extension Mobility, Attendant Console, Cisco Agent Desktop, and Cisco Unified Manager Assistant are examples of applications that require a PIN to be entered from the end user. The PIN is authenticated against the CUCM database, not against the LDAPv3 server.

It is best practice to configure CUCM to query a Microsoft Active Directory (AD) Global Catalog (GC) server for faster response times. Configure the LDAPv3 server information in the LDAPv3 Authentication page to point to the IP address or hostname of a domain controller that has the Global Catalog role enabled, and configure the LDAPv3 port as 3268. This will enable queries against a Microsoft Global Catalog server.

The use of Global Catalog for authentication becomes more efficient if the users belong to multiple Microsoft AD domains. It allows CUCM to authenticate users immediately without having to follow referrals. Point CUCM to a Global Catalog server and set the LDAPv3 user search base to the top of the root domain.

Microsoft AD forests that encompass multiple trees require additional considerations. A single LDAPv3 search base cannot cover multiple namespaces. CUCM must use a different mechanism to authenticate users across discontiguous namespaces.

Figure 6-18 *LDAPv3 Authentication Overview*

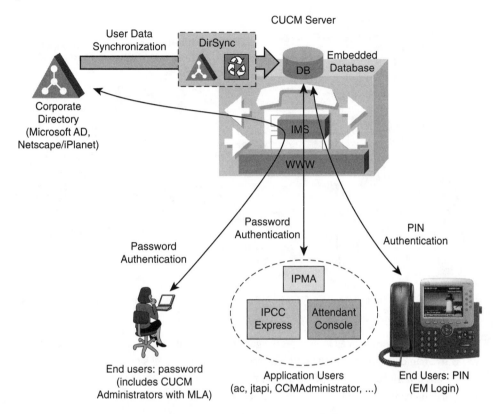

To support synchronization with an AD forest that has multiple trees, you must use the UserPrincipalName (UPN) attribute as the user ID within CUCM. The CUCM LDAPv3 authentication configuration page does not allow the LDAPv3 Search Base field when the User ID field uses the UPN. The LDAPv3 configuration page will display the note "LDAPv3 user search base is formed using userid information."

The user search base is derived from the UPN suffix of each user, as shown in Figure 6-19. In this example, a Microsoft AD forest consists of two trees: avvid.info and vse.lab. Because the same username may appear in both trees, CUCM has been configured to use the UPN to uniquely identify users in its database during the synchronization and authentication processes.

A user named John Doe exists in both the avvid.info tree and the vse.lab tree. Figure 6-19 and the steps that follow illustrate the authentication process for the first user, whose UPN is jdoe@avvid.info.

Figure 6-19   *LDAPv3 Authentication When Using Microsoft AD with Multiple Domains or Trees*

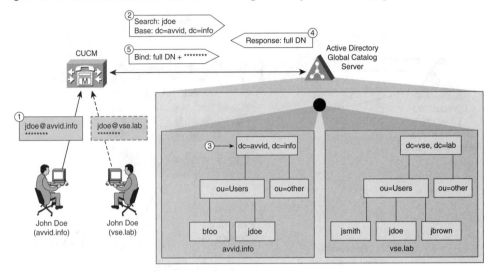

1. The user authenticates to CUCM via HTTPS with its username (which corresponds to the UPN) and password.

2. CUCM performs an LDAPv3 query against a Microsoft AD Global Catalog server. The username is specified in the UPN (information before the @ sign). The LDAPv3 search base is derived from the UPN suffix (information after the @ sign). In Figure 6-19, the username is jdoe, and the LDAPv3 search base is "dc=avvid, dc=info".

   Microsoft AD identifies the correct Distinguished Name corresponding to the username in the tree specified by the LDAPv3 query. In this case, "cn=jdoe, ou=Users, dc=avvid, dc=info".

3. Microsoft Active Directory responds via LDAPv3 to CUCM with the full Distinguished Name for this user.

4. CUCM attempts an LDAPv3 bind with the Distinguished Name provided and the password initially entered by the user. The authentication process then continues as in the standard case.

Support for LDAPv3 authentication with Microsoft AD forests containing multiple trees relies exclusively on the approach just described. Therefore, support is limited to deployments where the UPN suffix of a user corresponds to the root domain of the tree where the user resides. If the UPN suffix is disjointed from the actual namespace of the tree, it is not possible to authenticate CUCM users against the entire Microsoft Active Directory forest. (It is, however, still possible to use a different attribute as the user ID and limit the integration to a single tree within the forest.)

LDAPv3 Authentication Configuration

The LDAPv3 synchronization configuration procedure includes the following steps:

Step 1   Add the CUCM directory user and assign administrator access rights in the LDAPv3 directory.

Step 2   Configure LDAPv3 authentication. Navigate to **System > LDAPv3 > LDAPv3 Authentication** to configure the CUCM directory user configured in the LDAPv3 directory, the user search base, and the LDAPv3 server(s). Check the **Use LDAP Authentication for End Users** check box, as shown in Figure 6-20.

Figure 6-20   *LDAPv3 Authentication When Using Microsoft AD*

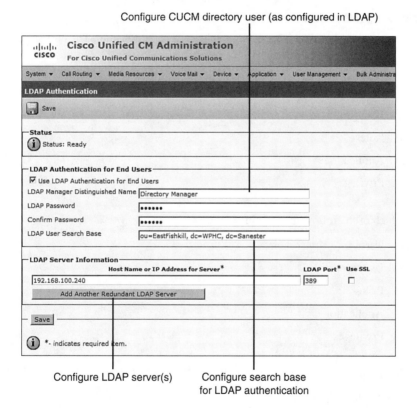

Configure CUCM directory user (as configured in LDAP)

Configure LDAP server(s)   Configure search base
                                  for LDAP authentication

Chapter Summary

The following list summarizes the key points that were discussed in this chapter:

■ CUCM has application users and end users.

■ Application and end users can be configured one by one using CUCM Administration.

■ LDAPv3 directories are centralized storage of user information.

■ CUCM can integrate with LDAPv3 for user provisioning.

■ CUCM can integrate with LDAPv3 for user authentication.

Review Questions

Use the questions here to review what you learned in this chapter. The correct answers are found in Appendix A, "Answers to Chapter Review Questions."

1. Users are assigned directly to which of the following?

    a. User groups

    b. Roles

    c. Applications

    d. Privileges

2. Which of the following contain resources?

    a. Users

    b. User groups

    c. Roles

    d. Applications

    e. Privileges

3. What type of user is accessible from the Directories button on the Cisco IP Phone?

    a. Application users

    b. Domain administrators

    c. Super users

    d. End users

4. What is the name of the technology that CUCM uses for user configuration data by default?

   a. SQL Server

   b. IDS database

   c. LDAPv3

   d. Microsoft Active Directory

   e. Netscape iPlanet

5. With which system can CUCM synchronize user data?

   a. Microsoft Active Directory

   b. SQL Server

   c. IBM Informix Database Server

   d. Microsoft Access database

   e. DC Directory Service

6. When synchronizing with Microsoft Active Directory, where does end-user authentication occur?

   a. CUCM

   b. DC Directory Service

   c. Microsoft Active Directory

   d. Internet Information Server

   e. IBM Informix Database Server

7. When synchronizing with Microsoft Active Directory, where does application-user authentication occur?

   a. CUCM

   b. DC Directory Service

   c. Microsoft Active Directory

   d. Internet Information Server

8. What service does Microsoft Active Directory synchronization rely on?

    a. LDAPv3

    b. IBM Informix Database Server

    c. Directory Synchronization

    d. CUCM

9. Users cannot be added to the CUCM user database directly when which option is enabled?

    a. LDAPv3 Authentication

    b. LDAPv3 Synchronization

    c. Backup and Restore System

    d. LDAPv3 User Search Base

CHAPTER 7

Endpoints

An important task of supporting a Unified Communications (UC) deployment is managing the endpoints. It is important to be able to distinguish between various Cisco UC endpoints that you may encounter during the course of deploying and administering a CUCM network. Understanding the boot and registration communication between a Cisco IP Phone and CUCM can be very valuable for troubleshooting purposes.

This lesson describes the various models of Cisco IP Phones and how they work within a Cisco IP Telephony (CIPT) solution. This module introduces the basic features of Cisco IP Phones, the IP phone boot and registration process, and the audio coders-decoders (codecs) that are supported by Cisco IP Phones. The lesson also describes third-party Session Initiation Protocol (SIP) and H.323 endpoints.

Chapter Objectives

Upon completing this lesson, you will be able to describe the general features and unique characteristics of the H.323, Skinny Client Control Protocol (SCCP), and SIP endpoints that interwork with CUCM, and you will be able to meet these objectives:

- Identify the endpoints supported by CUCM.

- Describe features of Cisco IP Phones.

- Describe the features supported by different Cisco IP Phone models.

- Describe the boot sequence of Cisco IP Phones.

- Identify third-party IP phones supported by CUCM.

- Describe how H.323 endpoints are supported by CUCM.

- Describe how SIP third-party IP phones are supported by CUCM.

CUCM Endpoints

A variety of endpoints, from Cisco and third-party manufacturers, can be used with CUCM. Endpoints include IP phones, analog gateways, and video endpoints.

CUCM has widespread support for the following protocols to be used for endpoints: SCCP, SIP, and H.323. Figure 7-1 illustrates some of the various protocol options to connect to CUCM.

Figure 7-1 *CUCM Endpoints*

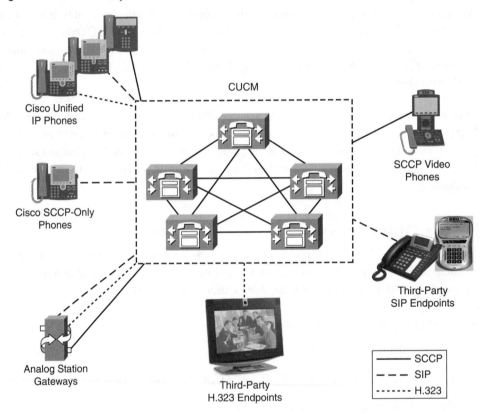

- **Type A phones**: These are the following Cisco Unified IP Phones: 7905, 7912, 7940, and 7960.

- **Type B phones**: These are the following Cisco Unified IP Phones: 7906, 7911, 7931, 7941, 7942, 7945, 7961, 7962, 7965, 7970, 7971, and 7975.

Cisco also offers software-based phones such as the older Cisco IP SoftPhone, Cisco IP Communicator (CIPC), and Cisco Unified Personal Communicator (CUPC). CIPC is a software-based version of the 7970 Cisco IP Phone. CIPC has always supported SCCP, and SIP support was added with CIPC 2.1. The CUPC requires a Cisco Unified Presence Server (CUPS) to register. The CUPS represents a UC client that operates as a phone, video device, and instant messenger client. CUPC can be used to promote a voice call into an audio-conference, video call, or videoconference if the network has sufficient resources. All of this can be done while using CUPC to instant message different people.

The Cisco Unified IP Phone 7902 and Cisco Unified IP Phone 7910 models support SCCP only and are no longer being sold (End of Sale [EoS]).

The Cisco Unified IP Phone 7985 is a desktop video phone, whereas the Cisco Unified IP Phone 7920 and 7921 models are wireless LAN (WiFi) phones. The Cisco Unified IP Phone 7935, 7936, and 7937 models are conference stations. The 7935 and 7936 endpoints support SCCP only.

> **NOTE**   The Cisco Unified IP Phone 7902, 7905, 7910, 7912, and 7935 are End of Sale (EoS). Cisco no longer sells these units, but it will continue to support them until the end of life (EoL) date.

Third-party products are available for most of the supported protocols. Nokia supports the Cisco Unified Mobile Communicator. Cisco Unified Mobile Communicator is a software client that is used on Nokia dual-mode mobile phones, allowing cellular PDA phones to register with CUCM. Tandberg and Sony produce various SCCP-enabled video endpoints, and IP blue offers an SCCP-based software IP phone that emulates standard Cisco 79xx phone lines. Many other third-party endpoints for SIP and H.323 can also be found on the market.

Endpoint Features

The features supported on the Cisco IP Phones vary by the device protocol in which the phone is running. The protocols can be categorized into three groups:

- **SCCP**: SCCP is a Cisco proprietary protocol and is typically used only by Cisco IP endpoints. Third-party companies such as Sony, Tandberg, and VTGO (IP blue) have licensed SCCP. SCCP offers a rich set of telephony features that are supported on most Cisco handsets.

- **Third-party SIP or H.323**: CUCM supports standards-based SIP and H.323 endpoints. The number of standardized telephony features, however, is limited when compared to the feature richness of SCCP.

■ **SIP support for Cisco IP Phones**: Cisco IP Phones using SIP support different features depending on which Cisco IP Phone is used. Many additional features are supported, compared to the SIP third-party phone support. Cisco SIP Type B phones support similar features when compared to those supported with SCCP. The number of features supported depends significantly on the Cisco IP Phone model being used.

Table 7-1 displays the support between various phone types and protocols. Third-party SIP and H.323 endpoints can be used with any other IP telephony devices or systems, including CUCM. Third-party SIP and H.323 are limited regarding the number of supported telephony features, when compared to Cisco SIP or SCCP IP Phones.

Table 7-1 *Endpoint Support*

	Third-Party SIP	Cisco IP Phone SIP	SCCP	Third-Party H.323
Third-Party PBX Support	Yes	No	No	Yes
Feature Support	Small	Type A phones: Medium Type B phones: High	Large	Large
Supported Phones	Third party	Type A and B	All Cisco phones Third-party SCCP phones	Third party

The Cisco Unified IP Phone models 7940 and 7960 can be loaded with a special firmware that provides RFC 3261 SIP support for third-party PBX systems. When these models interact with CUCM, both SIP and SCCP implementations provide more features than the phones operating on a third-party SIP proxy server. This option is used more by customers who connect to other IP communication systems but want to take advantage of the superior voice quality and look and feel of the Cisco IP Phones. Some Internet telephony service providers (ITSP) offering standard SIP telephony services provide their customers with preconfigured Cisco Unified IP Phone models 7940 or 7960 to be used to connect to their SIP proxy servers.

The Cisco Unified IP Phone models 7905 and 7912 can also be loaded with an H.323 firmware to be used with third-party PBX vendors using H.323.

Cisco IP Phones with SIP support a different number of features depending on whether the phone is a Type A or B model. Type A models include the 7905, 7912, 7940, and 7960. Type A phones support a large number of features but many fewer features than SCCP. The

Type A phones also have a different screen appearance when compared to their SCCP counterparts. Type B SIP phones support many more features than Type A SIP phones but do not have feature parity with their SCCP counterparts.

Cisco IP Phone Models

Cisco IP Phones range from entry-level phones employing a single directory number, one-way speakerphones, and no display to high-end phones with high-resolution, color, touch-screen displays and Gigabit Ethernet connectivity. Differences in hardware capabilities include the following:

- **Screen**: Different models have screens with different resolution, size, color, and touch-screen capabilities.

- **Codec support**: All Cisco IP Phones support G.711 and G.729 codecs. Most of the Cisco IP Phones support the Cisco wideband audio codec. All Type B phone models support the Internet low-bandwidth codec (iLBC) at 15.2 kbps, and G.722 wideband audio codec at 64 kbps. The G.722 audio codec requires a high-fidelity handset that ships only with the 79x2 and 79x5 phone models. Other Type B phones require a high-fidelity handset upgrade to support the G.722 audio codec.

- **LAN**: Most Cisco IP Phones have a PC port so that a PC can be connected to the network without requiring its own switch port. Different phone models support different speeds on the PC and switch port of the IP phone.

- **Phone buttons**: The number of IP phone buttons differs per phone model.

- **Speakerphone and headset support**: Most Cisco IP Phones offer speakerphone and headset support.

- **Number of lines**: The number of lines varies per phone model from one to eight. Twenty-eight lines can be added to most of the phones with the purchase of two 7914 sidecar modules.

- **Other features**: Some IP phones provide other special features such as video, WiFi support, or dedicated support for use in conference rooms. The 7936 and 7937 phones support external microphones to provide coverage to large conference rooms.

Entry-Level Cisco IP Phones

The Cisco Unified IP Phone models 7906 and 7911 fill the communication needs of cubicle, retail, classroom, or manufacturing. These phones are satisfactory to users conducting low to moderate telephone traffic without use of advanced features. Four dynamic soft keys guide users through core business features and functions, while a pixel-based display combines intuitive features, calling information, and Extensible Markup Language (XML) services allowing IP phone service applications.

The Type B entry-level phones mentioned support security features, including encrypted signaling and media. Encrypted voice traffic and security concepts are covered in *Cisco Unified Communications IP Telephony, Part 2*. All Type B entry-level phones support IEEE 802.3af Power over Ethernet (PoE), Cisco in-line power, or local power through an optional power adapter.

Midrange Cisco IP Phones

Midrange Cisco Unified IP Phones (7940, 7941, 7942, 7960, 7961, and 7962 models) address the communications needs of those that make frequent use of the phone system. Users providing a majority of their business services through telephone communications normally require a phone with more features than the entry-level phones. They provide a high-quality speakerphone and four dynamic soft keys that guide users through call features and functions. A built-in headset port and an integrated Ethernet switch are standard with these phones. The phones also include audio controls for the full-duplex, high-quality, hands-free speakerphone, handset, and headset.

All Type B phone models have LED-based line keys that allow call states to be represented by different colors. These phones also support the iLBC and G.722 audio codecs.

> **NOTE**   For a detailed list of features per phone model, see the data sheets for the Cisco Unified IP Phone 7900 series products.

High-End Cisco IP Phones

High-end Cisco Unified IP Phones include the 7945, 7965, 7970, 7971, and 7975 models. These phones demonstrate the latest advances in Unified Communications technology, including G.722 wideband audio support, backlit color display, and an integrated Gigabit Ethernet chipset. They address the needs of executives and managers with significant phone traffic.

All Cisco IP Phones include a display for easy access to communication information, date and time display, calling party name and number, called party name and number, and presence information. The Cisco IP Phones also accommodate XML applications that take advantage of the display. The phones provide direct access to two to eight telephone lines (or a combination of lines, speed dials, and direct access to telephony features), four or five interactive soft keys that guide you through call features and functions, and an intuitive four-way (plus Select key) navigation cluster. A hands-free speakerphone and handset designed for high-fidelity wideband audio are standard, as is a built-in headset connection. XML and presence are covered in more detail in later chapters.

Other Cisco IP Phones

Other Cisco Unified IP Phones and endpoints include the following models:

- **Cisco Unified IP Phone 7985**: The 7985 is a personal desktop video phone for the Cisco UC solution. The Cisco Unified IP Phone 7985 offers executives and managers a productivity-enhancing video phone that enables instant, face-to-face communication between physically disparate locations. The 7985 contains a video camera, LCD screen, speaker, keypad, and handset incorporated into one easy-to-use unit.

- **Cisco Unified IP Conference Station 7936**: This conference station combines speakerphone conferencing technologies with Cisco voice communication technologies. The 7936 is an IP-based, hands-free conference station. The new Cisco Unified IP Conference Station 7937 is a Cisco-designed conference room solution that has a much newer look and feel compared to the 7936 phone based on Polycom technology.

- **Cisco Unified Wireless IP Phone 7921**: This phone provides a solution with an intelligent wireless infrastructure. This wireless phone supports a host of calling features and voice-quality enhancements. Because the Cisco Unified Wireless IP Phone 7921 is designed to grow with system capabilities, features will keep pace with new system enhancements. The 7921 is an 802.11g WLAN phone that supports XML applications and extension mobility. The older 7920 WLAN phone did not support XML applications or extension mobility and was limited to 802.11b wireless support.

- **Cisco Unified IP Phone 7931**: The 7931 phone meets the communication needs of retail, commercial, and manufacturing workers, and anyone with moderate telephone traffic but specific call requirements. Dedicated hold, redial, and transfer keys facilitate call handling in a retail environment. Illuminated mute and speakerphone keys give a clear indication of speaker status. A pixel-based display with a white backlight makes calling information easy to see and delivers a large number of physical buttons that can be used for lines and speed dials.

Cisco IP Phones integrate seamlessly into a Cisco Unified network infrastructure. Cisco IP Phones provide the following network-related features:

- **Cisco Discovery Protocol Version 2(CDP)**: Cisco IP Phones generate CDPv2 messages, common in most other Cisco network products. Cisco IP Phones listen for CDP announcements sent out by Cisco Catalyst switches and desktop PCs. With CDP, a Cisco Catalyst switch can *configure* the phone's voice VLAN. CDP is also useful for tracking telephony devices when 911 is called. Cisco Emergency Responder is an enhanced 911 server that finds mobile users in a dynamic work environment. The Cisco Emergency Responder server is notified by CUCM when there is a new phone registration in the cluster. Cisco Emergency Responder contacts the switches and routers to physically find the device. CDP announcements from the IP phone and IP Communicator make this discovery process viable. The Cisco Unified Video Advantage client also uses CDP to associate the video-enabled PC to the IP phone. Cisco Unified Video Advantage is covered later in this book.

- **DHCP**: Cisco IP Phones can have static IP configurations entered at the IP phone or dynamic IP addresses assigned from a DHCP server.

- **MAC address-based device identification**: Cisco IP Phones are identified by the burned-in MAC address of the IP phone. This allows the device to be moved between subnets and simplifies DHCP configuration because no specific IP address is required for an individual phone.

- **TFTP**: Cisco IP Phone configurations are downloaded from the TFTP server component in CUCM. CUCM dynamically generates device-specific configuration files and makes them available for download at one or more TFTP servers. Cisco IP Phones obtain the IP address of the TFTP server via DHCP (option 150) and load the appropriate configuration file based on the MAC address. A phone with a MAC address of 012345012345 will request a configuration file of 012345012345.cnf.xml from the TFTP server. All configuration files are based on the XML programming language.

- **PoE**: Cisco IP Phones do not require wall power. The phones obtain power over Ethernet from a PoE-compliant LAN switch. Various Cisco Catalyst switches provide Power over Ethernet in different capacities. The older Catalyst switches with power support provide Cisco power only, whereas the newer switches provide both IEEE 802.3af and Cisco power. PoE eliminates the need for extra power adapters and cabling at user workspaces. It also allows power backup in a centralized location in situations where the phone system must be operational during a power outage.

- **PC port**: Cisco IP Phones allow PCs to be connected to a PC port at the IP phone and then share the uplink toward the switch. The voice VLAN feature of Cisco Catalyst switches separates the phone and PC traffic into different VLANs on a single access port at the LAN switch.

Cisco IP Phones: Boot Sequence

The Cisco IP Phone has a standard startup process consisting of several steps. The steps are illustrated in Figure 7-2 and outlined as follows:

Step 1 **PoE**: The Cisco IP Phone obtains power from the switch. The switch continuously sends a small voltage on the transmit pins. The voltage sent by the switch is then looped back in hardware from the IP phone back to the switch's receiving pins. The switch has now detected an in-line power-requiring device, and the Cisco switch generates the port's default power allocation. The default power allocation is 10 watts with Cisco proprietary PoE and 15.4 watts with the IEEE 802.3af in-line power specification. Type B Cisco phones support IEEE power and Cisco power, but the IEEE specification did not exist when Cisco manufactured the Type A phones. The 79x2 and 79x5 phones require IEEE or wall power bricks. The Cisco power option does not supply enough power to power these phones.

Step 2 **Loading the stored phone image**: The Cisco IP Phone has nonvolatile flash memory where the phone's firmware image is stored. At startup, the phone runs a bootstrap loader that loads the phone image from flash memory. Using this image, the phone initializes its software and hardware.

Step 3 **Configuring VLAN**: A Cisco Catalyst switch uses CDP to inform the Cisco IP Phone which voice VLAN the phone should use for all VoIP traffic. An application-specific integrated circuit (ASIC) in the phone's hardware is used to create Ethernet 802.1q frames before transmitting the traffic on the switch port. The ASIC also gives the phone 1p3q1t (one priority queue, three normal queues, and one drop threshold) QoS capabilities and allows the phone to act like a three-port switch. The Cisco IP Phone does not support the weighted random early detection (WRED) congestion-avoidance protocol. The one threshold is set to tail drop (100 percent queue utilization).

Step 4   Obtaining an IP address: Cisco IP Phones use DHCP by default to obtain an IP address, subnet mask, default gateway, and TFTP server (option 150). The phone sends out a Layer 2 broadcast to the Ethernet layer 2 broadcast address of FF-FF-FF-FF-FF-FF. The DHCP server receives this broadcast and returns an IP address lease from the DHCP scope for the Cisco IP Phones, which contains an IP address, default gateway, subnet mask, and TFTP server (option 150). If DHCP is not used in the network, a static network configuration must be assigned to each IP phone locally. If the DHCP server does not respond, the IP phone will make use of the DHCP scope stored in NVRAM. DHCP information will be in NVRAM only if the phone has previously obtained a lease from the DHCP server.

Step 5   Requesting the configuration file and the profile file: The TFTP server has configuration files. A configuration file includes parameters for connecting to CUCM and information about which image load a phone should be running.

The IP phone first requests its SEP<*mac-address*>.cnf.xml file from the TFTP server. If the TFTP server does not respond, the IP phone falls back to the last used configuration stored in NVRAM. If the TFTP server responds, but the SEP<*mac-address*>.cnf.xml file is not found on the server, the phone requests the XMLDefault.cnf.xml file. The XMLDefault.cnf.xml file is used to request an auto-registration configuration. Auto registration is disabled by default. CUCM dynamically generates a directory number and configuration file for the IP phone if auto registration has been provisioned.

If cryptographic features are enabled in CUCM, the phone then attempts to download a certificate trust list (CTL) in addition to the phone configuration file.

Step 6   Registering: The configuration file includes a prioritized list of CUCM servers that are configured in CUCM as a CallManager group. After obtaining the file from the TFTP server, the phone attempts to register with the highest-priority CUCM in the CallManager group using SCCP over TCP port 2000.

Figure 7-2 *Cisco IP Phone: SCCP Boot Process*

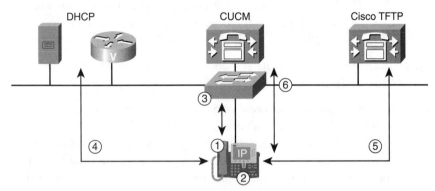

The boot sequences for SIP phones are similar to those used for SCCP phones. There are three main differences:

- **SEP<*mac*>.cnf.xml**: The SIP phones get their entire configuration from the configuration file. The SEP<*mac-address*>.cnf.xml file is much larger for SIP than for SCCP.

- **Dial plan file (optional)**: The Cisco SIP phones can download and use local dial plans. Third-party SIP phones can be configured with local dial plans, but they cannot be configured and downloaded from CUCM. Third-party phone configuration takes place on the third-party device.

- **Soft key file**: The SIP phones download their soft key sets in an XML soft key file, whereas SCCP phones receive these soft key states as part of the SCCP call-control signaling.

Steps 1 through 4 of the SCCP boot process are identical in both Cisco SIP Phones and Cisco SCCP Phones. The steps in Figure 7-3 follow the step list that follows, but all the steps of Figure 7-2 are also performed by the Cisco SIP Phones. Figure 7-2 illustrates a high-level overview of the network integration of the Cisco IP Phone, and 7-3 illustrates the details of the files and messages exchanged between the IP phone and the TFTP and CUCM servers. The step list that follows assumes the SIP phone has obtained power, the voice VLAN, and a DHCP scope from the DHCP server. Cisco SCCP and SIP Phones have a similar boot and registration process. The primary differences have been highlighted in the three previous bullet points.

Step 1 The SIP phone boots and downloads a CTL file from the TFTP server. The CTL file contains a set of X.509v3 certificates and is used only when CUCM cluster security has been enabled. Cluster security is covered in *Cisco Unified Communications IP Telephony, Part 2.*

Step 2 The SIP phone requests its SEP<*mac-address*>.cnf.xml file from the Cisco TFTP server.

Step 3 If the SIP phone has not been provisioned before boot time, the SIP phone downloads the default configuration file XMLDefault.cnf.xml from the TFTP server. The default configuration file is used only if auto registration has been enabled. Auto registration using SIP requires a file containing a parameter called *auto_registration_name*. If this parameter is blank, the SIP phone will not auto-register. If this parameter is not blank, the SIP phone will attempt to auto-register.

Step 4 The SIP phone requests a firmware upgrade (Load ID file), if one was specified in the configuration file. This process allows the phone to upgrade the firmware image, allowing it to operate with future versions of CUCM. Each version of CUCM updates the firmware of the Cisco IP Phones so that they can properly communicate with CUCM. After the image has been downloaded and authenticated with the Cisco self-signed X.509v3 certificate, the SIP phone reboots to load the new image. This process might require many reboots to incrementally upgrade the firmware of the IP Phone.

Step 5 The Cisco IP Phone registers with the highest-priority CUCM server. The default SIP configuration file indicates whether the SIP phone should connect using User Datagram Protocol (UDP) port 5060 (default) or TCP. The TCP transport layer IP is supported and configurable on Type B phones only.

Booting for Type B Cisco IP Phones is slightly different from this procedure, which describes the boot sequence of Type A Cisco IP Phones. Type B Cisco IP Phones first download the SIPdefault.cnf file, which contains the default configuration parameters shared by all SIP phones that use the TFTP server. The Cisco SIP Phone continues requesting the SIP<*mac*>.cnf file to receive its individual configuration file.

Figure 7-3 *Cisco IP Phone: SIP Boot Process*

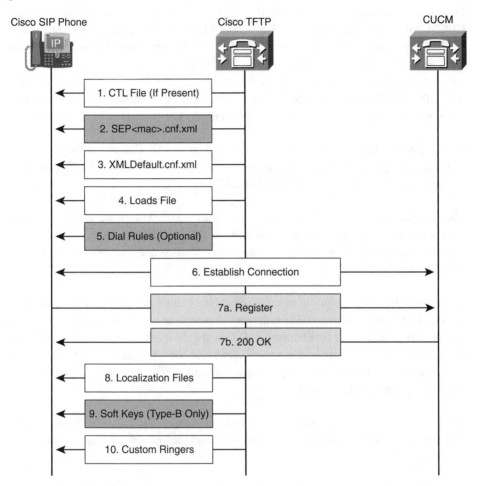

H.323 Endpoint Support

H.323 phones support multiple lines and can be audio, video, or data networking end-points. H.323 terminals are synonymous with endpoints. The H.323 terminal language is used in the H.323 standard. CUCM supports voice calls from H.323 terminals natively. CUCM can also integrate with H.323 video endpoints using an H.323 gatekeeper. *Cisco Unified Communications IP Telephony, Part 2* explains the H.323 video integration in further detail.

H.323 phones do not register with CUCM. H.323 devices are configured by IP address or fully qualified domain name (FQDN). H.323 gateways always show up as unregistered in CUCM. An unregistered Media Gateway Control Protocol (MGCP) is a bad thing, but H.323 gateways will always show up as unregistered because of their point-to-point nature. CUCM directs calls to the IP address of the H.323 gateway and accepts calls to the H.323 gateway over the H.225 call-control signaling TCP port 1720. There is no further integration with either H.323 gateways or gatekeepers. Third-party H.323 devices (terminals, gateways, and gatekeepers) can register with the gatekeeper or integrate directly with CUCM.

Configuration of H.323 devices must be performed on both CUCM and on the phone itself. Dial plan configuration must be configured on each device. Third-party H.323 phones consume two device license units (DLU) in CUCM.

The Cisco Unified IP Phone 7905 can be loaded with an H.323 firmware. If H.323 firmware is loaded, the phone is treated like a third-party H.323 endpoint and needs to be configured as a third-party H.323 phone, rather than as a Cisco Unified IP Phone 7905. The 7905 is an EoS device.

Examples of H.323 endpoints include Microsoft NetMeeting and H.323 video devices from Sony, Polycom, and Tanberg. H.323 endpoints often register with H.323 gatekeepers. H.323 gatekeepers contain dial plan elements and allow the devices to perform dynamic e.164 aliasing. Dynamic e.164 aliasing is a process in which the user specifies the phone number that the device is in charge of. The gatekeeper dynamically loads a configuration based on the device phone number specified.

H.323 endpoints support a small subset of features compared to Cisco IP Phones using SCCP or SIP. The features that are not supported include, but are not limited to, the following:

■   H.323 phones need to be configured by their IP address in CUCM rather than by a MAC address-based device ID.

■   Phone button templates and soft key templates are not supported. Each device user interface varies by vendor and product.

- Telephony features and applications such as the following:

  —IP phone services

  —CUCM Assistant

  —Cisco Unified Video Advantage

  —Call Pickup

  —Barge

  —Presence

The high-level configuration steps for H.323 phone implementation are as follows:

1. The H.323 phone is added to CUCM with its IP address and directory numbers specified.

2. The H.323 phone is configured with the IP address of CUCM.

SIP Third-Party IP Phone Support in CUCM

CUCM supports RFC 3261–compliant third-party SIP phones. Support for third-party SIP phone features varies greatly from Cisco SIP IP Phone features. Third-party phones have only RFC 3261 SIP Version 2 support, whereas Cisco SIP Phones have many Cisco SCCP features that have been rewritten to work in a native SIP protocol stack.

Two different types of third-party SIP phones can be added to CUCM. Third-party SIP phones may be added as basic or advanced phones. Third-party SIP basic phones support one line appearance and consume three DLUs. Third-party SIP advanced phones support up to eight lines and video but consume six DLUs. Basic and advanced third-party SIP phones offer the same telephony features.

Third-party SIP phones register with CUCM but do not use a MAC address–based device ID. CUCM uses SIP digest authentication to identify a registering SIP third-party SIP phone.

Both CUCM and the third-party SIP phone have to be configured with a username and password for digest authentication to work properly. CUCM refers to this item as a digest user in which a user is associated with the phone in both the phone and user configuration pages. The third-party device must also be configured with a matching username.

SIP standards and drafts supported by CUCM include the following:

- RFC 3262: *PRACK*

- RFC 3264: *SDP offer/answer*

- RFC 3311: *UPDATE*

- RFC 3515: *REFER*

- RFC 3842: *MWI Package*

- RFC 3891: *Replaces Header*

- RFC 3892: *Referred-by Mechanism*

- draft-levy-sip-diversion-08.txt: *Diversion Header*

- draft-ietf-sip-privacy-04.txt: *Remote-Party-Id Header*

The following audio and video standards are supported for third-party SIP phones:

- Audio:

    —Audio codecs: G.711 mu-law, GSM Full-rate, G.723.1, G.711 A-law, G.722, G.728, G.729

    —RFC 2833: *DTMF (Telephony-event)*

- Video:

    —Video codecs: H.261, H.263, H.263+, H.263++, H.264

> **NOTE**   For more information about the support of these standards, see the *Cisco SIP IP Administrator Guide, Version 8.0 - Compliance with RFC 3261*:
>
> http://www.cisco.com/en/US/products/sw/voicesw/ps2156/products_administration_guide_chapter09186a00807f47e3.html

Cisco is working with key third-party vendors who are part of the Cisco Technology Development Partner Program. These partners are developing solutions that leverage the new CUCM and CUCM Express SIP capabilities. These vendors include Linksys, IPCelerate, Research In Motion, IP blue, and Grandstream.

Cisco is also participating in an independent third-party testing and interoperability verification process being offered by tekVizion. This independent service has been established to enable third-party vendors to test and verify the interoperability of their endpoints with CUCM and CUCM Express.

Third-party SIP phones support only a few features compared to Cisco IP Phones using SCCP or SIP. The features that are not supported include but are not limited to the following:

- MAC address registration

- Phone buttons template

- Soft key templates

- Telephony features and applications such as the following:

    —IP phone services

    —CUCM Assistant

    —Cisco Unified Video Advantage

    —Call Pickup

    —Barge

    —Presence

SIP Third-Party Authentication

Digest authentication allows CUCM to act as a server to challenge the identity of a SIP device when it sends a request to CUCM. When digest authentication is enabled for a phone, CUCM challenges all SIP phone requests except keepalive messages. CUCM does not support responding to challenges from SIP phones.

CUCM can challenge SIP devices connecting through a SIP trunk and can respond to challenges received on its SIP trunk interface.

CUCM digest authentication is used to determine the identity of a third-party SIP phone. The phones cannot be authenticated via MAC address like SCCP devices because third-party SIP phones do not register by MAC address. Digest authentication is the industry standard.

CUCM can ignore the keyed hash that is provided in a digest authentication response and check only if the provided username exists and is bound to a third-party SIP phone. This is the default behavior. Alternatively, CUCM can be configured to check that the key that was used at the third-party SIP phone to generate the keyed hash matches the locally configured key (called digest credentials) at the end-user configuration in CUCM.

Third-party SIP phones cannot be configured by using the CUCM TFTP server. Instead, they need to be configured using the native phone configuration mechanism, which is usually a web page or a TFTP file. The device and line configuration in the CUCM database must be manually synchronized with the native phone configuration (for example, extension 1002 on the phone and 1002 in CUCM). In addition, if the directory number of a line is changed, it must be changed in both CUCM Administration and in the native phone configuration mechanism.

Third-party SIP phones include their directory number in the registration message. They do not send a MAC address. Third-party SIP phones identify themselves with digest authentication. The SIP REGISTER message includes a header with a username and the keyed hash, as shown in the following example:

```
Authorization: Digest
  username="3rdpsip",realm="ccmsipline",nonce="GBauADss2qoWr6k9y3hGGVDAqnLfoLk5",
  uri="sip:172.18.197.224",algorithm=MD5,response="126c0643a4923359ab59d4f5349455
  2e"
```

CUCM receives the registration message and searches for an endpoint that matches the provided username in the SIP message (**3rdpsip** in the preceding example). CUCM uses the digest credentials configured for that user to verify the keyed hash (**response="126c0643a4923359ab59d4f53494552e** in the preceding example).

NOTE   CUCM must be explicitly configured to verify the keyed hash. By default, CUCM searches only for the end-user name.

CUCM searches for a third-party SIP phone that is associated with the end user and verifies that the configured directory number matches the one provided by the third-party SIP phone in its registration message. If the phone is found and the directory number is the same, the third-party SIP phone registers with CUCM.

To add a third-party SIP phone in CUCM, follow these steps:

Step 1   Configure an end user in CUCM and specify the digest credentials.

Step 2   Add the third-party SIP phone in CUCM and configure its directory number.

> **NOTE**   When you are configuring the third-party SIP phone in CUCM, a dummy MAC address can be specified. The MAC address is not used to identify the device but is required inside the CUCM configuration database.

Step 3   Associate the third-party SIP phone with the end user.

Step 4   Configure the third-party SIP phone with the IP address of the CUCM, end-user ID, digest credentials, and directory number.

Chapter Summary

The following list summarizes the key points that were discussed in this chapter:

- CUCM supports SIP, SCCP, and H.323 protocols for endpoints.

- Feature differences exist between SIP, SCCP, and H.323 endpoints and between different IP phone models.

- Cisco IP Phones follow a process during the boot cycle. The Cisco IP Phone learns its voice VLAN ID and IP configuration, and a configuration is downloaded from the TFTP server.

- Third-party H.323 phones are configured on both CUCM and in the phone-configuration interface.

- Third-party SIP phones register by their directory number and a username, provided by digest authentication.

Review Questions

Use the questions here to review what you learned in this chapter. The correct answers are found in Appendix A, "Answers to Chapter Review Questions."

1.   Choose the Type A phones from the following list. (Choose three.)

   a.   7905

   b.   7912

   c.   7940

   d.   7941

2. What protocol is used by default on Cisco IP Phones?

   a. SCCP

   b. SIP

   c. H.323

   d. MGCP

3. Which type of SIP device has the highest number of features?

   a. Type A

   b. Type B

   c. Third party

   d. Cisco IP Phone on third-party SIP device

4. Which audio codecs does every Cisco IP Phone support? (Choose two.)

   a. G.711

   b. G.729

   c. G.722

   d. G.723

5. Which protocol or technology is required to provide the phone with firmware and a configuration file?

   a. Cisco Discovery Protocol

   b. TFTP

   c. FTP

   d. Power over Ethernet

6. How many watts of power does the IEEE 802.3af power specification deliver?

   a. 10 watts

   b. 15.4 watts

   c. 13.2 watts

   d. 9.6 watts

7. What protocol or technology is required to provide an IP address, subnet mask, default gateway, and option 150 to a Cisco IP Phone?

    a. Cisco Discovery Protocol

    b. TFTP

    c. FTP

    d. Power over Ethernet

8. What protocol or technology is required for power delivery to the Cisco IP Phone?

    a. Cisco Discovery Protocol

    b. TFTP

    c. FTP

    d. Power over Ethernet

9. Which protocol is used to communicate with the Cisco IP Phone VLAN?

    a. Cisco Discovery Protocol

    b. TFTP

    c. FTP

    d. Power over Ethernet

10. How are third-party SIP phones authenticated in CUCM?

    a. MAC address

    b. Transport layer security

    c. Digest authentication

    d. Secure hashing algorithm

CHAPTER **8**

Cisco Catalyst Switches

Deploying IP telephony requires planning how the IP phones will be powered and how the voice network will be combined with the data network, while ensuring voice calls maintain high quality.

Cisco Catalyst switches provide three primary features that aid an IP telephony deployment: in-line power, voice VLANs, and class of service (CoS). Power over Ethernet (PoE) can save on wiring costs and simplify management. Multiple VLANs must be enabled on a port because voice and data packets are placed on different VLANs. The dual-VLAN access port approach saves money by reducing the number of switch ports necessary for the deployment.

This lesson discusses the three major functions that Cisco Catalyst switches perform in an IP telephony network and describes how to configure a Cisco Catalyst switch to enable these functions.

Chapter Objectives

Upon completing this chapter, you will be able to configure both the Cisco IOS Catalyst and the Cisco CatOS switches to support Cisco IP Phones, third-party IP phones, and software-based phones, and you will be able to meet these objectives:

- Describe the role and features of Cisco LAN switches in a Cisco Unified Communications (UC) solution.

- Describe how power can be provided to IP phones by Cisco LAN switches.

- Configure Cisco LAN switches to provide power to IP phones.

- Describe how voice VLAN support can be provided to IP phones that have a PC attached to their PC port.

- Describe why allowed VLANs on trunk ports should be limited.

- Describe how to configure voice VLANs in Cisco IOS LAN switches.

- Describe how to configure voice VLANs in Cisco CatOS LAN switches.

Cisco LAN Switches

Cisco Catalyst switches can provide three primary features to assist the IP telephony deployment:

- **In-line power**: In-line power capabilities allow a Cisco Catalyst switch to send power over Ethernet to a Cisco IP Phone or other in-line power-compatible devices (wireless access points) without the need for an external power supply. In-line power is commonly referred to as Power over Ethernet (PoE). There are currently two popular types of PoE delivery used in Cisco IP Telephony (CIPT). IEEE 802.3af-compliant PoE is a standards-based power-delivery mechanism that any vendor can support. The Cisco prestandard version was developed by Cisco to accommodate the PoE need in the marketplace before there was an industry standard. The IEEE 802.3at PoE standard was ratified in late 2007 and not used in IP telephony as of the writing of this book. IEEE 802.3at is required for 802.11n access points. Type A phones support only Cisco power, whereas Type B phones support both Cisco power and IEEE 802.3af power. Most Cisco IP Phones have two physical connections. One is labeled SW and used to connect to the switch port; the other is labeled PC and used to connect to the personal computer. The SW interface can receive in-line power; the PC port cannot.

- **Voice VLAN support**: One or more network devices can be connected to the back of the Cisco IP Phone. Voice VLANs place IP phone traffic into a VLAN separate from the desktop computers connected to the PC port of the phone.

- **CoS marking**: CoS marking is data link layer marking (Layer 2 of the OSI reference model) that is used to prioritize traffic over switches. Prioritizing voice traffic is critical in IP telephony networks. If voice traffic is not given priority, poor voice quality may result. Voice traffic might suffer because it must wait in a queue behind large data frames during periods of high congestion.

The following switches in the Cisco Catalyst family were shipping as of the writing of this book:

- **Cisco Catalyst modular switching**: The Cisco Catalyst 6500 series delivers up to 96 ports of PoE delivery over Ethernet-based ports. Line card speed capabilities vary between 10BASE-T/100BASE-T and 10BASE-T/100BASE-T/1000BASE-T connectivity. The Cisco Catalyst 4500 series delivers up to 48-port 10/100/1000 PoE line cards. Some line cards support both IEEE 802.3af and Cisco prestandard in-line power, whereas others support only Cisco prestandard in-line power, and some line cards do not support in-line power at all. The quality of service (QoS) queuing capabilities vary by line card on the 6500 series platform. The 6500 has line cards that do not support QoS, cards that have standard QoS, and cards that have enhanced QoS. The enhanced QoS cards support more queues than the standard QoS line cards.

NOTE Overall power calculation has to be performed when power supply redundancy is desired. When too many PoE ports are used, power supply redundancy might fail because of excessive load caused by PoE ports. To aid in power calculations, check out the Power Calculator at http://www.cisco.com/go/powercalculator. You must be a registered user of Cisco.com to access the Power Calculator.

- **Cisco Catalyst stackable switching**: The Cisco Catalyst 3750 series offers 48- and 24-port FastEthernet switches that comply with 802.3af and Cisco prestandard PoE. The Cisco Catalyst 3560 series offers 48- and 24-port FastEthernet switches that support both the industry standard 802.3af and Cisco standard PoE.

- **Cisco EtherSwitch modules**: The Cisco 36- and 16-port 10/100 EtherSwitch modules for Cisco 2600, 2800, 3700, and 3800 series routers offer branch office customers the option to integrate switching and routing in one platform. These modules can support Cisco prestandard PoE and provide straightforward configuration, easy deployment, and integrated management in a single platform.

Providing Power to Cisco IP Phones

Most Cisco IP Phone models can use the following three options for power:

- **PoE**: Power-source equipment (PSE) inserts PoE to the powered device after a powered device (PD) negotiation phase.

- **Midspan power injection**: Some switches and modular switch blades do not support PoE. A midspan power source may be used instead of an Ethernet switch providing PoE. The midspan power injector is connected between the LAN switch and the powered device and inserts power on the Ethernet cable to the powered device. A major technical difference between the midspan and in-line power mechanism is that midspan power is delivered on the FastEthernet unused pairs (pins 4, 5, 7, and 8), whereas a PoE-capable switch delivers power over the used Ethernet and FastEthernet pairs (pins 1, 2, 3, and 6). Gigabit Ethernet uses all four pairs. Cisco sells midspan power injectors.

- **Wall power**: Wall power requires a DC converter to connect the IP phone to a wall outlet.

NOTE Cisco IP Phones do not ship with a wall power supply. The wall power supply must be ordered separately from the Cisco IP Phone.

Cisco provides two types of in-line power delivery:

- **Cisco original implementation of PoE**: Cisco was the first to develop PoE. The original Cisco (prestandard) implementation supports the following features:

    —Provides –48 V DC at up to 6.3 to 7.7 watts (W) per port over data pins 1, 2, 3, and 6.

    —Supports most Cisco devices (IP phones and wireless access points).

    —Uses a Cisco proprietary method of determining whether an attached device requires power. Power is delivered only to devices that require power.

- **802.3af PoE**: Cisco has been driving the evolution of PoE technology toward standardization by working with the IEEE and IEEE member vendors to create a standards-based means of providing power from an Ethernet switch port. The IEEE 802.3af standard supports the following features:

    —Specifies –48 V DC at up to 15.4 W per port over data pins 1, 2, 3, and 6 or the spare pins 4, 5, 7, and 8. Cisco Catalyst switches provide 802.3af PoE using pins 1, 2, 3, and 6.

    —Enables a new range of Ethernet-powered devices.

    —Standardizes the method of determining whether an attached device requires power. Power is delivered only to devices that require it. The IEEE 802.3af standard supports power classification, which allows a powered device to communicate a signature that defines the maximum power requirement. The PSE reads the power signature and budgets the correct amount of power for the powered device. This is less than the full 15.4 W that class 3–powered devices require.

A switch without power classification reserves the maximum 15.4 W of power for every port. This behavior may result in oversubscription of the available power supplies. Over-subscription will cause a condition in which devices requiring power will be denied because all the switch power has been preallocated.

Power classification defines these five classes:

- **0 (default)**: 15.4 W reserved
- **1**: 4 W
- **2**: 7 W
- **3**: 15.4 W
- **4**: Reserved for future expansion

All Cisco 802.3af-compliant switches support power classification.

Cisco Prestandard Power over Ethernet Device Detection

A 147-Hz tone is sent to the phone, and the phone hardware loops back the signal to the switch port. This process occurs using the same fast link pulse (FLP) process used to auto-negotiate port speed and duplex settings on FastEthernet interfaces. The switch detects the 147-Hz tone and begins delivering the default power allocation (10 W by default) configured power to the IP phone or other in-line power-capable endpoint. The Cisco IP Phone then sends a Cisco Discovery Protocol (CDP) Version 2 trigger message with the Power field set to the phone's power requirement (6.3 W for the 7960 phone). Figure 8-1 shows Cisco prestandard device detection.

Figure 8-1 *Cisco Prestandard Device Detection*

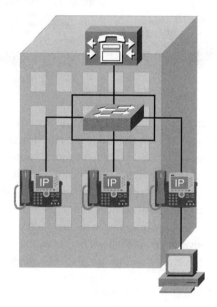

IEEE 802.3af Device Detection

The PSE detects a powered device by applying a voltage in the range of –2.8 V to –10 V on the transmit pins of the Category 5 (or higher) cable. The switch will receive this tone back only if the PD is IEEE 802.3af compliant. The Cisco IP Phone (PD) has a 25-k ohm signature resistor that allows it to loop back this tone. Compliant PDs must support this resistance method. If the appropriate resistance is found, the Cisco Catalyst switch delivers power. Figure 8-2 shows the IEEE 802.3af PoE device-detection process.

Figure 8-2 *IEEE 802.3af Device Detection*

Cisco Catalyst 6500

Cisco Catalyst 4500

Cisco Catalyst 3750

Cisco EtherSwitch Network Module

Cisco Catalyst 3560

As demonstrated in Example 8-1, the **set port inlinepower** command can be used on a switch that is running Cisco Catalyst Operating System (CatOS) software. The two modes are **auto** and **off**. All switch ports are set to auto negotiate (**auto**) by default. In the **off** mode, the switch does not provide power on the port even if an in-line power-capable device is connected. In auto mode, the switch provides power on the port only if an IP phone was discovered on the port. Examples of devices running Cisco CatOS include the Cisco Catalyst 6500 and earlier Supervisor modules on the 4500 platform (Supervisor I and II). Most companies have converted their Catalyst 6500 switches to Native IOS mode and no longer use CatOS. CatOS feature development has been discontinued.

Example 8-1 *CatOS Power Configuration Command*

```
CatOS>(enable) set port inlinepower mod/ports ?
auto   Port inline power auto mode
off    Port inline power off mode
```

Use the following interface configuration command on switches that are running native Cisco IOS Software to change the default in-line power configuration (Catalyst 6500, 4500, 3550, 3750, and 3560 switches):

```
CSCOIOS(config-if)# power inline {auto | never}
```

The PD discovery algorithm is set to auto mode by default. The PD discovery algorithm is disabled if the **power inline** command is configured to **never**.

> **NOTE** The Cisco Catalyst 6500 series can run either Cisco CatOS software or native Cisco IOS Software if the switch Supervisor Engine has a Multilayer Switch Feature Card (MSFC). The Cisco Catalyst 4500 and 4000 series can also run Cisco Catalyst software or native Cisco IOS Software, depending on the Supervisor Engine. Most Supervisor modules run native Cisco IOS Software.

Use the commands shown in Example 8-2 and 8-3 to display a view of the power allocated on Cisco Catalyst switches. The switch shows the default allocated power as 10 W in addition to the in-line power status of every port.

Example 8-2   *CatOS Power Display Command*

```
CatOS>(enable) show port inline power 7
Default Inline Power allocation per port: 10.000 Watts (0.23 Amps @42V)
Total inline power drawn by module 7: 75.60 Watts (1.80 Amps @42V)
Port    InlinePowered      PowerAllocated
        Admin    Oper      Detected        mWatt       mA @42V
....    .....    ....      ........        ........    ...........
7/1     auto     off       no              0           0
7/2     auto     on        yes             6300        150
7/3     auto     on        yes             6300        150
7/4     auto     off       no              0           0
7/5     auto     off       no              0           0
7/6     auto     off       no              0           0
7/7     auto     off       no              0           0
```

Example 8-3   *Native Cisco IOS Power Display Command*

```
Switch# show power inline
Interface         Admin    Oper    Power ( mWatt )    Device
..........        .....    ....    ...............    ......
FastEthernet9/1   auto     on      6300               Cisco 6500 IP Phone
FastEthernet9/2   auto     on      6300               Cisco 6500 IP Phone
FastEthernet9/3   auto     off     0                  n/a
```

Voice VLAN Support on Cisco IP Phones

The Cisco IP Phone contains an integrated three-port 10/100 or 10/100/1000 switch depending on the phone model. The ports are illustrated in Figure 8-3 and used as follows:

- Port 0 is an internal interface that carries the Cisco IP Phone traffic.

- Port 1 connects to a PC or other Ethernet device.

- Port 2 connects to the access layer switch. In-line power can be used at port 2.

Figure 8-3 *Cisco IP Phone Ports*

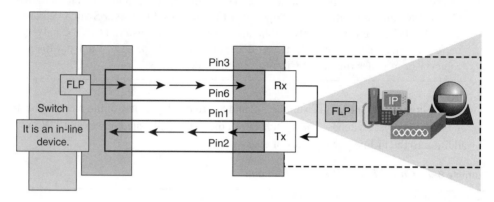

The switch port states can be configured in one of the following trust states:

- **Trusted**: The IP phone sends IEEE 802.1q tagged frames with IEEE 802.1p prioritizations to indicate Layer 2 CoS priority value, and the switch port trusts the CoS markings of the IP phone.

- **Untrusted (default)**: The switch does not trust the IP phone CoS marking and rewrites the priority value to 0.

- **Configured CoS priority level**: The IP phone changes the 802.1p header with a new CoS priority value if the PC used 802.1p with a different CoS priority level than the new priority value. The IP phone is capable of re-marking only Layer 2 CoS. If the PC is not doing 802.1q trunking, the IEEE 802.1p CoS values will never be marked.

The trust boundary is configured at the switch port with the **mls qos trust** command options.

The traffic that is sent by the IP phone should normally be trusted, but the switch port must be configured for this trust level. The trust configuration can be one of the following:

- **802.1q**: In the voice VLAN, tagged with a Layer 2 CoS priority value

- **802.1p**: In the access VLAN, tagged with a Layer 2 CoS priority value

- **Untagged**: In the access VLAN, untagged, with no Layer 2 CoS priority value

If CDP is enabled on the switch port, the switch instructs the IP phone to use one of the three listed options based on the **voice vlan** command.

Single VLAN Access Port

All Cisco Catalyst switch ports are configured as single-VLAN access ports by default. A single-VLAN access port is typically used for third-party IP phones or IP softphones. It is not recommended to configure Cisco Catalyst switch ports connected to Cisco IP Phones in this way. A single-VLAN access port should be configured with the voice VLAN.

It is not recommended to put both the IP phone and attached PC into the same VLAN. Separating voice and data services into different VLANs allows IP subnets to be treated separately for QoS and network security applications. The single-VLAN access point concept is illustrated in Figure 8-4.

A single-VLAN access port

- Can be configured as a secure port

- Allows physical separation of voice and data traffic

- Works with both Cisco and non-Cisco IP Phones

- Supports IP phones to leverage 802.1p for CoS

Non-Cisco switches are typically configured as single-VLAN access ports because they usually do not support the voice VLAN feature. Cisco Catalyst switches connected to third-party IP phones are also configured in this way because of the lack of the voice VLAN feature.

Figure 8-4 *Single-VLAN Access Port*

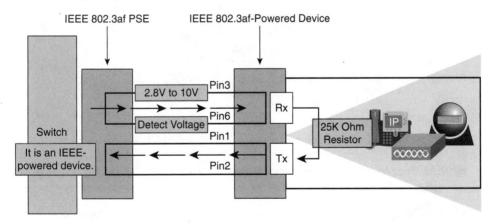

Multi-VLAN Access Port

Multi-VLAN access ports are supported by almost all Cisco Catalyst switches. All data devices connected to the PC port of the phone reside on the access (data) VLAN. A separate voice VLAN is normally used when combining voice and data on the same network infrastructure. Catalyst switches running CatOS software refer to the voice VLAN as an auxiliary VLAN.

The placement of IP phones in a separate voice VLAN makes it easier for customers to automate the process of deploying IP phones. IP phones boot and reside in the voice VLAN if the switch is configured to support them. The switch provides the IP phone with the appropriate VLAN ID through CDP Version 2 announcements at boot time.

Administrators can implement multiple VLANs on the same port by configuring an access port with two VLANs configured. An Ethernet frame-tagging mechanism must exist to distinguish among VLANs. 802.1q is the IEEE standard for tagging frames with a VLAN ID number. The IP phone sends tagged 802.1q frames with the VLAN ID that the switch communicated to it. The PC sends untagged frames (native Ethernet frames), and the switch ASIC tags the frame with an 802.1q trunk header, which has the configured access VLAN. When the switch receives a frame from the network destined for the PC, it removes the 802.1q trunk header and forwards a native untagged Ethernet frame to the PC. The IP phone marks all phone traffic in the voice VLAN. Figure 8-5 shows a multi-VLAN access port.

Figure 8-5 *Multi-VLAN Access Port*

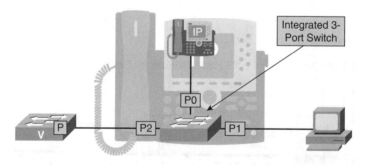

The following are some advantages in implementing multi-VLAN access ports:

- The Voice VLAN ID can be either discovered using CDPv2 or configured on the IP phone.

- This solution creates a scalable IP addressing scheme that can be easily accomplished via additional DHCP scopes. Most IP subnets have more than 80 percent of their available IP addresses leased. The voice VLAN (IP subnet) allows the introduction of a large number of new devices into the network without modifying the existing IP addressing scheme.

■ Dual-VLAN access ports allow for the logical separation of data and voice traffic. The voice and data VLAN segregation creates an environment where security and QoS policy can be tailored for the voice network.

■ This solution allows the connection of multiple devices on a single-switch access port.

802.1q Trunk Port

An 802.1q trunk port can be used to connect to an IP phone. The multi-VLAN access port is the best practice for connecting a Cisco IP Phone to a Cisco Catalyst switch. 802.1q trunk ports provide a solution for connecting Cisco IP Phones to third-party vendor switches. 802.1q trunk ports can also be used when connecting third-party IP phones to Cisco Catalyst switches. Some older Cisco switches do not support a multi-VLAN access port (3524-PWR).

Frames of the native VLAN on a .1q trunk port are always transmitted and received as untagged. Personal computers send their Ethernet frames untagged even though most network interface cards (NIC) support .1q trunking. When an IP phone is inserted between the PC and the switch port, the PC frames will be untagged, whereas the IP phone frames will be tagged with the voice VLAN. Figure 8-6 displays the logical connectivity achieved when an 802.1q trunk port is connected to an IP phone with a PC.

Figure 8-6 *802.1q Trunk Port*

If the voice VLAN feature is enabled on a trunk port, the port will not allow any other tagged frames on the port. 802.1q trunk ports allow all VLANs by default, unless configured to do otherwise.

Cisco IP Phones trunk port considerations include the following:

■ Spanning-tree PortFast cannot be enabled on trunk ports of some very old Cisco Catalyst switches. This causes a condition where the IEEE 802.1d Spanning Tree Protocol (STP) must run on the port connected to the IP phone. STP can take up to 50 seconds before it allows traffic to be forwarded on the port.

■ 802.1q trunk ports cannot be configured as a secure port.

Native Cisco IOS VLAN Configuration

Example 8-4 shows the configuration of a single-VLAN access port. The switch is configured to transmit and receive CDPv2 frames to enable the Cisco IP Phone to transmit voice traffic in the IEEE 802.1p (Layer 2 CoS or Priority bits) field of the 802.1q trunk header, tagged with VLAN ID 0 (VLAN field). The switch inserts the 802.1p voice traffic into the configured access VLAN of 261.

Example 8-4 *Single-VLAN Access Port Configuration*

```
Console(config)# interface FastEthernet0/1
Console(config-if)# switchport mode access
Console(config-if)# switchport voice vlan dot1p
Console(config-if)# switchport access vlan 261
Console(config-if)# spanning-tree portfast
```

Example 8-5 shows a multi-VLAN access port configuration where the voice traffic is sent on VLAN 261 and the data traffic is sent on access VLAN 262.

Example 8-5 *Multi-VLAN Access Port Configuration*

```
Console(config)# interface FastEthernet0/1
Console(config-if)# switchport mode access
Console(config-if)# switchport voice vlan 261
Console(config-if)# switchport access vlan 262
Console(config-if)# spanning-tree portfast
```

The **switchport mode access** command configures the switch port to be an access (nontrunking) port. Table 8-1 provides a switch command reference that shows many of the commands that are used in the configuration examples.

Table 8-1 *Switch Command Reference*

Command	Description
switchport mode access	Configures the switch port to be an access (nontrunking) port.
spanning-tree portfast	Causes a port to enter the spanning-tree forwarding state immediately, bypassing the listening and learning states. You can use PortFast on switch ports that are connected to a single workstation or server (as opposed to another switch or network device) to allow those devices to connect to the network immediately.

Table 8-1 *Switch Command Reference (Continued)*

Command	Description
switchport access vlan *data_VLAN_ID*	Configures the interface as a static access port with the access VLAN ID (262 in this example). The VLAN range is 1 to 4094. All untagged traffic received on the port will be colored into this VLAN by the ASIC.
switchport voice vlan {*voice_vlan_ID* | **dot1p** | **none** | **untagged**}	When configuring the way in which the Cisco IP Phone transmits voice traffic, note the following syntax information: • Enter a voice VLAN ID to send CDPv2 packets that configure the Cisco IP Phone to transmit voice traffic in 802.1q frames, tagged with the voice VLAN ID and a Layer 2 CoS value. (The default is 5.) Valid VLAN IDs are from 1 to 4094. The switch puts the 802.1q voice traffic into the voice VLAN. • Enter the **dot1p** keyword to send CDPv2 packets that configure the Cisco IP Phone to transmit voice traffic in 802.1p frames, tagged with VLAN ID 0 and a Layer 2 CoS value. (The default is 5 for voice traffic and 3 for voice control traffic.) The switch puts the 802.1p voice traffic into the access VLAN. • Enter the **untagged** keyword to send CDPv2 packets that configure the Cisco IP Phone to transmit untagged voice traffic. The switch puts the untagged voice traffic into the access VLAN. • Enter the **none** keyword to allow the Cisco IP Phone to use its own configuration and transmit untagged voice traffic. The switch puts the untagged voice traffic into the access VLAN.

In Example 8-6, VLAN 261 is used for voice traffic, whereas VLAN 262 is used for data traffic. The voice VLAN will be tagged by the ASIC in the Cisco IP Phone, and the switch ASIC will tag the native VLAN traffic from the PC into VLAN 262. All other VLANs are explicitly blocked from the trunk interface.

Example 8-6 *802.1q Trunk Port Configuration*

```
Console(config)# interface FastEthernet0/1
Console(config-if)# switchport trunk encapsulation dot1q
Console(config-if)# switchport mode trunk
Console(config-if)# switchport trunk native vlan 262
Console(config-if)# switchport voice vlan 261
Console(config-if)# switchport trunk allowed vlan 261
```

Example 8-7 displays the output from a Native Cisco IOS switch trunk verification command. The **show interface trunking** command is useful, too.

Example 8-7 *Trunk Port Verification*

```
Class-1-Switch# show interfaces fastethernet 0/4 switchport
Name: Fa0/4
Switchport: Enabled
Administrative Mode: static access
Operational Mode: static access
Administrative Trunking Encapsulation: negotiate
Operational Trunking Encapsulation: native
Negotiation of Trunking: Off
Access Mode VLAN: 262 (VLAN0262)
Trunking Native Mode VLAN: 1 (default)
Voice VLAN: 261 (VLAN0261)
```

CatOS VLAN Configuration

Example 8-8 shows the configuration of a single-VLAN access port. The switch is configured to transmit and receive CDPv2 frames, enabling the Cisco IP Phone to transmit voice traffic in 802.1p frames, tagged with VLAN ID 0. The switch inserts the 802.1p voice traffic into the configured access VLAN of 261, which is used for voice traffic.

Example 8-8 *Single-VLAN Access Port*

```
Console>(enable) set port auxiliaryvlan 2/1-3 dot1p
Console>(enable) set vlans 262 2/1-3
Console>(enable) set trunk 2/1-3 off
```

Example 8-9 shows a multi-VLAN access port configuration where the voice traffic is sent to voice VLAN 261 (auxiliary VLAN) and the data is using the access VLAN 262.

Example 8-9 *Multi-VLAN Access Port*

```
Console>(enable) set port auxiliaryvlan 2/1-3 261
Console>(enable) set vlans 262 3/1-3
Console>(enable) set trunk 2/1-3 off
```

In 802.1q trunking, all VLAN packets are tagged on the trunk link, except the native VLAN packets. The native VLAN packets are sent untagged on the trunk link. Therefore, the native VLAN is used for the data traffic coming in from the workstation attached to the Cisco IP Phone. By default, VLAN 1 is the native VLAN on all switches.

In Example 8-10, VLAN 262 is set as the native VLAN, is untagged, and will be used by the data traffic. VLAN 261 is tagged with 802.1q tagging and will be used by the voice traffic.

In Cisco CatOS, you can change the native VLAN by issuing the **set vlan vlan-id** *mod/port* command, where *mod/port* is the trunk port. The **set trunk** command enables you to configure trunk ports and to add VLANs to the allowed VLAN list for existing trunks. The voice VLAN is configured with the **set port auxiliary vlan** command.

Example 8-10 *Multi-VLAN Access Port*

```
Console>(enable) set trunk 2/1-3 on
Console>(enable) clear trunk 2/1-3 1-4096
Console>(enable) set vlan 262 2/1-3
Console>(enable) set port auxiliary vlan 261 2/1-3
Console>(enable) set trunk 261 2/1-3
```

The status of the auxiliary VLAN on a port or module can be verified in two ways:

■ The **show port auxiliaryvlan** *vlan-id* command enables you to show the status of that auxiliary VLAN with the module and ports where it is active, as demonstrated in Example 8-11.

Example 8-11 *CatOS VLAN Trunking Verification*

```
Console> (enable) show port auxiliaryvlan 222

AuxiliaryVlan AuxVlanStatus Mod/Ports
------------- ------------- ----------
222           active        1/2,2/1-3
```

The **show port** [*module/port*] command enables you to show the module, port, and auxiliary VLAN with the status of the port, as demonstrated in Example 8-12.

Example 8-12 *CatOS VLAN Verification*

```
Console> (enable) show port 2/1
...
Port  AuxiliaryVlan AuxVlan-Status
----- ------------- --------------
 2/1  222           active
...
```

Chapter Summary

The following list summarizes the key points that were discussed in this chapter:

- Cisco LAN switches can supply in-line power to IP phones.

- Two types of PoE delivery are supported by Cisco LAN switches.

- PoE delivery methods can be configured on Cisco LAN switches.

- Cisco LAN switches can be configured to support voice traffic in three different ways: single-VLAN access port, multi-VLAN access port, and trunk port.

- Only required VLANs should be allowed on a trunk port.

- Access and trunk ports can be configured to support Cisco IP Phones.

- Voice VLAN configuration can be verified using Cisco CatOS and Cisco IOS commands and tools.

Review Questions

Use the questions here to review what you learned in this chapter. The correct answers are found in Appendix A, "Answers to Chapter Review Questions."

1. What is the maximum power level generated by the Cisco original power implementation?

    a. 6.3 W

    b. 10 W

    c. 15 W

    d. 15.4 W

2. What is the maximum power level generated by the IEEE 802.3af Power over Ethernet specification?

    a. 6.3 W

    b. 10 W

    c. 15 W

    d. 15.4 W

3. Which Cisco platform does not support IEEE 802.3af power?

    a. 4500

    b. 6500

    c. 3750

    d. EtherSwitch network module

4. On which unshielded twisted-pair cable pins is midspan power injection delivered?

    a. 1, 2, 3, 6

    b. 1, 2, 4, 5

    c. 4, 5, 7, 8

    d. 3, 4, 5, 6

5. On which unshielded twisted-pair cable pins is Power over Ethernet delivered?

    a. 1, 2, 3, 6

    b. 1, 2, 4, 5

    c. 4, 5, 7, 8

    d. 3, 4, 5, 6

6. Which protocol delivers VLAN information to the Cisco IP Phone?

    a. Cisco Discovery Protocol

    b. TFTP

    c. FTP

    d. Power over Ethernet

7. Which port configuration must be used with third-party phones?

    a. Single-VLAN access port

    b. Multi-VLAN access port

    c. Trunk port

8. Which port configuration does *not* support spanning-tree PortFast?

    a. Single-VLAN access port

    b. Multi-VLAN access port

    c. Trunk port

9. What mechanism is used to detect a Cisco IP Phone with the Cisco original power implementation?

    a. Cisco Discovery Protocol

    b. 25-k ohm resistor in phone

    c. Fast link pulse

    d. Power always injected

10. What command is used in Native IOS to turn off in-line power?

    a. **power inline off**

    b. **power inline never**

    c. **power inline auto**

    d. **power inline inactive**

CHAPTER 9

CUCM Configuration

Moves, adds, and changes (MAC) are important functions in the day-to-day activities of a Cisco Unified Communications Manager (CUCM) administrator.

CUCM provides various tools to accomplish the MAC tasks.

This chapter describes how to implement Skinny Client Control Protocol (SCCP) and Session Initiation Protocol (SIP) phones (Cisco and third party) in CUCM. This chapter also covers securing the IP phone.

Chapter Objectives

Upon completing this chapter, you will be able to configure Cisco SCCP and SIP phones and third-party SIP phones in CUCM. This chapter also covers the securing of Cisco IP Phones. This chapter targets the following objectives:

- Identify the endpoint configuration elements and tools for adding phones.

- Describe how auto registration works.

- Describe how to enable auto registration for automatic insertion of new phones to the CUCM configuration database.

- Describe how the CUCM BAT and CUCM TAPS tools can be used to add IP phones.

- Describe how to use CUCM BAT to add phones to CUCM.

- Describe how to manually add phones to CUCM.

- Describe Cisco IP Phone configuration settings that can be used to harden the IP phone.

Endpoint Configuration Tools and Elements Overview

There are four ways to add IP phones to CUCM:

■   Auto registration

■   Bulk Administration tool (BAT)

■   Tool for Auto-Registered Phone Support (TAPS)

■   Manual configuration

Auto registration allows Cisco IP Phones to be added to CUCM without the administrator having to first compile a list of MAC address for the endpoints. Auto registration automatically populates phone configuration data, so it is impossible to migrate phone settings from the existing phone system. Configuration changes can be made to the phone using CUCM Administration.

CUCM BAT allows bulk insertion, deletion, or updating of various devices and features, including phones. BAT requires the MAC addresses of the IP phones for phone insertion. Dummy MAC address population is an option in the tool, but dummy MAC addresses can not be used without TAPS.

TAPS leverages BAT and auto registration to deploy phones in a greenfield deployment. TAPS requires a separate Cisco Customer Response Solution (CRS) server but allows the flexibility of auto registering phones to lower deployment times. Administrators must familiarize themselves with the installation and configuration of the Cisco CRS server. BAT is used to configure the phones and users, but the phones are added with dummy MAC addresses. The real MAC address of the phone is associated with the phone during TAPS enrollment. TAPS enrollment occurs when the end user dials the CTI route point associated with the CRS server running TAPS. The end user enters the directory number of the phone, and the configuration file for that phone in the TFTP server is downloaded to the phone. TAPS is not recommended for deployments of fewer than 50 phones because of the amount of time required to set up TAPS.

Manual phone insertion is the easiest mechanism to configure, but it can be tedious and time consuming in a large deployment. The administrator must compile a list of the MAC address of the IP phones and ensure that this is correctly entered when creating device records for the phones. The MAC addresses of the phones can be added by bar-code scanning the MAC address UPC code on the back of the phone or on the phone box. Bar-code scanning requires the purchase of a USB-based bar-code scanning device.

Endpoint Basic Configuration Elements

There are mandatory and optional configuration details. It is advisable to never use any of the default mandatory items. Three examples of this are the call manager group, region, and location. The device pool and region do not need to be specified, but they are mandatory. The default values will not work in most environments, but they can be modified. Instead of modifying the default values, these elements can be copied, renamed, and reconfigured. Rename the elements in a way that allows the administrator to clearly define the goal of the configuration element. A device pool named NYC-CCMG is probably a Cisco Communications Manager group for the New York City office. Endpoint configuration elements that this chapter covers include the following:

- CUCM Group

- Regions

- Locations

- Date/Time Group

- CUCM Group

- Regions

- Locations

- Phone NTP Reference

- Presence Group

- Device Pool

- Security Profile

- Softkey Templates

- Phone Button Templates

- SIP Profile (SIP Phones Only)

- Common Phone Profile

Device Pool

Device pools define common characteristics that can be applied to many devices. The device pool structure supports the separation of user and location information. The device pool contains only device- and location-related information. The Common Device Profile Configuration window records all the user-oriented information such as type of softkey template that is used and locale information. The Common Device Profile was introduced in CallManager 5.0. Each device must be associated with a device pool and with a common device configuration.

The following mandatory components must be assigned to a device pool:

- CUCM group

- Date/time group

- Region

- Softkey template

- SRST reference

The device pool combines all the individual configuration settings into a single logical construct. The device pool can then be assigned to devices, such as IP phones, gateways, and trunks. To create, modify, or delete a device pool in CUCM, use the CUCM Administration web page and navigate to **System > Device Pool**. Click **Add New** to display a configuration screen similar to the one shown in Figure 9-1.

Figure 9-1 *Device Pool Configuration*

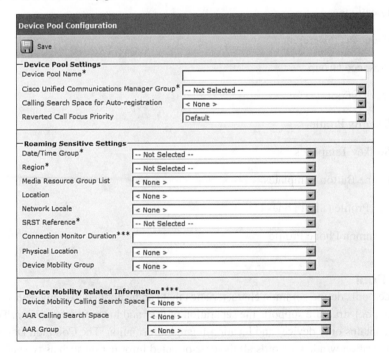

Phone Network Time Protocol Reference

The phone Network Time Protocol (NTP) references can be configured in CUCM Administration to ensure that a SIP phone gets its date and time directly from an NTP server. The SIP phone will use the date header in the SIP 200 OK response message to the phone's SIP REGISTER if an NTP server is unavailable. SCCP phones obtain time information within the SCCP signaling.

The phone NTP reference must be selected in a date/time group to become active. A hierarchy of phone NTP references can be configured in the date/time group.

The date/time group configuration is referenced from a device pool, and the device pool is assigned to a device at the device configuration page. The date/time group configuration descriptions are as follows:

- **IP Address**: Enter the IP address of the NTP server that the SIP phone should use to get its date and time.

- **Description**: Enter a description for the phone NTP reference. CUCM Administration automatically propagates the information in the IP Address field to the Description field, but it can be edited.

- **Mode**: From the drop-down list box, choose the mode for the phone NTP reference. The values available are as follows:

    —**Directed Broadcast**: This is the default NTP mode; in this mode, the phone accesses date/time information from any NTP server but gives the listed NTP servers (1st = primary, 2nd = secondary) priority. For example, if the phone configuration contains NTP servers where A = primary NTP server and B = secondary/backup NTP server, the phone uses the broadcast packets (derives the date/time) from NTP server A. If NTP server A is not broadcasting, the phone accesses date/time information from NTP server B. If neither NTP server is broadcasting, the phone accesses date/time information from any other NTP server. If no other NTP server is broadcasting, the phone derives the date/time from the CUCM 200 OK response to the REGISTER message.

    —**Unicast**: In this mode, the phone sends an NTP query packet to the specified NTP server. If the phone gets no response, the phone accesses date/time information from any other NTP server. If no other NTP servers respond, the phone derives the date/time from the CUCM 200 OK response to the REGISTER message.

CUCM currently does not support the multicast and anycast NTP modes. If either of these modes is selected, CUCM defaults to the directed broadcast mode.

To create or modify a phone NTP reference in CUCM, use the CUCM Administration web page. Navigate to **System > Phone NTP Reference**. Click **Add New** to display the same configuration screen shown in Figure 9-2. Phone NTP references can be added, deleted, or modified from the Phone NTP Reference Configuration page.

Figure 9-2 *Phone NTP Reference*

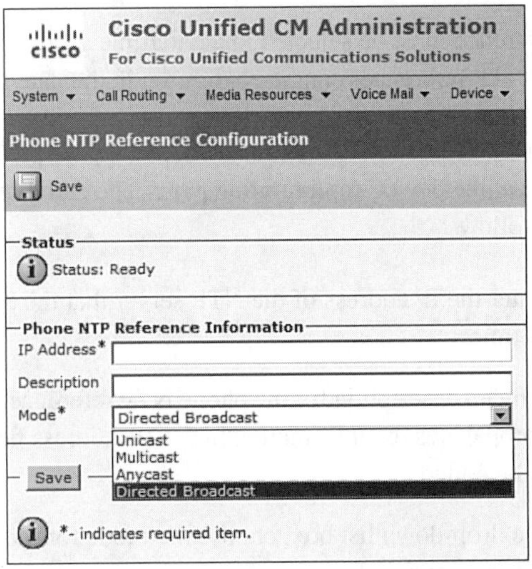

Date/Time Groups

Date/time groups are used to define the time zone a device should use for the local time the end user will be in. Each device is assigned to a device pool, and each device pool has one assigned date/time group.

Installation of CUCM automatically configures a default date/time group that is called CMLocal. CMLocal synchronizes to the active date and time of the operating system on the server where CUCM is installed. After installing CUCM, the settings of CMLocal can be changed.

To create, modify, or delete a date/time group in CUCM, use the CUCM Administration web page and navigate to **System > Date/Time Group**. Click **Add New** to display a configuration screen similar to the one displayed in Figure 9-3.

Figure 9-3   *Date/Time Group Configuration*

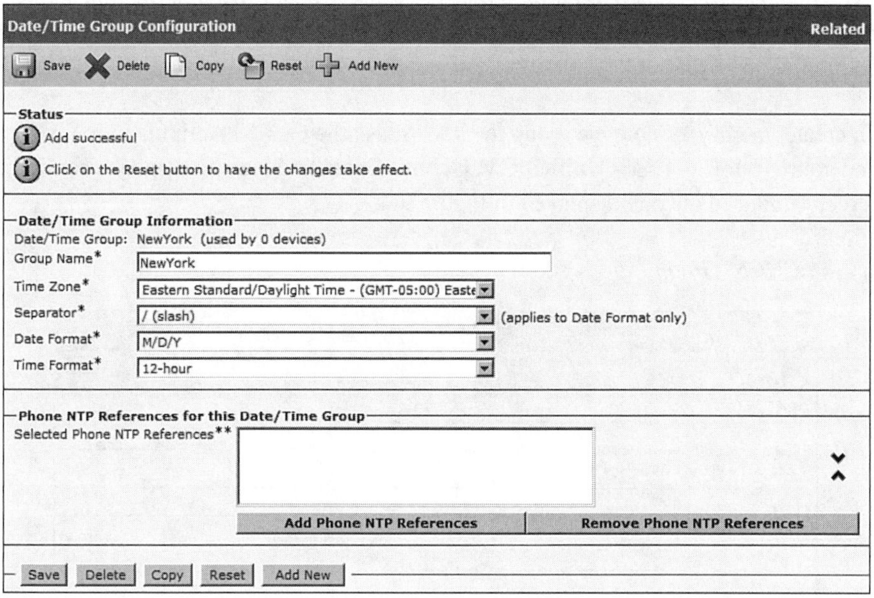

Cisco Unified CM Group

A CUCM group specifies a prioritized list of up to three CUCMs.

The first CUCM in the list serves as the primary CUCM for that group, the next member of the list (from the top) serves as the secondary CUCM, and the third the tertiary (third) CUCM.

If the primary CUCM in the CUCM group is not available, the device tries to register to the second CUCM that is listed in the group, and on the third if the secondary is unavailable. The Cisco IP Phone always maintains an active TCP 2000 (SCCP) connection open to two CUCMs. Keepalives are sent every 30 seconds to each CUCM to guarantee reachability.

CUCM groups provide important features for the CUCM system:

- **Redundancy**: Up to three CUCM servers can be defined for each CUCM group. The Cisco IP Phone has five CUCM references, but only three of them can be populated by the CUCM group.

- **Call processing load balancing**: The administrator can control active device registrations by configuring multiple CUCM groups and using different primary servers for each group. This distributes the control of devices and call-processing load.

For most systems, there is a need for multiple CUCM group configurations, and a single CUCM can be assigned to multiple groups to achieve better load distribution and redundancy. Different CUCM groups are configured in different device pools that collect phone configuration settings.

To create, modify, or delete a group in CUCM, use the CUCM Administration web page and go to **System > Cisco Unified CM Group**. Click **Add New** to display a configuration screen similar to the one displayed in Figure 9-4.

Figure 9-4   *CUCM Group*

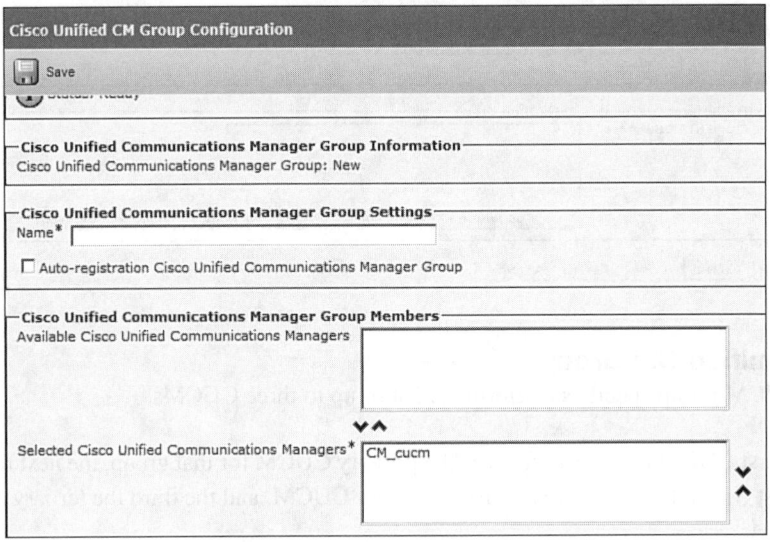

Regions

Regions are used to specify the audio and video codec that is used per call within and between regions. The configured audio codec determines the type of audio compression used per audio call.

The video call bandwidth comprises the sum of the audio and video bandwidth of the video call.

> **NOTE**   The default audio codec for all calls through CUCM specifies G.711. If there is no plan to use any other audio codec, it is not required to change region configuration.
>
> CUCM allows a maximum of 500 regions.

To create, modify, or delete a region in CUCM, use the CUCM Administration and navigate to **System > Region**. Click **Add New** to display a configuration screen similar to the one in Figure 9-5. Choose a destination region, and then select the audio codec and video call bandwidth as appropriate between the regions.

Figure 9-5 *Regions*

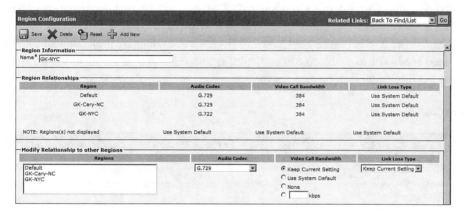

Locations

Use locations to implement call admission control (CAC) in a centralized call-processing system. CAC enables the administrator to limit the number of audio and video calls placed over the WAN. WAN availability is limited only by the amount of bandwidth that is available for audio and video calls configured in the priority queue (PQ) of the quality of service (QoS) configuration.

> **NOTE** If CAC is not used to limit the audio and video bandwidth on IP WAN links, an unlimited number of calls can be active on that link at the same time. This situation can cause the quality of all audio and video calls to degrade as the link becomes oversubscribed.

In a centralized call-processing system, a single CUCM cluster provides call processing for all locations on the IP telephony network. The CUCM cluster usually resides at the main (or central) location, along with other devices such as phones and gateways. The remote locations contain additional devices, but no CUCM. IP WAN links connect the remote locations to the main location.

CUCM has no concept of bandwidth limitations without a CAC mechanism. CUCM believes that bandwidth is infinite, causing a condition where 100 G.711 phone calls could be routed over a T1 link that has QoS provisioned to accommodate 7 phone calls. Devices can be provisioned into different locations, and then the interlocation bandwidth would limit the number of calls that can be routed over the WAN links. When a call is rejected from being routed over the WAN, the call can be rerouted over the PSTN links, and a toll charge would probably apply. When the call is rerouted, the end user will see a No Bandwidth, Re-Routing message on the LCD display of the phone.

To create, modify, or delete a location in CUCM, use the CUCM Administration web page and go to **System > Location**. Click **Add New** to display a configuration screen similar to the one displayed in Figure 9-6. Choose the location and configure the amount of audio and video bandwidth available to that particular location. These configurations should align to the PQ bandwidth that the data network team has provisioned across the IP WAN links.

Figure 9-6 *Locations*

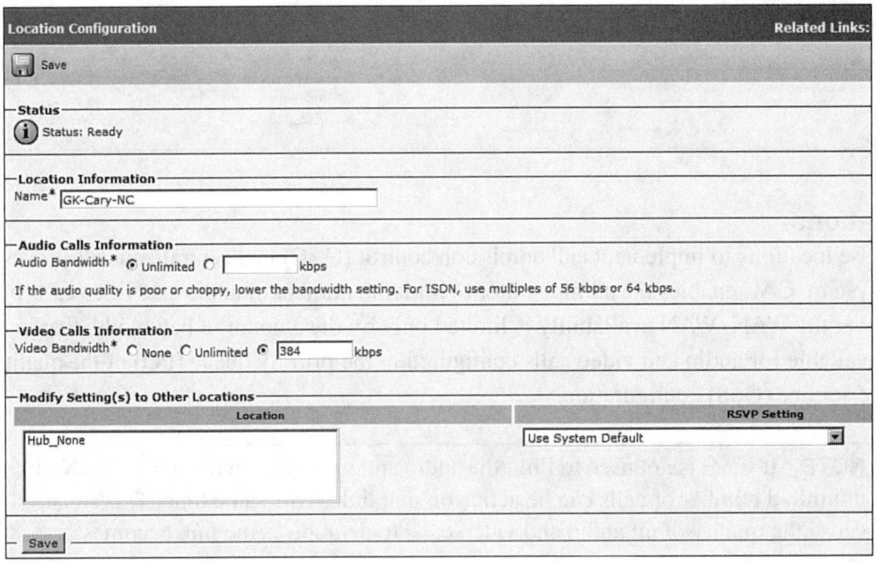

Phone Security Profile

The Phone Security Profile window includes security-related settings such as device security mode, Certificate Authority Proxy Function (CAPF) settings, digest authentication settings (for SIP phones only), and encrypted configuration file settings. A security profile must be applied to all phones that are configured in CUCM Administration. Administrators can make use of existing security profiles that have security disabled.

To create, modify, or delete a security profile in CUCM, use the CUCM Administration web page and go to **System > Security Profile > Phone Security Profile**. Click **Add New**, and then select the phone type from the Phone Security Profile Type drop-down menu. Click **Next**. Select the phone security profile protocol from the drop down-menu (SCCP or SIP) and click the **Next** button. A configuration screen similar to that shown in Figure 9-7 will display. Security parameters are covered in more detail in *Cisco IP Telephony Part 2*.

Figure 9-7   *Phone Security Profile*

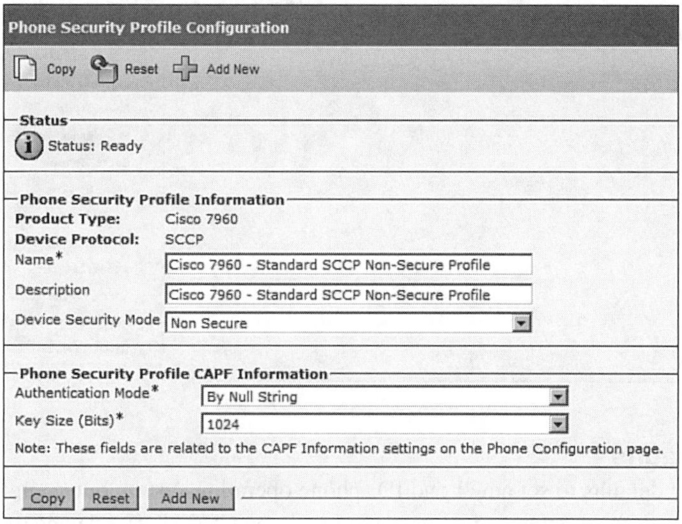

Device Settings

Device settings include default settings, profiles, templates, and common device configurations that can be assigned to the device or device pool. Some of the common elements in device settings are described over the next few pages. Figure 9-8 displays the options that are available from the Device Settings submenu.

Figure 9-8 *Device Settings*

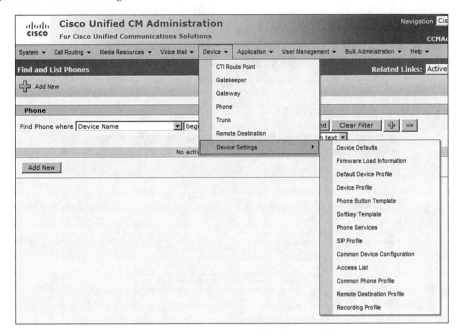

Device Defaults

Use device defaults to set new Load ID (phone operating system binary image) default characteristics for the types of devices used with the CUCM. The device defaults apply to all auto-registered devices of that type within a CUCM cluster. A different Phone Load Name (Load ID) can be specified at the device configuration page after the device has registered. The following device defaults can be set for each device type to which they apply:

- **Device load**: Lists the firmware load that is used with a particular type of hardware device

- **Device pool**: Allows the administrator to choose the device pool that is associated with each type of device

- **Phone button template**: Indicates the phone button template that is used by each type of device

To set device defaults from the CUCM Administration web page, go to **Device > Device Settings > Device Defaults**. Modify the settings that you want to modify and click **Save**. Figure 9-9 displays the options available from the Device Defaults Configuration page.

Figure 9-9 *Device Defaults Configuration*

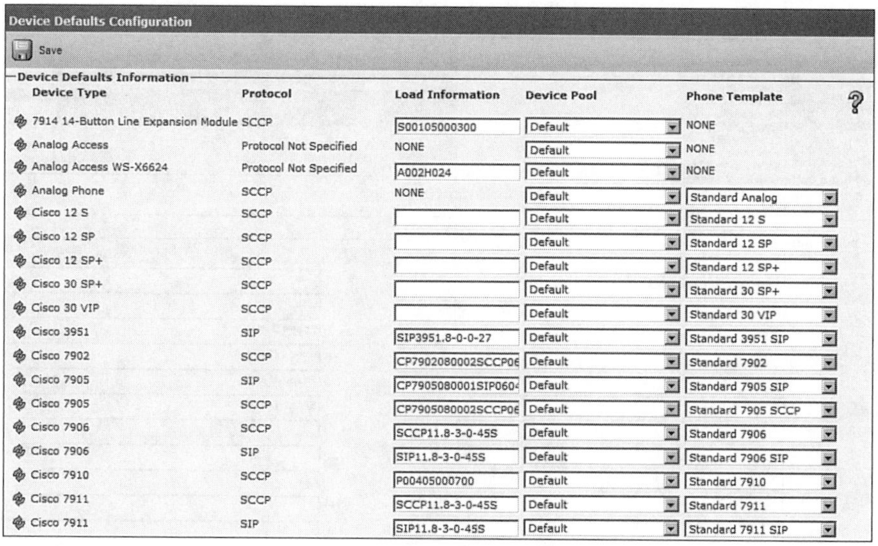

Device Defaults Configuration

Save

Device Defaults Information

Device Type	Protocol	Load Information	Device Pool	Phone Template
7914 14-Button Line Expansion Module	SCCP	S00105000300	Default	NONE
Analog Access	Protocol Not Specified	NONE	Default	NONE
Analog Access WS-X6624	Protocol Not Specified	A002H024	Default	NONE
Analog Phone	SCCP	NONE	Default	Standard Analog
Cisco 12 S	SCCP		Default	Standard 12 S
Cisco 12 SP	SCCP		Default	Standard 12 SP
Cisco 12 SP+	SCCP		Default	Standard 12 SP+
Cisco 30 SP+	SCCP		Default	Standard 30 SP+
Cisco 30 VIP	SCCP		Default	Standard 30 VIP
Cisco 3951	SIP	SIP3951.8-0-0-27	Default	Standard 3951 SIP
Cisco 7902	SCCP	CP7902080002SCCP06	Default	Standard 7902
Cisco 7905	SIP	CP7905080001SIP060	Default	Standard 7905 SIP
Cisco 7905	SCCP	CP7905080002SCCP06	Default	Standard 7905 SCCP
Cisco 7906	SCCP	SCCP11.8-3-0-45S	Default	Standard 7906
Cisco 7906	SIP	SIP11.8-3-0-45S	Default	Standard 7906 SIP
Cisco 7910	SCCP	P00405000700	Default	Standard 7910
Cisco 7911	SCCP	SCCP11.8-3-0-45S	Default	Standard 7911
Cisco 7911	SIP	SIP11.8-3-0-45S	Default	Standard 7911 SIP

Phone Button Template

Creating and using phone button templates provides a fast way to assign a common button configuration to a large number of Cisco Unified IP Phones.

CUCM includes several default phone button templates. When adding phones, one of these templates must be assigned to the phones.

All phones must have at least one line assigned. The remaining buttons can be used for additional lines, speed dials, privacy buttons, or service URLs. CUCM 6.0 also supports programmable line keys (PLK) on Cisco Type B phones. PLKs enable supplementary service phone features such as call hold, park, transfer, and conference to be applied to physical buttons on the phone.

Before adding any IP phones to the system, create phone button templates with all the required combinations of phone button templates for all IP phone models in use.

To create, modify, or delete a phone button template in CUCM, use the CUCM Administration web page and navigate to **Device > Device Settings > Phone Button Template**. Click **Find** and choose an existing phone button template to display a configuration screen similar to the one displayed in Figure 9-10.

Figure 9-10 *Phone Button Template*

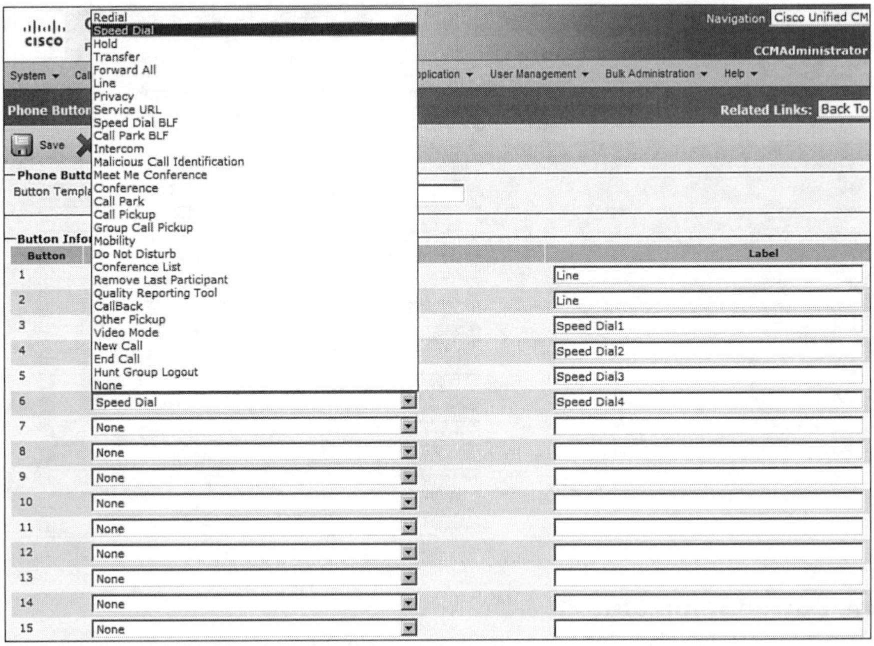

Softkey Template

Softkey template configuration allows the administrator to manage softkeys on Cisco IP Phones. CUCM supports two types of softkey templates: standard and nonstandard. Applications that support softkeys can have one or more standard softkey templates that are associated with them; for example, CUCM has the Standard Feature and the Standard User softkey templates that are associated with it. Standard softkey templates cannot be modified or deleted. To create a new softkey template, copy one of the templates, edit it and save it with a new name, or create a new one from scratch.

Choose **Device > Device Settings > Softkey Templates** to access the Softkey Template Configuration window in CUCM Administration. Click **Find** and choose an existing softkey template. If the softkey template is a default, the softkey template positions cannot be modified. Click the **Copy** button and rename the softkey template. Click **Save**. The Configure Softkey Layout Related Link is selected in the upper-right portion of the screen by default. Click the **Go** button. Select a call state to modify the softkey templates for and move the softkeys from the Unselected Softkeys to the Selected Softkeys (and vice versa) of the screen by selecting the softkey and clicking the left and right arrow buttons. Softkey positions can be modified, too, by clicking the up and down arrows. Different softkeys are available on the phone depending on the call state (on-hook, off-hook, phone ringing, and so on). Figure 9-11 displays the configuration of a softkey template.

Figure 9-11 *Softkey Template*

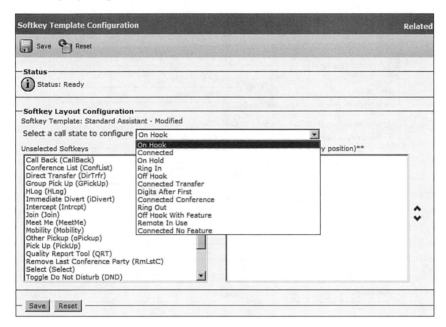

SIP Profile

A SIP profile comprises the set of SIP attributes that are associated with SIP trunks or SIP endpoints. SIP profiles include information such as name, description, timing, retry, call pickup Uniform Resource Identifier (URI), and so on. The profiles contain some standard entries that cannot be deleted or changed.

> **NOTE** A SIP URI consists of a call destination configured with a user@host format, such as xten3@CompB.cisco.com or 2085017328@10.21.91.156:5060.

A default SIP profile exists, called the Standard SIP Profile, which can be assigned to SIP phones on the SIP Phone Configuration page. The Standard SIP Profile cannot be deleted or modified. To create a new SIP profile, copy the default SIP profile, edit it, and save it with a new name or create a new one from scratch. SIP profiles can be accessed by navigating to **Device > Device Settings > SIP Profile** in CUCM Administration. The SIP Profile Configuration page is shown in Figure 9-12.

Figure 9-12 *SIP Profile*

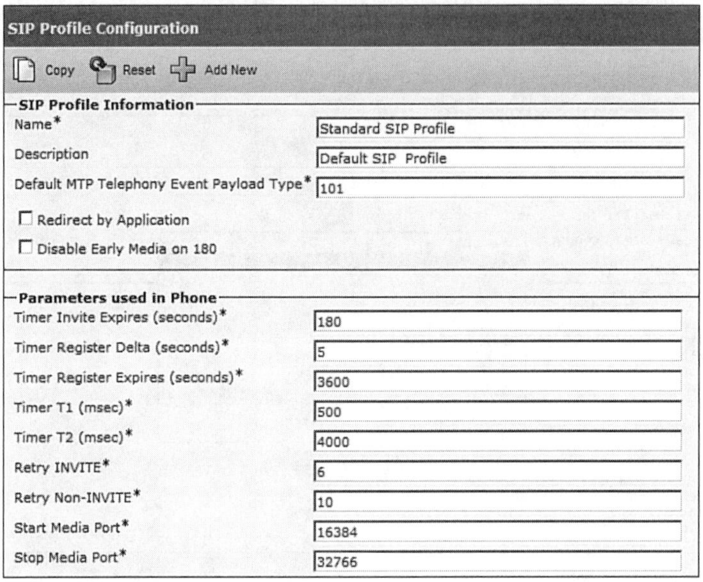

Common Phone Profiles

Common phone profiles include phone configuration parameters such as the phone password (for supported Cisco IP Phones), Do Not Disturb (DND), and personalization settings, including end-user access to background images. After a common phone profile has been configured, use the Phone Configuration window to associate an SCCP or SIP phone with it.

Administrators can chose to use the default Standard Common Phone Profile that is created when CUCM is installed, if no specific settings are required.

Common phone profiles can be accessed by navigating to **Device > Device Settings > Common Phone Profile** in CUCM Administration. The Common Phone Profile Configuration page is displayed in Figure 9-13.

Figure 9-13   *Common Phone Profile*

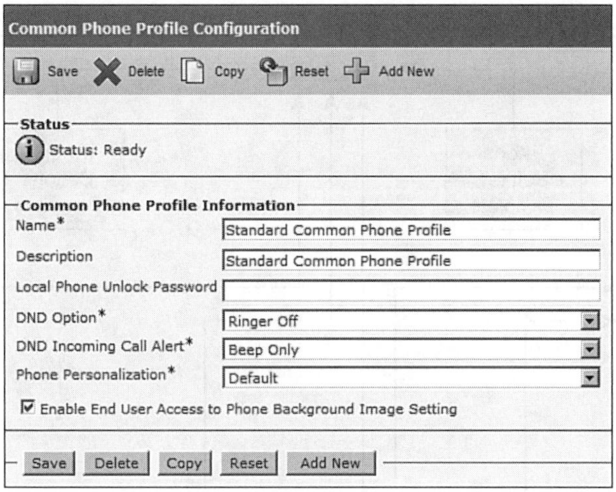

Phone Configuration Element Relationship

In Figure 9-14, an NTP reference is applied as an element to the date/time group, and the date/time group is applied as an element of the device pool configuration. The device pool is one of the elements in the device record of an IP phone, allowing the IP phones to inherit settings configured at the device pool level.

Some elements can be applied to both the device pool and the phone configuration, in which case the value applied to the phone configuration will have higher priority. The Locations element is an example of a configuration element that can be configured at the device and device pool level. This is normally done when there is a group of phones that should be configured in the same manner, but one option differs.

Some of the elements apply to only specific device types (for example, a SIP profile applies only to SIP devices). Figure 9-14 uses arrows to display the relationships between the configuration elements.

Figure 9-14 *Phone Configuration Element Relationship*

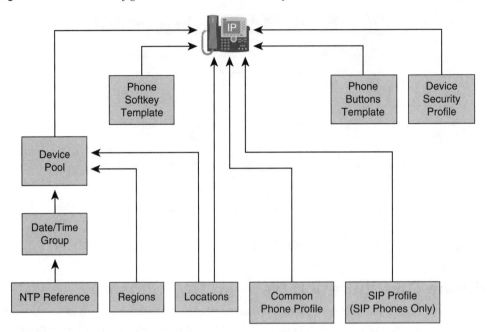

IP Phone Auto Registration

Auto registration allows CUCM to issue extension numbers to new IP phones, which is similar to the way in which the DHCP server issues IP addresses.

With auto registration configured and enabled, when a new IP phone boots and attempts to register with CUCM for the first time, CUCM issues an extension number from a configured range. After CUCM issues the extension, it adds the phone to its configuration database with the used device ID (MAC address) and the assigned extension.

If a specific extension is intended to be used for a phone, the automatically assigned extension has to be modified.

Auto registration eases only one small part when adding a high number of IP phones: The MAC addresses of the phones are automatically added to the CUCM configuration database. The extensions, however, still have to be modified per phone.

If a large number of phone settings need to be changed, CUCM BAT can be used to alter the phone configurations.

NOTE   For large deployments, the CUCM Auto-Register Phone tool can be used, which allows specific extensions to be assigned to individual phones based on user input.

Auto registration is supported by all Cisco IP Phones and does not affect IP phones that are already configured.

Auto registration occurs as part of the IP phone startup process, at the point where the IP phone tries to download its configuration file from the TFTP server. Assuming the IP phone has a MAC address of 0015C5AABBDD, the following will happen:

1. The Cisco IP Phone attempts to download configuration from the TFTP server. The TFTP server does not contain a configuration file for this phone (that is, SEP0015C5AABBDD.cnf.xml) because the phone does not have a unique configuration in CUCM. Each preconfigured phone in CUCM will have a unique XML configuration file corresponding to the configuration in CUCM. The TFTP server returns "Read Error" to the IP phone TFTP request.

2. The IP phone then queries the TFTP server for the XmlDefault.cnf.xml file. CUCM automatically creates a phone device record in the configuration database and assigns a directory number (DN) to the first line of the device based on the auto-registration DN range. A configuration file (SEP0015C5AABBDD.cnf.xml) is created and added to the TFTP server.

3. The IP phone updates its firmware if the load information defined in the configuration file is an older or newer version than the one the phone is currently running.

4. The IP phone registers to the CUCM server configured for auto registration and specified in the file XmlDefault.cnf.xml.

Administrators should carefully evaluate auto registration before implementing it, because its use can pose a security risk to the network. Auto registration allows anyone with physical access to the voice network to connect an IP phone and use it, whether authorized or not. Auto registration is turned off by default. The security risks of auto registration can be minimized by applying partitions to all route patterns in the system. This topic is covered in more detail in Chapter 13, "Calling Privileges."

A range of DNs must be configured on CUCM for auto registration. CUCM assigns the next available DN out of the configured range. One DN is assigned per IP phone. The administrator cannot control which DN will be allocated on a per-device basis.

The default protocol for auto-registered IP phones is set globally within the cluster and can be set to either SIP or SCCP. For endpoints that are both SIP and SCCP capable, it automatically converts the endpoint firmware to match to the default auto-registration protocols. Endpoints that support only one protocol will still be able to auto register even if the auto-registration protocol is set to the other protocol.

Auto-Registration Configuration

There are four steps involved in configuring for auto registration; the fourth step is optional, although commonly required:

Step 1   Verify that the desired auto-registration default protocol is selected.

Step 2   Ensure that auto registration is enabled on one CUCM group.

Step 3   Configure CUCM member servers of that group selectively to be used for auto registration, and if enabled on a particular server, set this server's DN range.

Step 4   (Optional) Reconfigure the automatically added phones, applying the individually required configuration settings. This can be done using CUCM BAT for groups of phones that share some settings or manually for each phone.

The default auto-registration protocol is an enterprise parameter, configured under **System > Enterprise Parameters**. This parameter specifies the protocol that should be used on Cisco IP Phones that support SCCP and SIP.

The default auto-registration protocol is SCCP. Restart all services for the parameter change to take effect. Figure 9-15 displays the auto-registration phone protocol enterprise parameter.

Figure 9-15   *Auto-Registration Phone Protocol*

Auto-Registration Phone Protocol

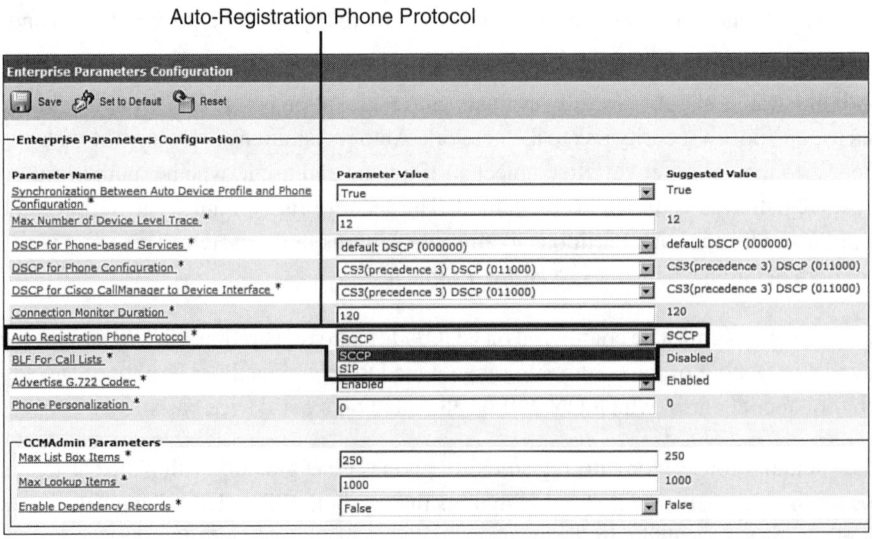

Auto registration can be enabled only on one CUCM group. Checking the Enable Auto-Registration check box on one CUCM group automatically disables the check box on the group that had auto registration enabled before (if applicable). Navigate to **System > Cisco Unified CM Group** and select the group that should provide the auto-registration service, and then check the Enable Auto-Registration check box. Figure 9-16 displays the default Cisco Unified CM Group Configuration page.

Figure 9-16 *Auto Registration: CUCM Group Configuration*

Enable Auto-Registration

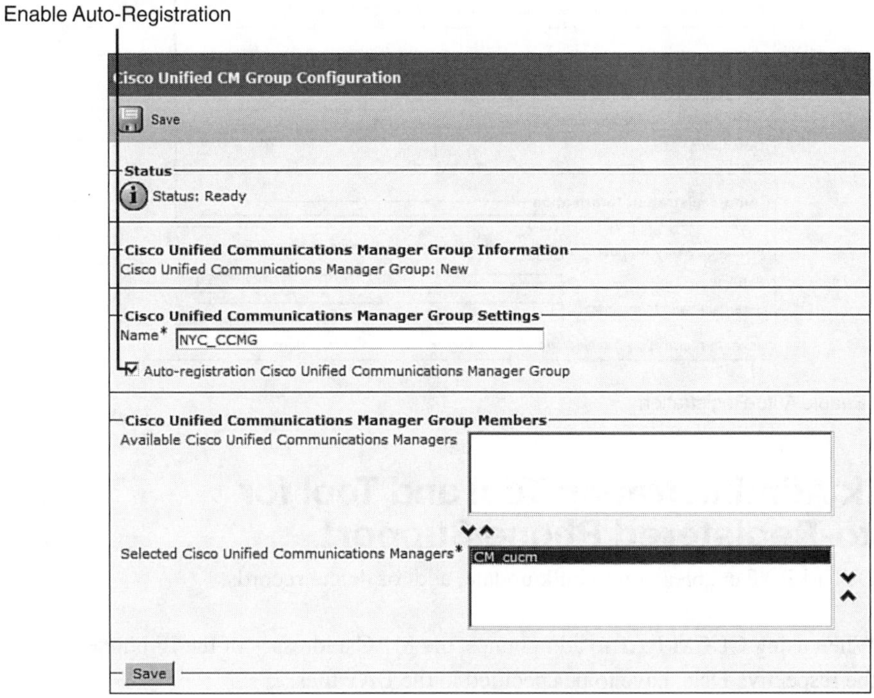

Complete these steps to enable auto registration on a specific CUCM server; this server has to be a member of the CUCM group that is configured for auto registration.

Step 1 From CUCM Administration, choose **System > CUCM**.

Step 2 Click **Find**, and then from the list of CUCM servers, choose the server that should be configured for auto registration.

Step 3 Under the Auto-Registration Information section, enter the appropriate DN range in the Starting and Ending Directory Number fields.

Step 4 Ensure that the Auto-Registration Disabled on this Cisco Unified Communications Manager check box is unchecked.

Step 5 Click **Save**.

Figure 9-17 displays the Cisco Unified CM Configuration page.

Figure 9-17   *Figure 9-17 Cisco Unified CM Configuration*

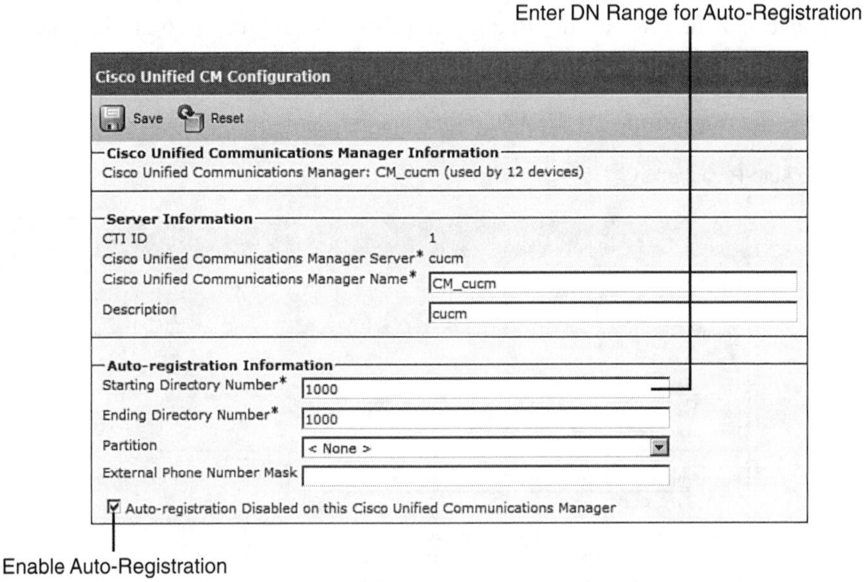

Bulk Administration Tool and Tool for Auto-Registered Phone Support

CUCM BAT enables you to bulk update, add, or delete records.

When using CUCM BAT to add phones, the MAC addresses of the IP phones, along with the respective DNs, have to be specified in the BAT files.

NOTE   The MAC address is printed in text and Universal Product Code (UPC) form, on both the shipping box of the IP phone and on the IP phone itself. This allows bar-code scanners to be used instead of manually typing MAC addresses into the BAT comma-separated value files.

The CUCM Auto-Register Phone tool is a set of Cisco CRS scripts that have to be installed onto a Cisco CRS server.

With the CUCM Auto-Register Phone tool, new phones and their DNs are added with dummy MAC addresses. Usually, CUCM BAT is used to create the unique configuration of each phone. After the phone records have been added to CUCM with CUCM BAT, the real

MAC addresses of the auto-registered phones have to be applied to each phone record created by BAT.

The correlation process is automated by placing a call from an auto-registered phone to an interactive voice response (IVR) application running on the Cisco CRS. When a phone user calls into the Auto-Register Phone application, the user is prompted to enter the desired DN.

At this stage, the system knows all the required information: the MAC address of the physical phone and the phone configuration record to be applied to the phone. The CUCM Auto-Register Phone tool will now update the CUCM configuration database accordingly by removing the phone record that was added by auto registration and by changing the dummy MAC address of the desired phone record to the one of the physical phone.

Tool for Auto-Registered Phone Support

The Tool for Auto-Registered Phone Support (TAPS) has the following requirements:

■ The TAPS service must be activated and running.

■ The CUCM TAPS plug-in has to be downloaded from the CUCM plug-in page and installed onto a Cisco CRS (Cisco Unified Contact Center) server.

■ Installation prerequisites for the CUCM TAPS are as follows:

—The CUCM publisher is running and integrated with the Cisco CRS.

■ After installation of the CUCM, TAPS optional parameters may be configured in Cisco CRS.

> **NOTE**   Details for installation, configuration, and integration of the Cisco CRS server are not part of this book. These concepts are covered in the Cisco course UCXXD. An AXL (AVVID XML Layer) admin account needs to be configured for Cisco CRS so that it can access and update the CUCM database. You can find additional information at Cisco.com.

TAPS: Phone Insert Process

Figure 9-18 illustrates the TAPS insertion process described here:

1. The administrator uses CUCM BAT to preconfigure phone device records with dummy MAC addresses.

2. A new phone is plugged into the network. It auto registers to CUCM, which creates a new devices records with a DN out of the auto-registration range.

3. The phone user dials the number of the CUCM Auto-Register Phone tool CRS application.

4. CUCM routes the call to CUCM Auto-Register Phone tool applications on Cisco CRS.

5. Cisco CRS prompts the user to enter the appropriate directory number. The number is then looked up in the phone configuration records that were previously added using CUCM BAT and which have a dummy MAC address.

6. Cisco CRS updates the dummy MAC address of the found phone record with the actual MAC address of the phone in the CUCM configuration database.

7. The IP phone downloads its newly created configuration file from CUCM TFTP.

Figure 9-18 *Auto-Registered Phone Tool: Phone Insertion Process*

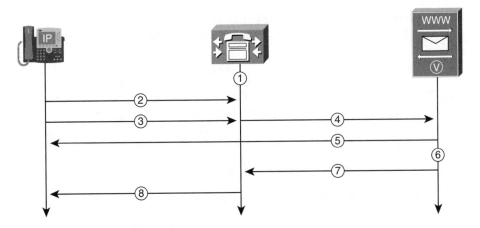

Bulk Administration Tool

The procedure for adding phones using BAT is as follows:

Step 1 Verify that the Bulk Provisioning Service has been activated.

Step 2 Configure the CUCM BAT template.

Step 3 Create the comma-separated values data input file.

Step 4 Validate the data input file.

Step 5 Insert the devices into the CUCM database.

Bulk Provisioning Service

You can verify the Bulk Provisioning Service (BPS) status from the Cisco Unified Service-ability pages available at https:<*ip-address*>/ccmservice. Alternatively, the serviceability pages can be loaded by choosing Cisco Unified Serviceability from the Navigation drop-down menu in the upper-right portion of the screen and clicking the Go button.

From the Serviceability pages, choose **Tools > Control Center — Feature Services** to verify that the Cisco BPS is running. If the service is not activated, go to **Tools > Service Activation** and activate the service.

Phone Template

Once the BPS has been activated, create a phone template. The phone template contains common parameters for phone configurations. The phone template must include the mandatory name field. Individual phone configuration parameters are entered in the comma-separated value (CSV) data file.

Before creating the template, make sure phone settings such as device pool, location, calling search space, button template, and softkey templates have already been configured in CUCM Administration. These settings cannot be created by CUCM BAT.

Follow these steps to create a phone template:

Step 1   From CUCM Administration, choose **Bulk Administration > Phones > Phone Template**. The Find and List Phone Templates window displays.

Step 2   Click the **Add New** button. The Add a New Phone Template window displays.

Step 3   From the Phone Type drop-down list, choose the phone model for which the template is to be created. Click the **Next** button.

Step 4   Choose the device protocol from the Select the Device Protocol drop-down list. Click **Next**. The Phone Template Configuration window displays with fields and default entries for the chosen device type.

Step 5   In the Phone Template Name field, enter a name for the template. The name can contain up to 50 alphanumeric characters (for example, Sales_7960).

Step 6   In the Device Information area, enter the phone settings that the phones to be added have in common. Some phone models and device types do not use all the attributes that are shown.

Step 7   After all the settings for this CUCM BAT phone template have been entered, click **Save**. This page is displayed in Figure 9-19.

Figure 9-19 *Phone Template Configuration*

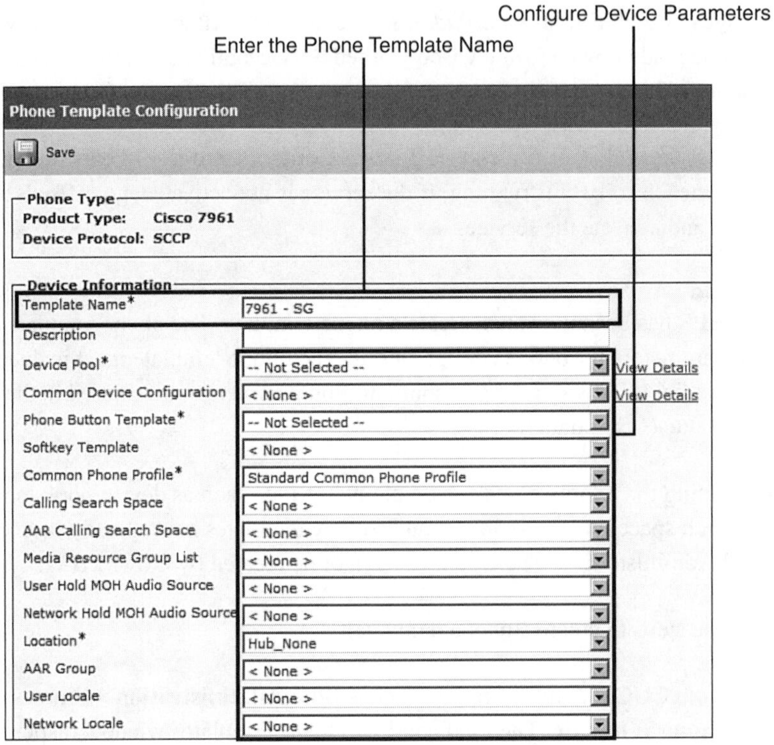

Line Template

The administrator clicks **Line [1] Add a new DN**. The Line Template Configuration window, shown in Figure 9-20, needs to be configured in the following way:

Step 1 Enter or choose the appropriate values for the line settings, such as partition, calling search space, presence, and others. Keep in mind that all phones added by this BAT job will use the settings that are chosen for this line.

Step 2 Click **Save**. CUCM BAT adds the line to the phone template configuration.

Step 3 Repeat the described procedure to add settings for any additional lines.

> **NOTE** The maximum number of lines that display for a CUCM BAT template depends on the model and phone button template that the administrator chose when the administrator created the CUCM BAT phone template.

Figure 9-20   *Line Template Configuration*

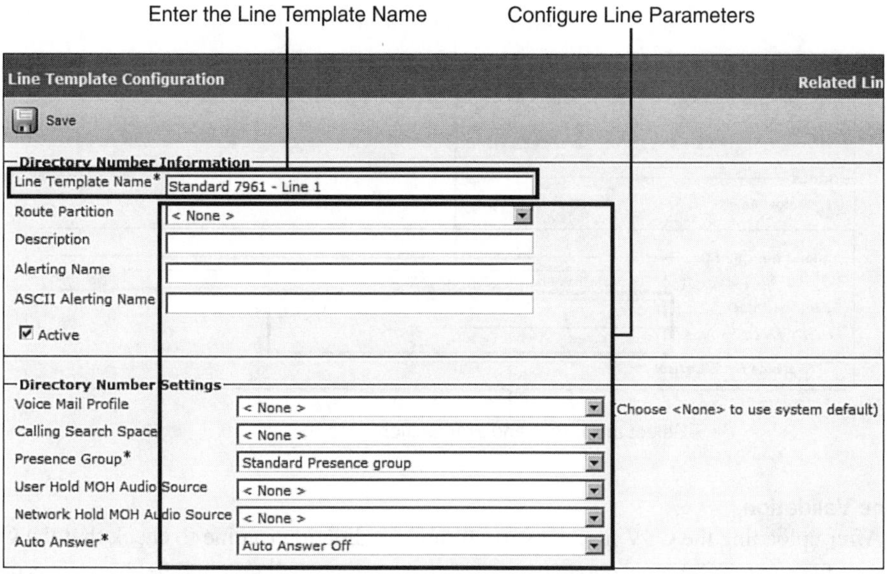

CSV File Upload

Follow these steps to upload the CSV file containing the device data to the CUCM server:

Step 1   Choose **Bulk Administration > Upload/Download Files**. The Find and List Files window displays (shown in Figure 9-21).

Step 2   Click **Add New**. The File Upload Configuration window displays.

Step 3   In the File text box, enter the full path of the file to be uploaded or click **Browse** and locate the file.

Step 4   From the Select the Target drop-down list, choose the target the file is to be used for (phones in this case).

Step 5   From the Transaction Type drop-down list, choose the transaction type for the file.

Step 6   If the file is to overwrite an existing file with the same name, check the **Overwrite File If It Exists** check box.

Step 7   Click **Save** and wait for updated status information; the status should be Successful.

Figure 9-21 *CSV File Upload*

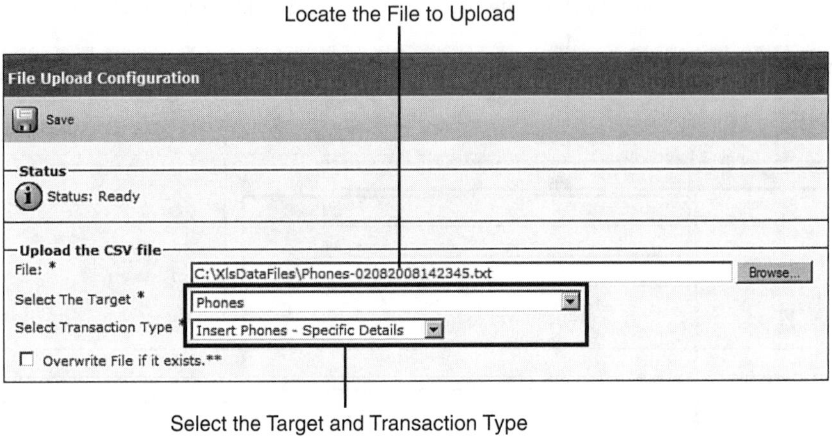

Phone Validation

After uploading the CSV file, the system runs a validation routine to check that the CSV data file and CUCM BAT phone template have populated all required fields, such as device pool and locations. The validation also checks for discrepancies with the first node database (for instance, an already existing entry with the same MAC address).

To validate the CSV data file phone records, follow these steps:

Step 1 Choose **Bulk Administration > Phones > Validate Phones**. The Validate Phones Configuration window displays (shown in Figure 9-22).

Step 2 Select the **Validate Phones Specific Details** radio button to validate phone records that use a customized file format or select the **Validate Phones All Details** radio button to validate phone records from an exported phones file that was generated using the All Details option.

Step 3 In the File Name drop-down list, choose the CSV data file that contains the unique details for the phones or other IP telephony devices. This is the file that was uploaded previously.

Step 4 For the Specific Details option, in the Phone Template Name drop-down list, the administrator can choose the CUCM BAT phone template that he created for this type of bulk transaction.

Step 5 To start the verification, click **Submit**.

Step 6 The job is submitted and gets executed immediately.

Check for the status of the verification. Only proceed to the next step if the verification was successful.

Figure 9-22 *Phone Validation*

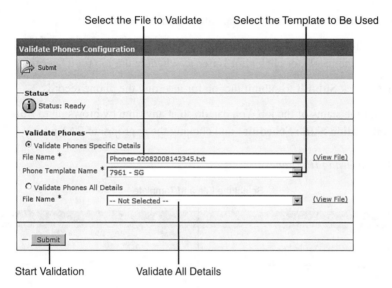

Inserting IP Phones into the CUCM Database

To start the bulk insertion of phones listed in the uploaded and verified data file, follow these steps:

Step 1   Choose **Bulk Administration > Phones > Insert Phones**. The Insert Phones Configuration window displays (shown in Figure 9-23).

Step 2   Either click the **Insert Phones Specific Details** radio button to insert phone records that use a customized file format, or click the **Insert Phones All Details** radio button to insert phone records from an exported phones file that was generated by using the All Details option.

Step 3   In the File Name drop-down list, the administrator can choose the CSV data file that he created for this specific bulk transaction.

Step 4   Checking the Override the Configuration check box overwrites the existing phone settings with the information that is contained in the file to be inserted.

In the Phone Template Name drop-down list, choose the BAT phone template that has been created for this type of bulk transaction. If an individual MAC address is not entered in the CSV data file, the Create Dummy MAC Address check box must be checked. This is used when the CUCM Auto-Register Phone tool is used.

Step 5   In the Job Information area, enter the job description.

Step 6   Click the **Run Immediately** radio button to insert the phone records immediately, or click **Run Later** to schedule the job for a later time.

Step 7   Click **Submit** to submit the job for inserting the phone records.

Check for the status of the job. You can do so at any time by browsing to **Bulk Administration > Job Scheduler** and clicking the appropriate BAT job.

Figure 9-23   *Inserting IP Phones*

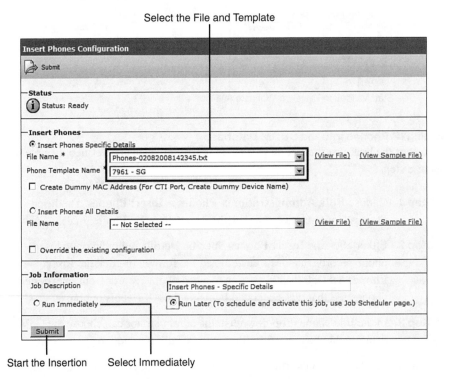

Manual Configuration

Manually adding new IP phones to the network is often tedious, but it can constitute a large part of day-to-day voice network management. Provisioning a Cisco SIP Phone is just like provisioning a SCCP phone.

The configuration procedure consists of these high-level steps:

Step 1   Add the IP phone.

Step 2   Configure the phone.

Step 3   Configure one or more DNs.

To manually add an IP phone to CUCM, go to **Device > Phone** and click the **Add New** button. Select the phone type (in Figure 9-24, a 7960 was selected). Select the device protocol that should be used with the Cisco IP Phone (SCCP or SIP), and click **Next** to get to the phone configuration page.

Figure 9-24   *Manual Phone Configuration*

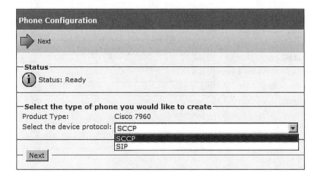

Each phone in the CUCM configuration database is uniquely identified by a device ID that is built from the phone's MAC address. The MAC address of a Cisco IP Phone is printed on a label at the back of the IP phone and can be viewed at the phone itself by pressing the Settings button.

In addition to the MAC address, the following mandatory parameters have to be set (as shown on Figure 9-25):

■   Device pool

■   Phone button template

■   Device security profile

All of these mandatory parameters have to be configured. Any configuration item on the screen with an asterisk (*) next to it is a required field. Many of these fields have default values. The only exceptions are the preceding three bullet point items.

Figure 9-25 *Manual Phone Configuration*

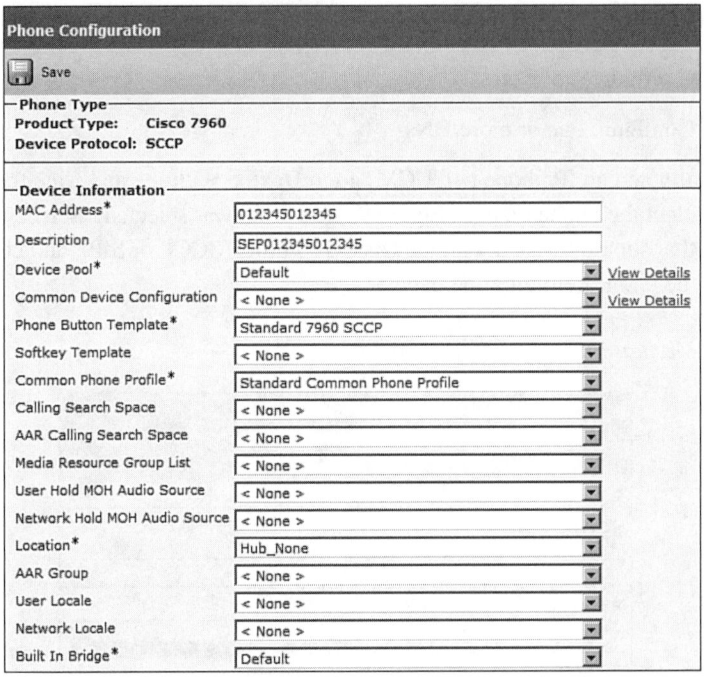

Follow this procedure to configure the directory number for the manually added IP phone:

Step 1 After the Phone is Saved, the left side of the Phone Configuration window will have an Associated Information column. Click the **Line [x] — Add a new DN** link to configure the first directory number.

Step 2 When the Directory Number Configuration window appears (shown in Figure 9-26), enter the DN of the IP phone in the appropriate field.

Step 3 Click **Save**.

Use the same procedure to configure additional lines if the phone has more than one line.

Figure 9-26 *Manual Phone Configuration*

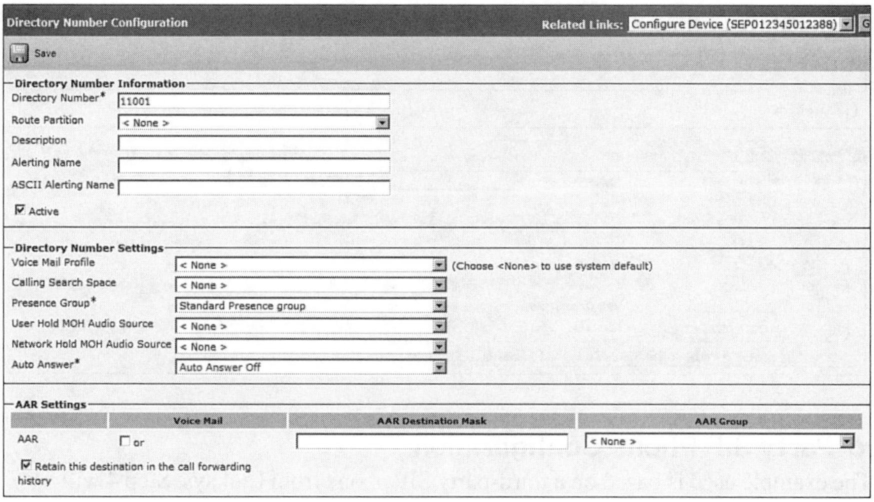

Endpoint Registration Verification

Figure 9-27 shows an example of a phone listing from the Find and List Phones function available by clicking the Find button at the **Device > Phone** menu. Successful phone registration can be verified by checking the following items:

■ Look at the Status column and verify that the phone is registered.

> **NOTE** If the phone is displayed as unregistered, the phone has previously registered but is no longer registered. If a phone is being reset, it is shown as unregistered during the short time until it reregisters with CUCM. If it is shown as unknown, it means that the phone has never successfully registered to the CUCM. If the phone is registered, its IP address is shown in the Status column. The IP address is used for CUCM to send signaling to.

■ Look at the IP Address column to verify whether the IP phone registered to the intended CUCM server.

By clicking the device name of a specific phone in the list, you can show the phone configuration page of the corresponding phone. The line configuration (DNs) parameters can be verified by clicking a line in the Phone Configuration page.

Figure 9-27 *Phone Registration Verification*

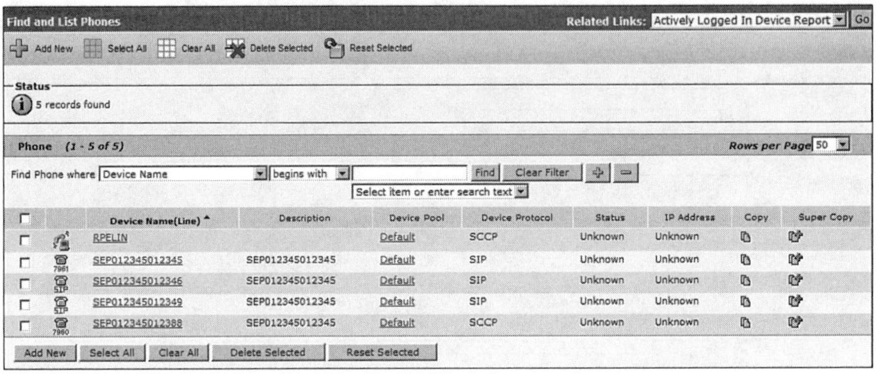

Third-Party SIP Phone Configuration

The example used is based on a third-party SIP phone from Linksys. Step 4 will vary based on the vendor of the SIP phone, but the first three steps are the same for other third-party SIP phones.

The high-level steps for adding a third-party SIP phone are as follows:

Step 1 Configure the end user in CUCM.

Step 2 Configure the device in CUCM.

Step 3 Associate the device to the end user.

Step 4 Configure the third-party SIP phone to register with CUCM.

Figure 9-28 displays the addition of an end user in CUCM to be used for the third-party SIP phone. Third-party SIP phones register with CUCM by sending their username and password in a process called digest authentication. Third-party SIP phones do not send their MAC address like SCCP or Cisco SIP Phones. A MAC address must be configured for a third-party SIP phone, but it can be an arbitrary value because there is no MAC address verification. To add a new end user, navigate to **User Management > End User** and click the **Add New** button. The end user must be associated with the third-party SIP phone after the SIP phone is created.

Figure 9-28 *End-User Configuration*

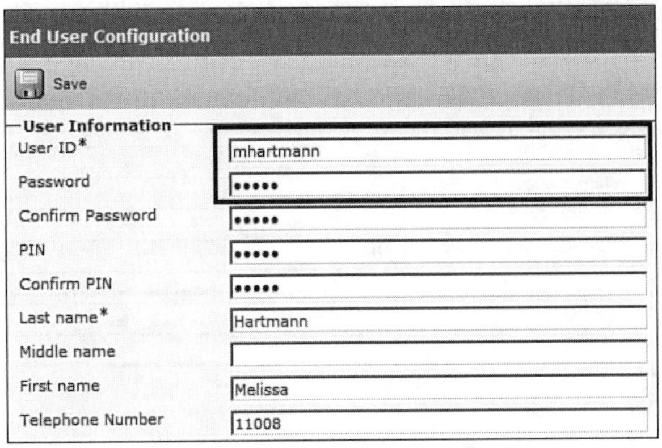

Figure 9-29 displays the addition of a new third-party SIP phone. Navigate to **Device > Phone** and click the **Add New** button. Choose **Third-Party SIP Device (Basic)** or **Third-Party SIP Device (Advanced)** from the Phone Type drop-down menu. A Basic third-party SIP phone can have only one line and consumes three device license units (DLU). An Advanced third-party SIP phone can have up to eight lines and consumes six DLUs. Third-party SIP devices must have a SIP profile.

Third-party SIP devices usually support RFC 2833 DTMF-Relay, which may cause compatibility issues with Type A Cisco IP Phones. Type A Cisco IP Phones require a media termination point (MTP) to communicate with a device that passes Dual-Tone Multifrequency digits in the RTP UDP channel (RFC 2833). MTPs are covered in detail in Chapter 15, "Media Resources."

The Digest User drop-down field must be populated with the end user configured in the preceding figure. After the phone has been configured with the digest user, update the end-user configuration by associating the end user with the third-party SIP phone.

Figure 9-29 *Third-Party SIP Phone Configuration*

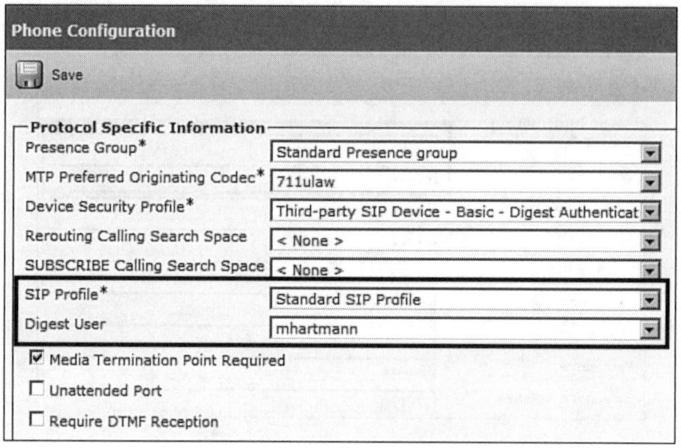

The final step to add a third-party phone takes place on the third-party phone itself. Therefore, the configuration depends on the product that is used. Figure 9-30 shows the configuration of a Linksys SPA 942 third-party SIP phone.

In the Proxy Address field of the third-party phone, specify the IP address or fully qualified domain name of CUCM.

The user ID has to be set to the DN that is assigned to the IP phone in CUCM. The auth ID has to match the digest user that was assigned to the phone in CUCM. The password needs to be set only if the digest credentials have been configured when configuring the end user and if the check box Enable Digest Authentication has been checked in the phone security profile.

> **NOTE** If the Enable Digest Authentication check box has not been checked in the phone security profile, only the username of the digest authentication is verified; the password (digest credentials in CUCM end-user configuration) is not checked.

Some third-party SIP phones do not have a separate user ID and auth ID. In this case, the user ID has to be set to the DN at the third-party SIP phone, and on the CUCM side, the end-user name has to be identical with the DN of the IP phone. The shown Linksys phone simulates that behavior when the Use Auth ID parameter is set to No. Figure 9-30 is a configuration display from the Linksys SPA 942 product.

Figure 9-30   *Third-Party SIP Phone Configuration*

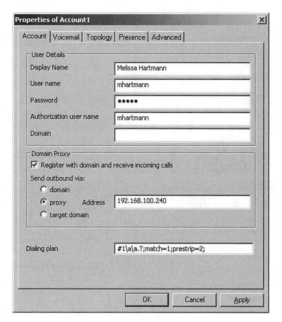

Hardening Cisco IP Phones

The IP phone is a target for attacks, just like all other components of the network. IP phone endpoints should be protected in a similar manner to servers in the environment. IP phones have default settings that make them vulnerable to attacks. There are several options available to harden IP phones and thus protect them against various attacks and infiltration methods.

The product-specific configuration parameters of Cisco IP Phones are set by default to achieve the greatest functionality but are not considered secure. To secure Cisco IP Phones, you can modify these settings:

■ **Disable Speakerphone and Disable Speakerphone and Headset**: Disable these features to prevent eavesdropping on conversations in the office by an attacker gaining remote control of the IP phone and listening to the sound near it.

■ **PC Port**: Disable the PC port to prevent a PC from connecting to the corporate network via the IP phone's PC port.

■ **Settings Access**: Disable or restrict access to the IP phone settings to avoid the risk that details about the network infrastructure could be exposed.

- **Gratuitous ARP**: Disable this feature to prevent GARP-based man-in-the-middle attacks.

- **PC Voice VLAN Access**: Disable this feature to stop the IP phone from forwarding voice VLAN traffic to the PC.

- **Web Access**: Disable access to the IP phone from a web browser to avoid the risk that details about the network infrastructure could be exposed.

Figure 9-31 displays the device-level security configuration options.

Figure 9-31 *IP Phone Security Configuration*

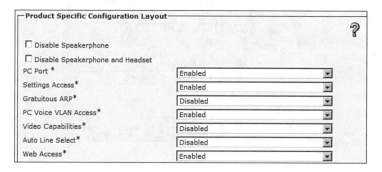

PC Port

The PC port should be disabled in special areas such as a lobby or areas where no additional PC access is allowed. This practice is not common otherwise, however, because it entails a major functionality constraint.

Settings Access

Disabling access to settings prevents anyone with physical access to the phone from gathering information about network settings (DHCP server, TFTP server, default router, and CUCM IP addresses). The network settings share information about the network that an attacker can leverage to launch attacks. CUCM Release 4.1 and later releases offer a restricted option for settings access. With restricted access, the user can modify the contrast and ringer settings but cannot access other settings.

Cisco IP Phones Web Services

A web browser can be used to connect to the HTTP server of the IP phone by browsing to the IP address of the phone. The HTTP server displays similar information that can be viewed directly on the IP phone using the Settings button, enhanced by some additional statistics.

Attackers can use the intelligence gained by discovering the network configuration to direct their attacks at the most critical telephony components, such as CUCM and the TFTP server. It is recommended that you disable web access to the phone if the highest level of security is desired. Figure 9-32 displays the information available by pointing a web browser to the IP address of the Cisco IP Phone. Notice that there are many hyperlinks on this page that access more information. The web services of the IP phone can prove useful for troubleshooting.

Figure 9-32   *Cisco IP Phone Web Services*

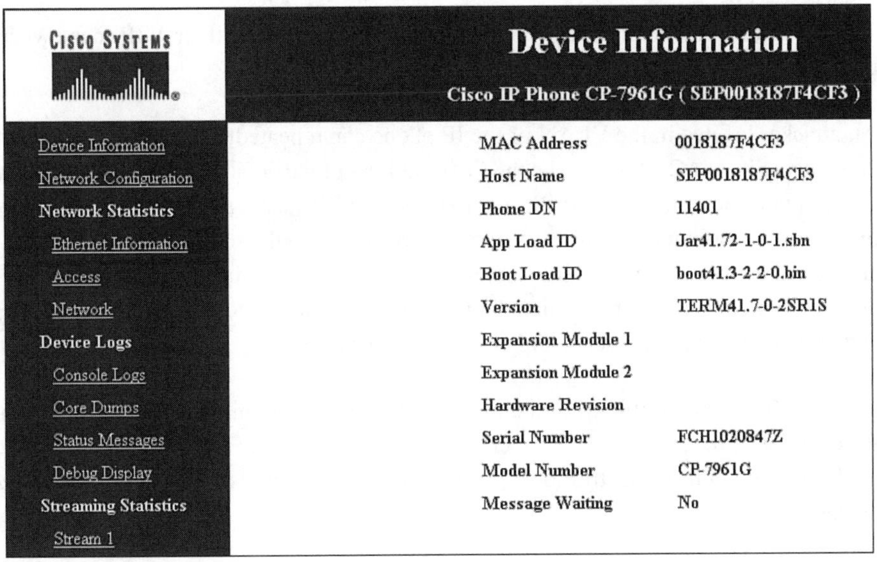

CISCO SYSTEMS	**Device Information**	
	Cisco IP Phone CP-7961G (SEP0018187F4CF3)	
Device Information	MAC Address	0018187F4CF3
Network Configuration	Host Name	SEP0018187F4CF3
Network Statistics	Phone DN	11401
Ethernet Information	App Load ID	Jar41.72-1-0-1.sbn
Access	Boot Load ID	boot41.3-2-2-0.bin
Network	Version	TERM41.7-0-2SR1S
Device Logs	Expansion Module 1	
Console Logs	Expansion Module 2	
Core Dumps	Hardware Revision	
Status Messages	Serial Number	FCH1020847Z
Debug Display	Model Number	CP-7961G
Streaming Statistics	Message Waiting	No
Stream 1		

When web access is disabled, the IP phone does not accept incoming web connections and does not provide access to sensitive information.

Disabling web access at the IP phone stops Extensible Markup Language (XML) push applications from working. If you want to use XML push applications on some IP phones, you cannot disable web access to the IP phone. An example of a push application is the emergency notification sent by Cisco Emergency Responder (Cisco ER).

Gratuitous Address Resolution Protocol

Address Resolution Protocol (ARP) normally operates in a request-and-response fashion. When a station needs to know the MAC address of a given IP address, it sends an ARP request. The device with the corresponding IP address replies and thus provides its MAC address. All receiving devices update their ARP cache by adding the IP and MAC address pair.

Gratuitous Address Resolution Protocol (GARP) packets are packets that announce the MAC address of the sender even though this information has not been requested. This technique allows receiving devices to update their ARP caches with the information. Usually such GARP messages are sent after the MAC address of a device has changed to avoid packets being sent to the old MAC address until the related entry has timed out in the ARP caches of the other devices.

GARP, however, can also be used by an attacker to redirect packets in a man-in-the-middle attack and therefore should be disabled.

Cisco IP Phones, by default, accept GARP messages and update their ARP cache whenever they receive a GARP packet.

An attacker located in the VLAN of the IP phone can repeatedly send out GARP packets announcing its MAC address to be the MAC address of the default gateway of the IP phone. The IP phone accepts the information, updates its ARP cache, and forwards all packets meant for the default gateway to the attacker. Software tools, such as Ettercap, allow the attacker to copy or modify the information and then relay it to the real destination. The user does not notice that someone is listening to the data stream so long as the attacker does not significantly increase the delay and does not drop packets.

In Figure 9-33, only traffic from the IP phone toward the default gateway is sent to the attacker; but if the attacker also impersonates the IP phone toward the router, the attacker could control bidirectional traffic. In this case, the router would also have to listen to GARP packets.

To prevent GARP-based attacks against an IP phone, you should disable the GARP feature of the IP phone.

> **NOTE** There are several ways to prevent GARP attacks. You can disable GARP on end devices, or you can use features such as Dynamic ARP Inspection (DAI) and IP Source Guard at switches.

Figure 9-33 *GARP Man-in-the-Middle Attack*

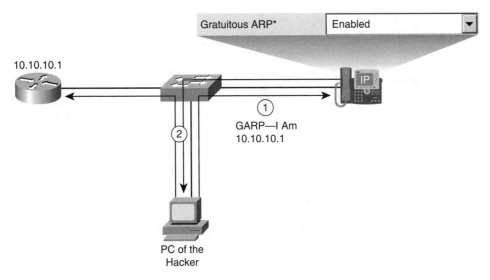

PC Voice VLAN Access

By default, an IP phone sends all traffic that it receives from the switch out its PC port (as shown in Figure 9-34). This enables the PC to see not only the traffic of the data VLAN (untagged Ethernet traffic) but also the traffic of the voice VLAN sourced and destined to the IP phone. When the PC receives voice VLAN traffic, the traffic can be captured, and hence the conversation can be sniffed with tools such as Wire Shark, available at http://www.wireshark.org.

The PC can also send packets to the voice VLAN if they are tagged accordingly. This capability breaks the separation of voice and data traffic, because the PC that is supposed to have access to the data VLAN can now send packets to the voice VLAN only, bypassing all access control rules (access control lists [ACLs] in routers or firewalls) that might be enforced between the two VLANs.

Usually the PC does not need access to the voice VLAN, and therefore you should block PC access to the voice VLAN.

NOTE   Some applications, such as call recording or supervisory monitoring in call center applications, require access to the voice VLAN. In such situations, you cannot disable the PC Voice VLAN Access setting.

Figure 9-34 *PC Voice VLAN Access*

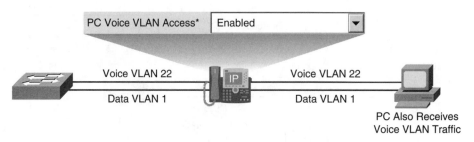

Two different settings are available for blocking PC VLAN access:

- **PC Voice VLAN Access can be disabled.**

  When a phone is configured this way, it does not forward voice VLAN-tagged traffic to the PC when it receives such frames from the switch. In addition, the phone does not forward voice VLAN-tagged traffic to the switch if it receives such frames from the PC. Although this setting is recommended for security, it makes troubleshooting more difficult because you cannot analyze voice VLAN traffic from a PC connected to the PC port of the IP phone. Whenever you need to capture voice VLAN traffic to analyze network problems, you must sniff the traffic on the network devices.

  This setting is supported on all current Cisco IP Phones with PC ports.

- **Span to PC Port can be disabled.**

  This setting has the same effect as the PC Voice VLAN setting, except it does not apply only to voice VLAN-tagged traffic, but to traffic tagged with any VLAN ID. With Span to PC Port disabled, the IP phone forwards only untagged frames.

  This setting is not available on Cisco Unified IP Phones 7940 and 7960.

NOTE   The Cisco Unified IP Phone 7912, which is end of sale, does not support either of the two settings.

Chapter Summary

The following list summarizes the key points that were discussed in this chapter:

- Some IP configuration settings are applied directly to the device, others by referencing configuration elements such as a device pool.

- IP phone auto registration automatically adds new Cisco IP Phones to the configuration database and assigns one DN to the IP phone.

- Auto-registration configuration includes the configuration of a DN range and activation of the feature on some servers of a CUCM group.

- The CUCM Tool for Auto-Registered Phone Support requires a Cisco CRS server on the network.

- CUCM BAT can be used to add and delete IP phones or to change their configuration.

- Manually adding IP phones is time consuming.

- Harden IP phones by disabling features that are not required.

References

For additional information, refer to these resources:

- **Cisco Unified Communications SRND Based on CUCM 6.x**: http://www.cisco.com/en/US/products/sw/voicesw/ps556/products_implementation_design_guide_book09186a008085eb0d.html

- **CUCM Bulk Administration Guide 6.0(1)**: http://www.cisco.com/en/US/docs/voice_ip_comm/cucm/bat/6_0_1/bat-wrapper.html

- **CUCM Administration Guide, Release 6.0(1)**: http://www.cisco.com/en/US/docs/voice_ip_comm/cucm/admin/6_0_1/ccmcfg/bccm.pdf

- **Working with the CUCM Auto-Register Phone Tool**: http://www.cisco.com/en/US/partner/docs/voice_ip_comm/cucm/bat/6_0_1/t15taps.html

Review Questions

Use the questions here to review what you learned in this chapter. The correct answers are found in Appendix A, "Answers to Chapter Review Questions."

1. Which of the following is not an option to set the time for a Cisco IP Phone?

   a. Manual settings configuration

   b. Phone NTP reference

   c. Cisco Unified Communications Manager registration

2. Which of the following configuration parameters are only required for SIP phones?

   a. Security profile

   b. SIP NTP reference

   c. Device pool

   d. SIP profile

3. Which phone NTP reference option generates a packet to the all hosts broadcast address?

   a. Unicast

   b. Multicast

   c. Anycast

   d. Directed broadcast

4. The date/time group is configured to which value by default?

   a. CMLocal

   b. NTP Reference

   c. Cisco Unified Communications Manager Publisher

   d. Eastern standard time (EST)

5. What parameter is not available in the device pool in CUCM 6.0?

   a. Softkey template

   b. Date/time group

   c. Region

   d. Cisco Unified Communications Manager Group

6. How many CUCM servers can be configured in a CUCM group?

    a. 2

    b. 3

    c. 4

    d. 5

7. What functionality does the region support?

    a. Call admission control

    b. Collection of configuration parameters

    c. Date and time configuration

    d. Audio codec selection

8. What functionality does the location support?

    a. Call admission control

    b. Collection of configuration parameters

    c. Date and time configuration

    d. Audio codec selection

9. Where must auto registration be enabled in CUCM? (Choose two.)

    a. Call Manager Group Configuration

    b. Device Settings Configuration

    c. Device Configuration

    d. Call Manager Configuration

10. The Bulk Administration tool does not require which parameter of the IP phone?

    a. IP address

    b. Phone type

    c. Phone protocol

    d. MAC address

CHAPTER **10**

Configuring Voice Gateways

CUCM deployments need a connection to the public switched telephone network (PSTN) to be able to place and receive external calls. PSTN connections are provided by gateways that interconnect traditional digital or analog telephony interfaces. Gateways are analogous to trunk cards in traditional PBXs, whereas CUCM trunks indicate call routing over an IP network. Gateways can use various protocols for signaling between CUCM. Media Gateway Control Protocol (MGCP) is the signaling protocol that is investigated in this chapter.

The purpose of this lesson is to describe the role and implementation of MGCP gateways to provide PSTN access to a CUCM environment.

Chapter Objectives

Upon completing this lesson, you will be able to describe the implementation of MGCP gateways in CUCM and be able to meet these objectives:

- Describe how gateway interfaces can be controlled by CUCM using MGCP.

- Describe how CUCM and Cisco IOS gateways support MGCP protocols.

- Describe how to configure an MGCP gateway in CUCM.

- Describe how to configure a gateway for MGCP.

Media Gateway Control Protocol Gateways

MGCP is a plain-text protocol used by call-control devices to manage IP telephony gateways.

MGCP (IETF RFC 2705) is a master/slave protocol that allows a call-control device (CUCM) to take control of a specific port on a gateway. MGCP has the advantage of centralized gateway administration and provides for scalable IP telephony solutions. CUCM controls the MGCP state of the configured ports of the gateway. MGCP allows centralized administration of the dial plan and gives CUCM per-port control of all gateway interfaces. The gateway interfaces are traditional time-division multiplexing (TDM) interfaces, including analog and digital interfaces, which can interconnect PBXs, voice-mail systems, plain old telephone service (POTS) phones, and other traditional device connections. MGCP is implemented with the use of a series of plain-text commands (Session Description Protocol [SDP]) sent over User Datagram Protocol (UDP) port 2427 from CUCM to the gateway.

It is also important to note that for an MGCP interaction to take place with CUCM, the gateway and gateway interface must have CUCM support. Use the Feature Navigator tool (http://www.cisco.com/go/fn) to make sure that the router or switch platform version of Cisco IOS Catalyst Operating System (CatOS) software is compatible with the CUCM version MGCP features.

Endpoint Identifiers

The MGCP call agent (CUCM) directs its commands to the gateway to manage an endpoint or a group of endpoints on the device. Endpoint identifiers address individual endpoint interfaces.

Endpoint identifiers consist of two logical parts. The first part is the local name of the endpoint (hostname of fully qualified domain name). The two parts are separated by an at symbol (@). If the local part represents a hierarchy, the subparts of the hierarchy are separated by a slash (/). The local ID may be representative of a particular gateway/circuit number, and the circuit number may in turn be representative of a circuit ID/channel number.

Figure 10-1 shows a gateway with two endpoint interfaces. The **show voice port summary** Cisco IOS command would display the hardware T1 or E1 voice WAN interface card (VWIC) in slot 1, subslot 1, port 1 (1/1/1) and the Foreign Exchange Station (FXS) analog interface in slot 2, subslot 1, port 1 (2/1/1). The T1 or E1 card provides the ability to trunk 24 (T1-CAS), 23 (T1-PRI), or 30 (E1) calls to the PSTN. The configuration of the T1 or E1 interface is done primarily in CUCM for MGCP gateways. The first of CUCM's two configured endpoints (S1/SU1/DS1-1@gw1.domain.com) indicates that the T1 interface was configured as an ISDN PRI using the DS1 (digital signal level 1) signaling specification. The second interface is an analog access line number (AALN) that indicates the interface is an FXS or Foreign Exchange Office (FXO) port. An FXS port generates dial tone to the device plugged into the RJ-11 port. End-user devices such as fax machines and analog phones are normally plugged into FXS ports. FXO RJ-11 ports accept dial tone and are normally connected to the PSTN to make and receive phone calls. MGCP gateways do not support caller ID services on FXO ports. If caller ID over analog FXO interfaces is a requirement, H.323 gateways should be used. H.323 is covered in a later chapter.

Figure 10-1 *MGCP Endpoint Nomenclature*

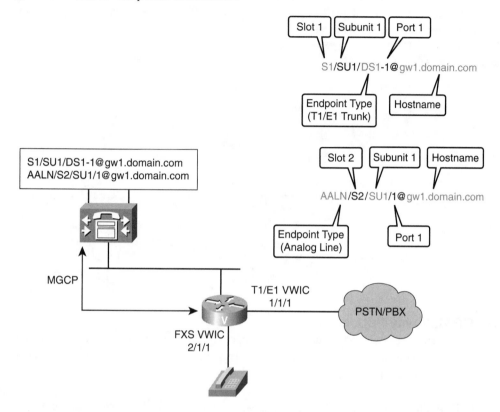

Both MGCP and Skinny Client Control Protocol (SCCP) are master/slave protocols; the CUCM is the master server for both protocols. SCCP and MGCP devices cannot operate without CUCM:

■ SCCP IP phones communicate directly with CUCM for all call setup signaling.

■ MGCP gateways communicate directly with CUCM for all call setup signaling.

Figure 10-2 displays a call that was received over an MGCP gateway to an SCCP IP phone. The MGCP communication from the gateway is sent to the CUCM for call processing. CUCM performs digit analysis on the received digits, and the lookup results in an SCCP endpoint. CUCM sends information to the gateway, allowing the gateway endpoint to play a ringback tone to the calling party. CUCM also sends SCCP signaling to the Cisco IP Phone, indicating that there is an incoming call. When the destination Cisco IP Phone end user answers the phone, CUCM coordinates the communication of the media path between the Cisco IP Phone and the MGCP gateway. The voice bearer traffic from the gateway to the IP phone uses Real-Time Transfer Protocol (RTP). RTP uses an even port number in the UDP port range of 16,384 through 32,767.

Figure 10-2 *MGCP Call Flow*

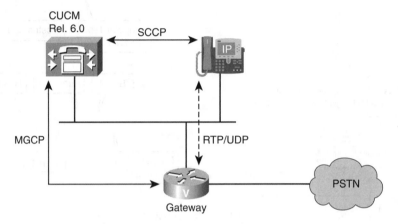

MGCP Gateway Support

MGCP support in CUCM includes a wide range of analog and digital interfaces that can be used on several Cisco router and switch platforms. Tables 10-1, 10-2, and 10-3 list MGCP-supported analog and digital features.

CUCM allows the Cisco IOS MGCP gateway to pull its MGCP-related configuration from the Cisco TFTP server. This eliminates the need for manual MGCP gateway configuration.

CUCM also supports Q.931 backhauling. Q.931 backhauling is supported on ISDN PRI, BRI, and E1 using common channel signaling (CCS). The MGCP call agent (CUCM) takes control of the ISDN D channel. The gateway sends CUCM all Q.931 call setup and teardown traffic over TCP port 2428.

Table 10-1 lists supported MGCP hardware.

Table 10-1 *MGCP Gateway Hardware Support*

Gateway	Supported Voice Hardware	Remarks
Cisco 3800	Analog FXS/FXO, T1 CAS (E&M Wink Start; Delay Dial only), T1/E1 PRI	Beginning with Cisco IOS Release 12.3.11T
Cisco 2800	Same as Cisco 3800	Beginning with Cisco IOS Release 12.3.8T4

Table 10-1   *MGCP Gateway Hardware Support (Continued)*

Gateway	Supported Voice Hardware	Remarks
Cisco 3700	Same as Cisco 3800	
Cisco 3640 and 3660	Same as Cisco 3800	
Cisco 2600/2600XM/VG200	Same as Cisco 3800	
Cisco 1751 and 1760	Same as Cisco 3800	
WS-X4604-GWY Module	Same as Cisco 3800	
Comm. Media Module (CMM)	T1 CAS FXS, T1/E1 PRI, FXS	
WS-X6608-x1 Module and FXS Module WS-X6624	T1 CAS E&M, T1 CAS FXS, T1/E1 PRI, FXS with WS-6624	
VG224	FXS only	
Cisco ATA 188	FXS only	

Table 10-2 lists supported MGCP analog features.

Table 10-2   *MGCP Analog Features*

Gateway	FXS	FXO	E&M	FXO, Battery Reversal	Analog DID	CAMA 911
Cisco 3800	Yes	Yes	No	Yes	No	No
Cisco 2800	Yes	Yes	No	Yes	No	No
Cisco 3700	Yes	Yes	No	Yes	No	No
Cisco 3640 and 3660	Yes	Yes	No	Yes	No	No
Cisco 2600 and 2600XM	Yes	Yes	No	Yes	No	No
VG200	Yes	Yes	No	Yes	No	No
Cisco 1751 and 1760	Yes	Yes	No	Yes	No	No
WS-X4604-GWY Module	Yes	Yes	No	No	No	No
Communication Media Module (CMM) 24FXS	Yes	N/A	N/A	N/A	N/A	N/A
FXS Module WS-X6624	Yes	N/A	N/A	N/A	N/A	N/A
VG224	Yes	N/A	N/A	N/A	N/A	N/A
Cisco ATA 188	Yes	N/A	N/A	N/A	N/A	N/A

Table 10-3 lists supported MGCP digital features.

Table 10-3   *MGCP Digital Features*

Gateway	BRI[*]	TI CAS (E&M)	T1 PRI	T1 QSIG	E1 PRI	E1 QSIG
Cisco 3800	12.4(2)T	Yes[†]	Yes[†]	Yes[†]	Yes[†]	Yes[†]
Cisco 2800	12.4(2)T	Yes[†]	Yes[†]	Yes[†]	Yes[†]	Yes[†]
Cisco 3700	12.4(2)T	Yes[†]	Yes[†]	Yes[†]	Yes[†]	Yes[†]
Cisco 3640 and 3660	12.4(2)T	Yes[†]	Yes[†]	Yes[†]	Yes[†]	Yes[†]
Cisco 2600 and 2600XM	12.4(2)T	Yes[†]	Yes[†]	Yes[†]	Yes[†]	Yes[†]
VG200	No	Yes	Yes	Yes	Yes	Yes
Cisco 1751 and 1760	12.3(14)T	Yes	Yes	Yes	Yes	Yes
WS-X4604-GWY Module	No	Yes	Yes	Yes	Yes	Yes
Communication Media Module (CMM) 6T1/E1	N/A	Yes	Yes	Yes	Yes	Yes
WS-X6608-T1/E1	N/A	Yes	Yes	Yes	Yes	Yes

[*]Cisco IOS 12.4(2)T supports BRI MGCP with the following hardware: NM-HDV2, NM-HD-XX, and on-board HWIC slots. BRI MGCP is also supported on older Cisco IOS releases with NM-1V/2V hardware.

[†]AIM-VOICE-30 modules require Cisco IOS Release 12.2.13T.

MGCP Configuration Server

When you are using the Configuration Server feature, the gateway- and interface-specific MGCP configuration commands are provided by CUCM in the form of an Extensible Markup Language (XML) configuration file that is downloaded by the Cisco IOS gateway from the CUCM TFTP server. This is the recommended approach to integrate Cisco IOS MGCP gateways with CUCM. The Cisco IOS gateway dynamically loads the necessary MGCP configuration commands from the XML file downloaded from the TFTP server.

When changes are made to the configuration in the CUCM database, a message is sent by CUCM to the MGCP gateway instructing the gateway devices to download the updated XML configuration file. Each device has an XML parser that interprets the XML file according to its device-specific requirements. Cisco MGCP gateways, for example, translate the content of the XML file into specific Cisco IOS commands for local execution.

Figure 10-3 illustrates the configuration and communication on and between CUCM and the MGCP gateway. Notice that the router requires only two configuration commands: **ccm-manager config** and **ccm-manager config server** *ip-address*.

Figure 10-3 *MGCP Configuration Server Communication*

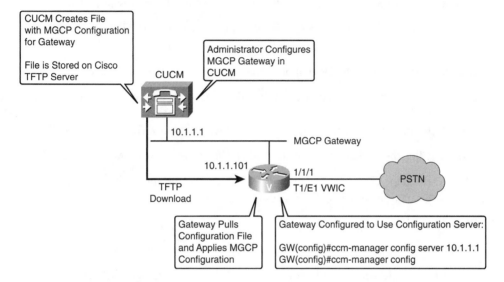

Q.931 Backhaul

A distinguishing characteristic of ISDN interfaces is the common channel signaling (Q.931) carried in the D channel (channel 24 in PRI interfaces and channel 17 in E1 interfaces). The gateway does not process or change this signaling data; it just passes it to CUCM through what Cisco calls the Q.931 backhaul channel. The gateway is still responsible for the termination of the Layer 2 signaling (Q.921 link access procedure over the D channel [LAP-D]). The gateway will not bring up the D channel unless it can communicate with CUCM to backhaul the Q.931 messages contained in the D channel.

A Q.931 backhaul channel is a logical TCP connection between CUCM and Cisco MGCP gateways. Q.931 backhaul forwards the Q.931 signaling traffic from an ISDN interface on a gateway over TCP port 2727 to a CUCM configured as an MGCP call agent.

MGCP Gateway Configuration: CUCM

MGCP gateway implementation includes configuration steps on *both* the CUCM (MGCP call agent) and the MGCP gateway that will be controlled.

The CUCM configuration steps for implementing an MGCP gateway are as follows:

Step 1   Add the MGCP gateway to CUCM.

Step 2   Configure the MGCP gateway in CUCM.

Step 3   Add one or more modules to the slots of the MGCP gateway in CUCM.

Step 4   Add voice interface cards, voice WAN interface cards, or high-density voice WAN interface cards to the configured modules.

Step 5   Configure the MGCP endpoints (one or more per voice interface card).

Follow these detailed configuration steps to add an MGCP gateway to CUCM:

Step 1   From CUCM Administration, choose **Device > Gateway**.

Step 2   Click the **Add New** button. The Add a New Gateway window will open.

Step 3   From the Gateway Type drop-down list, choose the appropriate MGCP gateway, as shown in Figure 10-4.

Step 4   Click **Next**.

Step 5   Choose **MGCP** from the Protocol drop-down menu and click **Next**.

Figure 10-4 displays the choosing of the Cisco 2811 router for an MGCP gateway configuration.

Figure 10-4   *MGCP Gateway Configuration*

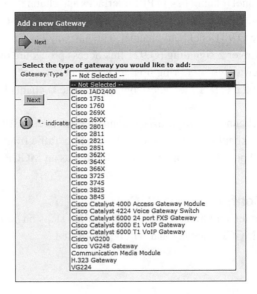

Figure 10-5 displays the selection of the MGCP protocol for the gateway configuration.

Figure 10-5 *MGCP Gateway Protocol Selection*

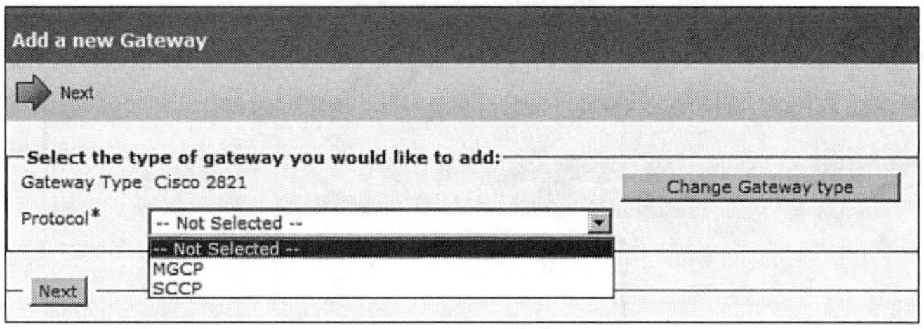

> **NOTE**   Some gateways support SCCP and MGCP, whereas few support only SCCP. The Protocol list box appears when adding a gateway that has support for both of these protocols. SCCP supports some features on analog FXS interfaces that are not available from MGCP-controlled FXS ports.

The configuration of an MGCP gateway depends on the selected platform. In Figure 10-4, a Cisco IOS 2811 router model has been selected.

The configuration of the MGCP gateway includes the following steps:

Step 1   Enter the hostname or fully qualified domain name of the gateway in the Domain Name field. The name has to match the hostname or the hostname and domain name (fully qualified domain name) of the Cisco IOS router.

Step 2   Enter a description for the gateway.

Step 3   Select a CUCM group.

Step 4   Configure the IDSN switch type.

Step 5   Click **Save**. Reset the gateway for the configuration changes to apply.

> **NOTE**   The ISDN switch type is configured globally in Cisco IOS routers. The ISDN switch type can also be set to a different value per ISDN interface. An interface command will always override the inheritance of a global command. The global ISDN switch type is also part of the gateway configuration in CUCM Administration. You can configure an interface-specific switch type at the MGCP endpoint level in CUCM Administration.
>
> To display help for the configuration parameters, click **?** on the page, or from the Help menu choose the **For This Page** option.

Figure 10-6 displays the MGCP Gateway Configuration page.

Figure 10-6 *MGCP Gateway Configuration*

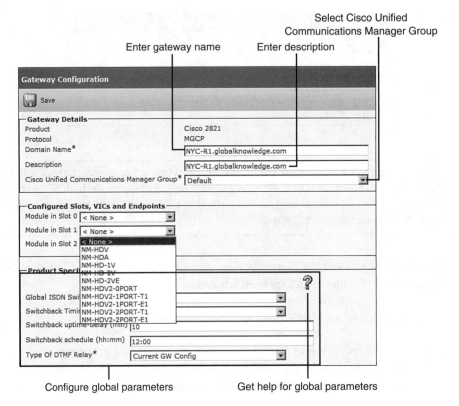

Endpoints are added by selecting voice modules and voice interface cards at the gateway configuration page. To add endpoints to a gateway, follow these steps:

Step 1 Locate the Configured Slots, VICs, and Endpoints section, and select the voice hardware module placed in the slot.

> **NOTE** Only voice modules have to be specified. If data network modules are used in a slot, you do not have to select them.

Step 2 Click **Save**. The subunits (voice interface cards slots) of the selected voice module will display.

Step 3 For each subunit (voice interface cards slot), select the subunit.

Step 4   Click **Save**. The endpoints of the selected voice interface card will display.

Step 5   Repeat Steps 4 to 5 for each subunit of a module. Repeat Steps 2 to 5 for each module of the gateway.

Figure 10-7 shows the voice module and voice interface card (VIC) selection process.

Figure 10-7   *MGCP Configuration*

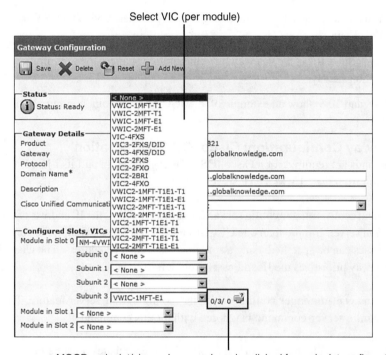

MGCP endpoint(s) are shown and can be clicked for endpoint configuration

> **NOTE**   Use the Cisco IOS command **show diag** on the gateway to display the modules and interface cards that the gateway is equipped with.

After adding voice modules and VICs in the Configured Slots, VICs, and Endpoints section of the gateway, the configuration endpoints of the VICs are displayed.

To configure an MGCP endpoint, follow these steps:

Step 1   Click the endpoint identifier (for example, 0/3/0).

Step 2   Select the device protocol or signaling for the endpoint. T1 and E1 interfaces support channel associated signaling (CAS) or command channel signaling (CCS) via ISDN PRI. Analog interfaces support ground-start and loop-start signaling. Select the protocol that should be used on the endpoint and click **Next**.

Step 3   Enter a description for the endpoint.

Step 4   Select the device pool that should be used by this endpoint.

Step 5   You can display help for any configuration parameters via **Help > For This Page**.

Step 6   Click **Save**. Reset the gateway for configuration changes to be committed to the gateway.

Figures 10-8 and 10-9 show an example of an MGCP E1 endpoint configuration.

MGCP Gateway Configuration: Cisco IOS Configuration

Two commands are required for a Cisco IOS MGCP gateway to pull its MGCP configuration from the CUCM TFTP server.

The command **ccm-manager config server** *ip-address* specifies the IP address of the TFTP configuration server. If more than one CUCM TFTP server is deployed in the cluster, a list of IP addresses can be specified using a space between each IP address. The Cisco IOS MGCP gateway prioritizes the IP addresses from left to right.

The command **ccm-manager config** enables the Configuration Server feature. The **ccm-manager config server** command is ignored without this command.

For the Configuration feature to work, the following prerequisites must be met:

■   The MGCP gateway and the CUCM TFTP server have IP connectivity.

■   The MGCP gateway and endpoints are configured in CUCM.

■   The hostname or fully qualified domain name (FQDN) of the Cisco IOS MGCP gateway has to match the CUCM MGCP gateway configuration.

If all these conditions are met and the gateway is configured with the **ccm-manager config** and the **ccm-manager config server** commands, the gateway can download its XML configuration file from the TFTP server.

The gateway then parses the XML file, converts the information to appropriate Cisco IOS configuration commands, and configures itself for MGCP operation.

Figure 10-8 *MGCP E1 Endpoint Configuration*

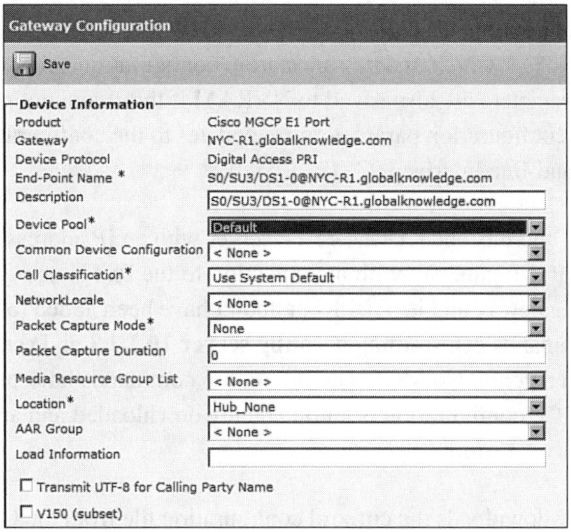

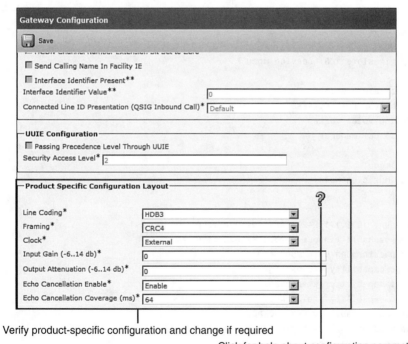

Figure 10-9 *MGCP E1 Endpoint Configuration (continued)*

The gateway registers with CUCM using the MGCP protocol.

After a successful configuration download, the MGCP gateway saves the running configuration to NVRAM, which updates the startup configuration. Any manually added configuration parameters are also saved to NVRAM if they were not previously saved. Manually added configuration parameters are updates to the configuration that were made using the command-line interface (CLI).

In Example 10-1, there is one CUCM TFTP server with an IP address of 10.1.1.1. There is a Cisco IOS MGCP gateway with a connection to the PSTN using an E1 interface (port 0/3/0). The gateway and its E1 PRI endpoint have been added to CUCM. At the gateway, the commands **ccm-manager config server 10.1.1.1** and **ccm-manager config server** have been entered. No MGCP configuration commands have been manually entered. The MGCP configuration is automatically downloaded and applied by the Configuration Server feature.

After the gateway downloads the cnf.xml configuration file from the CUCM TFTP server, the following MGCP commands are added to the router.

Example 10-1 *Configuring MGCP Gateway Registration*

```
controller E1 0/3/0
 framing crc4
 linecode hdb3
 pri-group timeslots 1-31 service mgcp
!
interface Serial0/3/0:15
 isdn switch-type primary-4ess
 isdn incoming-voice voice
 isdn bind-l3 ccm-manager
!
ccm-manager mgcp
ccm-manager music-on-hold
!
mgcp
mgcp call-agent 10.1.1.1 2427 service-type mgcp version 0.1
mgcp rtp unreachable timeout 1000 action notify
mgcp modem passthrough voip mode nse
mgcp package-capability rtp-package
mgcp package-capability sst-package
mgcp package-capability pre-package
no mgcp package-capability res-package
no mgcp package-capability fxr-package
no mgcp timer receive-rtcp
mgcp sdp simple
mgcp rtp payload-type g726r16 static
```

MGCP Gateway: Registration Verification

MGCP gateways register with CUCM in a manner similar to SCCP phones. Each endpoint in the CUCM MGCP gateway configuration can be verified to obtain the registration status. Similar registration verification information is available from the gateway router via Cisco IOS commands. The **show ccm-manager** command in Example 10-2 shows that the MGCP gateway has a CUCM group that includes only one CUCM and that the gateway is currently registered. There are some useful statistics, too.

Example 10-2 *Verifying MGCP Gateway Registration*

```
Router# show ccm-manager
MGCP Domain Name: Router
Priority Status Host
==============================================================
Primary Registered 10.16.240.124
First Backup    None
Second Backup None
Current active Call Manager: 10.16.240.124
Backhaul/Redundant link port: 2428
Failover Interval: 30 seconds
Keepalive Interval: 15 seconds
Last keepalive sent: 00:45:31 (elapsed time: 00:00:04)
Last MGCP traffic time: 00:45:31 (elapsed time: 00:00:04)
Last failover time: None
Switchback mode: Graceful
MGCP Fallback mode: Not Selected
Last MGCP Fallback start time: 00:00:00
Last MGCP Fallback end time: 00:00:00
PRI Backhaul Link info
 Link Protocol: TCP
 Remote Port Number: 2428
 Remote IP Address: 10.16.240.124
 Current Link State: OPEN
 Statistics:
   Packets recvd: 32
   Recv failures: 0
   Packets xmitted: 32
   Xmit failures: 0
 PRI Ports being backhauled: Slot 1, port 0
!
Configuration Auto-Download Information
=========================================
No configurations downloaded
Current state: Automatic Configuration Download feature is disabled Configuration Error
  History:
FAX mode: cisco
```

Although the MGCP gateway is registered, the endpoint in question might not be registered. The **show mgcp endpoints** command is useful to see which endpoints have registered. The output in Example 10-3 indicates that the T1 in slot 1/0 has registered all 24 channels as a PRI.

Example 10-3   *Verifying Endpoint Registration*

```
Router# show mgcp endpoints
Interface T1 1/0
!
ENDPOINT-NAME          V-PORT  SIG-TYPE ADMIN
S1/ds1-0/1@AV-2620-4 1/0:23 none up
S1/ds1-0/2@AV-2620-4 1/0:23 none up
S1/ds1-0/3@AV-2620-4 1/0:23 none up
S1/ds1-0/4@AV-2620-4 1/0:23 none up
S1/ds1-0/5@AV-2620-4 1/0:23 none up
S1/ds1-0/6@AV-2620-4 1/0:23 none up
S1/ds1-0/7@AV-2620-4 1/0:23 none up
S1/ds1-0/8@AV-2620-4 1/0:23 none up
S1/ds1-0/9@AV-2620-4 1/0:23 none up
S1/ds1-0/10@AV-2620- 1/0:23 none up
S1/ds1-0/11@AV-2620- 1/0:23 none up
S1/ds1-0/12@AV-2620- 1/0:23 none up
S1/ds1-0/13@AV-2620- 1/0:23 none up
S1/ds1-0/14@AV-2620- 1/0:23 none up
S1/ds1-0/15@AV-2620- 1/0:23 none up
S1/ds1-0/16@AV-2620- 1/0:23 none up
S1/ds1-0/17@AV-2620- 1/0:23 none up
S1/ds1-0/18@AV-2620- 1/0:23 none up
S1/ds1-0/19@AV-2620- 1/0:23 none up
S1/ds1-0/20@AV-2620- 1/0:23 none up
S1/ds1-0/21@AV-2620- 1/0:23 none up
S1/ds1-0/22@AV-2620- 1/0:23 none up
S1/ds1-0/23@AV-2620- 1/0:23 none up
```

Chapter Summary

The following list summarizes the key points that were discussed in this chapter:

- MGCP provides centralized gateway administration and highly scalable gateway solutions. It allows CUCM to take control of a specific port on a voice gateway.

- CUCM supports various MGCP gateway router platforms and interfaces. The gateway MGCP configuration can be provided by CUCM for TFTP download.

- To configure MGCP in CUCM, add an MGCP gateway, add voice modules, add VICs, and then configure the VICs.

- Configure Cisco IOS MGCP gateways to pull the configuration from CUCM to reduce manual configuration efforts.

References

For additional information, refer to these resources:

- **Session Description Protocol**: http://www.ietf.org/rfc/rfc2327.txt

- **Media Gateway Control Protocol**: http://www.ietf.org/rfc/rfc2705.txt

- **CUCM Solution Reference Network Design**: http://www.cisco.com/go/srnd

- **Cisco NetPro Forums**: www.cisco.com/go/netpro

- **Cisco-VoIP E-Mail Distribution List**: http://puck.nether.net

- **Cisco Feature Navigator**: http://www.cisco.com/go/fn

- **Cisco IOS MGCP Gateway Support for Cisco CallManager Network Specific Facilities**: http://www.cisco.com/en/US/products/sw/iosswrel/ps5012/products_feature_guide09186a0080181117.html

- **CUCM Administration Guide, Release 6.0(1)**: http://www.cisco.com/en/US/docs/voice_ip_comm/cucm/admin/6_0_1/ccmcfg/bccm.pdf

- **Cisco CallManager and Cisco IOS Interoperability Guide—Configuring MGCP Gateway Support for CUCM**: http://www.cisco.com/en/US/partner/products/ps6441/products_configuration_guide_chapter09186a00805583bd.html

Review Questions

Use the questions here to review what you learned in this chapter. The correct answers are found in Appendix A, "Answers to Chapter Review Questions."

1. Which type of protocol is MGCP?

    a. Proprietary

    b. Master/slave

    c. Peer to peer

    d. Clustered

2. MGCP is closest in operation to which of the following protocols?

    a. H.323

    b. SIP

    c. SCCP

    d. Megaco/H.245

3. What technology or protocol does an SCCP phone use to send media to an MGCP gateway?

    a. SCCP

    b. MGCP

    c. RTP

    d. Transcoder

4. Which of the following interfaces does not support caller ID with MGCP gateways using CUCM?

    a. FXO

    b. FXS

    c. PRI

    d. T1-CAS

5. What parameter is not available in the device pool in CUCM 6.0?

    a. Soft key template

    b. Date/time group

    c. Region

    d. CUCM group

6. What two commands are required to configure MGCP for automatic configuration from the CUCM?

    a. **ccm-manager config server**

    b. **mgcp**

    c. **ccm-manager redundant-host**

    d. **ccm-manager call-agent** *ip-address*

    e. **ccm-manager config**

7. Q.931 backhaul opens which socket with CUCM?

   a. UDP 2427

   b. UDP 16384

   c. TCP 2000

   d. TCP 2428

CHAPTER 11

Call Routing Components

The dial plan is the essence of an IP telephony system. Dial plan is at the core of the user experience because it defines the rules that govern how a user reaches any destination.

Endpoint addressing and path selection are the most important components of a dial plan when it gets to call routing. This lesson describes endpoint addressing, digit analysis, and path selection in a Cisco Unified Communications Manager (CUCM) deployment.

Chapter Objectives

Upon completing this lesson, you will be able to describe and configure CUCM numbering plans, directory numbers, route groups, route lists, route patterns, route filters, digit analysis, and urgent priority to place public switched telephone network calls. You will also be able to meet these objectives:

- Describe the concept of endpoint addressing, including on-net versus off-net dialing and the uniform on-net dial plan length.

- Describe the concept of call routing in CUCM.

- Describe how CUCM analyzes digits.

- Describe features that relate to call routing.

- Describe how CUCM performs path selection.

- Describe how to configure CUCM path selection.

Endpoint Addressing

Reachability of internal destinations is provided by assigning directory numbers (DN) to all endpoints (IP phones, fax machines, and analog phones) and applications (voice mail, auto attendants, and conferencing systems).

The number of dialable extensions determines the quantity of digits needed to dial extensions. A four-digit abbreviated dial plan cannot accommodate more than 10,000 extensions (from 0000 to

9999). A leading digit of 0 is normally not used in dial plans because it is dedicated to operator functionality. A leading digit of an 8 or 9 is also normally restricted because either one of these digits is used to make outgoing calls to the public switched telephone network (PSTN). If we assume access code 9 is used, the access code and operator functionality reduce the number range to 8000 dialable patterns (1000 to 8999). Customers may want to distinguish each site by a different leading digit, too. This would reduce the scalability of the system to eight sites if each site would receive a different leading digit (1 to 8). Each site could have 1000 directory numbers (1000 to 1999 as an example). A four-digit dial is not very popular with large organizations. Most organizations use at least a five-digit dial plan.

If direct inward dial (DID) is enabled for incoming PSTN calls, PSTN phone numbers directly dial internal directory numbers. This restricts the internal directory numbers used by the DID range purchased from the PSTN provider.

Endpoints dial each other using the four- or five-digit dial plan that was assigned to the phones. Each call made by a Cisco IP Phone is categorized as one of the following:

- **On-net**: These are all calls that remain within one telephony system or IP network (an internal call from one IP phone to another IP phone). These calls may involve multiple CUCM clusters. The administrators can control how calls made between CUCM clusters are categorized.

- **Off-net dialing**: These are calls that are placed from one telephony system to another telephony system. Most off-net calls are routed across gateways or trunks to the PSTN.

- **Abbreviated dialing**: This is when an off-net destination is dialed by an internal number (for example, dialing a four-digit extension to reach colleagues on their home office PSTN number). CUCM has to map the abbreviated number to the appropriate full PSTN number in this case.

In Figure 11-1, an IP phone located in the headquarters (extension number 2003) dials 3001 to reach an IP phone located at Site 1 over the IP WAN. Both devices are part of the same CUCM cluster. No toll charges are incurred for the call, and the call is classified as an on-net call.

The IP phone with extension 2002 dials 95552001, and the call is routed to a PSTN destination through a PSTN gateway. The call is classified as an off-net call.

The IP phone with extension 2001 dials 4001, which is an IP phone located at Site 2. CUCM Express is used for call processing at Site 2, and no IP WAN link connects the sites. Because Site 2 cannot be reached over an IP WAN and the service provider (PSTN) requires ten-digit dialing to properly route the call, a CUCM translation pattern is matched, and the call is manipulated from four-digit dialing to ten-digit dialing. Translation patterns are covered in more detail in the next chapter.

Figure 11-1 *Endpoint Dialing*

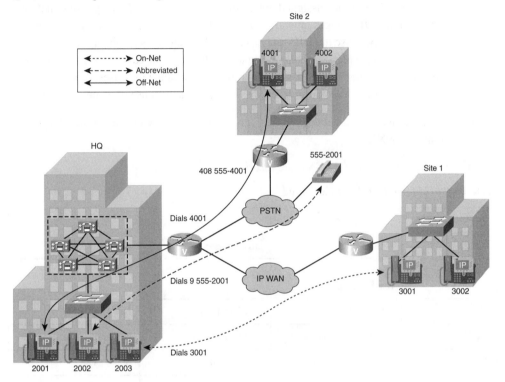

Uniform On-Net Dial Plan Example

A dial plan should be designed so that all extensions within the system are reached in a uniform way. A fixed number of digits is used to reach a given extension from any on-net origination point. Uniform dialing is desirable because of the simplicity it presents to users. A user does not have to remember different ways to dial a number when calling from various locations.

Table 11-1 is an example of a four-digit uniform on-net dial plan. Various sites in Table 11-1 were assigned numbers in the following ways:

- Site A, the company headquarters, requires more than 1000 extensions, so two ranges of numbers have been retained (1XXX and 5XXX). Note that the corresponding DID ranges must also be retained from the site's local exchange carrier (LEC).

- Site B has been assigned the range (2XXX), allowing for up to 1000 extensions.

- Site C was assigned a four-digit range, but it has been split between 100 DID extensions (415 555-30XX) and up to 900 non-DID extensions. If growth requires more extensions for DID, any unassigned numbers from the non-DID range could be used.

- Sites D and E were each assigned 500 numbers from the 4XXX range. Note that their corresponding DID ranges must match each of the site's respective portions of the 4XXX range. Because the DID ranges are for different sites (probably from different PSTN service providers), more coordination effort is required to split ranges between sites. As the number of sites assigned within a given range increases, it becomes increasingly difficult (sometimes impossible) to make full use of an entire range.

- Site F's range is split between 900 DID numbers (6[0–8]XX) and 100 non-DID numbers (69XX).

- The ranges 7XXX and 8XXX are reserved for future use.

Table 11-1   *Uniform Dial Plan Example*

Directory Number Range	Usage	DID Ranges	Non-DID Ranges
0XXX	Excluded: 0 is used to reach the operator.		
1XXX	Site A extensions.	418 555 1XXX	Not applicable
2XXX	Site B extensions.	919 555 2XXX	Not applicable
3XXX	Site C extensions.	415 555 30XX	3[1–9]XX
4[0–4]XX	Site D extensions.	613 555 4[0–4]XX	Not applicable
4[5–9]XX	Site E extensions.	450 555 4[5–9]XX	Not applicable
5XXX	Additional Site A extensions.	418 555 5XXX	Not applicable
6XXX	Site F extensions.	514 555 6[0–8]XX	69XX
7XXX	Future extensions.		
8XXX	Future extensions.		
9XXX	Excluded: 9 used as access code.		

When the enterprise consists of few sites, such an approach can be used with few complications. Large enterprises (in terms of number of extensions and sites) may face more of the following challenges in designing a uniform dial plan:

■ The number of extensions necessary can exceed the range afforded by the number of digits being considered for the dial plan. For instance, if more than 8000 extensions are required (considering the exclusions of the 0XXX and 9XXX ranges), the system may require that an abbreviated dial plan use more than four digits.

■ Matching on-net abbreviated extensions to DID numbers means that when a new DID range is obtained from a local exchange carrier, it cannot conflict with the preexisting on-net abbreviated dial ranges. For example, if the DID range of 415 555-1XXX exists in a system using a four-digit uniform abbreviated dial plan, and DID range 650 556-1XXX is also being considered, it might be desirable to increase the number of digits for on-net dialing to five. In this example, the five-digit on-net ranges 51XXX and 61XXX would not overlap.

■ Most systems require the exclusion of certain ranges because of off-net access codes and operator dialing. In such a system where 9 and 0 are reserved codes, no dial plan (uniform or not) could accommodate on-net extension dialing that begins with 9 or 0. This means that DID ranges could not be used if they would force the use of 9 or 0 as the first digit in the dial plan. For instance, in a five-digit abbreviated dial plan, the DID range 415 559-XXXX (or any subset thereof) could not be used. In this example, alternatives include increasing the length of the abbreviated dialing to six or more digits or avoiding any DID range whose last five digits start with 9.

Call Routing

CUCM automatically "knows" how to route calls to internal destinations within the same cluster, because it is configured with the DNs of its associated devices. This can be compared to directly connected networks at a router in IP routing. Route patterns must be configured to route calls to the PSTN. This is equivalent to static routes in an IP router. The call routing table of CUCM is built on registered devices and statically entered route patterns that point to external destinations.

Figure 11-2 has a basic routing table that consists of the following entries:

■ 2001, 2002, and 2003 are DNs of phones configured in CUCM located at the headquarters.

■ There is a second site, Site 1, with CUCM Express and phones using extensions in the range of 3000 to 3999. To be able to route calls to this external system, CUCM at the headquarters requires an entry in its routing table for destination 3XXX (X is a wildcard digit in route patterns that matches any dialed digit) that refers to the CUCM Express located at Site 1 via an H.225 trunk.

- At the headquarters, there is a PSTN gateway. To route calls out to the PSTN, a route pattern 9.! is configured in CUCM, which points to the headquarters PSTN gateway. The exclamation point (!) is a wildcard character that matches on one or more digits. Usage of the dot and the ! is explained in more detail later in this chapter.

Figure 11-2 *Call Routing*

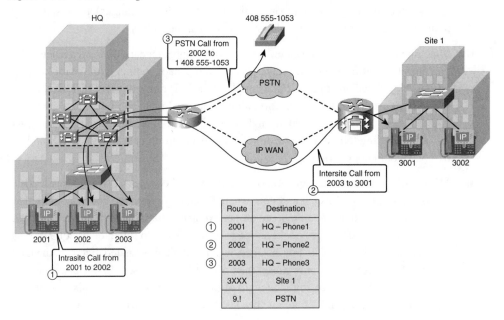

Three calls are placed in the example shown in Figure 11-2:

- **(1) 2001 to 2002**: This is an on-net call. The dialed number 2002 is looked up in the call routing table, and the call is sent to the appropriate IP phone.

- **(2) 2003 to 3001**: The dialed number 3001 matches the entry that refers to a trunk pointing to CUCM Express at Site 1. A call setup message is sent from CUCM to CUCM Express. This call is classified as on-net because the call is still on the company IP network.

- **(3) 2002 to 9 1 408 555-1053**: This call is sent to the PSTN because it matches the route pattern 9.!. CUCM will be configured to strip off the PSTN access code 9 before sending the call out to the PSTN through the headquarters gateway. This call is classified as off-net because it is traversing a PSTN gateway.

Call Routing Table Entries

In the preceding example, the call routing table of CUCM was composed of directory numbers and route patterns. Additional routing components can be configured and are added to the call routing table as possible call routing destinations. Table 11-2 shows a list of possible call routing table entries. All routing components shown in the table are discussed further in this book.

Table 11-2 *Call Routing Destinations*

Routing Component	Description
Directory numbers	Numbers assigned to endpoints and applications. Used for internal routing within a cluster.
Translation pattern	Used to translate the called-party number to a different number.
Route pattern	Used to route calls to remote destinations (PSTN, remote CUCM cluster, and so on).
Hunt pilot	Used to distribute calls (simplified automatic call distribution functionality).
Call-park numbers	Allows the holding of a call on a number to be retrieved by any other phone in the network.
Meet-me numbers	Allows conference call controller to set up a conference call for multiple parties.

Route Patterns

The CUCM call routing database includes the directory numbers of Cisco IP Phones and computer telephony integration (CTI) ports configured in the system, because these entries are entered in the IBM Informix Database Server (IDS) by CUCM administration. CUCM does not know about any phone numbers that are configured on external systems. Gateway and trunks allow CUCM to communicate with external systems. CUCM is configured with route patterns that will be steered through various gateways and trunks to reach the PSTN, remote clusters, and traditional PBXs. The call routing might require various wildcard parameters to implement robust call-processing logic. Table 11-3 covers the wildcard parameters that route patterns can use in CUCM.

The @ wildcard is a special macro function that expands into a series of patterns representing the entire national *numbering plan* for a certain country. For example, configuring a single unfiltered route pattern such as 9.@ with the North American Numbering Plan (NANP) really adds more than 100 individual route patterns to the CUCM dial plan database.

Table 11-3 *Route-Pattern Wildcards*

Wildcard	Description
x	Single digit (0–9, *, #)
@	North American Numbering Plan
!	One or more digits (0–9, *, #)
[x–y]	Generic range notation
[^x–y]	Exclusion range notation
.	Terminates access code
#	Terminates interdigit timeout
<wildcard>?	Matches 0 or more occurrences of any digit that matches the previous wildcard
<wildcard>+	Matches one or more occurrences of any digit that matches the previous wildcard

It is possible to configure CUCM to accept other national numbering plans. When this is done, the @ wildcard can be used for different numbering plans, even within the same CUCM cluster, depending on the value selected in the Numbering Plan field on the Route Pattern Configuration page.

The @ wildcard can be practical in several small and medium deployments, but it can become harder to manage and troubleshoot in large deployments. Certain components of the numbering plan can be matched by the use of route filters.

International destinations are usually configured using the ! wildcard, which represents one or more digits. In North America, the route pattern 9.011! is typically configured for international calls. In most European countries, the same result is accomplished with the 0.00! route pattern.

The ! wildcard is also used for deployments in countries where the dialed numbers can be of varying lengths. In such cases, CUCM does not know when the dialing is complete and waits for 15 seconds (by default) before sending the call. This delay can be reduced in any of the following ways:

- Reduce the T.302 timer service parameter. It is best practice to set this value to 4 to 5 seconds to prevent premature transmission of the call before the user is finished dialing.

- Configure a 9.011! second route pattern ending with an interdigit timeout expiration wildcard. (The # symbol is used for this functionality in most systems.) Instruct the users to dial the # at the end of their international calls. This action is analogous to pressing the Send button on a cell phone.

The Urgent Priority check box in the route-pattern configuration is often used to force immediate routing of certain calls as soon as a match is detected, without waiting for additional digits or the T302 timer to expire. In North America, if the patterns 9.911 and 9.[2–9]XXXXXX are configured and a user dials 9911, CUCM usually has to wait for the T302 timer before routing the call because further digits may cause the 9.[2–9]XXXXXX to match (overlapping dial plan). If urgent priority is enabled for the 9.911 route pattern, CUCM makes its routing decision as soon as the user has finished dialing 9911, without waiting for the T302 timer.

If enbloc dialing is used and the provided number is longer than the urgent pattern, the urgent pattern is not considered because all the digits are analyzed as one string.

Translation patterns always have urgent priority enabled. The check box on the configuration page is grayed out. It cannot be disabled. The urgent priority information is displayed so that the call-processing logic of a translation pattern can be understood. This can be best understood through an example. In a dial plan consisting of a translation pattern of 100 and a directory number of 1001, extension 1001 would never receive a call from a Skinny Client Control Protocol (SCCP)-based phone. As soon as CUCM matches on 100, the call-processing logic routes the call. In an overlapping dial plan scenario such as the one mentioned, CUCM normally waits for additional digits or for the T.302 timer to expire. The differentiating quality is that translation patterns have urgent priority checked and the call is translated as soon as the digits match.

Route-Pattern Examples

Table 11-4 includes some route-pattern matching examples using various wildcard parameters. The X wildcard matches on the * and # Dual Tone Multifrequency (DTMF) keys even though these are rarely included in phone numbers. The [X–Y] generic range notation matches only one digit. A range of [13–59] matches exactly one digit (a 1, 3, 4, 5, or 9). This range does not signify 13 to 59. A comma is an illegal character in the regular expression language used in route-pattern processing.

The 13! appears twice in Table 11-4, once with a pound sign (#) and once without it. The ! poses a call routing dilemma. CUCM will never know when the user is dialing digits because the exclamation point can match an infinite number of dialed digits. CUCM routes all calls that include ! when the T.302 interdigit timeout expires. The T.302 timer is 15 seconds by default. To alleviate the post-dial delay incurred by waiting for this timeout to expire, a second route pattern can be provisioned with the # to terminate the interdigit timeout. CUCM does not implicitly know how to process the interdigit timeout unless it's put into a route pattern. If the pound is not in the route pattern, the user cannot dial this digit unless the PreDot IntlAccess IntlDirectDial DDI is used.

Table 11-4   *Route-Pattern Matching Using Wildcard Processing*

Route Pattern	Result
1234	One exact dialed digit: 1234.
1*1X	Matches dialed digits 1*10 to 1*19, 1*1* and 1*1#.
12XX	Matches dialed digits 1200 to 1299, 12**, 12*#, 12#*, and 12##.
13[25–8]6	Matches dialed digits 1326, 1356, 1366, 1376, and 1386.
13[13–59]X	1310–1319, 1330–9, 1340–9, 1350–9, 1390–9. The * and # have been excluded for brevity.
13[^3–9]6	1306, 1316, 1326, 13*6, 13#6.
13!	13 followed by one or more digits.
13!#	13 followed by one or more digits and then ended with a #.

Digit Analysis

In practice, when multiple potentially matching patterns are possible, the destination pattern is chosen based on the following criteria:

1. When a user dials the string 1200, CUCM compares it to the patterns in its call routing table. In this case, there are two potentially matching patterns, 1XXX and 12XX. Both of them match the dialed string, but 1XXX matches a total of 1000 potential strings (1000 to 1999), whereas 12XX matches only 100 potential strings (1200 to 1299). 12XX is selected as the destination of this call because it is the closest match.

2. When the string 1212 is dialed, there are three potentially matching patterns: 1XXX, 12XX, and 121X. 121X matches only ten strings, whereas the other two route patterns match many more strings (explained in the previous step). 121X is the closest match and is selected as the matching pattern of the call.

When an endpoint goes off-hook, CUCM begins the digit analysis process. Every number in the call routing database is an initial match unless the phone is configured as a private line automatic ringdown (PLAR) line. PLAR is used on a directory number to automatically dial a destination and requires the configuration of a calling search space. This functionality is discussed further in Chapter 13, "Calling Privileges."

SCCP phones send their digits one by one as they are dialed unless the number is dialed without lifting the handset and the Dial softkey is pressed (hotdial). Hotdial functionality sends all dialed digits in one SCCP call setup message (enbloc) and the behavior of the digit analysis will differ. Analog interfaces (FXO, FXS) also send their digits digit by digit, whereas H.323 and ISDN send their digits in one Q.931 setup message (enbloc) by default. The method of forwarding digits is important to understand to determine how digit analysis will match on a route pattern when there is an overlapping dial plan.

As each digit in Figure 11-3 is received, CUCM can reduce the number of potential matches of the dialed digits against the call routing database. As soon as an exact match is found, digit analysis returns a current match, and call routing occurs immediately.

Figure 11-3 *Digit-by-Digit Analysis*

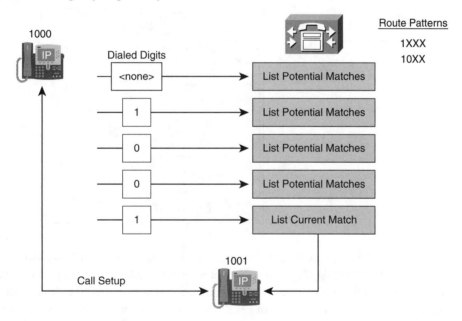

The dial plan in Figure 11-3 includes a directory number of 1001, and two route patterns (1XXX and 10XX). The dialed number is 1001, but CUCM has three matching patterns when the third digit is received. When the final digit is received, there is only one pattern that matches the dialed digits. Because there are no more digits to be collected, the call is routed immediately.

Digit collection is stopped as soon as an entry in the call routing table is matched in its full length and no other (longer) potential matches exist. In Figure 11-4, a user dialed 1111. CUCM interprets the number digit by digit. After the first two digits have been analyzed in

> **NOTE**   Session Initiation Protocol (SIP) phones use enbloc dialing in one SIP INVITE message by default. Keypad Markup Language (KPML) can be implemented on Type B SIP phones to emulate SCCP digit-by-digit behavior. If digits are received enbloc, the entire received dial string is checked against the call routing database. This differs greatly from the digit-by-digit analysis used by SCCP-controlled phones.

this example, only one potential match is left (the first entry) because all other entries in the call routing table require a different digit than 1 at the second position. CUCM continues collecting digits until it receives 4 digits (1111); now the first entry is fully matched and used to route the call.

Figure 11-4 *Digit Collection Example*

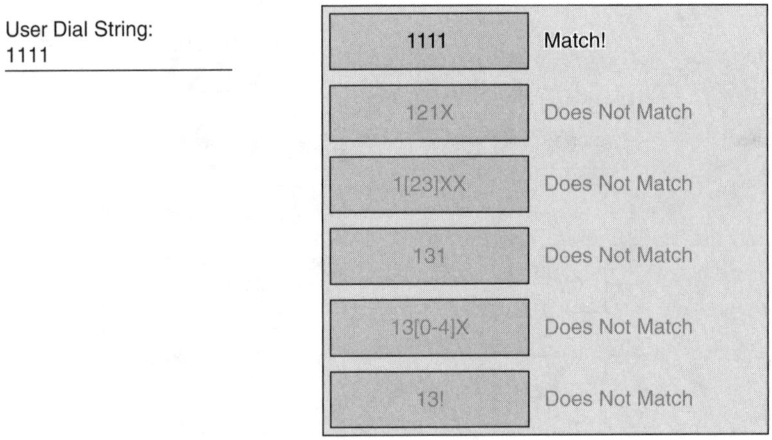

User Dial String:
1111

1111	Match!
121X	Does Not Match
1[23]XX	Does Not Match
131	Does Not Match
13[0-4]X	Does Not Match
13!	Does Not Match

In Figure 11-5, the user dialed 1211. After interpreting these digits, CUCM has two matches: 121X and 1[23]XX and no additional potential matches that are longer (which would require waiting for more digits). Digit collection is stopped, and the closest-match routing logic is applied. Route pattern 121X represents 10 potential matches, and route pattern 1[23]XX represents 100 potential matches that start with 12. The first entry is the closest match and will be used to route the call.

Figure 11-5 *Closest-Match Routing Example*

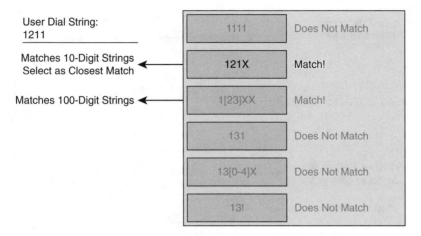

In Figure 11-6, a user dials 1311—CUCM has three potential matches at this time: 13[0–4]X, 1[23]XX, and 13!. The last entry represents a variable-length route pattern because it can potentially match on more digits. CUCM has to wait because the user might provide additional digits. CUCM will not wait an indefinite time for additional digits, however. After the T.302 interdigit timer expires (15 seconds by default), CUCM attempts to route the call based on the closest-match logic. If there are no other matching patterns at this time, CUCM issues a reorder tone or a recorded annunciator message to the calling party. In this example, there are two matching route patterns, but 13[0–4]X is the closest pattern representing only 10 possible numbers, whereas 1[23]XX has 100 potential matches, and 13! represents an unlimited number of potential matches.

Assume that the user dialed only three digits: 131. CUCM would match all three route patterns at this time, but after the interdigit timeout expired, only one route pattern would match: 13!.

These wildcards can be helpful when creating a PSTN dial plan in North America like that in Table 11-5. Most of the route patterns include a 9 as an access code and a dot (.) used as a delimiter for digit-stripping rules. Later in this chapter, we discuss digit discard instructions (DDI), which allow CUCM to strip digits preceding the dot (access code).

Figure 11-6 *Interdigit Timeout*

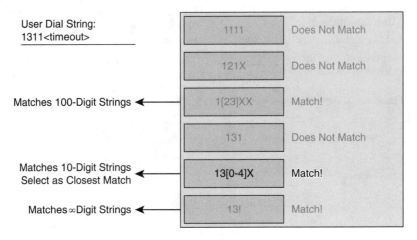

Table 11-5 *North America PSTN Dial Plan*

Route Pattern	Description
911	Emergency call routing without access code
9.911	Emergency call routing with access code
9.[2–8]11	3-digit service codes (for example, 411 for information)
9.[2–9]XX XXXX	7-digit local dialing
9.[2–9]XX [2–9] XXXX	10-digit local dialing
9.1[2–9]XX [2–9]XX XXXX	11-digit long-distance dialing
9.011!	International dialing (variable-length dialing)
9.011!#	International dialing (variable-length dialing with interdigit termination)

Digit Forwarding

Table 11-6 displays a summary of the digit-forwarding methods supported in CUCM for different types of devices.

SIP devices support enbloc dialing by default. Enbloc dialing sends the entire dialed string in a single SIP INVITE message. KPML is an IETF SIP standards-based extension that Cisco supports. KPML allows digits to be sent one by one. Although Cisco supports KPML, multivendor interoperability might prove difficult because most vendors do not support this standard. SIP dial rules offer yet another option that can be used in SIP devices. SIP dial rules are downloaded to the phone and processed inside the SIP phone. A SIP phone can detect invalid numbers and play a reorder tone without sending any signaling messages to CUCM.

Trunks and ISDN PRIs send their digits enbloc by default, but they can both be configured for overlap sending and receiving, allowing digits to be sent or received one by one over an ISDN PRI.

Table 11-6 *Digit-Forwarding Behavior*

Device	Signaling Protocol	Addressing Method
IP phone	SCCP	Digit by digit
	SIP	Enbloc KPML SIP dial rules
Gateway	MGCP/SIP/H.323	Enbloc Overlap sending and receiving (ISDN PRI only)
Trunk	H.323/SIP	Enbloc Overlap sending and receiving (ISDN PRI only)

SCCP Phones: User Input

IP phones using SCCP report every user input event to CUCM immediately. As soon as the user goes off-hook, a signaling message is sent from the phone to the CUCM server with which it is registered. The phone can be considered to be a terminal, where all decisions resulting from the user input are made by dial plan configured on the CUCM server.

As other user events are detected by the phone, they are relayed to CUCM individually. A user who goes off-hook and then dials 1000 triggers five individual signaling events from the phone to CUCM. All the resulting feedback provided to the user (screen messages, playing dial tone, secondary dial tone, ringback, reorder, and so forth) are commands issued by CUCM to the phone in response to the dial plan configuration.

It is neither required nor possible to configure dial plan information on IP phones running SCCP. All dial plan functionality is contained in the CUCM cluster, including the recognition of dialing patterns as user input is collected.

If the user dials a pattern that is denied by CUCM, a reorder tone is played to the user as soon as that pattern becomes the best match in CUCM digit analysis. For example, if all calls to the 976 area code are denied, a reorder tone is sent to the user's phone as soon as the user dials 91976.

Figure 11-7 *SCCP Phones: User Input*

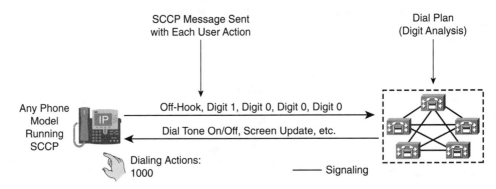

SIP Phones: User Input

Type A phones (Cisco Unified IP Phone models 7905, 7912, 7940, and 7960) do not support KPML. They do support SIP dial rules, which are configured in CUCM and downloaded to the IP phone at boot time.

Type B phones (Cisco Unified IP Phone models 7911, 7941, 7961, 7970, and 7971) support KPML and SIP dial rules.

Type A SIP Phones: No Dial Rules

Type A phones without SIP dial rules (default) do not deliver a dial tone to the calling party when the calling party goes off-hook with the handset, speakerphone, or headset. All digits are sent after the user completes dialing and clicks the Dial softkey. This function is similar to the Send button used on cellular phones.

Figure 11-8 illustrates a user making a call to extension 1000. The user has to dial 1000 followed by clicking the Dial softkey or the # key. The phone then sends a SIP INVITE message to CUCM for digit analysis.

Figure 11-8 *SIP Type A Phones: No Dial Rules*

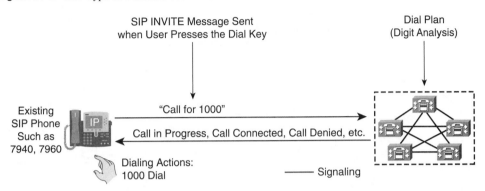

Type A SIP Phones: Dial Rules

SIP dial rules allow SIP phones to emulate the functionality of a SCCP phone. When the user goes off-hook, a dial tone is received, and digits are processed against the local SIP dial rule in real time. If a user dials a pay service beginning with 9 1-900, the call is immediately dropped. Users are accustomed to hearing a reorder tone when a call cannot be routed. SIP dial rule pattern rejection does not result in a reorder tone. Whereas the loss of reorder tone might be seen as a deficit, SIP dial rules have positive network bandwidth and CUCM processor overhead advantages. SCCP uses many small signaling messages sent between the IP phone and CUCM. These constant SCCP messages result in delay when the IP phone and CUCM are separated by large geographical boundaries. The SCCP messages also use up a small amount of bandwidth across the expensive WAN data circuits and utilize processor and memory overhead on CUCM. SIP dial rules eliminate the need to send signaling across the network between the IP phone and CUCM.

When a permitted call occurs on the phone, the SIP INVITE message is sent enbloc to CUCM. The user does not need to press the Dial key. If you do not use SIP dial rules or KPML, the end-user community will have to be retrained, because the phone will need to be operated differently. SIP dial rules allow Type A phones to emulate SCCP and traditional phone systems, while also providing processing and signaling benefits.

Figure 11-9 shows a phone configured to recognize all four-digit patterns beginning with 1 and that has an associated timeout value of 0. All user input actions matching the pattern will trigger the sending of the SIP INVITE message to CUCM immediately, without requiring the user to press the Dial key. Type A phones using SIP dial rules offer a way to dial patterns not explicitly configured on the phone. If a dialed pattern does not match a SIP dial rule, the user can press the Dial key or wait for interdigit timeout.

If a particular pattern is recognized by the phone but blocked in the dial rule, the call is immediately ended. The user will not receive a reorder tone, but the session will end.

Figure 11-9 *SIP Type A Phones: Dial Rules*

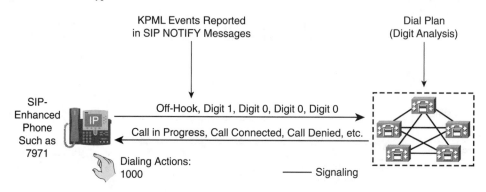

Type B SIP Phones: No Dial Rules

Type B IP phones offer functionality based on the KPML standard to report user activities. Each user input event generates a KPML message to CUCM. This mode of operation emulates a similar end-user experience to that of phones running SCCP.

Every key the end user presses triggers an individual SIP message. SIP NOTIFY messages are sent to CUCM to report a KPML event corresponding to the key pressed by the user. This messaging enables CUCM digit-by-digit analysis to recognize partial patterns as the user dials them. If a pattern beginning with 9 1-900 is blocked, a reorder tone is sent to the calling party.

Users of Type B SIP phones do not need to click the Dial softkey to indicate the end of user input. In Figure 11-10, a user dialing 1000 would be provided call progress indication (either a ringback tone or reorder tone) after dialing the last 0, without having to press the Dial softkey. This behavior is consistent with the user experience of phones running SCCP.

Figure 11-10 *SIP Type B Phones: No SIP Dial Rule*

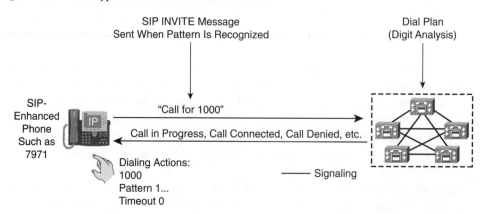

Type B SIP Phones: Dial Rules

Type B IP phones can be configured with SIP dial rules so that dial pattern recognition is accomplished by the phone.

Type B IP phones using SIP dial rules offer only one way to dial patterns not explicitly configured on the phone. If a dialed pattern does not match a SIP dial rule, the user has to wait for the interdigit timeout before the SIP NOTIFY message is sent to CUCM. Unlike Type A IP phones, Type B IP phones do not need the Dial softkey clicked to indicate the end of dialing. When on-hook dialing is used, the user can click the Dial softkey at any time to trigger the sending of all dialed digits to CUCM in one SIP INVITE message.

If a particular pattern is permitted by the phone but blocked by CUCM, the user must dial the entire dial string before receiving an indication that the call is rejected by the system. Dial rules should be configured to be more restrictive than the calling restrictions applied at the CUCM call-processing layer.

In countries whose national numbering plan is not easily defined with static route patterns, CUCM can be configured for overlap sending and overlap receiving. Overlap sending changes the way gateways pass digits on Q.931 gateways. To enable overlap sending, check the Allow Overlap Sending box on the Route Pattern Configuration page.

Overlap receiving allows CUCM to receive dialed digits one by one from a PRI PSTN gateway. To enable overlap receiving, set the OverlapReceivingFlagForPRI service parameter to True.

CUCM Path Selection

Path selection is an essential dial plan element. After matching an entry in the call routing table, CUCM has to select how and where to route the call. Most CUCM calls are routed across IP trunks or gateways. CUCM allows multiple paths to be configured for a route pattern for resiliency purposes.

Figure 11-11 shows a scenario in which a user has dialed a long-distance PSTN number starting with an access code of 9, 1 for the long-distance operator, 408 for the area code, followed by 526 for the exchange (office code), and a four-digit subscriber number of 4000. These dialed digits have matched the route pattern of 9.14085264XXX. The primary path for the call routing is the H.225 trunk over the IP WAN. The H.225 trunk is pointed to the H.323 gatekeeper, which will provide call admission control in distributed multicluster call-processing environments. If not enough bandwidth is available to route the call, the H.323 gatekeeper returns an admission rejection, and the call is rerouted across the PRI gateway to the PSTN.

Path-Selection Elements

Route patterns are strings of digits and wildcards configured in CUCM. Route patterns can point directly to a trunk or gateway device, but the device would not be available for any other route patterns, and there cannot be redundancy if the device is not available or is out of resources. It is best practice to point a route pattern to a route list logical entity. Route lists are a prioritized list of route groups that allow digit manipulation to be configured on a per-route group. A route group points to one or more devices that are selected based on a distribution algorithm (circular or top down). The route list and route group elements provide the greatest level of flexibility for call routing and digit manipulation.

Figure 11-11 displays the call routing logic of route pattern, route list, route groups, and devices. The processing order is top down from the route pattern down to the devices, but the configuration order is bottom up.

Figure 11-11   *CUCM Call-Processing Logic*

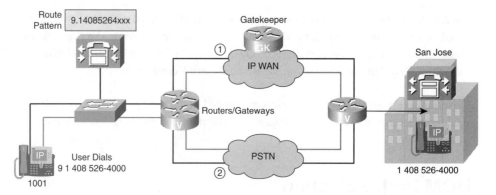

Path-Selection Configuration

To implement path selection in CUCM, the call processing logic must be built from the bottom up. When the route group is created, devices are added to the route group. If the devices do not exist yet, there will be nothing to relate to the route group. The following steps have to be performed in the given order:

Step 1   Add devices (gateways and trunks).

Step 2   Build route groups from available devices.

Step 3   Build route lists from available route groups.

Step 4   Build route patterns pointing to route lists.

Route Group

A route group is a list of devices (gateways and trunks). It is recommended to put such devices into the same route group that have identical digit-manipulation requirements, because digit manipulation can be configured only once per route group during route list configuration.

> **NOTE**   A route group can be configured for circular distribution (round-robin) or top-down distribution. Circular distribution is used for load sharing resources, whereas the top-down distribution is used to prioritize gateway usage within a route group. Multiple gateway resources can be in the same route group.

Figure 11-12 displays the call routing logic of CUCM. Notice that there are two gateway resources to the PSTN in the route group. The route group can be configured with the top-down distribution algorithm to use the resources of gateway 1 first and then the resources of gateway 2. This configuration would prove useful in a scenario where gateway 1 and 2 are pointed to different service providers with different negotiated rates. If the same rate is paid to both providers, circular routing is a viable solution that allows load sharing calls across both gateways.

Figure 11-12   *Route Groups*

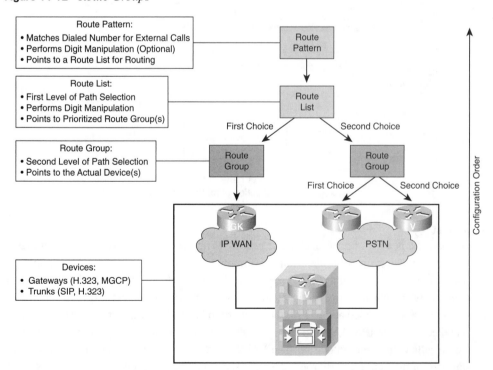

Figure 11-13 displays a screen capture of a Route Group Configuration page. To access this configuration page, navigate to **Call Routing > Route/Hunt > Route Group** from CUCM Administration. The route group should be given a descriptive name. If all the resources in the route group will be used to access the PSTN and there is only one PSTN route group in the CUCM cluster, use a name of PSTN_RG. Best practice is to use a naming nomenclature that includes the configuration item's functionality. The PSTN_RG route group name ends with _RG to signify that the configuration item is a route group. Choose the distribution mechanism from the Distribution Algorithm drop-down menu. Select the gateway or trunk resource that you want to add to the route group from the Available Devices section of the page and click the **Add to Route Group** button.

Figure 11-13 *Route Group Configuration*

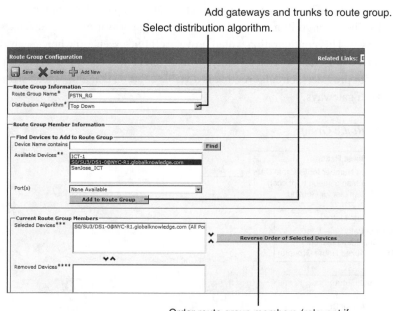

Route List

A route list is a list of prioritized route groups. When configuring a route list, digit manipulation can be set up per route group within the route list. Figure 11-14 is an example of call routing where the first route group is an IP WAN route group distributing calls over a trunk between clusters. If five-digit dialing is used internally and between sites, no digit manipulation is needed at the IP WAN route group level. If the call is rejected by the H.323 gatekeeper or the IP WAN is down, the call is routed over the PSTN. The PSTN will not route calls with five-digit dialing. The PSTN route group will need to prefix the necessary number of digits to properly route the call. Assuming that 11-digit dialing is necessary to

route the call over the PSTN and direct inward dialing is in effect at the destination, six digits are needed to be prefixed to the dialed digits to properly route the call over the PSTN.

Figure 11-14 *Route Lists*

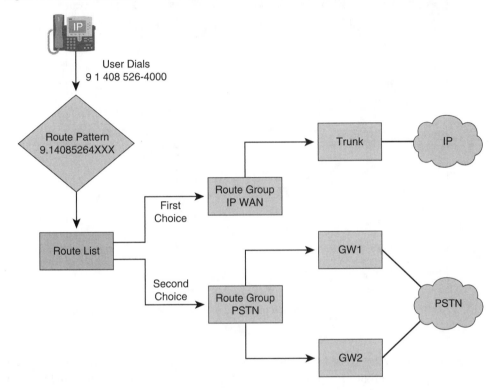

Figure 11-15 displays a route list configuration in which two route groups have been added
to a route list. The route groups are in a prioritized order with the top route group being
the highest priority and the bottom routed group the lowest priority. IP-WAN_RG has the
highest priority, and PSTN_RG has the lower priority. If calls cannot be set up using a trunk
of the IP_WAN_RG route group, the PSTN_RG route group is used to route the call.
CUCM attempts to route the call from all the devices of that route group according to the
route group distribution algorithm (circular or top down). Use good naming nomenclature
when configuring route lists that identify the functionality of the route list. If the route list
is being used to route calls between New York and San Jose, the name SanJose_RL works
well.

Figure 11-15   *Route List Configuration*

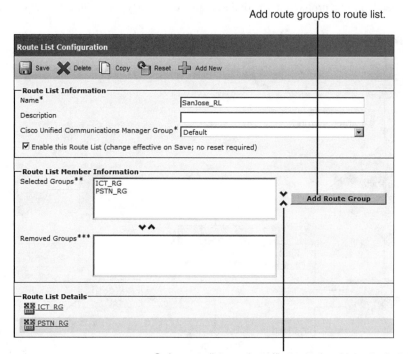

Add route groups to route list.

Order route list members (first entry has highest priority).

At the bottom of the Route List Configuration page, the Route List Details hyperlinks can be configured per route group. This is where digit manipulation can be configured for each route group that is a member of the route list.

Figure 11-16 illustrates two sites of an enterprise (San Jose and Philadelphia) in which each phone has a 5-digit extension and a corresponding 11-digit long-distance PSTN DID number. CUCM has replaced an existing system in which users dialed seven digits for all intersite calling. The dial plan is capable of using five-digit dialing to call between the locations, but the solution will use seven digits because the existing system used seven digits or the company expects a certain amount of expansion.

At the CUCM in Philadelphia, a route pattern of 52.64XXX is configured for intersite calls toward San Jose. The route pattern points to a route list with two route groups. The primary route group includes a trunk, and the secondary route group includes a group of PSTN gateways. Depending on the chosen path, the following digit-manipulation requirements apply for a call placed from Philadelphia to 526-4000:

- **Calls routed over the intercluster trunk**: The first two digits (52) of the called number (526-4000) have to be stripped so that the receiving CUCM in San Jose finds the five-digit number as a configured directory number on one of its IP phones. In addition, the calling party number has to be changed from a five-digit extension to a seven-digit intersite route pattern (prefix 55 to calling party number). The placement of the dot (.) is critical in this scenario. The called party DDI will be configured as pre-dot to remove the 52 from the dialed number. The result will forward only the dialed digits 64000 to San Jose for digit analysis.

- **Calls routed over the PSTN**: The called number has to be extended to a full 11-digit long-distance number by prefixing 1408 to the dialed 7-digit number. The result is an 11-digit long-distance number of 1 408 526-4000. The San Jose gateway has been configured with an inbound call routing significant digits set to 5. CUCM will analyze only the last five digits of the received pattern. Alternatively, most providers customize the number of dialed digits forwarded from the PSTN to the company's dial plan requirements. The circuit may have been ordered so that only five digits are received from the PSTN.

More information about digit-manipulation configuration is provided in the next chapter.

Figure 11-16 *Intercluster Call Routing Example*

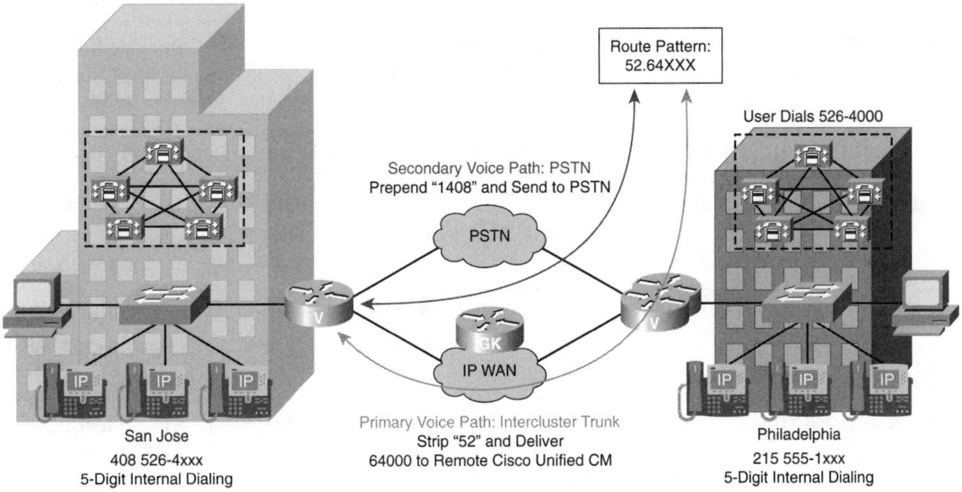

Route Pattern:
52.64XXX

User Dials 526-4000

Secondary Voice Path: PSTN
Prepend "1408" and Send to PSTN

PSTN

IP WAN

San Jose
408 526-4xxx
5-Digit Internal Dialing

Primary Voice Path: Intercluster Trunk
Strip "52" and Deliver
64000 to Remote Cisco Unified CM

Philadelphia
215 555-1xxx
5-Digit Internal Dialing

Route Filters

Route filters can be used only with the @ route pattern to match certain elements or special numbers of a numbering plan. A route filter applied to a pattern not containing the @ wildcard is ignored.

The logical expression entered with the route filter can be up to 1024 characters, excluding the Not-Selected fields.

For large-scale deployments, use explicit route patterns rather than the @ wildcard and route filters. This practice also facilitates management and troubleshooting because all patterns configured in CUCM are easily visible from the Route Pattern Configuration page.

Tags serve as the core component of a route filter. A tag applies a name to a subset of the dialed-digit string. For example, the NANP number 972 555-1234 comprises LOCAL-AREA-CODE (972), OFFICE-CODE (555), and SUBSCRIBER (1234) route filter tags. Table 11-7 provides the complete list of tags available for the NANP.

Table 11-7 *NANP Tags*

Tag	Description
AREA-CODE	This 3-digit area code in the form [2–9]XX identifies the area code for long-distance calls.
COUNTRY CODE	These 1-, 2-, or 3-digit codes specify the destination country for international calls.
END-OF-DIALING	This single character identifies the end of the dialed-digit string. The # character serves as the end-of-dialing signal for international numbers that are dialed within the NANP.
INTERNATIONAL-ACCESS	This 2-digit access code specifies international dialing. Calls that originate in the United States use 01 for this code.
INTERNATIONAL-DIRECT-DIAL	This 1-digit code identifies a direct-dialed international call. Calls that originate in the United States use 1 for this code.
INTERNATIONAL-OPERATOR	This 1-digit code identifies an operator-assisted international call. This code specifies 0 for calls that originate in the United States.
LOCAL-AREA-CODE	This 3-digit local area code in the form [2–9]XX identifies the local area code for 10-digit local calls.
LOCAL-DIRECT-DIAL	This 1-digit code identifies a direct-dialed local call. NANP calls use 1 for this code.

Table 11-7 *NANP Tags (Continued)*

Tag	Description
LOCAL-OPERATOR	This 1-digit code identifies an operator-assisted local call. NANP calls use 0 for this code.
LONG-DISTANCE-DIRECT-DIAL	This 1-digit code identifies a direct-dialed, long-distance call. NANP calls use 1 for this code.
LONG-DISTANCE-OPERATOR	These 1- or 2-digit codes identify an operator-assisted, long-distance call within the NANP. Operator-assisted calls use 0 for this code, and operator access uses 00.
NATIONAL-NUMBER	This tag specifies the nation-specific part of the digit string for an international call.
OFFICE-CODE	This tag designates the first 3 digits of a 7-digit directory number in the form [2–9]XX.
SATELLITE-SERVICE	This 1-digit code provides access to satellite connections for international calls.
SERVICE	This 3-digit code designates services such as 911 for emergency, 611 for repair, and 411 for information.
SUBSCRIBER	This tag specifies the last 4 digits of a 7-digit directory number in the form XXXX.
TRANSIT-NETWORK	This 4-digit value identifies a long-distance carrier. Do not include the leading 101 carrier access code prefix in the TRANSIT-NETWORK value. Refer to TRANSIT-NETWORK-ESCAPE for more information.
TRANSIT-NETWORK-ESCAPE	This 3-digit value precedes the long-distance carrier identifier. The value for this field specifies 101. Do not include the 4-digit carrier identification code in the TRANSIT-NETWORK-ESCAPE value. Refer to TRANSIT-NETWORK for more information.

- **Example 1**: A route filter that uses AREA-CODE and the operator DOES-NOT-EXIST selects all dialed-digit strings that do not include an area code (for example, seven-digit calls).

- **Example 2**: A route filter that uses AREA-CODE, the operator ==, and the entry 515 selects all dialed-digit strings that include the 515 area code (equivalent to a route pattern 515XXXXXXX or 1515XXXXXXX).

- **Example 3**: A route filter that uses AREA-CODE, the operator ==, and the entry 5[2–9]X selects all dialed-digit strings that include area codes in the range of 520 to 599.

- **Example 4**: A route filter that uses TRANSIT-NETWORK, the operator ==, and the entry 0288 selects all dialed-digit strings with the carrier access code 1010288.

Route patterns and translation patterns can be configured to block the pattern. Patterns that are blocked prevent calls to the blocked pattern cluster-wide.

Call Classification

Route patterns are classified as off-net (by default) if the Provide Outside Dial Tone check box is selected in the route pattern. The assumption is that the route pattern is being used to route a call off of the cluster.

The Allow Device Override parameter can be checked at the route-pattern level. The device override changes the call classification method for outgoing calls if the device the call is routed over has a different call classification than the route pattern matched. The device override may be used when a route pattern points to a route list with multiple path selections. The first path for route patterns used between clusters is usually an intercluster trunk, which should be considered to be an on-net call because it uses the IP network. If the call fails over to the secondary path, the PSTN gateway is used, and the enterprise might want to classify the call differently.

The classification is used by several features, including the following:

- **Call forward settings**: Call forward can be configured differently for internal (on-net) versus external (off-net) calls.

- **Block off-net to off-net transfers**: This is a toll-fraud prevention feature that ensures that the company telephony infrastructure is not misused to connect two external parties (usually separated by a long distance) by an internal facilitator.

- **Drop conference when no on-net party remains**: This is a toll-fraud prevention feature that ensures that a conference is dropped when only external parties remain in the conference. If this setting is not enabled, an internal facilitator could again try to connect two external parties (this time by setting up a conference and then dropping out, leaving the two external parties alone in the conference).

Chapter Summary

The following list summarizes the key points that were discussed in this chapter:

- A uniform on-net dial plan provides unique endpoint addressing by fixed-length directory numbers.

- Call routing is when CUCM processes incoming call requests by looking up the dialed number in its call routing table.

- CUCM can receive dialed digits one by one or enbloc.

- CUCM allows multiple, prioritized paths to be selected for a given route pattern.

- Route lists, route groups, and devices are configured to implement path selection.

- CUCM configuration includes special call routing features such as numbering plans and route filters, a wildcard for variable-length numbers, blocked patterns, patterns with urgent priority, and classification of calls.

References

For additional information, refer to these resources:

- **Session Description Protocol**: http://www.ietf.org/rfc/rfc2327.txt

- **Media Gateway Control Protocol**: http://www.ietf.org/rfc/rfc2705.txt

- **CUCM Solution Reference Network Design**: http://www.cisco.com/go/srnd

- **Cisco NetPro Forums**: www.cisco.com/go/netpro

- **Cisco-VoIP E-Mail Distribution List**: http://puck.nether.net

- **Cisco Feature Navigator**: http://www.cisco.com/go/fn

- **Cisco IOS MGCP Gateway Support for Cisco CallManager Network Specific Facilities**: http://www.cisco.com/en/US/products/sw/iosswrel/ps5012/products_feature_guide09186a0080181117.html

- **CUCM Administration Guide, Release 6.0(1)**: http://www.cisco.com/en/US/docs/voice_ip_comm/cucm/admin/6_0_1/ccmcfg/bccm.pdf

- **Cisco CallManager and Cisco IOS Interoperability Guide**—Configuring MGCP Gateway Support for CUCM: http://www.cisco.com/en/US/partner/products/ps6441/products_configuration_guide_chapter09186a00805583bd.html

Review Questions

Use the questions here to review what you learned in this chapter. The correct answers are found in Appendix A, "Answers to Chapter Review Questions."

1. Which of the following is not a dialing method?

    a. PSTN

    b. On-net

    c. Off-net

    d. Abbreviated

2. What dial plan element is used to match the dialed digits for call routing to another cluster or the PSTN?

    a. Route pattern

    b. Route list

    c. Route group

    d. Gateway

    e. Trunk

3. What dial plan element is responsible for changing the dialed digits?

    a. Directory numbers

    b. Translation pattern

    c. Route pattern

    d. Hunt pilot

    e. Meet-me numbers

4. Which of the following wildcards represent the North American Numbering Plan (NANP)?

    a. @

    b. !

    c. X

    d. T

    e. #

5.   Which of the following wildcards represent one or more digits?

   a.   @

   b.   !

   c.   X

   d.   T

   e.   #

   f.   #

6.   Which of the following wildcards represent the termination of the interdigit timeout?

   a.   @

   b.   !

   c.   X

   d.   T

   e.   #

7.   Which two of the following patterns does the route pattern 13[13–49]X match?

   a.   13130

   b.   13199

   c.   1310

   d.   1319

CHAPTER 12

Digit Manipulation

Users of a phone system need to communicate with a variety of destinations. Destinations are located within the same site, different sites within the same company, and other companies located within the same country or different countries. Completing various types of calls often requires dialing access codes or prefix numbers. It is often prudent to restrict users from dialing certain destinations that incur high costs, such as 1-900 numbers.

Users should be provided with a dial plan with the lowest amount of complexity. Digit manipulation, the ability of Cisco Unified Communications Manager (CUCM) to add or subtract digits to comply with a specific internal or national numbering plan, is the key to providing transparent dialing and creating a unified dialing plan for end users.

This lesson describes digit manipulation tools that allow a CUCM administrator to implement flexibility and transparent dial plans. It describes external phone number masks, digit prefix and digit stripping, transformation masks, translation patterns, and significant digits.

Chapter Objectives

Upon completing this lesson, you will be able to use digit manipulation techniques to change calling-party (caller ID) and called-party (dialed digits) information, and be able to meet the following objectives:

- Describe when to use digit manipulation in CUCM.

- Describe CUCM digit manipulation operation.

- Identify CUCM digit manipulation configuration options.

- Describe how to use external phone number masks.

- Describe how to use translation patterns.

- Describe how to use transformation masks in CUCM.

- Describe how to use digit stripping in CUCM.

- Describe how to use significant digits in CUCM.

CUCM Digit Manipulation

Digit manipulation is often used to change calling-party numbers for caller ID purposes on outgoing PSTN calls. Digit manipulation is also used to strip public switched telephone network (PSTN) access codes before extending calls to the PSTN. Other uses of digit manipulation involve expanding or modifying abbreviated dialing options. Inbound calls from the PSTN may be ten digits in length, whereas the internal dial plan is only four or five digits. These inbound calls would need to have the E.164 PSTN numbers converted to the internal dial plan, which could be significantly smaller. It is normally required to manipulate the calling-party (initiator) and called-party (destination) numbers when routing a call to the PSTN. The PSTN access code needs to be stripped from the called number before sending it out to PSTN. Most organizations use the number 8 or 9 as the access code to the PSTN. The calling-party number also needs to be changed from the abbreviated internal extension number to a full E.164 PSTN number to allow for easier redial.

CUCM Digit Manipulation Overview

In Figure 12-1, an IP phone with extension 1002 calls a phone on the PSTN with a phone number of 408 555-111. The user at extension 1002 must first dial a PSTN access code of 9 to direct a call to the PSTN. It is important to strip the 9 from the called number before sending the call to PSTN; otherwise, the PSTN switch will not be able to route the call, and the user will receive a reorder tone because no numbers on the PSTN in North America begin with a 9 (except for 911 for emergency call routing). The calling-party number needs to be expanded to a full PSTN number so that the PSTN user can see the proper, routable caller ID of 706 555-1002, and not the extension of 1002, which is not routable on the PSTN. This functionality will provide proper caller ID, which can be used by a variety of features.

> **NOTE**   In some countries, the calling-party number must be set to the correct PSTN number of the used PSTN subscriber line or trunk.

Table 12-1 displays some often used digit manipulation requirements and the method in which they are handled in CUCM.

Figure 12-1 *Digit Manipulation Overview*

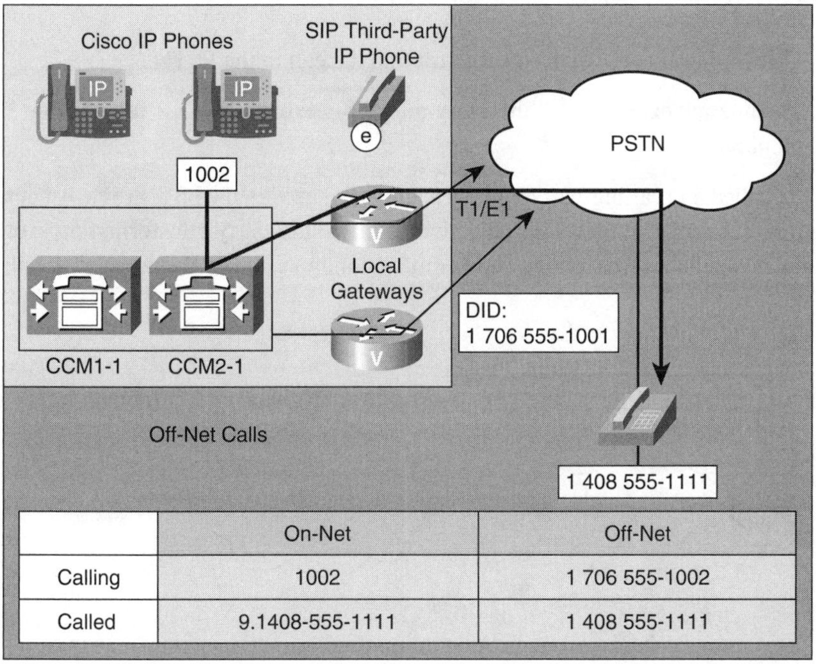

Table 12-1 *Digit Manipulation Methods*

Requirement	Call Type	Method
Expand calling-party directory number to full E.164 PSTN number	Internal to PSTN	Use calling-party's external phone number mask. The calling-party transformation in route pattern or route list provides additional manipulation.
Strip PSTN access code	Internal to PSTN	Use digit stripping in the route pattern or route list.
Expand abbreviated number	Internal to internal	Use called-party transformation in the translation pattern.
Convert E.164 PSTN called-party directory number to internal number	PSTN to internal	Use called-party transformation in the translation pattern, or use significant digits.
Expand endpoint directory numbers to accomodate overlapping dial plan	Internal to internal PSTN to internal	Use called-party transformation in the translation pattern.

Figure 12-2 illustrates an internal caller dialing a PSTN number using a PSTN access code 9 followed by the 11-digit PSTN number, where the following digit manipulations occurs:

1. CUCM discards the digit 9 before routing the call to the PSTN.

2. The internal extension calling-party number is expanded to the full 11-digit PSTN number.

Simple called and calling-party transformations are used in the PSTN route list at the route group level to achieve these two objectives. The calling-party transformation is often dependent on the external phone number mask configuration on the directory number (DN).

Figure 12-2 *Outgoing Call to PSTN*

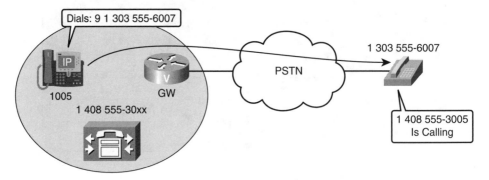

Figure 12-3 illustrates an incoming PSTN call to an internal phone, which is routed as follows:

1. The PSTN phone calls the full E.164 number of the destination; the call is received by the PSTN gateway with ten digits. Digit manipulation occurs on the gateway or on CUCM to convert the full E.164 number to the internal dial plan. The gateway configuration in CUCM is the easiest place to manipulate the incoming digits.

2. The destination DN can also be converted using a translation pattern that matches the digits received from the provider. Translation patterns are not necessary to change the incoming E.164 number to an internal directory number unless the incoming number does not map directly or additional digit manipulation is required. To make it easier for the IP phone user to call back the number, the calling-party transformation mask of the translation pattern can be used to insert 91 to the caller's number. This step is optional because the IP phone user can always edit the number and manually add access code 9 and possibly the long-distance code 1 before calling back the PSTN number.

3. The IP phone receives the call, and the call is listed in the Received Calls menu.

Figure 12-3 *Incoming Call from PSTN*

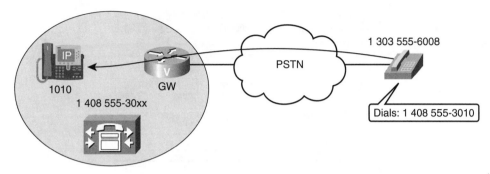

External Phone Number Mask

The external phone number mask is a DN configuration attribute. The external phone number mask of the first DN of the phone is also used for the following functions:

- Change the display of the main phone number at the top of the LCD screen. A DN of 15001 with an external phone number mask of 21255XXXXX would result in a displayed phone number of 212 551-5001. Any user on the phone can instantly identify the PSTN direct inward-dialing number by viewing the LCD of the phone.

- Automated alternate routing (AAR) technology uses the external phone number mask to manipulate digits for PSTN outbound dialing when bandwidth is not available for a guaranteed-quality call over the WAN. The AAR call will be rerouted out the PSTN using the full phone number of the destination as determined by the application of the external phone number mask.

- Change the display of the caller ID for all calls in which the call classification is off-net. In a four-digit dial plan, the caller ID is changed to the full ten-digit PSTN direct inward-dialing phone number.

Figure 12-4 displays the configuration of the external phone number mask at the directory number configuration page. This page is accessed by navigating to the following:

- **Device > Phone > Find**. Click a phone, and then click the DN that you want to configure on the Directory Number Configuration page.

Figure 12-5 displays the configuration of a route pattern that will be used to route calls to the PSTN. The Calling Party Transformations section includes a check box to use the calling-party's external phone number mask for the calling-party presentation on the PSTN.

Figure 12-4 *Directory Number Configuration: External Phone Number Mask*

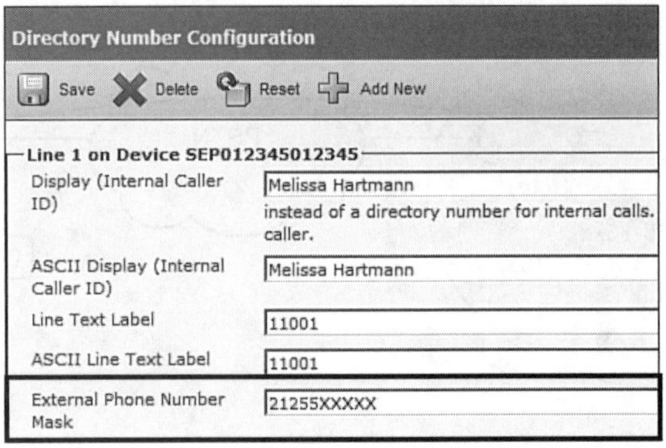

Figure 12-5 *Route-Pattern Configuration: External Phone Number Mask*

CUCM Digit Prefix and Stripping

The Digit Prefix feature prepends digits to a number. Any phone keypad digits from 0 to 9, and the * and # digits, can be prepended to the calling or called numbers.

The Digit Prefix feature can be applied to a calling-party or a called-party number and configured under the corresponding transformation setting in the route-pattern, route-list, or translation-pattern configuration.

Figure 12-6 displays the calling- and called-party prefix configuration available at the route-pattern, route-list, and translation-pattern configuration areas.

Digit discard instructions (DDI) remove parts of the dialed digit string before passing the number on to the adjacent system. A DDI removes a certain portion of the dialed string (for example, when an access code is needed to route the call to the PSTN, but the PSTN switch does not expect that access code).

Digit stripping is configured under the called-party transformations by selecting a DDI. It can be configured at route patterns and at route groups of a route list.

For North American Numbering Plan (NANP) patterns (@), the entire range of DDIs is supported; with non-@ patterns, only DDIs <None>, NoDigits, and PreDot can be used.

Figure 12-6 *Digit Manipulation: Prefix Digits*

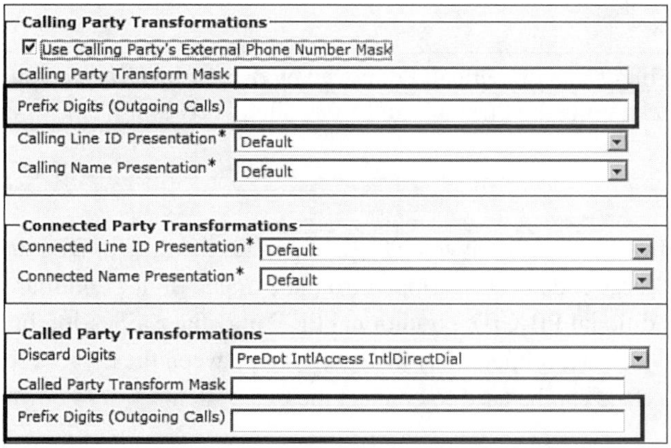

For the PreDot DDI to work, the route pattern has to include a period (.) delimiter. DDIs are available at the route-pattern and route-list (route-group link) levels, as shown in Figure 12-6 (discard digits).

Table 12-2 displays different DDIs and how they would apply to a route pattern of 9.5@ with some dialed digit examples. An access code with two digits before the @ symbol is not used in most systems, but has been used in the example to illustrate the flexibility of DDIs. The digits that would be discarded appear in bold and are highlighted.

Table 12-2 *Digit Discard Instructions*

Instructions	Discarded Digits	Used For
PreDot	**95** 1 214 555 1212	Removes access code
PreAt	**95** 1 214 555 1212	Removes all digits that are in front of a valid numbering plan pattern
11D/10D@7D	**95 1 214** 555 1212	Removes PreDot/PreAt digits and local or long-distance area code
11D@10D	**95 1** 214 555 1212	Removes long-distance identifier
IntlTollBypass	**95 011 33** 1234 #	Removes international access (011) and country code
10-10-Dialing	**95 1010321** 1 214 555 1212	Removes carrier access (1010) and following carrier ID code
Trailing #	95 1010321 011 33 1234 **#**	Removal of # sign for PSTN compatibility

PreDot and NoDigits DDIs are the only DDIs that can be used if the pattern *does not* contain the @ sign.

> **NOTE**   Trailing # is automatically removed by default by CUCM. You can turn off this behavior by changing the Strip # Sign from Called Party Number CM service parameter to False.

Figure 12-7 illustrates a call in which CUCM applies the PreDot DDI to the 9.8*XXX* route pattern. The access code of 9 is stripped from the dialed digits, and four digits of 8123 are routed to a traditional PBX. The traditional PBX may have a Session Initiation Protocol (SIP) trunk to CUCM, or there may be a gateway between the devices so that a traditional telephony interface can be used to connect the two systems.

Figure 12-7   *PreDot Digit Discard Instructions*

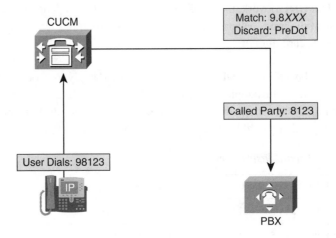

Figure 12-8 illustrates the PreDot 10-10-Dialing DDI applied to the 9.@ route pattern. This compound DDI strips the access code (9) from the dialed number (91010288 1 214 555-1212), removes the carrier selection (1010) and carrier identification code (288), and then sends the 11-digit long-distance phone number 1 214 555-1212 to the gateway device. Removing the 10-10 dialing parameters guarantees that long-distance calls will be billed by the preferred carrier. Most organizations contract minimum guarantees with the long-distance provider of their choice. Although end users might believe that they are saving the company money by routing the call across an advertised carrier, they may be incurring additional costs to the organization. This compound DDI works only if the @ symbol is part of the route pattern. Translation patterns could perform the same functionality without introducing a route pattern with the @ symbol into the dial plan.

Figure 12-8 *Compound Digit Discard Instructions*

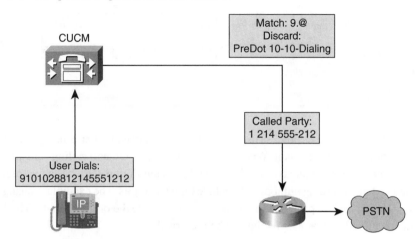

CUCM Transformation Masks

Dialing transformations allow the call-routing component to modify either the calling (initiator) or called (destination) digits of a call. Transformations that modify the calling number (automatic number identification, ANI) are calling-party transformations; transformations that modify the dialed digits (dialed number identification system, DNIS) are called-party transformations.

Transformation masks use mask operations that allow the suppression of leading digits, the modification or preservation of digits, and the insertion of digits.

A mask operation requires two pieces of information: the number to mask and the mask itself.

In the mask operation, CUCM overlays and aligns the number with the mask so that the last character of the mask aligns with the last digit of the number. CUCM uses the corresponding digit of the number wherever the mask contains an X. If the number is longer than the mask, the mask obscures the extra digits.

Figure 12-9 illustrates an approach typically used to change the ANI of internal callers when they make calls to the PSTN. In this example, the five-digit extension of 45000 is changed to a ten-digit pattern for the purposes of caller ID on the PSTN. Caller ID refers to the presentation of the calling-party name and number, whereas ANI refers only to the calling number. Caller ID is being used in this book to represent the presentation of the calling-party number. In the example, the mask applied to 45000 has changed the 45 of the calling party to 36, and five digits are prefixed before the number so that users connected to the PSTN can return phone calls to the presented number.

Figure 12-9   *Transformation Mask Operation*

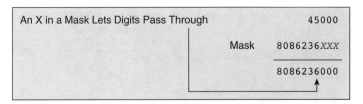

Figure 12-10 illustrates a process in which a ten-digit phone number is being changed into an internal five-digit extension. When a mask is applied to either a calling- or called-party number, the digits are matched from right to left. If a ten-digit pattern has a five-digit mask applied to it, the resulting number will include only five digits. The example is changing the 65 to a 45. If a digit is provided in a mask, it will override the original digits. The X character will allow the original digit to be preserved.

Figure 12-10   *Transformation Mask Operation*

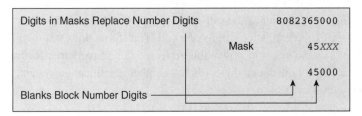

Transformation masks are configurable at route patterns, translation patterns, and route lists (per route group).

The calling- and called-party transformation settings that are assigned to route groups in a route list override the corresponding transformation settings that are assigned to a route pattern. Route-pattern transformations apply only when a route pattern is pointed directly to a gateway. Route patterns are normally pointed to a route list. Multiple route patterns can point to the same route list, but multiple route patterns cannot point directly to the same gateway. Inserting gateways into route groups allows the gateways to be used for many different route patterns.

Transformation masks are usually applied at the route-list level. In this way, a different transformation mask can be assigned for each route group in the route list.

Most calls between clusters of the same company have two route groups: a PSTN route group and an IP WAN route group. The IP WAN route group includes one or more intercluster or SIP trunks, and the PSTN route group may contain one or more gateways that connect to the PSTN. When CUCM uses a trunk from the IP WAN route group, CUCM forwards the internal extension number (five digits if the internal dial plan is using five-digit dialing). When CUCM forwards a call to a gateway in the PSTN route group, the network administrator applies a mask that transforms the number into an E.164-compliant phone number that can be routed over the PSTN.

Translation Patterns

CUCM uses translation patterns to manipulate digits before routing a call. The translation pattern can also be used to block certain patterns. Translation patterns are useful to manipulate the caller ID of incoming PSTN calls to allow the users to quickly return phone calls using the redial and missed-calls functionality. The caller ID from the PSTN may include only 10 digits while the system requires 11 digits prefixed with an access code of 9 to properly route outgoing calls. The translation pattern can prefix a 9 and a 1 to all incoming PSTN calls.

Digit manipulation and translation patterns are used frequently in cross-geographical distributed systems where, for instance, the office codes are not the same at all locations. In these situations, a uniform dialing plan can be created and translation patterns applied to accommodate the unique office codes at each location. Additional examples where translation patterns can be used are as follows:

■ Security desks and operator desks (abbreviated dialing)

■ Hotlines with a need for private line automatic ringdown (PLAR) functionality (security phones in elevators or on a college campus)

■ Extension mapping from a public to private network

Translation patterns use route-pattern style matching and transformation-mask digit manipulations. The resulting pattern is then re-analyzed by the system. The new pattern may match another translation pattern where digit transformation can occur once again. Eventually, the call is routed or blocked. To prevent call-routing loops, CUCM passes digits through translation patterns for only ten iterations.

Figure 12-11 illustrates the operation of a translation pattern. A translation pattern matches the dialed digits in a similar manner to the matching of a route pattern. The primary difference between route patterns and translation patterns is that translation patterns do not have a final call-routing destination (route list, gateway, or trunk). Translation patterns exist only to manipulate digits.

Figure 12-11 *Translation Patterns*

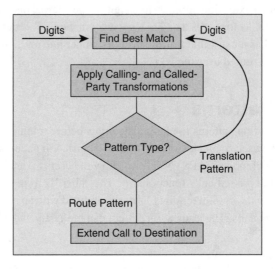

To configure a translation pattern, navigate to **Call Routing > Translation Pattern**, as shown in Figure 12-12. The translation pattern identifies the dialed digit string to match and the calling- or called-party transformation settings that should be applied.

If the Block This Pattern radio button is selected, a cause code must be selected. Choose a value from the drop-down box:

■   No Error

■   Unallocated Number

■   Call Rejected

■   Number Changed

■   Invalid Number Format

■   Precedence Level Exceeded

The transformation settings are not applicable if the Block This Pattern radio button is selected.

If the translation pattern contains an @ sign, a numbering plan and route filter can be selected to match certain number patterns of the selected numbering plan.

Translation patterns are processed as urgent priority by default, and the Urgent Priority check box cannot be removed from a translation pattern. An overlapping dial plan involving a translation pattern could result in call-routing issues.

Figure 12-12 *Translation Pattern Configuration*

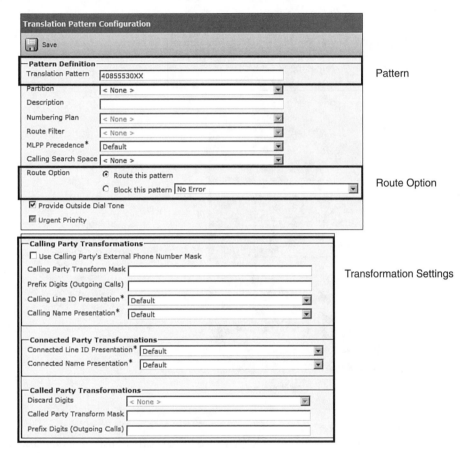

When the direct inward dialing (DID) range from the central office (CO) does not match the internal DN range, a translation pattern can be used to map the PSTN number to the internal DNs.

Figure 12-13 shows a scenario in which a company has a PSTN DID range of 408 555-1XXX, whereas the internal four-digit extensions begin with 4XXX. When the company receives an incoming call, the company uses a translation pattern that matches the assigned PSTN DID range (408 555-1XXX). The called-party transformation mask of 4XXX is applied against the translation pattern of 408 555-1XXX, resulting in a 4XXX dialed number. After CUCM applies the transformation mask, it performs a new call-routing lookup for the translated four-digit number, finds the DN in its call-routing table, and routes the call to the corresponding IP phone.

Figure 12-13 *Translation Pattern Example*

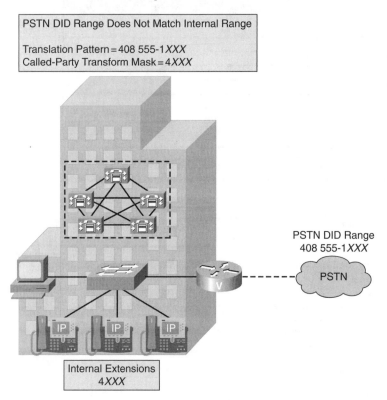

An additional translation pattern of XXXX with a called-party transformation mask of 4111 can be used to route calls of unidentified extensions to the company operator. Assume that the DN of 4333 no longer exists in the system because that user (Dennis) won the lottery for $10 million and decided that he was going to play his guitar all day long instead of working. When a call comes in from the PSTN to 408 555-1333, the call is translated to 4333. Because 4333 no longer exists, it matches the generic XXXX translation pattern, and the call is routed to the company operator at extension 4111. Josephine (the company operator) instructs the outside caller that Dennis can be reached on his cell phone because he is home playing Metallica on his guitar.

Significant Digits

The Significant Digits feature instructs CUCM to analyze the configured number of least-significant digits of the called number for incoming calls received by a gateway or trunk. Setting the Significant Digits to 5 on a PSTN gateway instructs CUCM to ignore all but the last five digits of the called number for routing incoming PSTN calls. This is the easiest approach to convert incoming PSTN called numbers to an internal extension, but it affects all calls received from that gateway. If there are variable-length extension numbers on the internal network, using significant digits is not the recommended approach for changing PSTN received digits to an internal dial plan.

In Figure 12-14, the PSTN gateway receives an incoming call with the destination number of 408 555-1010 through a gateway. If Significant Digits = 4 is configured under the gateway configuration in CUCM, CUCM strips off all digits except the last four (1010), looks up this number (1010) in its call-routing table, and forwards the call to the IP phone configured with that DN.

Figure 12-14 *Significant Digits Example*

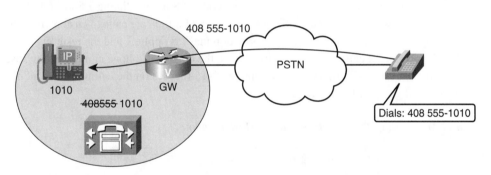

NOTE   In contrast to using translation patterns to map E.164 numbers to internal DNs on incoming PSTN calls, this solution performs only one call-routing table lookup. The Significant Digits feature is a more processor-friendly alternative than translation patterns, but this approach will not allow the same flexibility as translation patterns.

You can configure significant digits in the gateway or trunk configurations under the Incoming Calls section. This parameter affects all calls received by the gateway or trunk.

Transformation Examples

Multiple transformations might take place when placing a phone call. Using external phone number masks instructs the call-routing component to use the external phone number of a calling station rather than its DN for caller ID information. The external phone number mask is applied on an individual line basis through the Directory Number Configuration screen on the device.

The route pattern matched for an outgoing call can apply another set of calling-party transformations before extending the call to the PSTN. This can prove useful when third-level Technical Assistance Center (TAC) support technicians make outgoing calls to customers. Company policy may dictate that third-level TAC engineers never give out their DID phone number to customers because all calls should be routed through the Cisco TAC.

Figure 12-15 illustrates the multiple levels of calling-party manipulation that may occur when the third-level support TAC engineer places a call back to the customer, Global Knowledge. The engineer's phone number of 35062 will appear as 214 713-5062 when calls are routed through any off-net devices because of the configured external phone number mask. The engineer dialed a special access code of 8 before dialing 1 800 COURSES to Global Knowledge. All calls with an access code of 8 indicate calls to customers from TAC engineers. The calling-party transformation mask is applied, and the resulting caller ID will appear as if calls were being placed from the main TAC phone number in San Jose, California (408 853-5000). Notice that Figure 12-16 focuses on the calling party and not the dialed digits (1 800 COURSES).

Figure 12-15 *Calling-Party Transformation Mask Example*

Directory Number	35062
External Phone Number Mask	21471XXXXX
	2147135062
Calling-Party Transformation Mask	40885XX000
Caller ID	4088535000

Figure 12-16 is an example of called-party modifications where the user dialed 10-10-321 to save the company money on the phone call. The route pattern of 9.@ was matched by the dialed digits of 9 10-10-321 1 808 555-1221. The DDI was configured to remove the 10-10-dialing. The resulting number is applied against the called-party transformation mask, which includes ten wildcard characters. The access code (9) and long-distance code (1) are removed from the dialed digits. An (8) is prefixed as a new access code because the call may be routed to a traditional PBX where an 8 is required as an access code to trunk the call to the PSTN.

Figure 12-16 *Called-Party Digit Manipulation*

Dialed Number	9 10–10–321 1 808 555–1221
Discard Digits	10–10–Dialing
	9 1 808 555–1221
Called-Party Transformation Mask	XXXXXXXXXX
	808 555–1221
Prefix Digits	8
Called Number	8 808 555–1221

Figure 12-17 is an example where the Unified Communications support group in Richardson, Texas, is placing calls to someone in the Routing support group in San Jose, California. Because the corporate policy is to not allow direct calls to members of the support team, the calling and called party will be manipulated to reflect the main hunt pilot used to distribute calls to support group members at each site.

1. User A, at extension 5062, dials 91234.

2. The route pattern of 9.1XXX matches the dialed digits.

3. A DDI of PreDot is applied to the called party. The resulting dialed digits are now 1234.

4. A calling-party transformation mask of X000 is applied to caller 5062.

5. The caller ID at the destination will now appear as if the call were placed from the hunt pilot of 5000 in Richardson, Texas.

6. A called-party transformation mask of X000 is applied to the dialed digits. 1234 is applied to the mask, and the resulting number is 1000.

7. San Jose receives a call destined for extension 1000 with a caller ID of extension 5000. The original call was destined to 9-1234 with a caller ID of 5062.

Figure 12-17 *Complex Digit Manipulation*

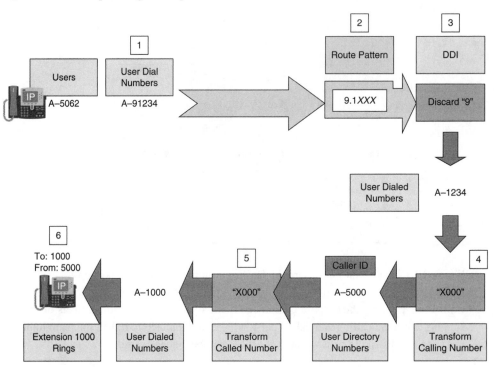

Chapter Summary

The following list summarizes the key points that were discussed in this chapter:

- In many call scenarios, it is required to manipulate the calling and called (dialed) string before routing the call.

- CUCM digit manipulation configuration main elements are external phone number mask, digit prefix and stripping, transformation masks, translation pattern, and significant digits.

- A CUCM external phone number mask designates the fully qualified E.164 address for the user's extension and is used to format caller ID information for outbound calls from the internal devices.

- The Digit Prefix option prepends digits to a pattern, and the Digit Stripping option strips off digits from a pattern.

- Transformation masks modify either the calling number or the called number (dialed digits).

■ Translation patterns can be used to either route or block certain patterns. When the digits match the translation pattern, CUCM performs the translation first before routing the call to another translation pattern or to a route pattern.

■ The Significant Digits feature instructs CUCM to pay attention to only the least-significant X digits of the called number for incoming calls from PSTN or from another CUCM cluster.

Review Questions

Use the questions here to review what you learned in this chapter. The correct answers are found in Appendix A, "Answers to Chapter Review Questions."

1. The external phone number mask modifies which of the following for calls routed to the PSTN?

    a. ANI

    b. DNIS

    c. Caller ID name

    d. Route pattern

2. What dial plan element is used to manipulate digits when a route pattern can be routed to multiple devices?

    a. Route pattern

    b. Route list

    c. Route group

    d. Gateway

    e. Trunk

3. Which of the following items do external phone number mask configurations not have an effect upon?

    a. Automatic number identification

    b. Automatic alternate routing

    c. Extension mobility

4. Calling-party modifications change which portion of a phone number?

    a. ANI

    b. DNIS

5. Called-party modifications change which portion of a phone number?

    a. ANI

    b. DNIS

    c. RDNIS

    d. Original calling party

6. Which of the following items is processed as urgent priority by default?

    a. Directory numbers

    b. 911

    c. Route patterns

    d. Translation patterns

7. Which of the following patterns does the 10-10-Dialing digit discard instruction apply to?

    a. 9.!

    b. 9.[2–9]XXXXXX

    c. 9.@

    d. 9.1[2–9]XX[2–9]XXXXXX

8. Which of the following digit discard instructions can be applied to a route pattern of 9.1[2–9]XX[2–9]XXXXXX?

    a. 10-10-Dialing

    b. 11D->10D

    c. PreDot

    d. PreDot 11D->10D

9. A directory number of 11001 with an external phone number mask of 212551XXXX would result in what phone number?

   a. 11001

   b. 212 551-1001

   c. 212 551-100X

   d. 212 551-1001

10. A number of 212 555-1212 with a called-party transformation mask of 646XXX3456 would result in which of the following numbers?

   a. 212 555-1212

   b. 646 555-1212

   c. 646 555-3456

   d. 212 646-1212

CHAPTER 13

Calling Privileges

Calling privileges are an important dial plan component. They are used to implement class of service (CoS), which restricts user calling capabilities. The calling restrictions are based on the calling device. Other applications of CoS include time-of-day call routing, vanity numbers, client matter codes (CMC), forced authorization codes (FAC), and private line automatic ringdown (PLAR).

This chapter describes the configuration tools that are used to implement calling privileges and discusses different usage scenarios.

Chapter Objectives

Upon completing this lesson, you will be able to explain the need and uses for calling privileges and to implement them in Cisco Unified Communications Manager (CUCM). You will also be able to meet these objectives:

- Describe the tools that CUCM supports for call-privilege implementation.

- Describe how partitions and calling search spaces work and how they are configured.

- Describe how time schedules and time periods work and how they are configured.

- Describe how CMC and FAC work and how they are configured.

- Identify applications for calling-privileges configuration elements.

- Describe how to implement CoS.

- Describe how to implement 911 emergency calls and vanity numbers.

- Describe how to implement time-of-day-based carrier selection.

- Describe how to implement PLAR.

Calling Privileges

Calling privileges control the available components of a call-routing database that are accessible to an endpoint. The primary application is the implementation of CoS. CoS is usually used to control telephony charges by blocking costly service numbers. Many organizations block international calls for most users and restrict long-distance dialing on common-area phones. CoS is also used to protect the privacy of some users. Executive managers may allow only those calls that have gone through their assistants, for example.

Calling privileges can also be used to implement special applications such as tail-end hop off (TEHO). TEHO allows organizations to save public switched telephone network (PSTN) toll charges by routing long-distance and international calls across the private IP WAN network before hopping off at the destination-site gateway to route a local PSTN call. TEHO is an application of least-cost routing (LCR), which has been in telephony networks for a very long time.

TEHO can greatly complicate a dial plan because of the additional configuration required to properly route calls on a per-site basis. In a multisite environment with PSTN gateways at each site, PSTN route patterns should always be routed to the local PSTN gateway; hence, the same route patterns have to exist multiple times (once per site in this example), and only the site-specific route patterns should be accessible by the devices located at this site.

Another application is time-of-day routing, where calls should take different paths depending on the time when the call is placed.

Table 13-1 provides a typical CoS implementation with calling classes and their allowed destination. These calling classes can then be assigned to devices or users.

In the example, class Internal allows only internal and emergency calls. Class Local adds the permission for local PSTN calls, class Long Distance also allows long-distance PSTN calls, and class International also enables international PSTN calls.

Table 13-1 *Class of Service Example*

Class of Service	Allowed Destinations
Internal	Internal
	Emergency
Local	Internal
	Emergency
	Local PSTN

Table 13-1 *Class of Service Example (Continued)*

Class of Service	Allowed Destinations
Long Distance	Internal
	Emergency
	Local PSTN
	Long-distance PSTN
International	Internal
	Emergency
	Local PSTN
	Long-distance PSTN
	International PSTN

Table 13-2 briefly describes the various call-privilege configuration elements that this chapter covers.

Table 13-2 *Call-Privileges Configuration Elements*

Element	Characteristic
Partition	Group of numbers with similar reachability characteristics (including route patterns, directory numbers, translation patterns, and so on)
Calling search space	Ordered list of accessible partitions applied to device to restrict call privileges
Time periods	Static days or recurring time intervals
Time schedules	Ordered list of time periods
CMCs	Used to track calls to certain destinations
FACs	Restrict outgoing calls to certain numbers

Partitions and Calling Search Spaces

A partition is a group of dialable patterns with similar accessibility. Any dialable pattern can be assigned to a partition. All phone numbers are in the null partition by default, and all devices have access to the null partition. As soon as a phone number is assigned to a different partition, the devices in the network will not be able to access that phone number without the configuration of a calling search space (CSS).

A CSS defines which partitions are accessible to a particular device. A device can call only those call-routing table entries located in partitions that are part of the CSS assigned to the device.

Partitions are assigned to call-routing targets. Any entry of the call-routing table, including voice-mail ports, directory numbers (DN), route patterns, translation patterns, meet-me conference numbers, and so on can be assigned to a partition.

CSSs are assigned to devices, which are the source of a call-routing request (phones, phone lines, gateways, trunks, voice-mail ports, and computer telephony integration [CTI] ports). Calls that come into the network from a gateway or trunk inherit the CSS assigned to the gateway or trunk.

By default, all entities that can be configured with a partition are in partition <None> (null partition), all entities that can be configured with a CSS are assigned with CSS <None> (null CSS).

Members of partition <None> are always accessible by sources of a call-routing request, regardless of the CSS applied to the calling party. Entities that do not have a CSS assigned can only access numbers that are in partition <None>. Partition <None> is commonly referred to as the null partition.

In Figure 13-1, various partitions and CSSs have been created. An easier way of understanding partitions and CSSs is to use an analogy of locks and key rings. If each house on a block has a different lock (partition), your key ring (CSS) would have to include many keys (to unlock different doors).

In Figure 13-1, DN 1 of Phone 1 has been configured in the lobby partition, and DN 1 of Phone 2 is in the employee partition, while Phone 3 and Phone 5 are both in the manager partition. Phone 4 has not been assigned to a partition. Following the analogy with locks and keys, there are three different types of locks (lobby, employee, and manager). Phone 4 does not have a lock. Phone 4 is therefore in the null partition, and everyone has access to call Phone 4.

When approaching CSSs from the perspective of key rings, Phone 1 has a key ring with the lobby and employee key on it. Phone 2 has a key ring with keys for the lobby, employee, and manager key ring. Phone 3 has a key ring with the lobby, employee, manager, and executive keys. The executive key is not seen in the example, but it will be used in the system for executive management. The key ring of Phone 4 contains only the lobby key. Phone 5 does not have any keys, which restricts Phone 5 to call only other DNs in the null partition.

As a result of this implementation of locks and keys, the following effective permissions apply:

- **Phone 1**: Like all other phones, this phone has access to all devices that do not have a lock applied (Phone 4 in this example). Phone 1 can access DN 1 on Phone 2 and Phone 4. Devices cannot access DNs in the same partition unless their CSS gives explicit permission to that partition.

- **Phone 2**: Phone 2 can access Phone 1, Phone 3, Phone 4, and Phone 5.

- **Phone 3**: Phone 3 can access Phone 1, Phone 2, Phone 4, and Phone 5.

- **Phone 4**: Phone 4 can access Phone 1 only, because the CSS has access only to the lobby partition.

- **Phone 5**: Like all other phones, this phone has access to all devices that do not have a lock applied (Phone 4 in this example). Phone 5 cannot unlock any locks because it does not have any keys. That means that Phone 4 can access only Phone 1.

Figure 13-1   *Calling Privileges: Partitions and Calling Search Spaces*

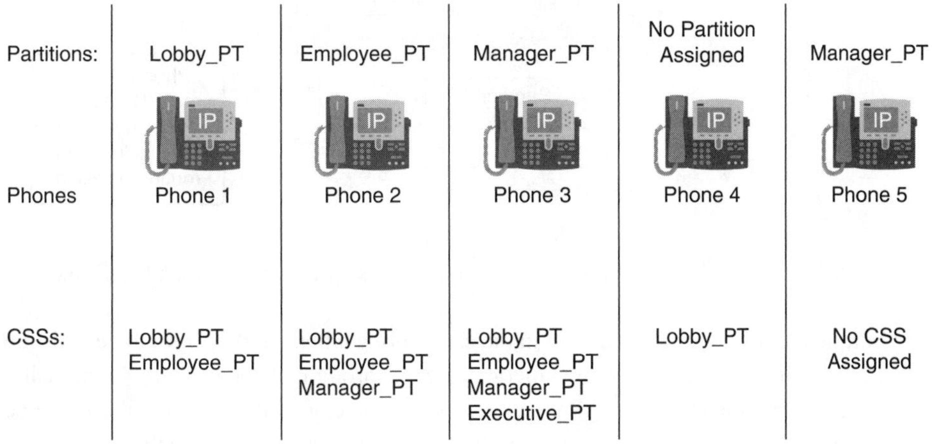

Partitions:	Lobby_PT	Employee_PT	Manager_PT	No Partition Assigned	Manager_PT
Phones	Phone 1	Phone 2	Phone 3	Phone 4	Phone 5
CSSs:	Lobby_PT Employee_PT	Lobby_PT Employee_PT Manager_PT	Lobby_PT Employee_PT Manager_PT Executive_PT	Lobby_PT	No CSS Assigned

Figure 13-2 illustrates a phone with a CSS that contains two partitions: Chicago and San Jose. A third partition, Atlanta, exists in the system but is not included in the CSS of the phone. Phone DNs are assigned to partitions as follows:

- DN 3001 (Phone 2-1) is assigned to partition Chicago.

- DN 2001 (Phone 1-1) is assigned to partition San Jose.

- DN 4001 (Phone 3-1) is assigned to partition Atlanta.

The user at the phone dials 3001, which is the DN of Phone 2-1. CUCM performs digit analysis against the dialed digits of 3001. The call-routing lookup will search only through the partitions configured in the CSS of the calling phone (Chicago and San Jose). CUCM finds a match in partition Chicago, because the DN of 3001 of Phone 2-1 is assigned to this partition. Because no other matches exist, routing is complete, and Phone 2-1 rings.

Figure 13-2 *Partition and CSS Example*

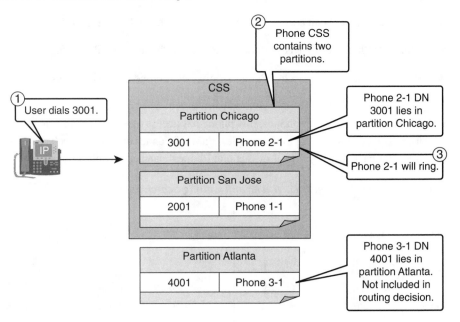

A CSS is an ordered list of partitions with the highest-priority partitions listed first.

Multiple identical entities can exist in the call-routing table, but they have to be in different partitions. It is advisable to route emergency calls through a local gateway in multisite centralized call-processing deployments. If 911 is the emergency number, there will be many iterations of the 911 route pattern in the system, but they must each be in a separate partition. Local call routing in a centralized call-processing approach will result in the creation of site-specific partitions and CSSs to guarantee that local PSTN resources are used.

Figure 13-3 *Multiple Best Matches Example*

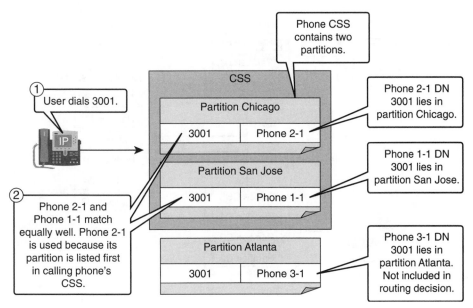

Figure 13-3 displays a CSS scenario in which the same dialed pattern matches multiple partitions. The CSS processing is based on the following order:

1.   Best match is searched.

2.   If multiple equally qualified matches exist (no single best match), the call routes through the partition in the CSS that is highest in the list. Many sources of call-routing requests (trunks, gateways, and translation patterns) have only one CSS. On IP phones, a different CSS can be applied per line and at the device level. If a CSS is specified only at the device level, each DN inherits the CSS of the device.

If CSSs are configured at both device and line level, the line from which the call is placed is considered first in the call-processing logic. CUCM concatenates the two CSSs and processes them in a top-down manner with the line CSS at the top of the list, as shown in Figure 13-4.

Figure 13-4   *Device and Line CSS Example*

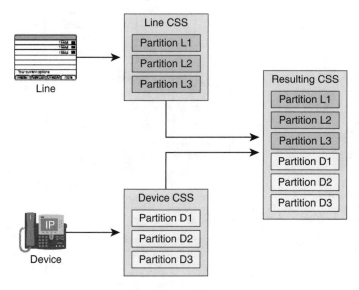

> **NOTE**   On CTI ports, the line and device CSS are processed in reverse order; the partitions of the device CSS are processed before the partitions of the line CSS.

In Figure 13-5, the line CSS of the calling party includes partitions San Jose and Chicago. The device CSS of the calling phone includes partition Atlanta.

Figure 13-5   *CSS Partition Order Example*

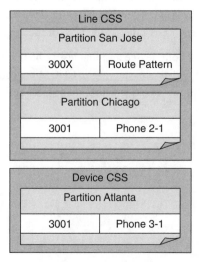

Route pattern 300X is in the San Jose partition, with DN 3001 assigned to both Phone 2-1 in the Chicago partition and Phone 3-1 in the Atlanta partition.

When the phone dials 3001, the following will happen:

CUCM interprets the dialed digits and searches for the closest match. The two DN entries in the call-routing table are more specific than the route pattern of 300X. Phone 2-1 is chosen because its partition is listed first in the concatenated CSS.

Figure 13-5 illustrates the line CSS having higher priority than the device CSS. If the line CSS and device CSS were reversed, the call would be sent to Phone 3-1. Notice that the CSS subsequently performs closest-match routing against all partitions in the CSS at the same time. If the CSS had been strictly processed on the San Jose partition before considering the Chicago or Atlanta partitions, 300X would have been the match. Instead, CUCM was aware of the closest match of 3001 in the other partitions. The partition order is used as a tiebreaker if there are multiple closest matches.

> **NOTE** It is a common misunderstanding that the first matching pattern (regardless of the quality of the match) that is found when searching through the partitions in the order specified in the CSS is used for call routing. If this were true, subsequent partitions of the CSS would only be looked at, if no match (of any kind) were found in the earlier partitions. This is not the case. All partitions are immediately considered for the best-match logic, and only if multiple best matches exist does the partition order become relevant.

Figure 13-6 is using partitions and CSS to implement four different classes of service:

- **Internal**: Allows internal calls only

- **Local**: Allows internal and local PSTN calls

- **Long Distance**: Allows internal, local PSTN, and long-distance PSTN calls

- **International**: Allows internal, local PSTN, long distance, and international PSTN calls

The following partitions are applied as described:

- **Phones**: This partition is applied to all phone lines.

- **Local-PSTN**: This partition is applied to route pattern 9.[2–9]XXXXXX

- **LD-PSTN**: This partition is applied to route pattern 9.1[2–9]XX[2–9]XX XXXX

- **Intl-PSTN**: This partition is applied to route pattern 9.011! and 9.011!#.

The following CSSs are configured, each implementing the corresponding service class:

- **CSS-Internal**: Containing partition Phones

- **CSS-Local**: Containing partitions Phones and Local-PSTN

- **CSS-LD**: Containing partitions Phones, Local-PSTN, and LD-PSTN

- **CSS-International**: Containing partitions Phones, Local PSTN, LD-PSTN, and Intl-PSTN

Figure 13-6   *CSS Example*

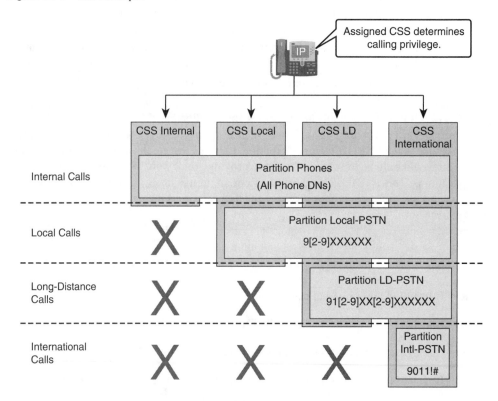

> **NOTE**   CSSs take on an inverted logical approach when assigned to devices such as Session Initiation Protocol (SIP) trunks, intercluster trunks, and gateways. Calls that are routed through a trunk or gateway take on the CSS applied at the device. In a multicluster distributed call-processing environment, it is not advised to allow emergency call routing across trunk links. Most organizations locally route emergency calls to the local public safety answering point (PSAP). It is common practice to restrict emergency call routing in the CSS applied to trunks.

Configuration of partitions and CSSs includes the following steps:

Step 1 Create partitions.

Step 2 Assign partitions to the DN, route-translation patterns, CTI ports, voice-mail ports, meet-me conference bridge numbers, call-park ranges, and any other number in the system.

Step 3 Create CSSs.

Step 4 Add partitions in the desired order into each newly created CSS.

Step 5 Assign CSSs to entities that can request lookups to the call-routing table to route a call; examples for such entities are phones and phone lines, trunks, gateways, and translation patterns.

> **NOTE** A translation pattern is a dialable pattern in the call-routing table. When a translation pattern is matched, it invokes a new call-routing request for the translated pattern. Which partition the translation pattern is in limits the devices that can access the translation pattern. The CSS of the translation pattern specifies the entries of the call-routing table that the translation pattern is allowed to see for the new call-routing request when it is trying to find the translated pattern in the call-routing table.

To add partitions in CUCM Administration, navigate to **Call Routing > Class of Control > Partition** and click the **Add New** button. Figure 13-7 shows the Partition Configuration page in CUCM. You can add up to 75 partitions in one insertion of partitions with a character limitation of 1475 characters. If more than 75 partitions are required, you may perform multiple insertions.

Partition names should not be lengthy because the CSS has a maximum length restriction of 1024 characters. A CSS is a string of partition names. The 1024-character limit includes separator characters between each partition name. (For example, the string "partition_1:partition_2:partition_3" contains 35 characters.) The maximum number of partitions in a CSS varies, depending on the length of the partition names and number of partitions. If individual CSSs are used on both the device and line level, the maximum character limit for the individual CSS is 512 (half the combined CSS clause limit of 1024 characters).

Figures 13-8 and 13-9 show the application of partitions, respectively, to a DN and route pattern.

Figure 13-7 *Partition Configuration*

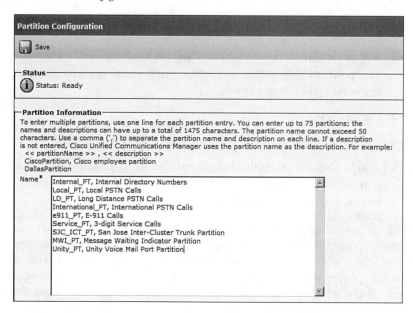

Figure 13-8 *Partition Application: Directory Number*

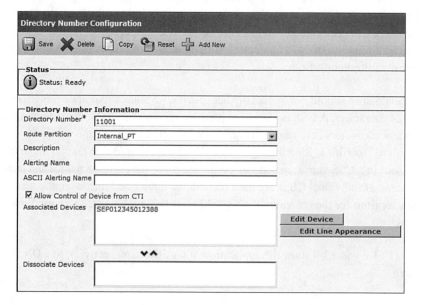

Figure 13-9 *Partition Application: Route Pattern*

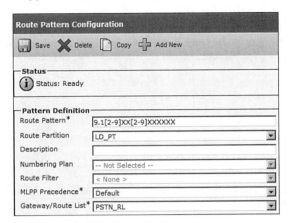

Figure 13-10 shows the Calling Search Space Configuration page. This page is accessible by navigating to the following CUCM Administration menu: **Call Routing > Class of Control > Calling Search Space**. Click the **Add New** button to add a new CSS. The CSS should be given a name that is descriptive of the desired functionality. LD_Calling Search Space would be descriptive of a CSS that allows long-distance, local, emergency, and internal dialing. Click a partition in the Available Partitions section of the configuration page and use the down arrow to move the partition to the Selected Partitions section. You can use the up and down arrows to the right of the Selected Partitions section to move the priority of the selected partition. The top of the list is the highest priority. The emergency partition should normally be at the top of the list.

Figure 13-11 displays the phone configuration page with a CSS applied. CSSs can be assigned to phones, phone lines, gateways, trunks, voice-mail pilots, voice-mail ports, CTI route points, CTI ports, translation patterns, and any other source of a call-routing request.

Figure 13-10 *CSS Configuration*

Add or remove highlighted partition to or from CSS.

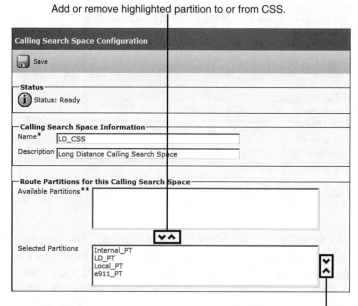

Change order of partitions in CSS by
moving highlighted partition up or down.

Figure 13-11 *CSS Configuration*

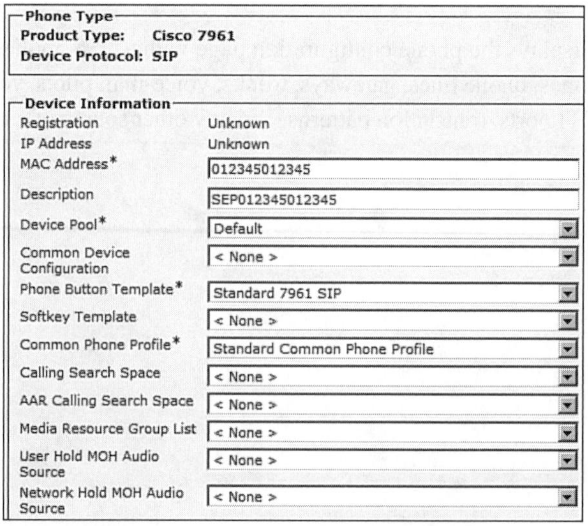

Time-of-Day Call Routing

Time-of-day routing can be implemented in CUCM by applying time and date attributes to partitions using time schedules and time periods. Time periods define time ranges or dates and are grouped into time schedules. Time schedules are then assigned to partitions.

A CSS that includes a partition that is associated with a time schedule has access only to the partition if the current date and time match the time and date information specified in the time schedule that is associated with the partition. If the configured time schedule does not fall into the current date and time, the partition is logically removed from the CSS.

> **NOTE**   It is highly advisable to use Network Time Protocol (NTP) when using time-of-day call routing.

Time-of-day routing can be used to route calls differently based on time in the following way:

- Identical route patterns are created and put into different partitions.

- At least one of these partitions has a time schedule applied.

- If the partition with the time schedule is listed first in CSSs, it will take precedence over other partitions *during the time that is associated with the partition*. If the current time does not match the configured time schedule, the partition that has the time schedule assigned is ignored, and the next partition becomes the partition with highest priority.

Examples of when time-of-day routing can be used include the following:

- Allowing international calls only during office hours

- Blocking international calls on holidays

- Using time-of-day routing to control the call-routing path based on the current time for maximum cost benefits:

   —Multiple providers for international calls might be available, some of them having different prices depending on the hours of the days (typically more expensive during business hours and less expensive during off-hours).

   —With time-of-day routing, international calls to certain countries can use the cheapest available provider based on the current time, and thus make use of the cheapest offer for any given time instead of using the same provider for calls to certain countries all the time.

A time period specifies a time range defined by start- and end- time and a repetition interval (days of week or specified calendar date). One or more time periods can be assigned to a time schedule. The same time period can be assigned to multiple time schedules.

A time schedule is a group of time periods. Time schedules are applied to partitions and thus make the partition inactive when the applied time schedule does not match the current date or time.

In Figure 13-12, the partition CiscoAustin_PT is accessible only from Monday to Friday from 8 a.m. to 5 p.m. (0800 to 1700) from a CSS that includes the partition.

Figure 13-12   *Time Periods and Schedules*

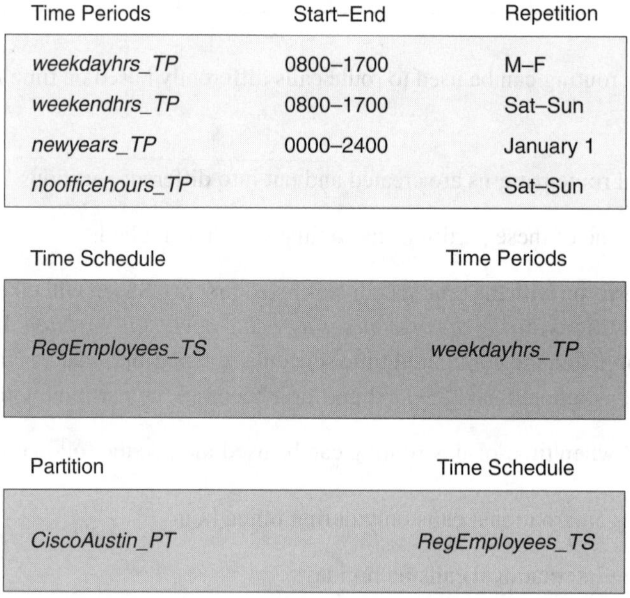

Time Periods	Start–End	Repetition
weekdayhrs_TP	0800–1700	M–F
weekendhrs_TP	0800–1700	Sat–Sun
newyears_TP	0000–2400	January 1
noofficehours_TP		Sat–Sun

Time Schedule	Time Periods
RegEmployees_TS	*weekdayhrs_TP*

Partition	Time Schedule
CiscoAustin_PT	*RegEmployees_TS*

You can use time-based CoS to allow international calls, for example, during only certain times of the day. Figure 13-13 is an example where international calls will be blocked on weekends and holidays (New Year's Day in the example). Multiple 9.011! route patterns must be created for this application. The first route pattern is put into the standard partition, which has no time schedule applied.

A second, identical route pattern is created, which is placed into the weekend partition. The phone's line CSS includes the weekend partition, while the device CSS includes the standard partition. The weekend partition is used to block the international call, because the route pattern has a *block this action* associated with it. The weekend partition will match only on weekends and New Year's Day.

Figure 13-13 *Time-Based Call-Routing Example*

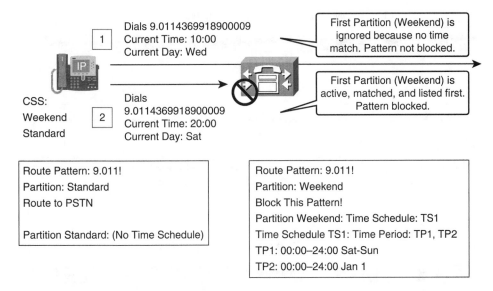

> **NOTE**   Route patterns and translation patterns can be configured with the parameter Block This Pattern to explicitly deny calls to certain patterns if the pattern was selected by the call-routing logic.

The steps to implement time-of-day routing are as follows:

Step 1   Create time periods.

Step 2   Create time schedules and associate them with time periods.

Step 3   Assign time schedules to partitions that should be active only during the time specified in the time schedule.

The CUCM Administration navigation to create a time period is **Call Routing > Class of Control > Time Period**. Click the **Add New** button. Use descriptive names in your time periods that include _TP in the name (for example, weekdays_TP). Figure 13-14 is an example of a time period configuration with a recurring time range every week from Saturday to Sunday. Figure 13-15 is a static date every year on January 1.

Time schedules are created by adding one or more time periods to a time schedule. Time periods are configured in the following navigation path: **Call Routing > Class of Control > Time Schedule**. Click the **Add New** button. Figure 13-16 shows a time schedule that includes two time periods.

Figure 13-14   *Recurring Time Period*

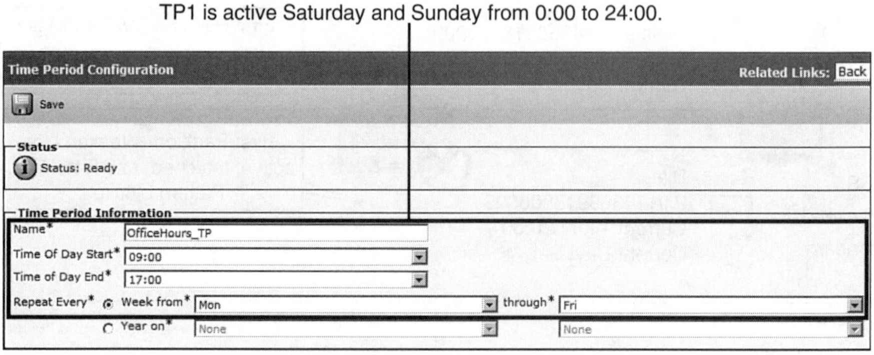

TP1 is active Saturday and Sunday from 0:00 to 24:00.

Figure 13-15   *Static Time Period*

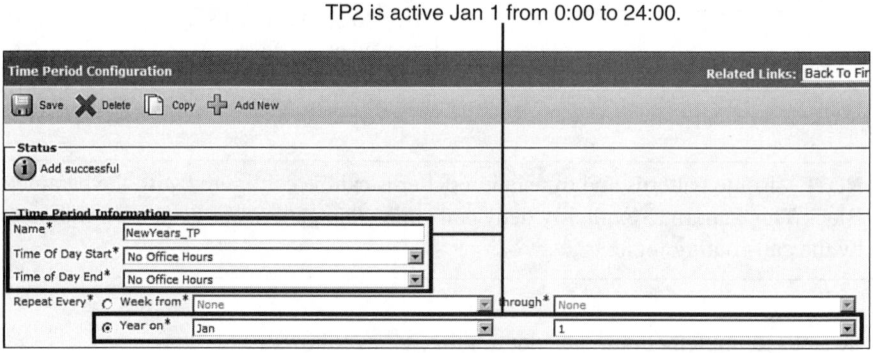

TP2 is active Jan 1 from 0:00 to 24:00.

Figure 13-16   *Time Schedule Configuration*

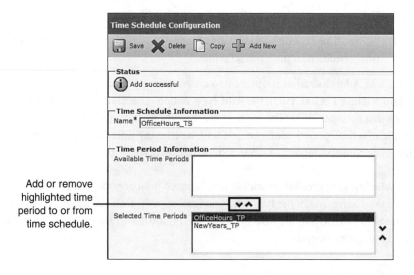

Add or remove highlighted time period to or from time schedule.

Time schedules are then assigned to partitions. In Figure 13-17, the time schedule OfficeHours_TS is applied to the International partition. The International_PT will only be included in the CSS during office hours.

Figure 13-17   *Time Schedule: Partition Application*

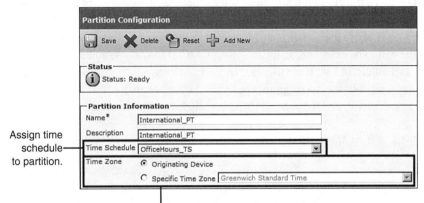

Set fixed time zone or use time zone of call originating device.

Client Matter Codes and Forced Authorization Codes

Client matter codes (CMC) and forced authorization codes (FAC) can be applied to route patterns.

CMCs are typically used in professional organizations where a great deal of business is transacted over the phone and clients are billed for such time. The CMC is added to call details records (CDR) to allow accounting and billing of calls based on their client matter. If a route pattern that has a CMC applied is matched, the user is prompted to enter a CMC for the call to be extended.

Valid CMCs are created in the system and associated with the company that will be paying for the services of the organization. For calls to be extended, users have to enter a valid CMC.

FACs are used to prevent calls from being placed by unauthorized users. Some organizations use unique FACs for every user in the system for legal or accounting reasons. We will investigate using FACs as another way of restricting calls similar to using CSSs. If a route pattern is matched to a pattern that has a FAC applied, the user is prompted to enter a FAC for the call to be extended. CSSs and FACs are not mutually exclusive; they can be used together.

Valid FACs are added to CUCM, and an authorization level is assigned to FACs. If a FAC is required for a route pattern, the minimum required authorization level has to be specified at the route pattern. Users have to enter a valid authorization code whose authorization level is equal to or greater than the level configured at the FAC-enabled router pattern.

Figure 13-18 illustrates a CMC application where UserA dials a number that matches a route pattern where the Require Client Matter Code parameter is checked. CUCM plays a tone to indicate to the user that a CMC has to be entered. The user has to enter a valid CMC for the call to be extended. In the example, CMCs 1234, 1244, and 3489 are configured. The user entered 1234. If the user does not terminate the code with the # sign, the user will have to wait until the interdigit timeout (T.302 timer) expires (15 seconds by default). The call is successful, and the entered CMC is included in the generated CDR.

Figure 13-18 *Client Matter Code: Successful Operation*

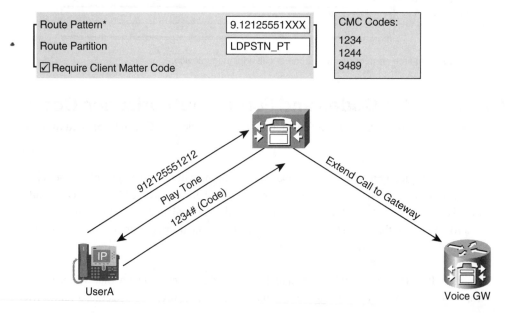

Figure 13-19 uses the same configuration as the preceding example, but this time UserA enters 5555 at the CMC prompt. This is not a valid CMC; therefore, the call is denied. A CDR is generated for the attempted call if the CDR Log Calls with a Zero Duration Flag CallManager service parameter has been enabled. Calls with zero duration flags are not logged in CDRs by default.

Figure 13-19 *Client Matter Code: Call Failure*

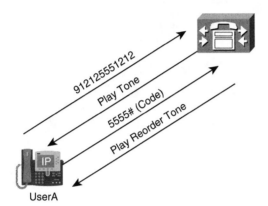

Route Pattern*	9.12125551XXX
Route Partition	LDPSTN_PT
☑ Require Client Matter Code	

CMC Codes:

1234
1244
3489

912125551212
Play Tone
5555# (Code)
Play Reorder Tone

UserA

Voice GW

In Figure 13-20, UserA dials a number that matches a route pattern where the Require Forced Authorization Code parameter is checked and the Authorization Level is set to 3. CUCM plays a tone to indicate to the user that a FAC has to be entered. The user has to enter a valid FAC with an authorization level of 3 or above for the call to be extended. At the prompt, the user enters 1888. Because the FAC level of the code was equal to or higher than the required authorization level, the call is successful, and the name of the entered FAC is included in the generated CDR.

Figure 13-21 has the same configuration as the preceding example, but this time UserA enters 1234 at the FAC prompt. The call is denied because the authorization level of the entered FAC is lower than the required level configured at the route pattern. A CDR is generated logging the attempted call.

Figure 13-20 *Forced Authorization Code: Successful Operation*

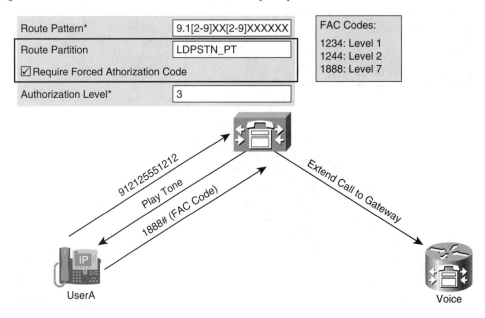

Figure 13-21 *Forced Authorization Code: Call Failure*

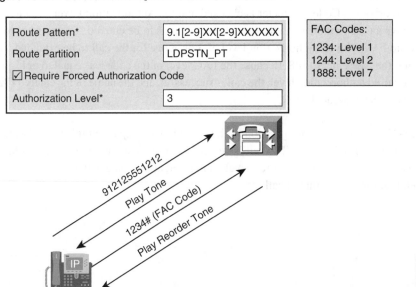

Class of Service Approaches

CoS applications in CUCM can be summarized as two distinctly separate implementations: the traditional approach and the line-device approach. This section investigates the difference between these two approaches and explains the advantages of using the line-device approach.

Figure 13-22 shows a simple single-site CoS deployment with four distinct classes of service. Four partitions and four CSSs have been created. The route patterns for each call type have been put into their respective partitions. The CSSs will be assigned to various devices in the infrastructure. This is as simple as CoS gets.

Figure 13-22   *Single Site with Four CoS Definitions*

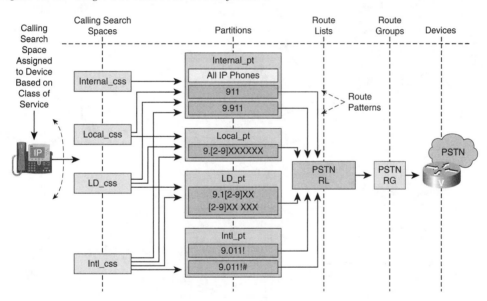

If the organization chooses to use the centralized call-processing model and an additional site is added to the cluster, four more site-specific partitions will need to be created, and four additional CSSs. In addition, the PSTN route patterns will need to be duplicated and put into their site-specific partitions. The challenge in this scenario is that partitions and CSSs need to provide two functions: 1) select the local PSTN gateway, and 2) control who is allowed to dial what number.

Figure 13-23 illustrates a summary of the partitions, CSSs, and route patterns necessary to achieve this solution. The solution includes four partitions per site: emergency partition, local partition, national partition, and international partition. The number of required partitions is calculated by multiplying the number of required classes of service by the number of sites. The example includes four classes of service per site. Implementations may involve considerably more partitions and CSSs per site.

> **NOTE** The traditional model of designing CoS in CUCM does not scale to large deployments involving 25 or more sites.

Figure 13-23 *Centralized Call Processing with Four CoS Definitions*

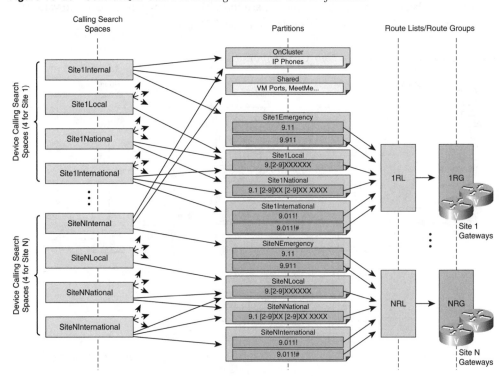

The traditional approach, outlined in the preceding section, can result in a large number of partitions and CSSs when applied to large multisite deployments with centralized call processing. This configuration is required because the device CSS is used to determine both the path selection (which PSTN gateway to use for external calls) and the CoS.

It is possible to significantly decrease the total number of partitions and CSSs needed by dividing the functions of site-specific routing and CoS between the line CSS and the device CSS. The use of both a line- and a device-based CSS is called the line-device approach.

In the line-device approach, CUCM performs a concatenation of both the line and device CSSs for each IP phone. Follow these rules to implement the line-device approach:

■ Use the device CSS to provide site-specific call-routing information (which gateway to select for PSTN calls). The device CSS will be an unrestricted CSS. This CSS is not used to enforce CoS.

■ Use the line CSS to block the route patterns that are not allowed by CoS (independent of the used PSTN gateway). This can be done effectively with translation patterns with a block action that are put into partitions that only the line CSSs have access to.

■ To implement the line device CSS approach, a per-site unrestricted CSS will be configured. This CSS will be applied at the phone configuration page to implement a device-based CSS. Recall that every DN (line) inherits this CSS by default. This CSS will contain a partition featuring route patterns that route the calls to the appropriate local gateway per site.

■ Create CSSs containing partitions featuring blocked route patterns for those types of calls not permitted by a user's CoS, and assign them to the lines of the user's phone. If a user has access to all types of calls except international, that user's line (or lines) should be configured with a CSS whose first partition includes a route pattern that blocks calls to 9.011!. Recall that CUCM will process the line CSS before the device CSS. Even though the international call is permitted at the device level, the international call is explicitly blocked at the line level CSS. As soon as CUCM matches on a pattern in the line CSS, the call is routed or blocked. The user placing the blocked call will hear a reorder tone or an annunciator message (if the annunciator media resource is active). Figure 13-24 illustrates this procedure.

Figure 13-24 *Line-Device CoS Approach*

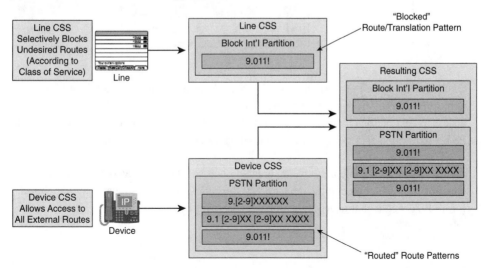

Figure 13-25 illustrates the line-device approach with multiple sites. This approach results in a significantly simpler configuration with many fewer partitions and CSSs.

Figure 13-25 *Line-Device CoS with Multiple Sites*

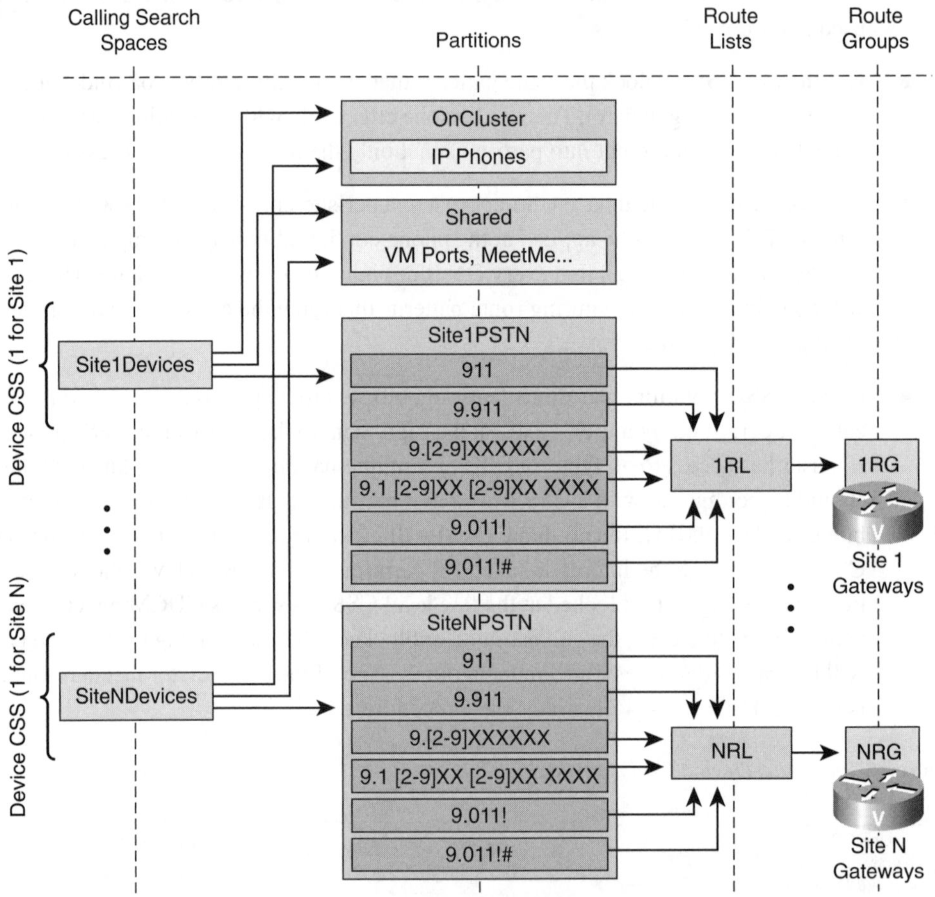

One partition is used per CoS that blocks those destinations that are not desired by the appropriate CoS. These partitions are included in the device's line CSS to always block access to destinations that are not permitted for the corresponding CoS, regardless of the PSTN gateway that is going to be used by devices of a certain location.

All possible PSTN route patterns are created once per PSTN gateway and put into a partition that is included at the device CSS, thus allowing the local gateway to be used for all PSTN calls that have not been blocked earlier by the line CSS.

This approach has the significant advantage that only a single, site-specific partition (and device CSS) is required for each site to allow local gateway selection, and only one partition per CoS (independent of the site) is required to perform CoS enforcement.

Instead of requiring the number of partitions determined by multiplying classes of service and sites, the number of partitions is determined by adding the required sites and classes of service.

A deployment with four sites and four classes of service using the traditional approach would result in 16 partitions, whereas the line-device approach results in only 8 required partitions.

911 and Vanity Numbers

911 is a single number to call for medical, fire, and police emergencies in the United States and Canada. Calls to 911 are routed to a public safety answering point (PSAP). The PSAP is the first-tier triage call center for emergency calls. PSAP operators dispatch medical, fire, and police resources as necessary.

Emergency calls have to be sent to a local PSAP through the local gateway. In a multisite deployment, all emergency calls are placed to the same number, but they need to be routed differently depending on the calling phone's physical location.

> **NOTE**   Emergency calling in the United States and Canada includes many additional aspects that are not covered in this book.

Vanity numbers provide access to a certain local service within an enterprise. Users should be able to dial the same number to access the appropriate locally provided service no matter where they are located. Some companies, for example, use the DTMF keypad word HELP (4357) to dial the IT help desk.

An example of vanity services is a number that connects users to local IT support. Vanity numbers are not limited to internal services; they could also be configured to reach external local services (taxi, travel agencies, and so forth) by using abbreviated dialing within the corporate dial plan.

A vanity number can be configured as a DN, a route pattern, a hunt pilot, or a translation pattern.

Implementing vanity numbers is similar to configuring selective PSTN outbreak (always using the local gateway for PSTN or emergency calls) and consists of the following steps:

Step 1   Create a site-specific partition per site.

Step 2   For each service, configure the same vanity number (route pattern, DN, hunt pilot, or translation pattern) once per site and put it into the site-specific partition created earlier.

Step 3   Put the appropriate site-specific partition into the CSS of the phones located at a site.

> **NOTE**   If abbreviated dialing is used to reach external local services (such as a local travel agency by dialing 7998), a translation pattern is used for the vanity number.

Figure 13-26 shows a vanity number for IT support that is configured as 7999. Both the New York and San Jose sites will use this same IT support vanity number. The DN of 7999 located in San Jose is put into the San Jose partition. The same DN is configured in the New York partition. Phones located in New York have partition New York listed first in their CSS; phones located in San Jose have partition San Jose listed first in their CSS.

If a San Jose user dials 7999, the call is routed to the IT help desk in San Jose because the New York DN of 7999 is not accessible by the San Jose phone. The San Jose CSS does not include the New York partition. The same call-routing theory applies to users in New York. Calls placed to 7999 in New York are routed to the local New York IT help desk.

Figure 13-26   *Vanity Number Example*

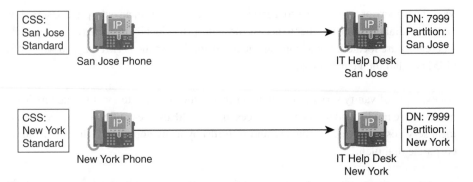

If the desired services are provided externally, a translation pattern is configured to translate the appropriate vanity number. Instead of memorizing a long number for the travel agency (which may change over time), users can be given a phone number that aligns to the corporate dial plan. The translation pattern will match on the dialed digits of 7998 and manipulate the digits to 1 914 555-1212 by using a called-party transformation mask. Over time, if there are changes to the external number, users will not need to know the new phone number. The CUCM administrator can reconfigure the called-party transformation mask. By creating the vanity number once per site and putting it into a site-specific partition, you can ensure that users always match the vanity number translation pattern for their respective site. This is achieved by including the site-specific partition in the phone CSS.

Figure 13-26 would use two translation patterns to achieve this objective. Each translation pattern would be placed in a site-specific partition. Configure the San Jose translation pattern with the PSTN number of the San Jose travel agency; configure the New York translation pattern with the PSTN number of the New York travel agency. Make sure that the translation patterns have CSSs assigned that allow them to use the local PSTN gateway for routing the calls out to the translated PSTN numbers.

Private Line Automatic Ringdown

Private line automatic ringdown (PLAR) is used when a phone should dial a predefined number as soon as the phone goes off-hook. PLAR is typically used with button-free security phones in elevators and stairways.

Implement PLAR in CUCM by following these steps:

Step 1   Configure a translation pattern where the pattern is empty (null string pattern), and put it into a partition.

Step 2   Configure the number to be dialed by the PLAR-enabled phone in the called-party transformation mask of the translation pattern.

Step 3   Configure the first line of the phone that should use PLAR with a CSS that includes only the partition that was applied to the translation pattern.

Step 4   Make sure that the CSS of the translation pattern has access to the transformed number. The translation pattern CSS is used when making the call-routing decision for the translated number.

When the phone goes off-hook, the off-hook event triggers call processing (digit analysis) on CUCM, where the null dialed string matches the translation pattern and is translated to the PLAR number. The call is then extended toward the PLAR destination. CUCM performs digit analysis as each digit is received from the phone, starting with the off-hook event. Different call-processing protocols (SIP, Skinny Client Control Protocol [SCCP], H.323) and calling methods send their dialed digits in different manners (enbloc or digit by digit), and thus the way in which a call is routed with an overlapping dial plan. This information is covered in more detail in Chapter 7, "Endpoints."

In Figure 13-27, a null-string translation pattern is created and put into partition PLAR1234. The called-party transformation mask is 1234. The translation pattern has a CSS assigned that includes partition Phones (the partition of destination 1234).

Figure 13-27   *PLAR Example*

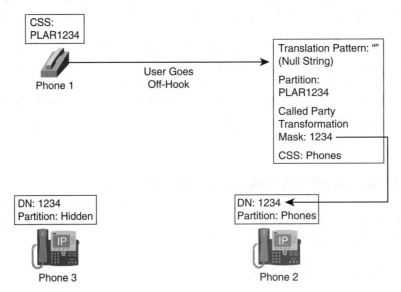

Phone 1 is configured with a CSS that contains the PLAR1234 partition (the partition of the translation pattern).

Two phones exist with DN 1234: Phone 2 is in partition Phones, and Phone 3 is in partition Hidden.

When Phone 1 goes off-hook, the null-string pattern is matched, and the translation pattern transforms the dialed null-string to 1234 and sends a call-routing request to CUCM. This request uses the CSS of the translation pattern (Phones) and therefore finds only a single match (Phone 2). The call is extended to Phone 2.

Chapter Summary

The following list summarizes the key points that were discussed in this chapter:

■ Calling privileges are configured to implement class of service (CoS) or special applications that require calls to be treated differently depending on the caller.

■ Partitions are groups of called numbers with identical reachability characteristics. Calling search spaces (CSS) are lists of partitions that the owner of the CSS has access to.

- Time schedules and time periods are used to activate or deactivate partitions within a CSS depending on time or date information.

- Client matter codes (CMC) are used to track calls to certain clients by requesting the CMC to be entered and adding it into call details records (CDR). Forced authorization codes (FAC) are used to allow access to route patterns only if an authorization code with a high-enough level is entered when requested.

- Calling-privileges applications include implementation of CoS, vanity numbers, time-based route or carrier selection, and PLAR.

- Complexity of CoS implementation at IP phones can be reduced by using the line-device approach, which allows the effective CSS to be composed of a line and device CSS (in this order).

- Vanity numbers provide access to local services by dialing the same number from any physical location.

- Time schedules and time periods can be used to route calls via different gateways or carriers depending on the time of the day or date to take advantage of the cheapest rate at any time.

- PLAR, a function where a phone is automatically connected to a predefined number when it goes off-hook, is implemented by using null-string translation patterns, partitions, and CSS.

Review Questions

Use the questions here to review what you learned in this chapter. The correct answers are found in Appendix A, "Answers to Chapter Review Questions."

1. What are the calling privileges of a user in the telephony system called?

   a. Class of service

   b. Calling search space

   c. Partition

   d. Capabilities

2. Phone numbers (directory numbers, partitions, translation patterns) are assigned to which dial plan element to achieve calling privileges?

   a. Calling search space

   b. Partition

   c. Class of service

   d. Route list

3. What is assigned to a phone or directory number to implement calling privileges?

   a. Calling search space

   b. Partition

   c. Class of service

   d. Route list

4. Which two elements are used to control how calls are routed based on the time of day?

   a. Time-based ACLs

   b. Time period

   c. Time range

   d. Time interval

   e. Time list

5. Which element is used to verify the calling privileges of a user after the digits have been dialed?

   a. Client matter code

   b. Partition

   c. Calling search space

   d. Forced authorization code

6. If a device contains both a device and line CSS, how will they be processed by CUCM?

   a. Line CSS overrides device CSS.

   b. Device CSS overrides line CSS.

   c. Both are concatenated. Line CSS is processed before device CSS.

   d. Both are concatenated. Device CSS is processed before line CSS.

7. Calling search spaces are *not* applied to which one of the following?

   a. Directory numbers

   b. Phones

   c. Translation patterns

   d. Voice-mail ports

   e. Route patterns

   f. Trunks

   g. Gateways

8. In the line-device CSS approach, the device CSS achieves which objective?

   a. Class of service

   b. Least-cost routing

   c. Site-specific call routing

   d. Tail-end hop off

9. A phone number that is used in the system to abbreviate the numbers that users need to remember is referred to as a what?

   a. Hunt pilot

   b. Route pattern

   c. Translation pattern

   d. Vanity number

10. A PLAR line uses which of the following dial plan elements?

   a. Route pattern

   b. Route list

   c. Translation pattern

   d. Directory number

CHAPTER **14**

Call Coverage

Many businesses have sales or service departments that handle inbound calls from customers. These businesses typically need several phone lines and a way to make the lines work together in a cohesive manner. If a representative is busy or not available, incoming calls to the group will rotate to available members of the group. The call is distributed in this way until it is answered or forwarded to an auto-attendant or voice mail. Hunt groups are the mechanisms that help these businesses manage inbound calls. A hunt group is a group of telephone lines that are associated with a common number. When a call comes in to the number associated with the hunt group, the call cycles through the group of lines until an available line is found. This process is known as hunting.

This lesson describes how to implement hunt groups and enable the other call-coverage features such as call forwarding, shared lines, and call pickup.

Chapter Objectives

Upon completing this lesson, you will be able to describe and configure call-coverage components in CUCM and be able to meet the following objectives:

- Identify call coverage options in CUCM.

- Describe call forwarding, shared lines, and call pickup.

- Describe call-hunting implementation in CUCM.

- Describe call-hunting options and line-group distribution algorithms.

- Describe the process of call hunting.

- Implement call hunting in CUCM.

Call Coverage

Call coverage is part of the dial plan. It ensures that all incoming calls are answered. The following call-coverage features are typically implemented for individuals:

- **Call forwarding**: If the called phone does not answer the call, the call should be forwarded to another phone or voice mail.

- **Shared lines**: A shared line is a directory number (DN) that is assigned to more than one device, allowing the call to be accepted on more than one phone.

- **Call pickup**: Call pickup allows a call that is ringing on a phone to be picked up at another phone.

In addition, there is a more complex and highly flexible feature providing call coverage called call hunting. Call hunting is based on a pilot number, which if directly called or used as a call-forward target allows hunting through multiple line groups. Several hunting algorithms exist, ranging from a round-robin selection of group members to a broadcast option that rings all members of a line group.

There are three primary types of call forwarding:

- **Call Forward All (CFA)**: The CFA feature forwards all calls unconditionally. CFA can be configured by the phone user from either the user web page (covered in Chapter 16, "User Features") or at the phone itself. If CFA is configured, the call is forwarded immediately without ringing the originally dialed phone. The CUCM administrator can also configure the CFA target.

- **Call Forward No Answer (CFNA)**: CFNA forwards calls if the call is not answered within a specified amount of time. CFNA can be configured by the administrator in CUCM Administration or by the phone user from the user web page.

- **Call Forward Busy (CFB)**: CFB forwards calls that are received while the IP phone is in use with another call. CFB can be configured by the administrator in CUCM Administration or by the phone user from the user web page.

The administrator can configure separate calling search spaces (CSS) for each call-forward type. For CFNA and CFB, different CSSs can be set for internal (on-net) calls and for external (off-net) calls. For CFA, a primary and a secondary CFA can be configured. These two get concatenated like a device and line CSS. For all call-forward scenarios, the corresponding call-forward CSSs are used; line and device CSSs are ignored. Therefore, if the system uses partitions, it is recommended to always set call-forward CSSs because otherwise forward operations are likely to fail. Figure 14-1 illustrates call forwarding.

Figure 14-1 *Call Forwarding*

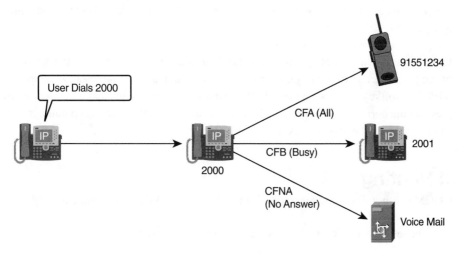

A shared line is implemented by assigning the same DN to multiple phones. If the number is called, all phones that are configured with this shared line number ring. The first user who accepts the call is connected to the caller, and all other phones stop ringing. Figure 14-2 illustrates shared lines.

Figure 14-2 *Shared Lines*

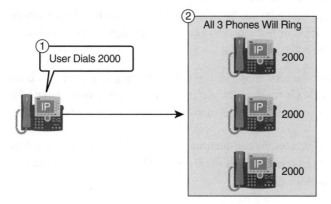

CUCM allows multiple lines to be grouped into call-pickup groups. Each pickup group is identified by a unique pickup group number. A phone line can be assigned to only one pickup group.

If a phone rings but there is nobody at the ringing phone to answer the call, another user can pick up the call by using the Pickup softkey if the ringing phone is in the same pickup group.

In the same situation, if the phone of the user who wants to pick up the call is not a member of the pickup group of the ringing phone, the user can use the *group pickup* feature (GPickup softkey) to pick up the call. When a user invokes the group pickup feature by pressing the corresponding softkey, the user has to enter the pickup group number of the ringing phone to be able to pick up the call.

Call Hunting

CUCM call-hunting implementation is composed of the following components:

- Phone DNs or voice-mail ports are assigned to line groups.

- Line groups are assigned to hunt lists. A hunt list can have one or more line groups. Line group hunt options and distribution algorithms can be specified to define how call hunting should be performed for the members of the line group.

- Hunt lists are assigned to hunt pilots. A hunt list is an ordered list of one or more line groups.

- Hunt pilots are the numbers that will match on dialed digits to invoke the hunting process. A hunt pilot can be called directly or a call may be forwarded to the hunt pilot from an IP phone that received a call and is configured to forward calls to the hunt pilot to provide call coverage.

While hunting, the forwarding configuration of line group members is not used. If the hunting algorithm is ringing a phone and the call is not answered, the CFNA setting of that phone is ignored, and the hunting algorithm goes on to the next line group member.

Figure 14-3 illustrates the call-hunting process and components. The hunt pilot in this example has been configured as 1 800 555-0111. Calls are distributed among the four DNs at the bottom of the figure.

Figure 14-3 *Call Hunting*

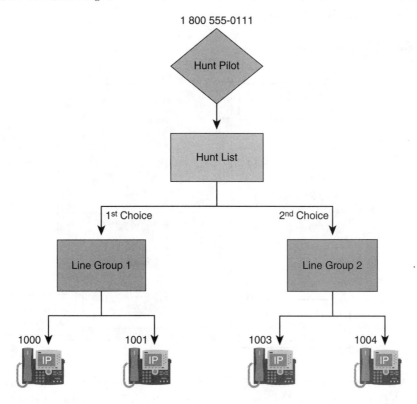

In the following example, two line groups are configured:

- **Agents line group**: Contains the DNs 2001 and 2002.

- **Operators line group**: Contains the DNs 2101 and 2102.

The line groups are assigned to the hunt list HelpDesk:

- The first line group is Agents.

- The second line group is Operators.

A hunt pilot of HelpDesk with the pattern 2222 is configured to use hunt list HelpDesk for call coverage.

Figure 14-4 and the list that follows illustrate the call-coverage components involved in distributing a call from the hunt pilot.

Figure 14-4   *Call-Hunting Process*

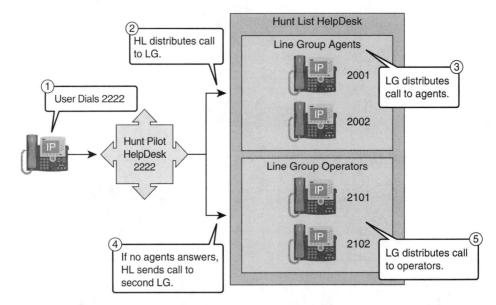

1. A call is received for extension 2222. The CUCM digit analysis result matches the hunt pilot number of 2222. The hunt pilot distributes the call to the hunt list HelpDesk.

2. The hunt list uses top-down processing of the line groups. The first line group of Agents is processed.

3. The line group distributes the call to agent DNs. Assuming the top-down call-distribution algorithm was selected, 2001 would ring, then 2002. The various call-distribution algorithms are covered later in this chapter.

4. If no agent answers, the hunt list sends the call to the second line group, Operators.

5. The line group Operators distributes the call to the operator DNs.

Hunt pilots are dialable patterns in the call-routing database (similar to route patterns, translation patterns, and DNs). The hunt pilot points to a hunt list. The hunt list points to one or more line groups, which include DNs.

Beginning with CUCM Release 4.1, calls can be redirected to a final destination when the hunting fails. Hunting may fail for one of the following reasons:

■   All hunting options have been exhausted, and the call has not been answered.

■   The maximum hunt timer has expired (configured at the hunt list level).

This call redirection is configured in the Hunt Forward Settings section of the Hunt Pilot Configuration page, and the destination for this redirect can be either of the following options:

■   A specific destination configured globally at the hunt pilot.

■   A personal preference, configured at the DN of the originally called number when hunting on behalf of that number fails. The personal preference is configured using the CFNC settings at the phone line.

You can implement the personal preferences option by configuring a user's phone so that the Forward No Answer field redirects the call to a hunt pilot, to search for someone else who can answer the call. If the call hunting fails, either because all the hunting options were exhausted or because a timeout period expired, the call can be sent to a destination personalized for the person who was originally called. For example, if the Forward No Coverage field is set to voice mail, the call will be sent to that person's voice-mail box when hunting fails.

The following considerations apply to calls handled by hunt pilots:

■   Call Pickup and Group Call Pickup are not supported on calls distributed by a hunt pilot. A member of the line group cannot pick up the hunt pilot call offered to another member in the line group, even if they belong to the same call-pickup group.

■   The hunt pilot can distribute calls to any of its line group members, regardless of the partition of the line group member. Class of service is not implemented in the call-coverage paradigm.

A hunt list is a prioritized list of line groups used for call coverage. Hunt lists have the following characteristics:

■   Multiple hunt pilots can point to the same hunt list.

■   Multiple hunt lists can contain the same line group.

■   A hunt list is a prioritized list of line groups; line groups are hunted in the order of their configuration in the hunt list.

Line groups control the order in which a call is distributed, and they have the following characteristics:

■ Line groups point to specific extensions, which are typically IP phone extensions or voice-mail ports.

■ The same extension may be present in multiple line groups.

■ Line groups are configured with a global distribution algorithm that is used to select the next line group member for hunting.

■ Line groups are configured with a hunt option that describes how hunting should be continued after trying the first member of the line group. The hunt option is configured per hunt failure event: No Answer, Busy, and Not Available.

■ The Ring No Answer Reversion (RNAR) timeout specifies how long the hunting algorithm rings a member of the line group before it continues hunting according to the line group No Answer hunt option setting.

Line group members are the endpoints accessed by line groups, and they can be of any of the following types:

■ Any SCCP endpoints, such as Cisco Unified IP Phone models VG248 or ATA 188

■ SIP endpoints

■ Voice-mail ports

■ H.323 clients

■ Foreign Exchange Station (FXS) extensions attached to an Media Gateway Control Protocol (MGCP) gateway

Computer telephony integration (CTI) ports and CTI route points cannot be added to a line group. Therefore, calls cannot be distributed to endpoints controlled through CTI applications such as Cisco Customer Response Solution (CRS), Cisco Unified IP Interactive Voice Response (IVR), and so forth.

Call-Hunting Options and Distribution Algorithms

Various hunt options are available at the line group configuration level. The default works for most implementations, but life is rife with options to accommodate the requirements of various organizations and collaborative groups. The following hunt options are available:

■ **Try Next Member, Then, Try Next Group in Hunt List (Default)**: Sends the call to the next idle or available member of this line group. If no more members are available in this line group, go to the next line group configured in the hunt list. If no more line groups are available, hunting stops.

- **Try Next Member, but Do Not Go to Next Group**: Sends the call to the next idle or available member of this line group. If no more members are available in this line group, hunting stops.

- **Skip Remaining Members, and Go Directly to Next Group**: Sends the call to the next line group. If no more line groups are available, hunting stops.

- **Stop Hunting**: Do not proceed to the next Line Group or next member.

The line group distribution algorithm specifies the order line in which group members should be used during the hunting process. The available algorithms are as follows:

- **Top down**: If you choose a top-down distribution algorithm, CUCM distributes the call to idle or available members starting from the first idle or available member at the top of the line group to the last idle or available member (bottom of the list). In Figure 14-5, a top-down distribution algorithm would extend the next call to 1000, then to 1001, then to 1002, then 1003, and back to 1000 depending on the line state of the destination DN. An important distinction in this model is that every new call attempts to use extension 1000, no matter how long the lines in the line group are idle. If extension 1000 is available every time there is a new call distributed, extension 1000 will receive the call. The user at extension 1000 would be very busy in this model.

- **Circular**: If you choose a circular distribution algorithm, CUCM distributes the call to idle or available members starting from the first member of the line group (1000). CUCM retains the most recently extended call target in memory and attempts to place the second call to the second member of the line group (1001). The third call is distributed to the third member of the line group (1002), and the fourth call is extended to the fourth member of the line group (1003). The circular distribution algorithm might appear to be the same as the top-down distribution algorithm, but it is much fairer in its distribution of calls.

- **Longest idle time**: If you choose a longest idle time distribution algorithm, CUCM distributes the call to the member that has been idle for the longest amount of time. Only members in the idle call state are considered by this distribution algorithm. Available and busy call states do not receive calls. A phone in the available state is servicing a call but can manage a second call. Figure 14-5 assumes that 1000 has been idle for 10 minutes and 1003 has been idle for 5 minutes. A longest idle time distribution mechanism extends the call to extension 1000.

- **Broadcast**: If you choose a broadcast distribution algorithm, CUCM distributes the call to all idle or available members of a line group simultaneously.

Distribution algorithms are configured once per line group in CUCM Administration.

Figure 14-5 *Line Group Distribution Algorithms*

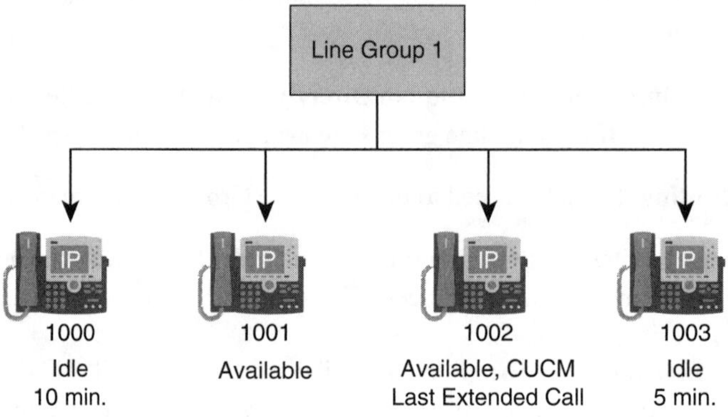

Call-Hunting Flow

The call-hunting flow in CUCM is as follows:

1. A direct call is placed to the hunt pilot number, or a call is forwarded to the hunt pilot number from a phone.

2. The hunt pilot starts the maximum hunt timer to monitor the overall hunting time. If the timer expires, hunting stops, and final forwarding is performed. The hunt pilot is logically associated with a hunt list.

3. The hunt list associated with the hunt pilot sends the call to the first line group configured in the hunt list.

    —The call is sent to the next line group member based on the distribution algorithm configured at the line group. Each line group is attempted until all resources are exhausted (or the maximum hunt timer expires).

4. If the call to the hunt pilot goes unanswered, hunt failure has occurred. Possible hunt failure reasons include no one answered the phone or everyone is busy servicing other customers.

Figure 14-6 illustrates the call-coverage distribution of a call destined to a hunt pilot of 7000.

Figure 14-7 illustrates the final forwarding options of the hunt pilot configuration.

If hunting stops (ring no answer or busy) and the hunt pilot is not configured for final forwarding, the call fails and a reorder tone is played.

If a final forwarding number is specified at the hunt pilot, the call is routed to the number.

If Use Personal Preference is selected, the call is routed as configured for Call Forward No Coverage at the phone line that invoked the call to the pilot number.

Figure 14-6 *Call-Hunting Flow*

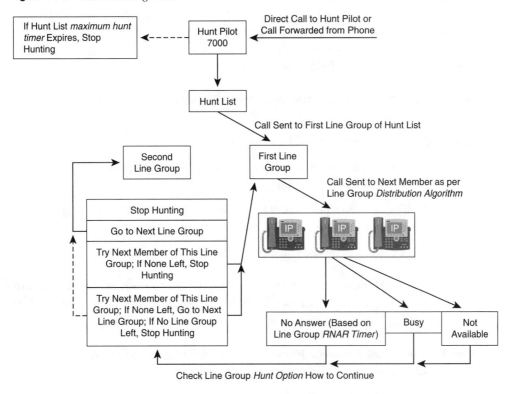

Figure 14-7 *Call-Hunting Flow*

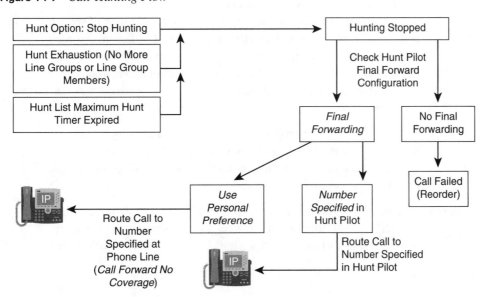

Call-Hunting Configuration

To access the line group, hunt list, and hunt pilot configuration windows in CUCM Administration, choose **Call Routing > Route/Hunt**.

When configuring hunting, follow these steps:

Step 1   Create the line groups, add members, and configure the distribution algorithm and hunt options.

Step 2   Create the hunt list and add the line groups.

Step 3   Create the hunt pilot, associate the hunt list with the hunt pilot, and configure hunt forward settings.

Step 4   Configure personal preferences on phone lines in the event that hunting ends with no coverage.

These steps are covered in more detail on the following pages.

The DNs that will become the members of the line group must already exist in the database before you can complete this procedure. The following steps describe the creation of a line group. The configuration of the line group is illustrated in Figure 14-8.

Step 1   Choose **Call Routing > Route/Hunt > Line Group** from CUCM Administration.

Step 2   Click the **Add New** button.

Step 3   Enter a name in the Line Group Name field. The name can contain up to 50 alphanumeric characters and can contain any combination of spaces, periods (.), hyphens (-), and underscore characters (_). Ensure that each line group name is unique to the route plan. Use a naming nomenclature that is brief and descriptive of the line group usage in the environment. It is good practice to append _LG to the line group name so that it can be easily identified.

Step 4   Configure the distribution algorithm, hunt options, and ring no answer reversion (RNAR) timeout as desired. The RNAR parameter limits the amount of time (in seconds) that each DN in the line group rings before CUCM reports a No Answer condition.

Step 5   Add members to the line group. To locate a DN, choose a route partition from the Partition drop-down list, enter a search string in the Directory Number Contains field, and click **Find**. To find all DNs that belong to a partition, leave the Directory Number Contains field blank and click **Find**. A list of matching DNs is displayed in the Available DN/Route Partition pane.

Step 6 In the Available DN/Route Partition pane, select a DN to add and click **Add to Line Group** to move it to the Selected DN/Route Partition pane. Repeat this step for each member that you want to add to this line group.

Step 7 In the Selected DN/Route Partition pane, choose the order in which the new DNs will be accessed in this line group. To change the order, click a DN and use the up and down arrows to the right of the pane.

Step 8 Click **Save** to add the new DNs and to update the DN order for this line group.

Figure 14-8 *Line Group Configuration*

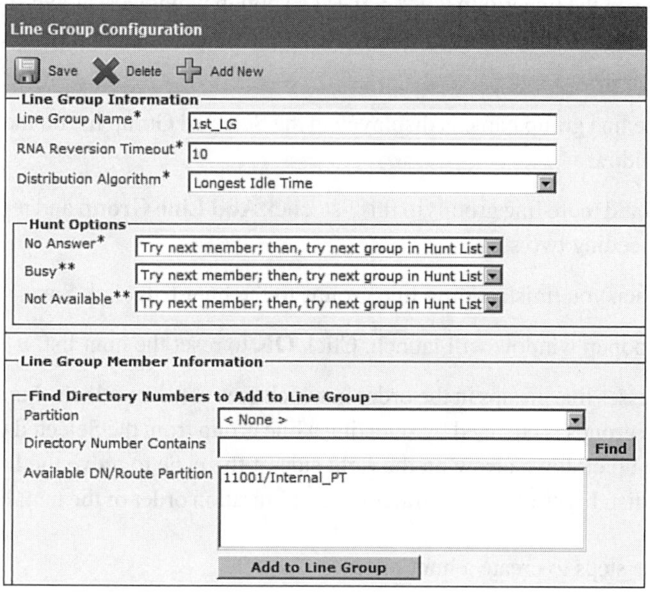

To add a hunt list, follow these steps:

Step 1 Choose **Call Routing > Route/Hunt > Hunt List**.

Step 2 Click the **Add New** button.

Step 3   In the Name field, enter a descriptive name for the hunt list functionality and append _HL to indicate that the item is a hunt list. The name can include up to 50 alphanumeric characters and can contain any combination of spaces, periods (.), hyphens (-), and underscore characters (_). Each hunt list name must be unique.

Step 4   Choose a CUCM group from the drop-down list.

Step 5   Click the **Save** button. The Hunt List Configuration window will display the newly added hunt list.

Step 6   Add at least one line group to the new hunt list. To add a line group, click **Add Line Group**. The Hunt List Detail Configuration window will open.

Step 7   From the Line Group drop-down list, choose a line group to add to the hunt list.

To add the line group, click **Save**. The popup window is shown stating that for the changes to take effect, you must reset the hunt list. Click **OK** to confirm the message.

The line group name is displayed in the Selected Group list on the right side of the window.

Step 8   To add more line groups to this list, click **Add Line Group** and repeat the preceding two steps.

Step 9   When you finish adding line groups to the hunt list, click **Save**.

Step 10 A popup window will launch. Click **OK** to reset the hunt list.

CUCM accesses line groups in the order in which they are shown in the hunt list. The access order of line groups is changed by selecting a line group from the Selected Groups pane and clicking the up or down arrow on the right side of the pane to move the line group up or down in the list. Figure 14-9 illustrates the configuration order of the hunt list configuration.

Follow these steps to create a hunt pilot:

Step 1   Choose **Call Routing > Route/Hunt > Hunt Pilot** from the menu.

Step 2   Click the **Add New** button.

Step 3   Enter the hunt pilot number in the Hunt Pilot field.

Step 4   Assign the hunt pilot to a hunt list using the Hunt List drop-down list.

Step 5   Scroll down to the bottom of the page to configure final forwarding settings and the maximum hunt timer.

Step 6   Click the **Save** button.

Figure 14-9 *Hunt List Configuration*

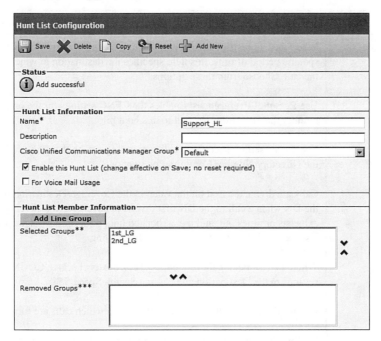

The hunt pilot configuration is illustrated in Figure 14-10. The Hunt Forward Settings pane of the Hunt Pilot Configuration window specifies the final forwarding settings and maximum timer values, as described in Table 14-1.

Figure 14-10 *Hunt Pilot Configuration*

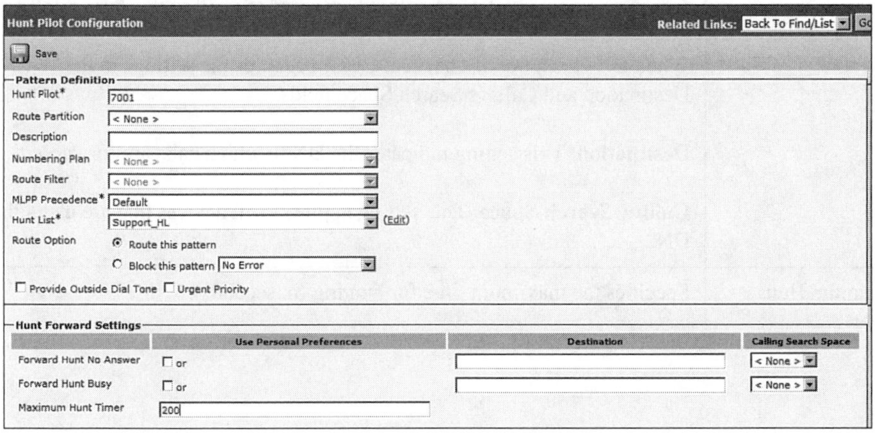

Table 14-1 *Hunt Forward Settings*

Setting	Description
Forward Hunt No Answer	When the call distributed through the hunt list is not answered within a specific period of time, this field specifies the destination to which to forward the call. Choose from these options: **Use Personal Preferences**: Enables the CFNC settings for the original called number that forwarded the call to this hunt pilot. The CFNC setting specifies a call-forwarding reason that you administer in the Directory Number Configuration window. Calls are diverted based on the value in the Coverage/Destination field of the DN when a call to the DN first diverts to coverage, and coverage either exhausts or times out, and the associated hunt pilot for coverage specifies Use Personal Preferences for its final forwarding. When the Use Personal Preferences check box is checked, CUCM ignores the settings in the Destination and Calling Search Space fields. **Destination**: This setting indicates the DN to which calls are forwarded. **Calling Search Space**: This setting applies to all devices that are using this DN.
Forward Hunt Busy	When the call distributed through the hunt list encounters only busy lines for a specific period of time, this field specifies the destination to which to forward the call. Choose from these options: **Use Personal Preferences**: Use this check box to enable the CFNC settings for the original called number that forwarded the call to this hunt pilot. When this check box is checked, CUCM ignores the settings in the Destination and Calling Search Space fields. **Destination**: This setting indicates the DN to which calls are forwarded. **Calling Search Space**: This setting applies to all devices that are using this DN.
Maximum Hunt Timer	Specifies the maximum time for hunting (in seconds).

The Directory Number Configuration window provides configuration options for internal and external forwarding based on whether a call is CFA or CFNA, as specified in Table 14-2.

Table 14-2 *Hunt Forward Settings*

Field	Description
Forward All	Specifies the forwarding treatment for calls to this DN if the DN is set to forward all calls. **Voice Mail**: Check this check box to use settings in the Voice Mail Profile Configuration window. When this check box is checked, CUCM ignores the settings in the Destination and Calling Search Space fields. **Destination**: This setting indicates the DN to which all calls are forwarded. Use any dialable phone number, including an outside destination. **Calling Search Space**: This setting applies to all devices that are using this DN.
Forward Busy Internal Forward Busy External	When the call distributed through the hunt list encounters only busy lines for a specific period of time, this field specifies the destination to which to forward the call. Choose from these options: **Use Personal Preferences**: Use this check box to enable the CFNC settings for the original called number that forwarded the call to this hunt pilot. When this check box is checked, CUCM ignores the settings in the Destination and Calling Search Space fields. **Destination**: This setting indicates the DN to which calls are forwarded. **Calling Search Space**: This setting applies to all devices that are using this DN.

continues

Table 14-2 *Hunt Forward Settings (Continued)*

Field	Description
Forward No Answer Internal	Specifies the forwarding treatment for internal or external calls to this DN if the DN does not answer.
Forward No Answer External	**Voice Mail**: Check this check box to use settings in the Voice Mail Profile Configuration window.
	When this check box is checked, CUCM ignores the settings in the Destination and Calling Search Space fields.
	Destination: This setting indicates the DN to which an internal call is forwarded when the call is not answered. Use any dialable phone number, including an outside destination.
	Calling Search Space: This setting applies to all devices that are using this DN.
Forward No Coverage Internal	This setting applies only if you configure one of the other forwarding fields (CFA, CFB, or CFNA) with a hunt pilot number in the Destination DN field.
Forward No Coverage External	For the hunt pilot settings, you must also configure the Forward Hunt No Answer or Forward Hunt Busy fields and check the Use Personal Preferences check box under the Hunt Forward Settings section in the Hunt Pilot Configuration window; otherwise, the Forward No Coverage configuration in the Directory Number Configuration window has no effect.

The following five examples explore the related call-forwarding options used at the Cisco IP Phone and the hunt pilot configuration. In Example 14-1, User A at DN 3000 has the DN configuration illustrated in Figure 14-11.

Example 14-1 *Call Forwarding Without Forward No Coverage Settings*

Figure 14-11 shows the following configuration:

- **CFB**: Call Forward Busy has two settings: Forward Busy Internal and Forward Busy External. Both forwarding options are set to 3001. This setting forwards both internal and external (PSTN) calls to 3001 when 3000 is busy. 3001 is probably the second line of the phone, but this cannot be determined from Figure 14-11 alone.

- **CFNA**: Call Forward No Answer has two settings as well: Forward No Answer Internal and Forward No Answer External. The CFNA setting in Figure 14-11 forwards internal calls to 3001, and external calls to 303 555-0111 when 3000 does not answer.

- **CFNC**: Call Forward No Coverage does not have a configuration. Any calls that are sent back to this phone from the hunt pilot for personal treatment will result in a reorder tone.

Figure 14-11 *Call Hunting: Example 14-1*

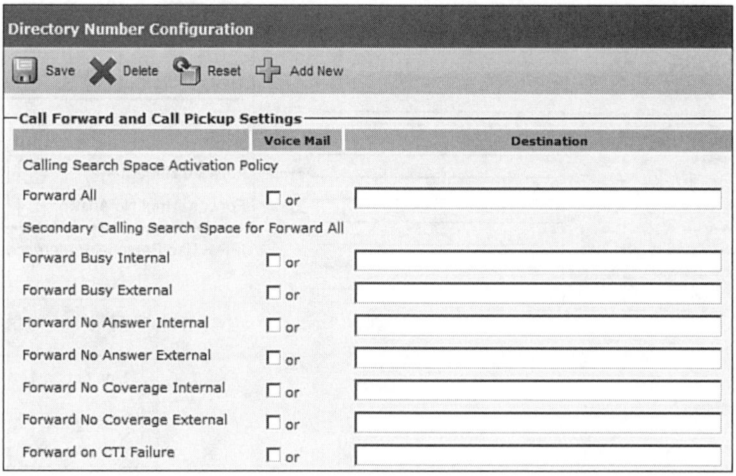

The following examples will discuss scenarios where the Hunt Pilot final forwarding rules are used. Example 14-2 is a scenario where no final forwarding rules were configured.

Example 14-2 *Forward No Coverage Examples*

User A at DN 3000 has the configuration shown in Figure 14-12 in the Directory Number Configuration window:

- **CFB**: When busy, incoming internal calls are forwarded to 3001, and external calls are forwarded to hunt pilot 7000.

- **CFNA**: When there is no answer, incoming internal calls are forwarded to 3001, whereas external calls are forwarded to hunt pilot 7000.

Hunt pilot 7000 is associated with hunt list abc and has four hunt parties equally distributed over Line Group 1 and Line Group 2. Hunt pilot 7000 has no final forwarding fields provisioned (default).

Question: What behavior results when an internal caller calls 3000 and user 3000 is busy?

Answer: The call forwards to line 3001.

Question: What behavior results when an external caller calls 3000 and user 3000 does not answer?

Answer: The call forwards to hunt pilot 7000, which will cause hunting to lines 3001, 3002, 4001, and 4002. If one of the hunt parties answers, the caller is connected to that party. If no hunt party answers, then, regardless of the reason, the caller receives a reorder tone (or an equivalent annunciator announcement).

Figure 14-12 *Call Hunting: Example 14-2*

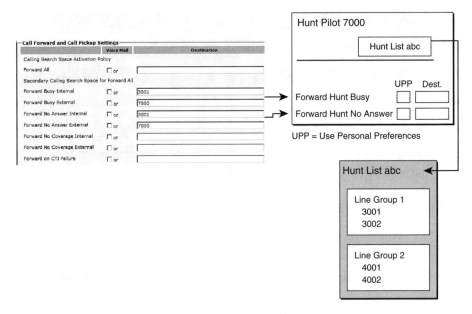

Example 14-3 *Call Coverage: Forward Hunt No Answer*

In call-hunting Example 14-3 in Figure 14-13, hunt pilot 7000 has the Forward Hunt No Answer field set to 3002, but all Forward Hunt Busy fields are empty.

Figure 14-13 *Call Hunting: Example 14-3*

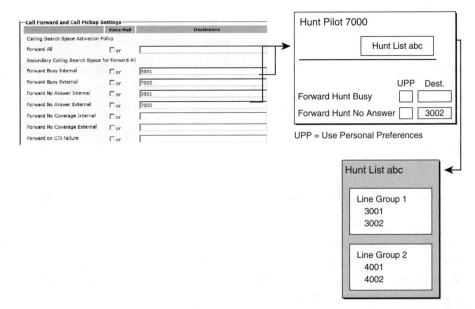

If an external caller calls 3000 and user 3000 does not answer, the call forwards to hunt pilot 7000, which causes hunting to lines 3001, 3002, 4001, and 4002. If one of the hunt parties answers, the caller is connected to that party.

If all hunt parties are busy, the caller receives a reorder tone. The reorder tone was sent because of the missing Forward Hunt Busy configuration in the hunt pilot.

If at least one hunt party is alerted (phone rings) but does not pick up, the call forwards to 3002 because 3002 is the value configured for the Forward Hunt No Answer field.

Example 14-4 illustrates a scenario where user personal preferences are used for the final forwarding for forward hunt busy. The forward hunt no answer calls to 3002.

Example 14-4   *Call Coverage: Forward Hunt Busy*

Figure 14-14 is different from Figure 14-13 because Forward Hunt Busy is configured at the hunt pilot level. The DN configuration also differs from previous examples because the DN has two Call Forward No Coverage numbers configured.

Figure 14-14   *Call Hunting: Example 14-4*

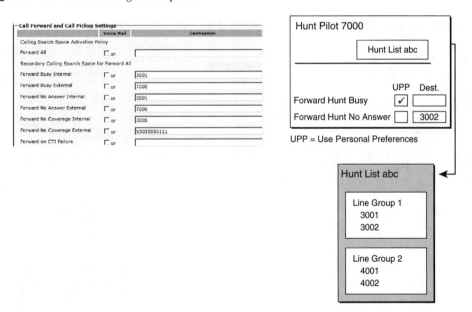

When an external caller calls 3000 and user 3000 does not answer, the call forwards to hunt pilot 7000, which hunts to lines 3001, 3002, 4001, and 4002.

If one of the hunt parties answers, the caller is connected to that party. If at least one party is alerted, but hunting exhausts the hunt list, the call is forwarded to 3002.

If all hunt parties are busy, the call is forwarded as configured by the DN that forwarded the call to the hunt pilot. The DN's Forward No Coverage External setting determines what happens to the call if the hunt pilot has Use Personal Preferences configured. In this case, the call will forward to 303 555-0111.

> **NOTE**   If the hunt pilot is configured to use personal preferences, the corresponding Forward No Coverage field should be set at the phone forwarding the call to the hunt pilot. A call forwarded from a phone to the hunt pilot leveraging personal preferences with no Forward No Coverage setting will result in a reorder tone. This is similar to the behavior when final forwarding settings are missing at the hunt pilot.

Example 14-5 illustrates a situation in which the Forward No Coverage External has not been configured. This missing configuration will cause any external calls forwarded to Hunt Pilots to result in reorder tone.

Example 14-5   *Call Coverage: Forward No Coverage External Missing*

Figure 14-15 has a similar configuration to Figure 14-14, but the DN does not have a Forward No Coverage External provisioned.

Figure 14-15   *Call Hunting: Example 14-5*

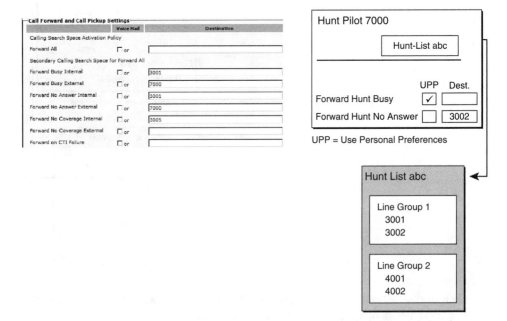

The RNAR timer for a line group determines how long hunting will ring a hunt party before moving to the next party in its list (assuming that the customer did not select the broadcast algorithm). This timer has a default value of 10 seconds.

In Figure 14-15, there are four hunt parties. How long will it take before hunting exhausts? It will take 40 seconds before hunting exhausts (10 seconds RNAR default × 4 hunt members).

Assume that the maximum hunt timer for hunt pilot 7000 is set to 25 seconds. The call must be answered within this hunt timer. In this example, the maximum hunt timer is 2.5 times the RNAR timer, which is 10 seconds.

If a user calls hunt pilot 7000, the call attempts to hunt for the four parties. If all the phones ring but no one picks up within 25 seconds, hunting terminates and the cause is treated as no answer. Hunting terminates after the third member has been alerted for 5 seconds (10 seconds RNAR on each of the first two members leaves 5 seconds before expiration of the 25 seconds maximum hunt time configured at the hunt pilot). The call forwards to 3002 because hunting failed with a No Answer condition.

Chapter Summary

The following list summarizes the key points that were discussed in this chapter:

- CUCM offers several features for call coverage, including call forwarding, shared lines, call pickup, and call hunting.

- In CUCM, IP phone lines can be configured with Call Forward All, Call Forward Busy, Call Forward No Answer, Call Forward No Coverage, and Call Forward Unregistered.

- Call hunting in CUCM uses the following elements: hunt pilots, hunt lists, line groups, and endpoints (lines and voice-mail ports).

- Call-hunting options are configured per line group and specify how to continue hunting when the selected line group member does not answer. The distribution algorithms, also configured per line group, specify how to select a line group member.

- During hunting, the hunt option, distribution algorithm, RNAR timeout, maximum hunt timer, and final forwarding settings are considered.

- Call-hunting implementation includes configuration of IP phone lines, line groups, hunt lists, and hunt pilots.

Review Questions

Use the questions here to review what you learned in this chapter. The correct answers are found in Appendix A, "Answers to Chapter Review Questions."

1. Which of the following is not a call-forwarding option that can be configured at the directory number of a phone?

   a. Call Forward Queue Exhaustion

   b. Call Forward All

   c. Call Forward Busy

   d. Call Forward No Coverage

2. Which calling search space will further restrict the Call Forward All capabilities of a phone?

   a. Phone CSS

   b. Directory Number CSS

   c. CFA CSS

   d. CFNA CSS

3. What two mechanisms will allow multiple phones to ring at the same time?

   a. Shared lines

   b. Call hunting

   c. Route pattern

   d. Route list

4. Which technology allows a call to be picked up on another phone in the same department?

   a. Shared line

   b. Call pickup

   c. Call hunting

   d. Group pickup

5. Which technology allows a call to be picked up on another phone in a different department?

   a. Shared line

   b. Call pickup

   c. Call hunting

   d. Group pickup

6. If a device contains both a device and line calling search space, how will they be processed by CUCM?

   a. Line CSS overrides device CSS.

   b. Device CSS overrides line CSS.

   c. Both are concatenated. Line CSS is processed before device CSS.

   d. Both are concatenated. Device CSS is processed before line CSS.

7. Which component of call hunting does a hunt pilot point to?

   a. Line group

   b. Line group members

   c. Telephony call dispatcher

   d. Hunt list

8. Which component of call hunting does a hunt list point to?

   a. Line group

   b. Line group members

   c. Telephony call dispatcher

   d. Hunt list

9. Which call-forwarding option is used when calls forwarded to the hunt pilot exhaust (final forwarding)?

   a. CFA

   b. CFB

   c. CFNB

   d. CFNC

   e. CFUR

10. Which line group distribution mechanism routes calls in a round-robin fashion between all the members of the line group?

  a.   Broadcast

  b.   Top down

  c.   Circular

  d.   Longest idle

CHAPTER 15

Media Resources

This chapter describes available hardware and software media resources and how they are configured in Cisco Unified Communications Manager (CUCM) to provide features such as conferences, transcoding, media termination, and music on hold (MoH). It also explains how to perform access control to media resources using media resource groups and media resource group lists.

Chapter Objectives

Upon completing this chapter, you will be able to describe CUCM media resources, including conferences, transcoding, media termination point (MTP), music on hold, and annunciator services. You will also be able to meet these objectives:

- Describe media resources.

- Describe how CUCM supports media resources.

- Describe conferencing.

- Configure conferencing media resource.

- Configure meet-me conferences.

- Describe and configure music on hold.

- Describe annunciators.

- Describe and configure media resources access control.

Media Resources

A media resource is a software- or hardware-based entity that performs media processing functions on the data streams to which it is connected. Media processing functions include mixing multiple streams to create one output stream (conferencing), passing the stream from one connection to another (MTP), converting the data stream from one compression type to another (transcoding), echo cancellation, signaling, termination of a voice stream from a time-division multiplexing (TDM) circuit (coding/decoding), packetization of a stream, and streaming audio (annunciation).

Not all the different media resources described in Table 15-1 are needed in every deployment. Software resources are provided by CUCM services, whereas hardware features are provided by digital signal processors (DSP). The DSP resources are hardware modules in the gateway router or switch. The software resources are controlled by the Cisco IP Voice Media Streaming application running on CUCM.

Table 15-1 introduces the different types of media resources.

Table 15-1 *Media Resource Functions*

Resource	Function
Voice termination	TDM legs must be terminated by hardware that performs coding/decoding and packetization of the stream. This is performed in DSPs on the gateway router.
Audio conferencing	A conference bridge joins multiple participants into a single call. It mixes the streams together and creates a unique output stream for each connected party.
Transcoding	A transcoder converts an input stream from one codec into an output stream that uses a different codec.
MTP	An MTP bridges the media streams and allows them to be set up and torn down independently.
Annunciator	An annunciator streams spoken messages and various call progress tones.
Music on hold	Music on hold provides music to callers when their call is placed on hold, transferred, parked, or added to a conference.

A *conference bridge* is a resource that joins multiple participants into a single call. It can accept a number of connections for a given conference, up to the maximum number of streams allowed for a single conference on that device. The conference bridge mixes the streams together and creates a unique output stream for each connected party. The output stream for a given party is the composite of the streams from all connected parties minus their own input stream. Some conference bridges mix only the three loudest talkers on the conference and distribute that composite stream to each participant minus their own input stream if they are one of the talkers. Software conferencing is limited to the G.711 audio codec.

> **NOTE** All hardware resource limitations are well documented in the media resource chapter of the SRND available online at http://www.cisco.com/go/srnd. It is best practice to use the Cisco DSP Calculator, which you can find at http://www.cisco.com/go/dspcalculator. The Cisco DSP Calculator requires Cisco.com membership access.

A *transcoder* takes the stream of one codec and converts it from one compression type to another compression type. For example, it could take a stream from a G.711 codec and transcode it in real time to a G.729 stream. In addition, a transcoder provides MTP capabilities and may be used to enable supplementary services for H.323 endpoints when required.

Two streams that use the same codec using different sampling intervals may also be connected.

A single-site deployment usually has no need for transcoding devices.

An *MTP* is an entity that accepts two full-duplex G.711 streams. It bridges the media streams and allows them to be set up and torn down independently. The streaming data received from the input stream on one connection is passed to the output stream on the other connection, and vice versa.

An *annunciator* is a software function of the Cisco IP Voice Media Streaming application that provides the ability to stream spoken messages or various call-progress tones from the system to a user. It is capable of sending multiple one-way Real-Time Transport Protocol (RTP) streams to devices such as Cisco IP Phones or gateways, and it uses Skinny Client Control Protocol (SCCP) messages to establish the RTP stream. The announcements may be customized by replacing the appropriate WAV file.

Music on hold (MoH) is an integral feature of the Cisco Unified Communications system. This feature provides music to callers when their call is placed on hold, transferred, parked, or added to an ad hoc conference.

Media Resource Support

CUCM offers software-based media resources. Start the IP Voice Media Streaming application to activate the following:

- Audio conferencing

- MTP

- Annunciator

- MoH

The following media resources are available only in hardware:

- Transcoding

- Voice termination

Audio conferencing and MTP media resources can also be offered by hardware media resources. MoH is a special case. Because of the potential WAN bandwidth utilization of MoH, the multicast streams of the server are normally scoped at the headquarters. Survivable Remote Site Telephony (SRST) can stream one media resource at branch locations.

The signaling between hardware media resources and CUCM most often uses SCCP to set up and tear down calls. All audio streams from any endpoint are always terminated by the media resources involved in the call. There is no direct IP phone-to-IP phone audio stream with media resources involved in the call flow.

The voice-termination function is needed when an incoming or outgoing TDM call is terminated on a gateway. The TDM leg is terminated by the Cisco IOS router's DSP and has to perform decoding, coding, and packetization functions.

There are two different audio streams in Figure 15-1, one inside the public switched telephone network (PSTN), the other one a VoIP audio stream using RTP transport.

Signaling messages are exchanged between the gateway and CUCM and between the telephony device and CUCM. The PSTN signaling is not considered in Figure 15-1.

Figure 15-1 *PSTN Voice Termination*

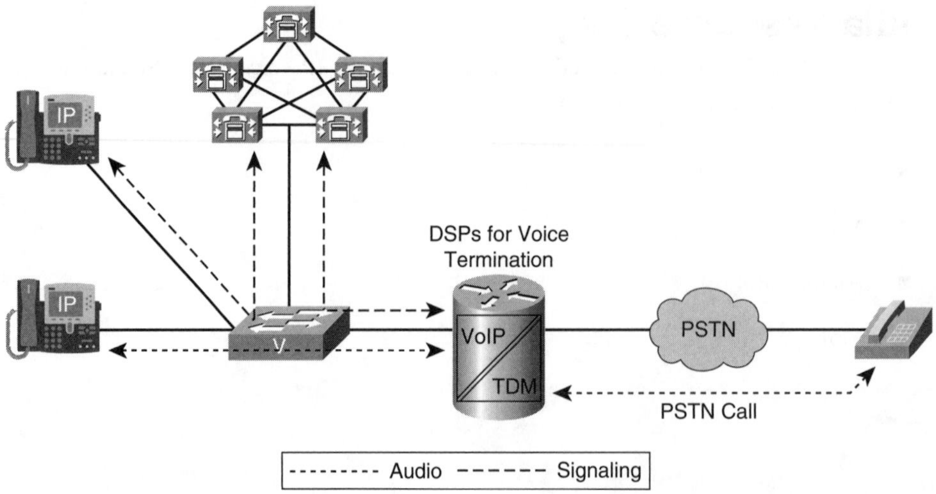

RTP bearer traffic streams are sent from the IP phones to the conference bridge resource mixing the audio. The conference resource mixes the audio streams and sends back a unique audio stream to the IP phones. The audio stream must subtract the audio stream of the person receiving the audio stream so that no echo is heard. Some conference devices, because of processing limitations, mix only the three loudest talkers.

Signaling messages (control traffic) are exchanged among the IP phones, CUCM, and the conferencing resource (if using a hardware resource or a version of Cisco Unified MeetingPlace). Cisco Unified MeetingPlace is not covered in this book.

NOTE The Cisco Press book *Voice and Video Conferencing Fundamentals* is an excellent resource for a more thorough understanding of audio conferencing and videoconferencing.

Most conference bridges that are under the control of CUCM use SCCP to communicate with CUCM. Session Initiation Protocol (SIP) support is increasingly being added to all the Unified Communications components.

CUCM does not distinguish between software- and hardware-based conference bridges when it processes a conference allocation request. Allocation of conferencing resources is covered in further detail later in this chapter. The number of individual conferences and maximum number of participants per conference varies based on the resource in use. Figure 15-2 illustrates that software conferencing is integrated into CUCM.

Figure 15-2 *Software Conferencing*

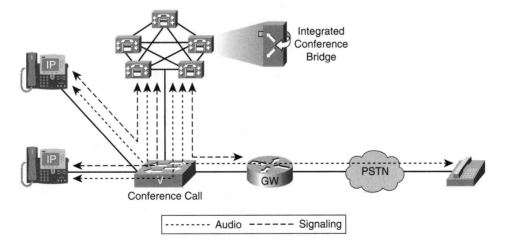

A transcoder converts an input audio stream using one audio codec into an output stream that uses a different audio codec. The transcoder in Figure 15-3 is implemented using DSP resources in the Cisco router. Transcoders are necessary when audio streams are using compressed audio codes (G.729 or iLBC), but the resource they are attempting to use accepts only G.711 calls. iLBC is the Internet Low Bandwidth Codec, which operates at 15.2 kbps. Most Cisco Unify voice-mail deployments use the G.711 audio codec for voice-mail storage to guarantee high quality.

Audio streams (RTP bearer channels) are set up between the telephony devices and the transcoder. Signaling messages are exchanged between the telephony devices and CUCM and between the transcoder resource and CUCM. DSP resources are required to perform transcoding. Those DSP resources are located in Cisco routers and switches.

Figure 15-3 *Transcoding Media Resources*

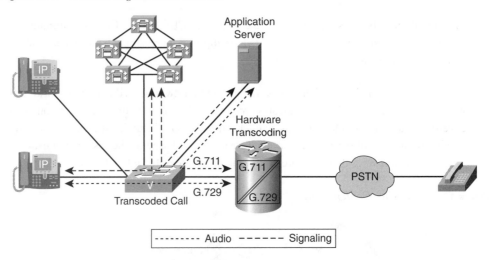

An MTP bridges two media streams and allows them to be set up and torn down independently.

An MTP can be used as an instance of translation between incompatible audio streams, to synchronize clocking, or to enable supplementary services for devices that do not support the empty capability set (ECS) option of the H.323 Version 2 protocol.

Audio streams exist between telephony devices and the MTP resource. Signaling messages are exchanged between the telephony devices and CUCM. Figure 15-4 illustrates a hardware-based MTP.

Figure 15-4 *Hardware MTP*

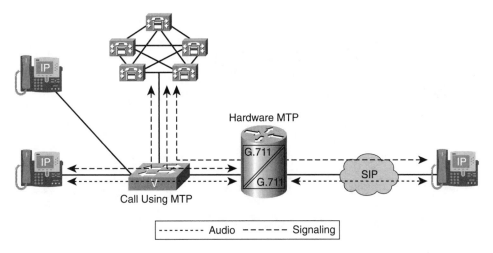

An annunciator is a function of the Cisco IP Voice Media Streaming application service that provides the ability to stream spoken messages or various call-progress tones from the CUCM system to a user.

The annunciator can send multiple one-way RTP streams to devices such as Cisco IP Phones or gateways, using SCCP messages to set up the RTP stream. Tones and announcements are predefined by the system. The announcements support localization and may also be customized by replacing the appropriate WAV file. The annunciator can support G.711 a-law, G.711 mu-law, G.729, and Cisco wideband audio codecs without transcoding resources.

Signaling messages are exchanged between telephony devices and CUCM. The audio stream is one way, from the annunciator to the telephony device. The annunciator is a software component of CUCM, as shown in Figure 15-5.

The MoH feature is part of the Cisco IP Voice Media Streaming (IPVMS) service running on CUCM. This feature provides music to callers when their call is placed on hold or a supplementary service is initiated. Supplementary services are not limited to, but include the following: transfer, park, and conference. When a supplementary service is initiated, the call is temporarily put on hold before the function is completed. Implementing MoH is relatively simple but requires a basic understanding of IP unicast and multicast traffic, MoH call flows, configuration options, server behavior, and requirements.

Figure 15-5   *Annunciator Services*

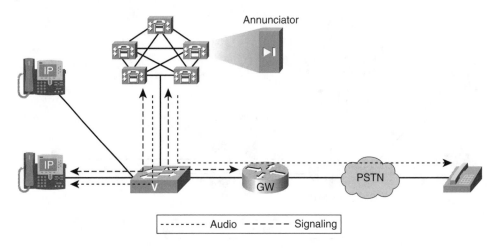

Audio streams are created between telephony devices and the MoH server. Signaling messages are exchanged between telephony devices and CUCM. Figure 15-6 illustrates the MoH component of CUCM.

Figure 15-6   *Music on Hold*

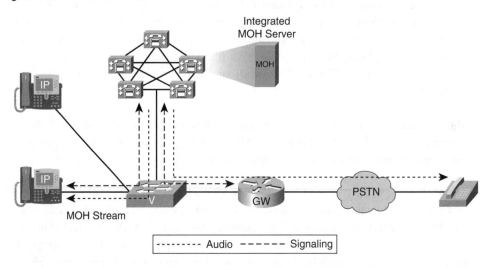

Conferencing

The CUCM supports hardware and software conference bridges.

The software-based conference bridge, implemented as a CUCM service, supports only conferences, using a single audio codec (G.711 or Cisco wideband).

Some hardware conference bridges can support multiple low bit-rate (LBR) stream types such as G.729, Global System for Mobile Communications (GSM), G.723, and iLBC. A mixed-mode conference is a conference in which multiple audio codecs are used for different audio streams. A mixed-mode conference bridge has the added burden of transcoding the RTP bearer streams. Mixed-mode conferences limit the number of conference participants and active conferences based on the capabilities of the hardware. There are multiple hardware conference bridge families that should be investigated.

> **NOTE**   Hardware conference capabilities are well documented in the *CUCM Solution Reference Network Design Guide* available at http://www.cisco.com/go/srnd. The DSP Calculator should also be used when designing a solution involving hardware media resources. As mentioned previously, the DSP Calculator is available at http://www.cisco.com/go/dspcalculator.

Software conferencing scalability is limited by the server platform CUCM is running on. Conferencing capabilities of the server are throttled by default because it is assumed that CUCM will be running call processing co-resident while providing conferencing capabilities. The number of streams can be tuned up to 64 ad hoc conference participants and 128 meet-me conference participants on a standalone server (dependent on the server hardware platform). A standalone server is dedicated to providing services to the CUCM, but it never performs call processing (call setup and teardown).

A hardware conference bridge can support multiple LBR audio stream types, including G.729, GSM, G.723, and iLBC.

All conference bridges that are under the control of CUCM currently use SCCP to communicate with CUCM.

CUCM allocates a conference bridge from a conferencing resource that is registered with the CUCM cluster. Both hardware and software conferencing resources can register with CUCM at the same time, and CUCM can allocate conference bridges from either resource. CUCM does not distinguish between these types of conference bridges when it processes conference allocation requests.

The number of individual conferences and maximum number of participants per conference varies by resource.

Cisco Conference Bridge Hardware

The following types of hardware conference bridge resources may be used on a CUCM system:

- Cisco Conference Bridge Hardware (Cisco Catalyst WS-X6608-T1 and WS-X6608-E1)

- Cisco IOS Conference Bridge (Cisco NM-HDV)

- Cisco Conference Bridge (Cisco WS-SVC-CMM and WS-SVC-CMM-ACT)

- Cisco IOS Enhanced Conference Bridge (Cisco NM-HDV2, NM-HD-1V/2V/2VE, PVDM2)

- Cisco Video Conference Bridge (CUVC-3510 or 3540)

Cisco Conference Bridge Hardware (Cisco Catalyst WS-X6608-T1 and WS-X6608-E1)

This hardware has eight DSPs that are physically associated to each port, and there are eight ports per card. The 6608 module is supported only in the Catalyst operating system of the 6500 series switch.

Configuration of the DSPs is at the port level, so all DSPs associated to a port perform the same function.

Conference bridges may have up to 32 participants, and each port supports 32 conference bridges.

For conferences with G.711 or G.723, there may be 32 conferences per port. If G.729 calls are used, there may be 24 conferences per port. The 6608-T1/E1 gateway module is end of sale (EoS).

Cisco IOS Conference Bridge (Cisco NM-HDV and 1700 Series Routers)

This hardware uses the PVDM-256K-type modules that are based on the C549 DSP chipset. Conferences using this hardware provide bridges that allow up to six participants in a single bridge.

The resources are configured per DSP for conference bridges.

The NM-HDV may have up to four PVDM-256K modules, whereas the Cisco 1700 series routers may have one or two PVDM-256K modules.

Each DSP provides a single conference bridge that can accept G.711 or G.729 calls.

The Cisco 1751 is limited to 5 conference calls per chassis, and the Cisco 1760 can support 20 conference calls per chassis.

Any PVDM2-based hardware, such as the NM-HDV2, may be used simultaneously in a single chassis for voice termination but may not be used simultaneously for other media resource functionality. The DSPs based on PVDM-256K and PVDM2 have different DSP farm configurations, and only one may be configured in a router at a time.

Cisco Conference Bridge (Cisco WS-SVC-CMM-ACT)

This Cisco Catalyst-based hardware provides DSP resources that may provide conference bridges of up to 32 participants per bridge.

Each module contains 4 DSPs that are individually configurable, and each DSP can support 32 conference bridges.

The G.711 and G.729 codecs are supported on these conference bridges without extra transcoder resources. However, transcoder resources are necessary if other codecs are used.

Cisco IOS Enhanced Conference Bridge (Cisco NM-HDV2, NM-HD-1V/2V/2VE, 2800 Series, and 3800 Series Routers)

Based on the Texas Instruments (TI) C5510 DSP chipset, the NM-HDV2 and the router chassis use the PVDM2 (Packet Voice DSP Modules - 2nd generation) modules for providing DSPs.

DSPs on PVDM2 hardware are configured individually as voice termination, conferencing, media termination, or transcoding resources. The DSPs on a single PVDM may be used as different resource types. Allocate DSPs to voice termination first, and then to other functionality as needed.

The NM-HDV2 (high-density voice) has four slots that will accept PVDM2 modules in any combination. The other network modules have fixed numbers of DSPs.

A conference based on these DSPs allows a maximum of eight participants. When a conference begins, all eight positions are reserved at that time. This means that unused DSP resources on the same DSP chip are not available for other conferences.

The PVDM2-8 is listed as having a DSP because it has a DSP that has half the processing capacity of the PVDM2-16. If the DSP on a PVDM2-8 is configured for G.711, it can provide (0.5 x 8) bridges/DSP = 4 conference bridges. PVDM2 modules are available in 8, 16, 32, 48, or 64 quantities. The number of resources uses a divisor of 16. A PVDM2-64 has 64/8, or 8 DSP resources, which will allow up to 64 conferences with 8 conference participants in each conference. The PVDM2 I/O limits the number of conference streams in this scenario because 512 (64×8) audio streams are possible with 64 conferences of 8 conference participants.

A DSP farm is a configuration parameter in Cisco IOS that specifies which codecs are supported for the DSPs that are working together (farming). A DSP farm that is configured for conferencing for G.711 provides 8 conferences. When configured to accept both G.711 and G.729 calls, a single DSP provides two conferences because it is also reserving its resources for performing transcoding of streams.

The I/O of an NM-HDV2 is limited to 400 streams, so ensure that the number of conference resources allocated does not cause this limit to be exceeded. If G.711 conferences are configured, no more than 6 DSPs (total of 48 conferences with 8 participants each) should be allocated per NM because 48×8 participants = 384 streams. If all conferencing is configured for both G.711 and G.729 codecs, each DSP provides only two conferences of eight participants each. In this case, it is possible to populate the network module (NM) fully and configure it with 16 DSPs (PVDM2-64) because there can only be 2 conferences with 8 participants (16) in each of the 16 DSPs ($16 \times 16 = 256$ streams).

Conferences cannot natively accept calls using the GSM codec. A transcoder must be provided separately for these calls to participate in a conference.

Meet-me conferences allow users to dial in to a conference. Ad hoc conferences allow the conference controller to add specific participants to the conference.

Meet-me conferences require that a range of directory numbers (DN) be allocated for exclusive use of the conference. When a meet-me conference is set up, the conference controller chooses a DN and advertises it to members of the group. The users call the DN to join the conference after the conference controller has set up the bridge using the MeetMe softkey.

Ad hoc conferences comprise two types: basic and advanced. In basic ad hoc conferencing, the originator of the conference acts as the controller of the conference and is the only participant who can add or remove other participants.

In advanced ad hoc conferencing, any participant can add or remove other participants; that capability is not limited to the originator of the conference. Advanced ad hoc conferencing also allows linking multiple ad hoc conferences. Set the Advanced Ad Hoc Conference Enabled cluster-wide service parameter to True to gain access to advanced ad hoc conferencing. Advanced ad hoc conferencing is also referred to as conference chaining.

Conferencing Media Resource Configuration

The following steps are required to configure media resources:

1. Configure software conference media resources (if desired).

   a. Enable the IP Voice Media Streaming application service.

   b. Configure IP Voice Media Streaming application service parameters.

   c. Configure desired software conferencing media resources.

2. Implement hardware conference media resources (if desired).

   a. Configure hardware media resources in CUCM.

   b. Configure hardware media resources in Cisco IOS.

   c. Verify that hardware media resources are registered with CUCM.

The Cisco IP Voice Media Streaming application service is activated in Cisco Unified Serviceability at **Tools > Service Activation**. At the top of the Service Activation window, the server on which services should be activated or deactivated has to be selected. After selecting the server, check the **IP Voice Media Streaming App** check box (Figure 15-7) and click **Save** to activate the service.

The Cisco IPVMS parameters are accessible via the CUCM Administration, **System > Service Parameters**. The following two conference bridge service parameters are illustrated in Figure 15-8:

■ **Call Count**: This parameter specifies the maximum number of conference participants that the conference bridge will support. Increasing this value above the recommended default might cause performance degradation on a CUCM server that is also performing call processing (co-resident). If this value needs to be tuned above the default, consider installing the Cisco IPVMS on a standalone server. Alternatively, hardware conferencing or a version of Cisco MeetingPlace can be used to offload conferencing processing from the call-processing server. The configurable range is 0 to 256, and the default is 48.

■ **Run Flag**: This parameter determines whether the conference bridge functionality of the Cisco IPVMS is enabled. Valid values specify True (enabled) or False. The default is True. All media resources are turned on by default when the Cisco IPVMS is activated. Each media service can be turned on or off individually via the service parameters or MoH server configuration.

Figure 15-7 *IP Voice Media Streaming Application Service Activation*

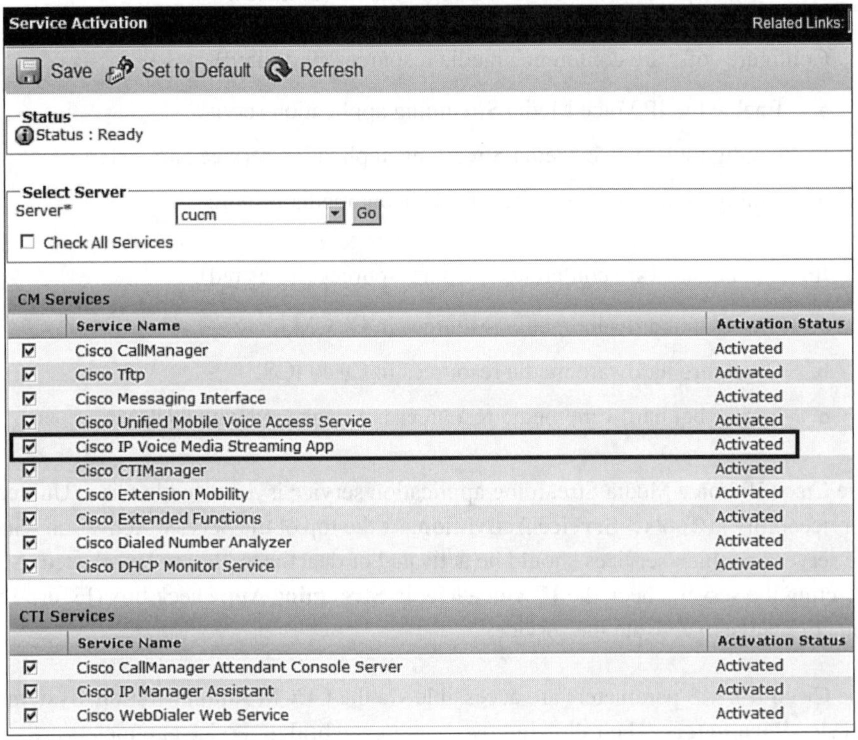

Figure 15-8 *IP Voice Media Streaming Application Service Parameters*

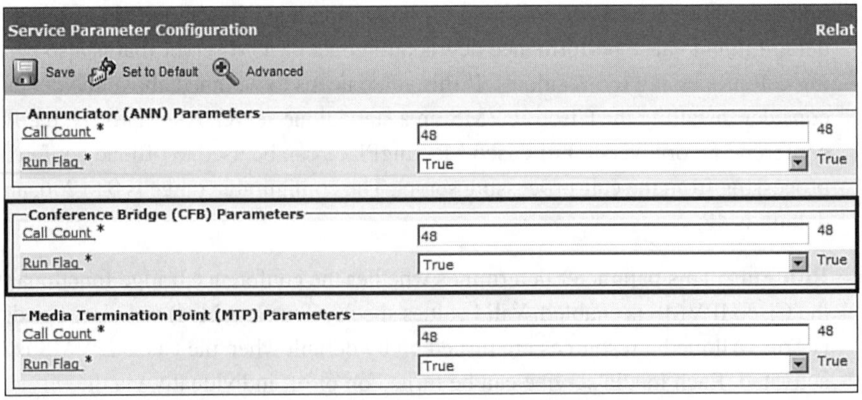

Figure 15-9 shows the default configuration of a software conference resource. The only configurable items are Name, Description, Device Pool, Common Device Configuration, and Location.

NOTE   The CUCM software conferencing media resource supports only the G.711 and Cisco wideband audio codecs. A hardware conference bridge or transcoder is necessary to allow devices that use other audio codecs to participate in a conference.

Figure 15-9   *IP Voice Media Streaming Application Service Parameters*

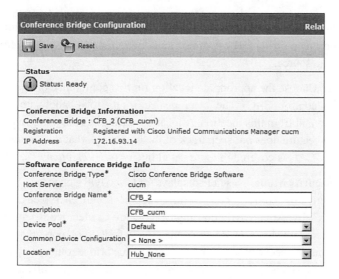

When adding a hardware conference bridge in CUCM, the type of conference bridge must match the hardware family used. The IOS Enhanced Conference Bridge used in Figure 15-9 represents an NM-HDV2 or NM-HD-1V/2V/2VE, as discussed earlier in this chapter. This particular type of conference bridge is configured by name, which must match between CUCM and the Cisco IOS router.

To add a hardware conference bridge, navigate to **Media Resources > Conference Bridge** and click the **Add New** button. The Conference Bridge Configuration window displays. Enter the appropriate settings for that particular conference bridge and click **Save**. Figure 15-9 is based on a Cisco IOS Enhanced Conference Bridge configuration. Configurable parameters vary by platform.

- **Conference Bridge Type**: Choose Cisco IOS Enhanced Conference Bridge.

- **Conference Bridge Name**: Enter a name for the conference bridge. The name must match the name of the conference media resource as configured at the Cisco IOS router.

NOTE The name of the Cisco IOS Enhanced Conference Bridge configured in CUCM must match the name of the conference bridge configured in the Cisco IOS router. The name is case sensitive. Good naming conventions should be used to easily identify the component. Prefix CFB (conference bridge), and then use a burned-in MAC address of the router. CFB012345012345 is an example of a hardware conference bridge in a router where the MAC address of 012345012345 is burned into the Gigabit Ethernet controller.

■ **Device Pool**: Choose a device pool. Best practice is to configure a separate device pool dedicated to media resources. A good naming convention recommendation is Media_Resources_DP.

■ **Common Device Configuration**: Choose the common device configuration to assign to the conference bridge. The common device configuration includes attributes such as MoH audio source.

■ **Location**: Choose the appropriate location for this conference bridge to enforce call admission control (CAC). The location specifies the total bandwidth that is available for calls to and from this location. A location setting of Hub_None means that the Locations feature does not keep track of the bandwidth that this conference bridge consumes. CAC is covered in more detail in *Cisco IP Telephony Part 2*.

■ **Device Security Mode**: This field displays for Cisco IOS Enhanced Conference Bridge because only this audio conference bridge supports secure encrypted conferencing starting in CUCM Version 6.0. If choosing Non Secure Conference Bridge, the nonsecure conference establishes a TCP port connection to CUCM on port 2000. Ensure this setting matches the security setting on the conference bridge; otherwise, the call will fail. The Encrypted Conference Bridge setting supports the secure conference feature. Refer to the *CUCM Security Guide* for secure conference bridge configuration procedures.

Figure 15-10 *Cisco IOS Enhanced Conference Bridge Configuration*

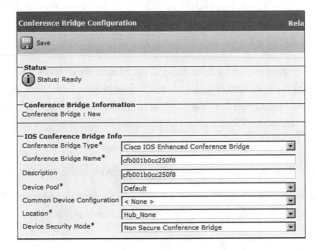

Example 15-1 is a configuration of a Cisco IOS Enhanced Conference Bridge. Each command is explained following the configuration example.

Example 15-1 *Cisco IOS Configuration*

```
voice-card 0
 dspfarm
 dsp services dspfarm

sccp local FastEthernet0/0.72
sccp ccm 10.1.1.1 identifier 1 version 6.0
sccp

sccp ccm group 1
 associate ccm 1 priority 1
 associate profile 1 register CFB001B0CC250F8

dspfarm profile 1 conference
 codec g711ulaw
 codec g711alaw
 codec g729ar8
 codec g729abr8
 maximum sessions 2
 associate application SCCP
 no shutdown
```

- **dspfarm** (DSP farm): To enable DSP farm service, use the **dspfarm** command in global configuration mode. The DSP farm service is disabled by default.

- **dsp services dspfarm**: To enable DSP farm services for a particular voice network module, use the **dsp services dspfarm** command.

- **sccp local**: To select the local interface that SCCP applications (transcoding and conferencing) use to register with CUCM, use the **sccp local** command in global configuration mode.

- **sccp ccm**: To add a CUCM server to the list of available servers and set various parameters, including IP address or DNS name, port number, and version number, use the **sccp ccm** command in global configuration mode.

- **sccp**: To enable the SCCP protocol and its related applications (transcoding and conferencing), use the **sccp** command in global configuration mode.

- **sccp ccm group**: To create a CUCM group and enter SCCP CUCM configuration mode, use the **sccp ccm** group command in global configuration mode.

- **associate ccm**: To associate a CUCM with a CUCM group and establish its priority within the group, use the **associate ccm** command in SCCP CUCM configuration mode.

- **associate profile**: To associate a DSP farm profile with a CUCM group, use the **associate profile** command in SCCP CUCM configuration mode.

- **dspfarm profile**: To enter DSP farm profile configuration mode and define a profile for DSP farm services, use the **dspfarm profile** command in global configuration mode.

- **codec** (DSP): To specify call density and codec complexity based on a particular codec standard, use the codec command in DSP interface DSP farm configuration mode.

- **associate application sccp**: To associate SCCP to the DSP farm profile, use the **associate application sccp** command in DSP farm profile configuration mode.

- **maximum sessions** (DSP farm profile): To specify the maximum number of sessions that are supported by the profile, use the **maximum sessions** command in DSP farm profile configuration mode.

- **no shutdown**: If you fail to use the **no shutdown** command, the DSP farm profile will display in the gateway but fail to operate.

To verify the Cisco IOS media resource configuration, use the **show** commands demonstrated in Example 15-2.

Example 15-2 *Verifying Cisco IOS Media Resource Configuration*

```
show sccp
SCCP Admin State: UP
Gateway IP Address: 10.1.1.101, Port Number: 2000
IP Precedence: 5
User Masked Codec list: None
Call Manager: 10.1.1.1, Port Number: 2000
                Priority: N/A, Version: 6.0, Identifier: 1
Conferencing Oper State: ACTIVE - Cause Code: NONE
Active Call Manager: 10.1.1.1, Port Number: 2000
TCP Link Status: CONNECTED, Profile Identifier: 1
Reported Max Streams: 16, Reported Max OOS Streams: 0
Supported Codec: g711ulaw, Maximum Packetization Period: 30
Supported Codec: g711alaw, Maximum Packetization Period: 30
Supported Codec: g729ar8, Maximum Packetization Period: 60
Supported Codec: g729abr8, Maximum Packetization Period: 60
Supported Codec: g729r8, Maximum Packetization Period: 60
Supported Codec: g729br8, Maximum Packetization Period: 60
Supported Codec: rfc2833 dtmf, Maximum Packetization Period: 30
Supported Codec: rfc2833 pass-thru, Maximum Packetization Period: 30
Supported Codec: inband-dtmf to rfc2833 conversion, Maximum Packetization Period: 30
```

Example 15-2 *Verifying Cisco IOS Media Resource Configuration (Continued)*

```
show sccp ccm group 1
CCM Group Identifier: 1
 Description: None
 Binded Interface: NONE, IP Address: NONE
 Associated CCM Id: 1, Priority in this CCM Group: 1
 Associated Profile: 1, Registration Name: CFB001B0CC250F8
 Registration Retries: 3, Registration Timeout: 10 sec
 Keepalive Retries: 3, Keepalive Timeout: 30 sec
 CCM Connect Retries: 3, CCM Connect Interval: 10 sec
 Switchover Method: GRACEFUL,Switchback Method: GRACEFUL_GUARD
 Switchback Interval: 10 sec, Switchback Timeout: 7200 sec
 Signaling DSCP value: cs3, Audio DSCP value: ef

show dspfarm profile 1

Dspfarm Profile Configuration
 Profile ID = 1, Service = CONFERENCING, Resource ID = 1
 Profile Description :
 Profile Admin State : UP
 Profile Operation State : ACTIVE
 Application : SCCP   Status : ASSOCIATED
 Resource Provider : FLEX_DSPRM   Status : UP
 Number of Resource Configured : 2
 Number of Resource Available : 2
 Codec Configuration
 Codec : g711ulaw, Maximum Packetization Period : 30 , Transcoder: Not Required
 Codec : g711alaw, Maximum Packetization Period : 30 , Transcoder: Not Required
 Codec : g729ar8, Maximum Packetization Period : 60 , Transcoder: Not Required
 Codec : g729abr8, Maximum Packetization Period : 60 , Transcoder: Not Required
 Codec : g729r8, Maximum Packetization Period : 60 , Transcoder: Not Required
 Codec : g729br8, Maximum Packetization Period : 60 , Transcoder: Not Required
```

Various CUCM service parameters are related to conferencing. The following conferencing options should be considered when leveraging the conferencing features of CUCM:

- **Suppress Music on Hold to Conference Bridge**: This parameter determines whether MoH plays to a conference when a conference participant places the conference on hold. Valid values specify True (the system does not play MoH to the conference when a conference participant presses the Hold button) or False. The default is True.

- **Drop Ad Hoc Conference**: This parameter determines how an ad hoc conference terminates. This is an important toll-fraud prevention setting, because inside facilitators can set up a conference call to expensive international numbers and then drop out of the call. Without the conference controller, international tariffs are billed back to the company in which the conference call was set up. Valid values are as follows:

—Never (default): The conference remains active after the conference controller and all on-net parties hang up. This default setting could result in potential toll fraud.

—When Conference Controller Leaves: Terminate the conference when the conference controller hangs up.

—When No On-Net Parties Remain in the Conference: Terminate the conference when there are no on-net parties remaining in the conference. This distinction is important because the conference controller might have to drop out of the call, but other business partners on the call should continue the conference. The When Conference Controller Leaves option would hang up the call when the conference controller left the conference.

- **Advanced Ad Hoc Conference Enabled**: This parameter determines whether advanced ad hoc conference features are enabled. Advanced ad hoc conference features include the ability for conference participants other than the conference controller to add new participants to an existing ad hoc conference (conference chaining); the ability for any noncontroller conference participant to drop other participants from the conference via the ConfList and RmLstC softkeys; and whether ad hoc conferences can be linked using features such as conference, join, direct transfer, and transfer. Valid values specify True (allow advanced ad hoc conference features) or False. The default is False.

- **Nonlinear Ad Hoc Conference Linking Enabled**: This parameter determines whether more than two ad hoc conferences can be linked directly to an ad hoc conference in a nonlinear fashion. Nonlinear conference linking occurs when three or more ad hoc conferences are linked directly to one other ad hoc conference. Linear conference linking occurs when one or two ad hoc conferences are linked directly to one other ad hoc conference. For this parameter to work, the Advanced Ad Hoc Conference Enabled service parameter must be set to True. Valid values specify True (allow nonlinear conference linking so that three or more ad hoc conferences can be linked to a single other conference) or False. The default is False. The Advanced Ad Hoc Conference Enabled service parameter must be set to True for the Nonlinear Ad Hoc Conference Linking Enabled service parameter to work.

- **Maximum Ad Hoc Conference**: This parameter specifies the maximum number of participants who are allowed in a single ad hoc conference. The value of this field depends on the capabilities of the software/hardware conference bridge. The maximum number of conference bridge participants for typical conference bridges follow:

Software, 64; Cisco Catalyst WS-X6608, 16; Cisco Catalyst 4000, 16; and NM-HDV, 6. Setting this value above the maximum capacity of the conference resource will result in failed entrance to a conference bridge if more ports than the specific conference bridge configuration allows are added. The range is 3 to 64. The default is 4.

- **Maximum Meet-Me Conference Unicast**: This parameter specifies the maximum number of participants that are allowed in a single meet-me conference. The value of this field depends on the capabilities of the software/hardware conference bridge. A software conference bridge is capable of conferencing up to 128 participants. When a conference is created, the system automatically reserves a minimum of three streams, so specifying a value less than 3 allows a maximum of three participants. The range is 1 to 128. The default is 4.

Meet-Me Conference Configuration

To add a range of numbers to be used for meet-me conferences in CUCM Administration, navigate to **Call Routing > Meet-Me Number/Pattern** and click **Add New**. Configure the new pattern with the following data:

- **Directory Number or Pattern**: Enter a meet-me number or number range.

- **Description**: Enter up to 30 alphanumeric characters for a description of the meet-me number.

- **Partition**: To use a partition to restrict access to the meet-me/number pattern, choose the desired partition from the drop-down list.

- **Minimum Security Level**: Choose the minimum meet-me conference security level for this meet-me number or pattern from the drop-down list:

    —Choose **Authenticated** to block participants with nonsecure phones from joining the conference.

    —Choose **Encrypted** to block participants with authenticated or nonsecure phones from joining the conference.

    —Choose **Non Secure** to allow all participants to join the conference.

Figure 15-11 shows a meet-me range of 100 numbers beginning with 4500 and ending with 4599. The numbers are not in a partition, which will allow any phone to set up a meet-me bridge by clicking the Meet-Me softkey and dialing one of the numbers in the meet-me number range. Subsequent meeting members will need to dial only the number of the bridge.

Figure 15-11 *Meet-Me Conference Bridge Configuration*

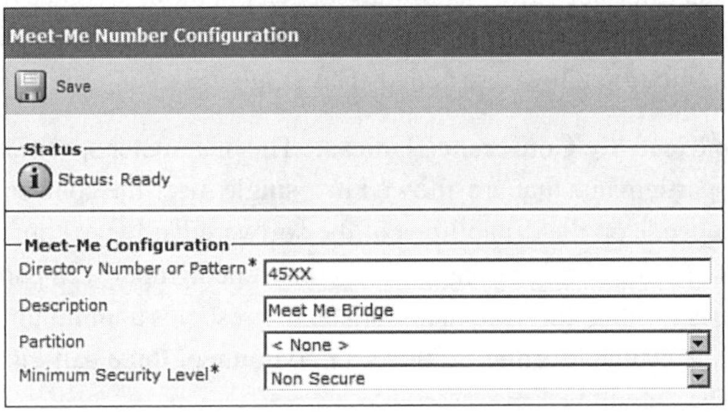

> **NOTE** Meet-me bridges do not offer any security, scheduling, or name-confirmation features. Security and scheduling features are offered by the Cisco MeetingPlace and Cisco MeetingPlace Express products. The conference controller could be given access to the ConfList softkey, which will allow the controller to view the conference partici-pants by caller ID information. The conference controller can individually remove users, but the conference controller does not have access to the users' line state information. Cisco MeetingPlace and MeetingPlace Express allow the conference controller to see which conference participant has a phone on hold. This is especially useful if MoH is being injected into the conference bridge. If the bridge has not been set up by the controller, callers to the meet-me number pattern receive a reorder tone.

Music on Hold

CUCM may be configured to provide MoH. The MoH feature has two main requirements:

- An MoH server must provide the MoH audio stream sources.

- CUCM must be configured to use the MoH streams provided by the MoH server when a call is placed on hold.

The integrated MoH feature enables users to place on-net and off-net callers on hold with music instead of the default "one on hold." The MoH source makes music available to any on-net or off-net device placed on hold. On-net devices include Cisco IP Phones and applications placed on hold. Off-net users include those connected through MGCP, SIP, and H.323 gateways. The MoH feature is also available for plain old telephony service (POTS) phones connected to the Cisco IP network through Foreign Exchange Station (FXS) ports.

It is also possible to configure multicast MoH streaming to leverage external media servers providing media streams. CUCM Express and Cisco Unified Survivable Remote Site

Telephony (SRST) gateways can be configured as media streaming servers for MoH, too. The CUCME and SRST router-based resources provide MoH by streaming one audio file stored in the router's flash memory or a fixed audio source connected through an optional E&M (ear and mouth) hardware interface. You can find detailed information about this feature in the *CUCM Solution Reference Network Design (SRND) Guide*.

The CUCM integrated MoH Server supports multicast and unicast for MoH streaming. The advantage of using multicast for MoH streaming over unicast is to save bandwidth and to reduce load on the MoH server. Saving bandwidth is normally not a major issue for campus LAN environments, but reducing load on the MoH server is always a big consideration. Reducing the number of media streams is especially advantageous when the MoH server is co-located on the same server as call processing. It is advisable to scope MoH traffic to the local site so that MoH does not consume WAN bandwidth. There are various ways of implementing multicast scoping and unicast filtering on the data network.

MoH audio codecs ($G.711_{ulaw}$, $G.711_{alaw}$, Cisco wideband, and G.729) are generated by CUCM when files with a .wav extension are uploaded to the MoH server. The recommended format for audio source files includes the following specifications:

■ 16-bit PCM WAV file

■ Stereo or mono

■ Sample rates of 48 kHz, 32 kHz, 16 kHz, or 8 kHz

If live audio (Muzak, radio broadcast) is a requirement, MoH can be generated from a fixed source. A sound card is required for a fixed audio source. The fixed audio source is connected to the audio input (line in) of the local sound card. The Cisco MoH USB audio sound card (MUSIC ON HOLD-USB-AUDIO=) must be used for connecting a fixed audio source to the MoH server. This USB sound card is compatible with all MCS platforms supporting CUCM Release 6.*x*.

This mechanism enables the use of radios, CD players, or any other compatible sound source. The stream from the fixed audio source is transcoded in real time to support the codec that was configured through CUCM Administration. The fixed audio source can be transcoded into G.711 (a-law or mu-law), G.729 Annex A, and wideband, and it is the only audio source that is transcoded in real time.

Before using a fixed audio source to transmit MoH, consider the legalities and the ramifications of rebroadcasting copyrighted audio materials. Consult your legal department for potential issues.

A unicast MoH stream is a point-to-point, one-way audio RTP stream between the server and one endpoint device. Unicast MoH uses a separate source stream for each connection. As more endpoint devices receive MoH, the number of MoH streams increases. If one hundred devices are on hold, there will be 100 independent streams of RTP traffic generated over the network between the server and the endpoints receiving the MoH. The number of streams can potentially have a negative effect on network throughput. Unicast MoH can be useful in networks where multicast is not enabled or where devices are not capable of multicast, thereby still allowing an administrator to take advantage of the MoH feature.

Multicast MoH streams are point-to-multipoint, one-way audio RTP stream between the MoH server and the multicast group IP address. Multicast MoH conserves system resources and bandwidth because it enables multiple users to use the same audio source stream to provide MoH. If 100 devices were simultaneously on hold, a single multicast RTP stream could be replicated over the network to all 100 resources. Bandwidth and server processor utilization would be greatly reduced. It is recommended to use a multicast IP address of 239.1.1.1 through 239.255.255.254 because these multicast addresses are implicitly scoped by the router because the IP packets are generated with a time to live (TTL) value of 2. Each data router decrements the TTL value by 1. When a TTL of 0 is reached, the packet is not forwarded by a router. A TTL of 0 has a drop operation.

The basic operation of MoH in a Cisco Unified Communications environment consists of a holding party and a held party. The holding party is the endpoint placing a call on hold, and the held party is the endpoint placed on hold, receiving MoH.

The MoH stream that an endpoint receives is determined by a combination of the user hold audio source identifier of the device placing the endpoint on hold (holding party) and the configured prioritized list of MoH resources of the endpoint placed on hold (held party). The user hold audio source configured for the holding party determines the audio file that will be streamed when the holding party puts a call on hold, and the held party's list of MoH resources determines the server from which the held party will receive the MoH stream.

Figure 15-12 illustrates an on-net phone being placed on hold by a phone with a different MoH audio source identifier and server configuration. Phone B places Phone A on hold. Phone B will instruct CUCM to place Phone A on hold with Audio Source 2 and the MoH server relevant to Phone B's configuration.

NOTE When multiple MoH servers are active in your network, make sure that all the configured MoH files are available on all MoH servers.

Figure 15-12 *Music on Hold: Resource Selection*

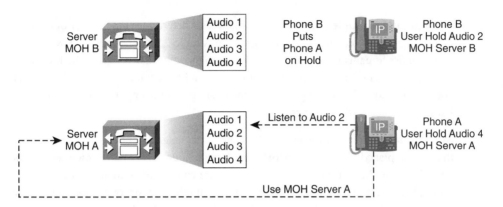

MoH Configuration

Configuration of MoH consists of four main steps. Additional configuration is required if multicast MoH is used.

Step 1   Plan MoH server capacity.

Step 2   Configure MoH audio sources:

    a.   Convert MoH audio files.

    b.   Configure MoH audio sources.

Step 3   Configure the MoH server.

Step 4   Configure MoH service parameters.

Step 5   (Optional) Configure multicast for MoH:

    a.   Configure audio sources for multicast MoH.

    b.   Configure the server for multicast MoH.

Capacity planning is crucial to ensure that the hardware can support the anticipated MoH volume of the network. The 7815 and 7825 servers allow up to 250 users to be placed on hold, and the 7835 and 7845 servers allow up to 500 users to be placed on hold (co-resident or standalone). If MoH sessions exceed the platform limitations, various issues can arise:

■   Poor MoH quality

■   Erratic MoH operation

■   Loss of MoH functionality

The following MoH server configuration parameters affect MoH server capacity:

- **Maximum Half Duplex Streams**: This parameter determines the number of devices that can be placed on unicast MoH. This value is set to 250 by default. The Maximum Half Duplex Streams parameter should be set to the value derived from the following formula: (Server capacity) – [(Number of multicast MoH sources) × (Number of MoH codecs enabled)]. The value of this parameter should never be set higher than the hardware capacity of the server.

- **Maximum Multicast Connections**: This parameter determines the number of devices that can be placed on multicast MoH. The default value is set to 30, which represents a maximum of 30,000. Multicast connections are configured in thousands of held parties because multicast is scalable. The Maximum Multicast Connections parameter should be set to a number that ensures that all devices can be placed on multicast MoH if necessary. Although the MoH server can generate only a finite number of multicast streams (204), a large number of held devices can join each multicast stream through the network multicast protocols. This parameter should be set to a number that is greater than or equal to the number of devices that might be placed on multicast MoH at any given time.

Typically, multicast traffic is accounted for based on the number of streams being generated; however, CUCM maintains a count of the actual number of devices placed on multicast MoH or joined to each multicast MoH stream. This method is different from the way multicast traffic is normally tracked. You can find additional information in the CUCM SRND (http://www.cisco.com/go/srnd).

CUCM ships with a default MoH audio file. To add additional MoH audio files, navigate to **Media Resources > MoH Audio File Management** from CUCM Administration (shown in Figure 15-13). Click the **Upload File** button, and browse the local directory structure for the WAV audio file.

Figure 15-13 *Music on Hold: Audio File Conversion*

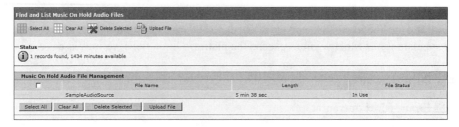

The uploaded file is automatically converted into four different audio formats. A file status of Translation Complete indicates that the audio file has been successfully converted. If any other status is displayed, or if the status remains open for a long period of time (conversion can take up to several minutes), the audio file translation failed. The uploaded audio file might be in the wrong file format or have improper audio qualities.

Navigate to **Media Resources > Music On Hold Audio Source** from CUCM Administration to configure the MoH audio sources, as illustrated in Figure 15-14. The MoH audio sources are identified by an MoH audio stream number from 1 to 51. Up to 50 prerecorded sources and 1 live audio source are available per CUCM cluster.

In the Music On Hold Audio Source Configuration window, select the MoH audio stream number of the audio source that you want to configure. Choose the MoH audio source file. The MoH audio source name defaults to the MoH audio source filename, but it can be modified. Enable continuous playing (repeat) of the audio file if desired.

Figure 15-14 *Music on Hold: Audio Source Configuration*

If a fixed audio source will be used, navigate to **Media Resources > Fixed MoH Audio Source** from CUCM Administration to configure a fixed MoH audio source. The source ID is 51 and cannot be modified. The name of the fixed MoH audio source has to be entered, and the fixed MoH audio source must be enabled. Figure 15-15 shows this configuration.

Figure 15-15 *Music on Hold: Fixed Audio Source Configuration*

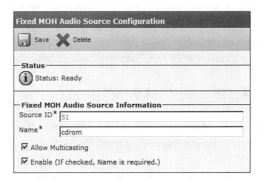

Navigate to **Media Resources > Music On Hold Server** from CUCM Administration to configure the MoH server parameters. Figure 15-16 illustrates the default configuration of the MoH media resource. Various parameters can be modified. It is best practice to use a media resource device pool. If MoH functionality is not desired on this server, but other services of the Cisco IPVMS are, the run flag should be set to No. If a fixed audio source that is physically connected to the server is used, the name of the audio source device has to be specified.

Figure 15-16 *Music on Hold: Server Configuration*

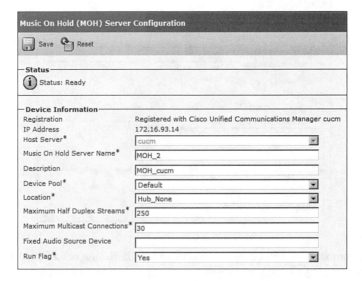

The following list of CUCM service parameters and the associated defaults are related to MoH:

■ Suppress MoH to Conference Bridge (True)

■ Default Network Hold MoH Audio Source ID (1)

■ Default User Hold MoH Audio Source ID (1)

■ Duplex Streaming Enabled (False)

To enable multicast MoH on an MoH server, the Multicast Audio Source Information section of the MoH server configuration window must be configured. Check the **Enable Multicast Audio Sources on This MoH Server** check box. The Base Multicast IP Address, Base Multicast Port Number, and Increment Multicast On parameters are automatically populated when you enable multicast MoH on the server. You can modify these values if desired. Figure 15-17 shows this section of the MoH Server Configuration page.

Figure 15-17 *Music on Hold: Server Configuration (Multicast Settings)*

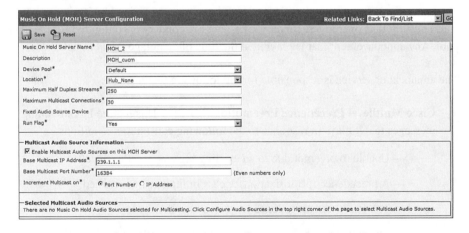

> **NOTE**   It is recommended to increment multicast on IP address rather than port number to avoid network saturation in firewall situations. This results in each multicast audio source having a unique IP address and helps to avoid network saturation.

All MoH audio sources that have been configured to allow multicasting are listed in the Selected Multicast Audio Sources section of the MoH Server Configuration window. Each audio source can have a different Max Hops value (default is 2). This parameter sets the TTL value in the IP header of the multicast MoH RTP packets to the specified value. The

TTL field in an IP packet indicates the maximum number of routers that an audio source is allowed to cross. If the Max Hops value is set to 1, the multicast MoH RTP packets remain in the subnet of the multicast MoH server.

> **NOTE**   When you are using multicast MoH for devices that are not in the same IP subnet, multicast routing has to be enabled in the IP network.

Check the **Allow Multicasting** check box for each MoH audio source. This applies to MoH audio sources and to fixed MoH audio sources.

Annunciator

An annunciator is automatically created in the system when the Cisco IPVMS is activated on a server. If Cisco IPVMS is deactivated, the annunciator is also deleted. A single annunciator instance can service the entire CUCM cluster if it meets the performance requirements. Additional annunciators can be configured for the cluster if necessary.

The annunciator registers with a single CUCM at a time, as defined by its device pool. It automatically fails over to a secondary CUCM if a secondary is configured for the device pool. Any announcement that is playing at the time of an outage is not maintained.

The annunciator service is responsible for the following features:

- **Cisco Multilevel Precedence Preemption (MLPP)**: This feature has streaming messages that it plays in response to the following call-failure conditions:

    —Unable to preempt due to an existing higher-precedence call.

    —A precedence (prioritization) access limitation was reached.

    —The attempted precedence level was unauthorized.

    —The called number is not equipped for preemption or call waiting.

- **Integration via SIP trunk**: SIP endpoints can generate and send tones in-band in the RTP stream, but SCCP cannot. An annunciator is used in conjunction with an MTP to generate or accept Dual-Tone Multifrequency (DTMF) tones when integrating with a SIP endpoint.

- **Cisco IOS gateways and intercluster trunks**: These devices require support for call-progress tone (ringback tone).

- **System messages**: During the following call-failure conditions, the system plays a streaming message to the end user:

  —A dialed number that the system cannot recognize

  —A call that is not routed because of a service disruption

  —A number that is busy and not configured for preemption or call waiting

- **Conferencing**: During a conference call, the system plays a barge-in tone to announce that a participant has joined or left the bridge.

The annunciator is configured to support 48 simultaneous streams by default. The maximum recommended is 48 for an annunciator running on the same server with the CUCM service (call processing).

If the server has only 10-Mbps connectivity, lower the setting to 24 simultaneous streams. A standalone server without the CUCM service can support up to 255 simultaneous announcement streams, and a high-performance server with dual CPUs and a high-performance disk system can support up to 400 streams. Multiple standalone servers can be added to support the required number of streams. The maximum streams are configured in the Cisco IPVMS service parameters.

The annunciator can be configured by navigating to **Media Resources > Annunciator** from CUCM Administration. Figure 15-18 shows the annunciator configuration.

Figure 15-18 *Annunciator Configuration*

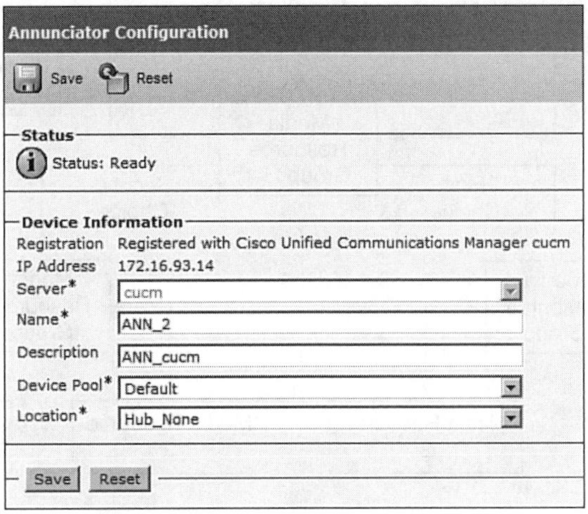

Media Resource Access Control

All media resources are located in a null media resource group by default. Usage of media resources is load balanced between all existing devices. Hardware resources are preferred in the selection algorithm based on their enhanced capabilities (multiple audio codec support) and the reduction of load on the CUCM.

Media resource management controls and manages the media resources within a cluster. The Media Resource Manager (MRM) service enhances CUCM features by making it easier for CUCM to control access to transcoder, annunciator, conferencing, MTP, and MoH resources.

Media resource groups (MRG) define logical groupings of media resources. MRGs create a logical collection of resources and are normally arranged to service a geographical location.

Media resource group lists (MRGL) specify a list of prioritized MRGs. An application can select required media resources from among the available resources according to the priority order that is defined in the MRGL. MRGLs are assigned to devices or device pools. Figure 15-19 illustrates the hierarchical processing order of media resources. MRGLs are similar to route lists, whereas MRGs are similar to route groups.

Figure 15-19 *Media Resource Management*

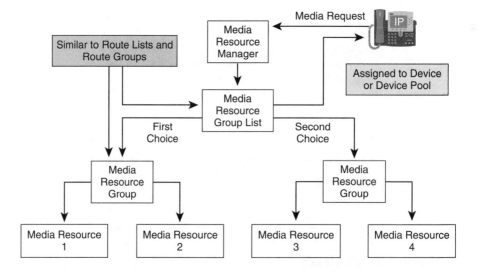

Figure 15-20 shows a media resource management scenario based on arbitrary values for learning purposes.

Figure 15-20 *Media Resource Management Example*

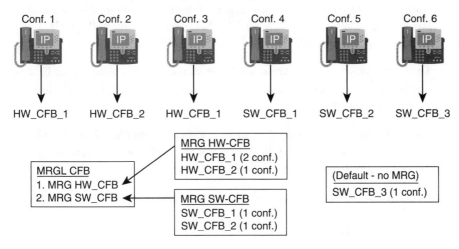

The five conference bridges in Figure 15-20 have the following capabilities:

- **HW_CFB_1**: 2 conference capacity

- **HW_CFB_2**: 1 conference capacity

- **SW_CFB_1**: 1 conference capacity

- **SW_CFB_2**: 1 conference capacity

- **SW_CFB_3**: 1 conference capacity

The following media resource groups have been configured:

- **MRG_HW-CFB**: HW_CFB_1 and HW_CFB_2

- **MRG_SW-CFB**: SW_CFB_1 and SW_CFB_2

- **SW_CFB_3**: Not assigned to an MRG

The MRGL of MRGL_CFB has MRG_HW-CFB configured as first priority and MRG_SW-CFB listed as second priority.

Assume that six conferences are established from devices that all use the MRGL_CFB MRGL. The conference bridges will be allocated in the following way:

- The first conference uses conference bridge HW_CFB_1. The second conference uses conference bridge HW_CFB_2, because the resources within an MRG are load shared and not used in the configured order. The third conference uses HW_CFB_1 again because there are available resources available in that conference bridge resource.

- The fourth conference uses a resource in the second media resource group because the first is out of resources. The fourth conference uses SW_CFB_1, and the fifth conference uses SW_CFB_2.

- The sixth conference does not find a free resource in either MRG, but it finds SW_CFB_3 in the default list. Resources not assigned to a media resource group can be used by any device.

Three configuration steps are required to configure media resource access control:

Step 1   Configure the MRGs.

Step 2   Configure the MRGLs.

Step 3   Assign the MRGLs to phones.

To add an MRG, navigate to **Media Resources > Media Resource Group** in CUCM Administration. At the Media Resource Group Configuration window, enter a name and description for the MRG and add the desired media resources to the MRG. An MRG configuration is illustrated in Figure 15-21.

To add an MRGL, navigate to **Media Resources > Media Resource Group List** in CUCM Administration. At the Media Resource Group List Configuration window, enter a name for the MRGL and add the desired MRG to the MRGL.

Because the order of MRGs within a MRGL specifies the priorities of the MRG, it is important to list the MRGs in the desired order. In Figure 15-22, hardware conference bridges should be used before software conference bridges.

Figure 15-21 *Media Resource Group Configuration*

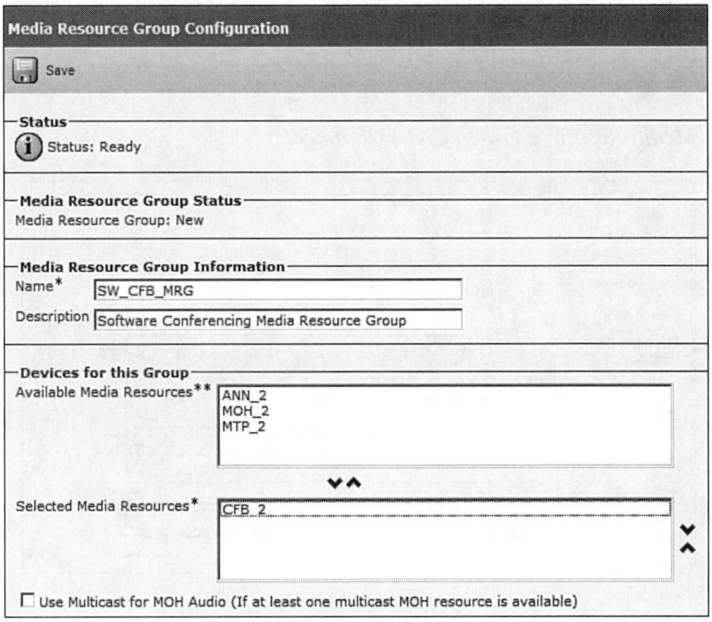

Figure 15-22 *Media Resource Group List Configuration*

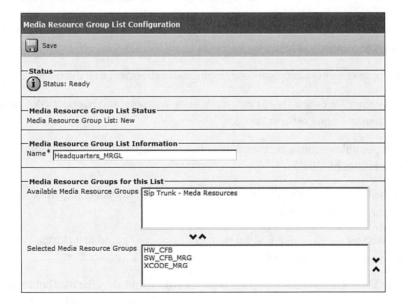

MRGLs can be assigned to devices (phones, trunks, or gateways) or to device pools. In Figure 15-23, an MRGL is assigned directly to an IP phone. If the device pool associated with the phone has a different MRGL, the phone configuration overrides the device pool inheritance.

Figure 15-23 *Media Resource Group List Assignment*

Chapter Summary

The following list summarizes the key points that were discussed in this chapter:

- Media resources are required for voice termination, audio conferencing, transcoding, MTP, annunciator, MoH.

- There are no direct endpoint-to-endpoint audio streams if a media resource is involved.

- Only some hardware-based conference bridges support mixed-mode conferences with participants using different codecs.

- It is possible to configure external conference bridges to enhance the conferencing capabilities of CUCM.

- If the Cisco IPVMS service is running, very few additional configuration steps are required to enable conferencing.

- A maximum of 51 unique audio sources can be configured in a cluster. For a fixed audio source, a Cisco MoH USB audio sound card is required.

- The MoH stream that an endpoint receives is determined by the user hold audio source of the device placing the endpoint on hold and the configured MRGL of the endpoint placed on hold.

- The annunciator streams spoken messages and various call-progress tones to devices supporting SCCP.

- The Media Resource Manager controls the media resources within a CUCM cluster. The media resources are shared within a cluster.

- To limit media resource access, MRGs and MRGLs must be configured and assigned.

Review Questions

Use the questions here to review what you learned in this chapter. The correct answers are found in Appendix A, "Answers to Chapter Review Questions."

1. Which of the following media resources act as a language translator?

   a. Transcoder

   b. Software conference bridge

   c. Annunciator

   d. Music on hold

2. Which of the following media resources require hardware (digital signal processors)?

   a. Conference bridge

   b. Music on hold

   c. Transcoding

   d. Annunciator

3. Which device protocol is used to set up media resources?

   a. SCCP

   b. H.323

   c. SIP

   d. MGCP

4. Which two scenarios require a media termination point?

   a. Mixed-mode audio conference

   b. RFC 2833 on Type A phone

   c. RFC 2833 on Type B phone

   d. Supplementary services on H.323 Version 1 endpoint

   e. Supplementary services on H.323 Version 2 endpoint

5. Which audio codec is supported in software conferencing?

   a. iLBC

   b. G.729

   c. G.722

   d. G.711

6. What are the two media resource deployment models?

   a. Standalone

   b. Centralized

   c. Co-resident

   d. Distributed

7. What are two types of valid conferences?

   a. Reservationless

   b. Ad hoc

   c. Scheduled

   d. Meet-me

   e. Broadcast

8. Which network technology limits the processor utilization of music on hold on CUCM?

   a. Multicast

   b. Broadcast

   c. Unicast

   d. Anycast

9. Which multicast IP address is used for local multicast?

   a. 255.255.255.255

   b. 239.1.1.1

   c. 225.1.1.1

   d. 235.1.1.1

10. What is the maximum number of MoH streams for a 7845 server?

   a. 48

   b. 250

   c. 500

   d. 96

CHAPTER 16

User Features

This chapter describes CUCM features such as call park, directed call park, Do Not Disturb (DND), hold reversion, intercom, call back, barge, privacy, and pickup. The chapter also explains how to configure these features. It provides information about softkeys, phone button templates, user web pages, and IP phone services.

Chapter Objectives

Upon completing this chapter, you will be able to describe and configure Cisco Unified Communications Manager (CUCM) user features and meet these objectives:

- Explain CUCM user features.

- Describe call park and directed call park.

- Describe call pickup and hold reversion.

- Describe DND, intercom, and Cisco Call Back.

- Describe barge and privacy.

- Describe user web pages.

- Describe IP phone services.

Call Park

The call park feature enables a user to park a call so that it can be retrieved from another telephone in the CUCM cluster.

An active call can be parked to a call park extension by pressing the Park softkey. When the Park key is pressed, the LCD screen displays the call park number for 10 seconds by default. This phone number can be dialed from another phone in the system, thus redirecting the call.

The call park feature works within a CUCM cluster. Each CUCM in a cluster must have its own call park extension numbers defined, because the call park configuration is done on a CUCM, not per cluster. Either a single directory number (DN) or a range of DNs can be defined for use as call park extension numbers, up to 100 call park numbers per CUCM cluster. call park numbers cannot overlap between CUCM servers.

CUCM can park only one call at each call park extension number.

Figure 16-1 shows how to use the Call Park feature, as follows:

1.   The user on Phone A calls Phone B.

2.   The user on Phone A wants to take the call in a conference room for privacy. The Phone A user presses the Park softkey.

3.   The CUCM server to which Phone A is registered sends the first available call park number, which displays on Phone A. The user on Phone A watches the display for the call park DN (so that he can dial that DN on Phone C).

4.   The user on Phone A leaves the office and walks to an available conference room where the phone is designated as Phone C. The user goes off-hook on Phone C and dials 1234 to retrieve the parked call.

5.   The system establishes the call between Phones C and B.

The call park feature can also be used across CUCM clusters.

Figure 16-1   *Call Park*

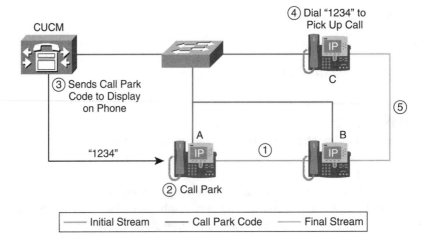

The call park feature is configured by navigating to **Call Routing > Call Park** in CUCM Administration. A maximum of 100 call park extension numbers can be provisioned per CUCM cluster. Each CUCM server must have its own portion of call park numbers carved out of the cluster wide maximum of 100 call park numbers. When a call gets parked, CUCM chooses the next call park extension number that is available and displays that number on the phone. The call park configuration is illustrated in Figure 16-2.

Figure 16-2 *Call Park Configuration*

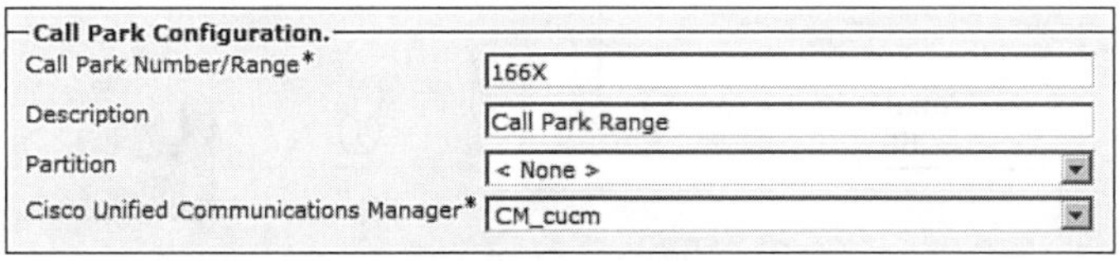

Directed call park numbers can be configured in the CUCM Directed Call Park Configuration window. Directed call park numbers exist cluster-wide. Phones that support the directed call park Busy Lamp Field (BLF) can be configured to monitor the busy/idle status of specific directed call park numbers. Users can also use the BLF to speed dial a directed call park number. The directed call park feature enables users to point the call to a number they use, whereas call park automatically assigns a DN.

CUCM can park only one call at each directed call park number. To retrieve a parked call, a user must dial a configured retrieval prefix followed by the directed call park number at which the call is parked. Configure the retrieval prefix in the Directed Call Park Configuration window.

Figure 16-3 shows the directed call park process explained in the list that follows:

1. Users A and B connect in a call.

2. To park the call, A presses the Transfer softkey and dials the directed call park number 80.

3. User A presses the Transfer softkey again to complete the directed call park transfer. This action parks A2 on directed call park number 80.

4. Phone C dials the directed call park prefix (21) followed by the directed call park number 80 to retrieve the call. After dialing the pattern of 2180, C connects to B.

5. If the call is not retrieved before expiration of the call park reversion timer configured in the service parameter, the call reverts to the configured reversion number.

Figure 16-3 *Directed Call Park*

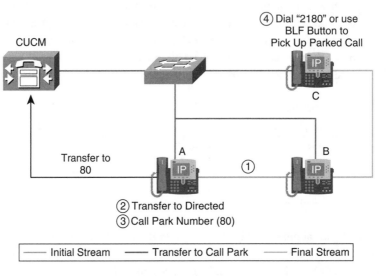

| Initial Stream | Transfer to Call Park | Final Stream |

Any phone that can perform a transfer can use directed call park. The directed call park feature does not require special installation. To configure directed call park, define a unique directed call park number or a range of directed call park numbers. 40XX configures a range of directed call parks (4000 to 4099).

> **NOTE** Cisco does not recommend configuring both directed call park and call park simultaneously. If both features are enabled, ensure that the call park and directed call park numbers do not overlap.

Directed call park is configured by navigating to **Call Routing > Directed Call Park** in CUCM Administration. The directed call park configuration is illustrated in Figure 16-4.

Figure 16-4 *Directed Call Park Configuration*

```
┌─Directed Call Park Information────────────────────────────┐
│ Number*                    [8X                          ]  │
│ Description                [Directed Call Park Range    ]  │
│ Partition                  [Internal_PT              ▼]   │
│ Reversion Number           [35                         ]  │
│ Reversion Calling Search Space [LD_CSS               ▼]   │
│ Retrieval Prefix*          [21]                           │
└───────────────────────────────────────────────────────────┘
```

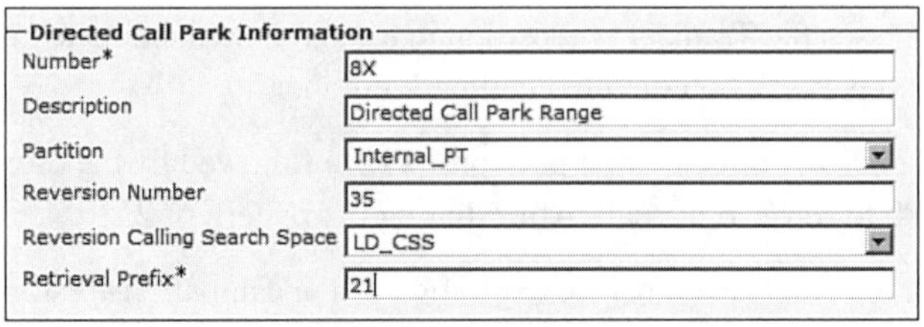

Call Pickup

The purpose of the call pickup feature is to enable a group of users who are seated near each other to cover incoming calls as a group. When a member of the group receives a call and is not available to answer it, any other member of the group can pick up the call from his own phone by using the PickUp softkey.

Three types of call pickup exist:

- **Call pickup**: Enables users to pick up incoming calls on any telephone within their own group. When the users press the PickUp softkey, CUCM automatically dials the appropriate call-pickup number associated with their DN. Because the other phone is in the same pickup group, the incoming call is redirected to the phone that clicked the PickUp softkey.

- **Group call pickup**: Enables users to pick up incoming calls destined to DNs on different pickup groups. Users press the GPickup softkey and dial the appropriate group number for the destination call-pickup group.

- **Other group call pickup**: Enables users to pick up incoming calls in a group that is associated with their own group. This type of call pickup is sometimes referred to as pickup chaining, and it is covered in the next subtopic.

Call-Pickup Example

Phone A and Phone B in Figure 16-5 are assigned to call-pickup Group A (4685). If Phone A is ringing, Phone B can go off-hook, press the PickUp softkey, and then press the Answer softkey. The call is diverted to Phone B.

Group Pickup Example

Phone C in Figure 16-5 belongs to call-pickup Group B with number 4688. Phone A and Phone B are in Group A call-pickup group (4685). When Phone C is ringing, Phone A can go off-hook, press the More softkey, the GPickup softkey, enter Group B's call-pickup number (4688), and then press the Answer softkey. The call is rerouted to Phone A.

Other group call pickup (OPickup) enables users to pick up incoming calls using call pickup even though the call is destined to a phone in a different call-pickup group. Call-pickup groups are associated to other call-pickup groups. CUCM automatically searches for incoming calls in the associated groups to make the call connection when the user activates this feature from a Cisco IP Phone. Use the OPickup softkey for this type of call pickup.

Figure 16-5   *Call Pickup and Group Call Pickup*

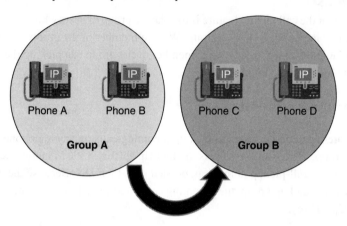

When more than one associated group exists, the priority of answering calls for the associated group goes from the first associated group to the last associated group. For example, Groups A, B, and C associate with Group X, and the priority of answering calls goes to Group A, then B, and then C.

Usually, within the same group, the longest alerting call (longest ringing time) is picked up first if multiple incoming calls occur in that group.

Call pickup, group call pickup, and other group call pickup can be automated by enabling the service parameter Auto Call Pickup Enabled. When this parameter is enabled, CUCM automatically connects users to the incoming call in their own pickup group, in another pickup group, or a pickup group that is associated with their own group after users press the appropriate softkey on the phone. This action requires only one keystroke. Auto Call Pickup connects the user to an incoming call. When the user presses a PickUp softkey on the phone, CUCM locates the incoming call and completes the call connection. If automation is not enabled, the user must press the PickUp and Answer softkeys to make the call connection.

To configure call pickup, a call-pickup number must first be configured and then associated to the DN. Call pickup is configured by navigating to **Call Routing > Call Pickup Group** in CUCM Administration. Enter a unique pickup group name and unique pickup group number. Access to call-pickup groups can be restricted by assigning a partition to the call-pickup group number. When this configuration is used, only the phones that have a calling search space (CSS) that includes the partition with the call-pickup group number can participate in that call-pickup group. Make sure that the combination of partition and group number is unique throughout the system. Figure 16-6 shows the call-pickup configuration.

Figure 16-6 *Call-Pickup Configuration*

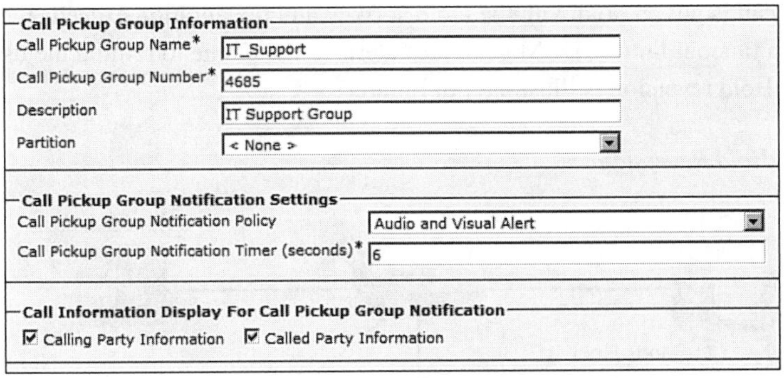

NOTE   In the Call Pickup Group Information section, you can specify pickup groups that should be associated with the current pickup group. The Other Group Call Pickup feature uses this list. The groups are searched sequentially, beginning with the first group in the list.

After the call-pickup group is added in CUCM, the group is assigned to the desired line from the Directory Number Configuration window. The call-pickup DN association is shown in Figure 16-7.

Figure 16-7 *Call-Pickup Directory Number Association*

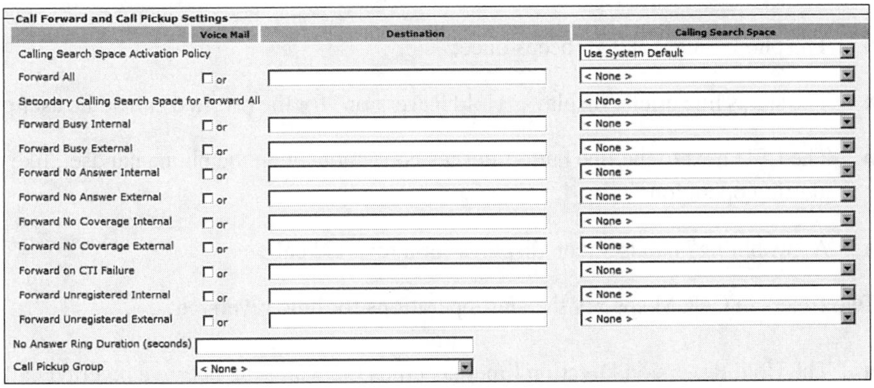

Hold Reversion

When a call is put on hold with the Hold softkey and the duration exceeds the hold-reversion timeout limit, CUCM generates alerts to the phone to remind the user to handle the call. Hold reversion is illustrated in Figure 16-8.

Figure 16-8 *Hold Reversion*

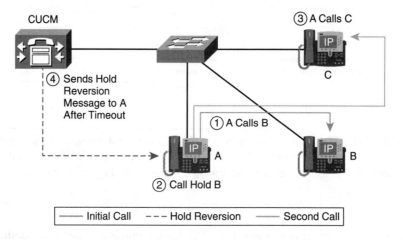

The types of alerts that are generated at the phone for reverted calls depend on the capabilities of the phone device. CUCM provides the following alerts when the Hold Reversion feature activates, depending on the capabilities of the phone and the firmware release that is installed:

■ The phone rings once or beeps once.

■ The status line briefly displays "Hold Reversion" for the reverted call at the user phone.

■ The LED next to the line button flashes continuously on the phone handset, like other alerting operations.

■ A "wobbling" handset icon displays for a reverted call.

Two timers in CUCM specify the alert operations for hold reversion:

■ The Hold Reversion Duration timer specifies the wait time before a reverted call alert gets issued to the phone of the holding party.

■ The Hold Reversion Notification Interval timer specifies the frequency of the periodic reminder alerts to the holding party phone.

A Hold Reversion Duration timer setting of 20 and a Hold Reversion Notification Interval timer setting of 30 means that CUCM will issue the first alert after 20 seconds and a reminder alert every 30 seconds thereafter.

You can configure hold reversion cluster-wide, as shown in Figure 16-9. Change the Hold Reversion Duration timer in the Service Parameters window to a value greater than 0. If the default system setting for reminder alerts is not desired, configure the Hold Reversion Notification Interval timer in the Service Parameters window. The default value specifies 30 seconds.

Figure 16-9 *Cluster-Wide Hold Reversion Configuration*

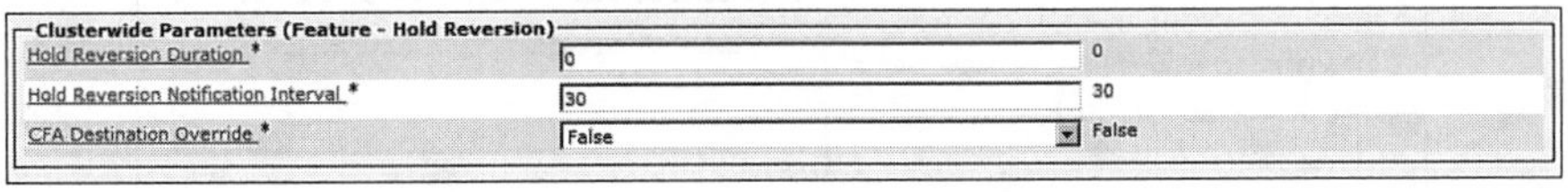

┌Clusterwide Parameters (Feature - Hold Reversion)─		
Hold Reversion Duration *	0	0
Hold Reversion Notification Interval *	30	30
CFA Destination Override *	False	False

To disable hold reversion for a line when the system setting is enabled, enter a value of 0 for the Hold Reversion Duration timer in the Directory Number Configuration window. If the field is left empty, CUCM uses the cluster timer setting.

To enable hold reversion for a line when the system setting is disabled, set the Hold Reversion Duration timer in the Directory Number Configuration window to a value greater than 0.

To enable reminder alerts, configure the Hold Reversion Notification Interval timer to a value greater than 0 in the same window or leave it blank to use the cluster setting.

To configure hold reversion timer settings that differ from the cluster settings when hold reversion is enabled, enter different values for the hold reversion timers in the Directory Number Configuration window.

Figure 16-10 shows the hold reversion DN configuration.

Figure 16-10 *Hold Reversion Directory Number Configuration*

┌Line Settings for All Devices─		
Hold Reversion Ring Duration (seconds)		Setting the Hold Reversion Ring Duration to zero will disable the feature
Hold Reversion Notification Interval (seconds)		Setting the Hold Reversion Notification Interval to zero will disable the feature

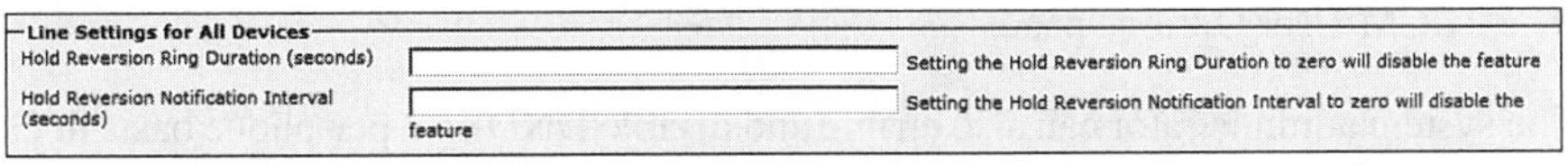

Call-focus priority specifies whether an incoming call or reverted call has priority. Incoming calls have priority by default.

An administrator configures the Reverted Call Focus Priority setting for a device pool, which is then assigned to a phone in CUCM Administration. The focus priority for the device pool that is associated with the phone applies to reverted and incoming calls that appear on the same line or on different lines on the phone device.

A priority value of Default means that incoming calls have priority. A priority value of Highest means that reverted calls have priority. The reverted call focus is configured at the device pool level, as illustrated in Figure 16-11.

Figure 16-11 *Reverted Call Focus Priority*

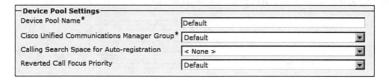

Do Not Disturb

The Do Not Disturb (DND) feature enables a user to turn off the ringer for an incoming call. The default ringer settings beep and flash. DND allows users to reconfigure the ringer settings when the DND softkey is pressed (beep, ring, both, or neither). This DND softkey is pressed directly on the Cisco Unified IP Phone and configured via the DND options from the User Options web pages.

When DND is enabled, all new incoming calls with normal priority honor the DND settings for the device. High-priority calls, such as Cisco Emergency Responder (Cisco ER) calls or calls with multilevel precedence and preemption (MLPP), ring on the device regardless of the DND settings.

The user can enable and disable DND by any of the following methods:

- Softkey

- Feature line key (programmable line keys)

- CUCM User Options pages

The system administrator can also enable and disable DND on a per-phone basis in CUCM Administration.

When DND is enabled, the Cisco Unified IP Phone displays the message "Do Not Disturb is active." The DND line button icon also turns into an empty circle, and on phones with LED buttons, the light turns amber when DND is active.

DND incoming call alert settings determine how the incoming call alert gets presented to the user when DND Ringer Off is enabled. The following list gives the available options:

- **Disable**: This option disables both beep and flash notifications of a call, but incoming call information still gets displayed.

- **Beep Only**: For an incoming call, this option causes the Cisco Unified IP Phone to play a beep tone only.

- **Flash Only**: For an incoming call, this option causes the Cisco Unified IP Phone to display a flash alert only.

DND Incoming Call Alert can be configured on a per-device basis. Figure 16-12 shows the phone configuration for DND.

Figure 16-12 *Phone Do Not Disturb Configuration*

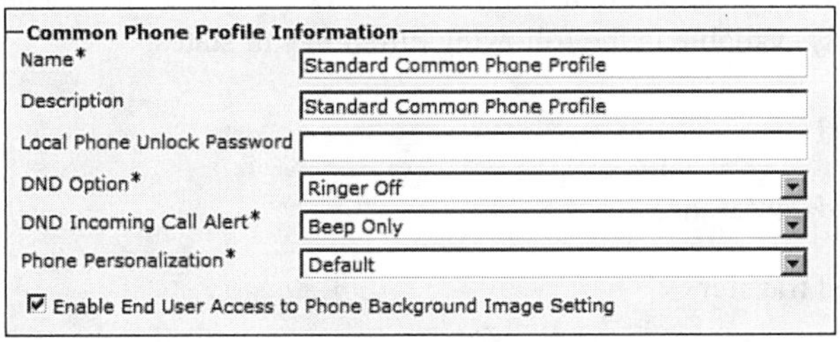

You can configure DND on a common phone profile. To add DND to a common phone profile, navigate to **Device > Device Settings > Common Phone Profile** and choose the phone profile that should be modified. In the Common Phone Profile Configuration window, configure the DND parameters DND Option and DND Incoming Call Alert, as shown in Figure 16-13.

Figure 16-13 *Common Phone Profile Common Phone Profile Configuration*

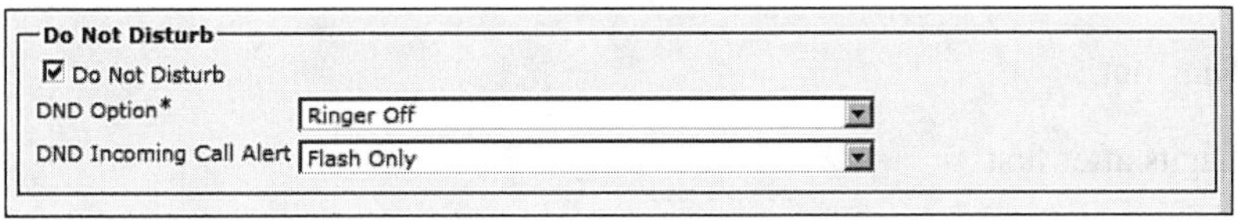

To add a DND softkey, navigate to **Device > Phone Settings > Softkey Template**, and add the DND softkey to a nonstandard softkey template in the Softkey Template Configuration window. Associate the template to the device. Figure 16-14 illustrates a softkey template configuration for the On Hook call state.

Figure 16-14 *Do Not Disturb Softkey Template Configuration*

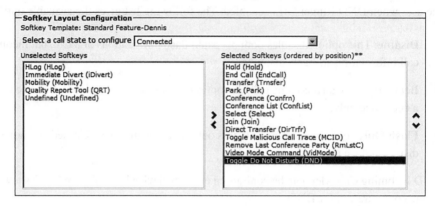

The softkey functions on the Cisco IP Phone change depending on the call state (connected in a call, connected in a conference, phone is on-hook, phone is off-hook, and so on). The DND softkey is available in the following different call states:

■   Connected

■   Connected conference

■   Connected transfer

■   Off-hook

■   Off-hook with feature

■   On hold

■   Remote in use

■   On-hook

■   Ring in

■   Ring out

■   Digits after first

Intercom

Intercom functionality is normally leveraged between administrative assistants and managers. The administrative assistants should not be allowed to hear the manager's conversation, but the manager would like immediate communication from the administrative assistant when, for example, an important business client is on hold at the administrative assistant's phone.

The CUCM intercom function allows a user to call a line of another user, which auto-answers with the line muted. The line must be configured as an intercom line, which causes the destination line to pick up in a one-way whisper conversation. A one-way whisper conversation does not allow the calling party to hear the manager to which the intercom call was routed. The recipient can press the Intercom softkey to convert the whisper conversation into a two-way intercom call.

Intercom is supported only on Cisco Type B phone models 7970, 79x1, 79x2, 79x5, and 7915.

The intercom feature involves the following configuration steps:

Step 1   Create an intercom partition.

Step 2   Verify the automatically generated intercom CSS or optionally replace it with a customized intercom CSS.

Step 3   Create the intercom DNs.

Step 4   Assign intercom DNs to phones.

> **NOTE**   When you create an intercom partition, the Administration interface automatically generates a corresponding intercom CSS with the same name. Customized intercom CSSs are required only if an intercom phone button should support multiple intercom targets and if access control is required to limit the targets that are available to the intercom phone button. The automatically generated intercom CSS does not need to be changed for a standard implementation of point-to-point intercom lines.

Navigate to **Call Routing > Intercom > Route Partition** from CUCM Administration to add one or more intercom partitions. Intercom partitions are created in the same way as normal partitions. Enter the partition name and description separated by a comma. Assuming standard point-to-point intercom lines, one intercom partition is required per intercom line. Figure 16-15 shows the configuration of intercom partitions.

Navigate to **Call Routing > Intercom > Intercom Calling Search Space** from CUCM Administration to configure an intercom CSS. This is required only if an intercom phone button should support multiple intercom targets and if access control is required to limit the targets that are available to the intercom phone button. Figure 16-16 shows the automatically created intercom CSS, which was created after the partition had been added in the previous step.

Figure 16-15 *Intercom Route Partition Configuration*

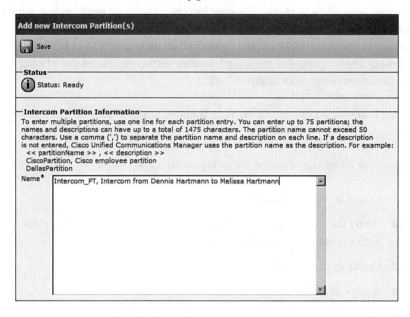

Figure 16-16 *Intercom CSS Configuration*

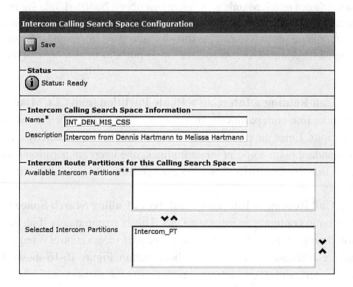

Navigate to **Call Routing > Intercom > Intercom Directory Number** in CUCM Administration to configure a new intercom DN. An intercom DN range will be specified. The values for the From and To fields can be the same if only one intercom DN is being added. Point-to-point intercom lines require a range of two DNs to be specified. Select the intercom partition, and enter a description and alerting name for caller identification (CLID) display. Select an intercom CSS.

If the range was not limited to a single DN, the description and alerting names should not be specific per intercom endpoint, or these values should be changed on the individual DNs after the range has been added.

After you add the intercom DN range, each intercom DN is shown in the list of intercom DNs and can be configured on its own. The intercom range is only a configuration tool to add multiple intercom DNs with similar settings in a single step. Intercom DN configuration is illustrated in Figure 16-17.

Figure 16-17 *Intercom Directory Number Configuration*

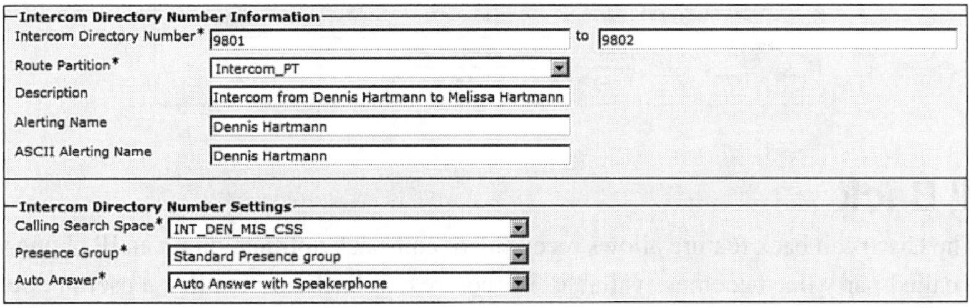

The line appearance of the intercom DN is not stored with the intercom DN but at the individual phone intercom line. Therefore, all fields are blank, and the entered values update only the intercom line appearance at the currently configured phone. Enter the display text that the receiving phone of an intercom call will display and the line text label that will be displayed next to the intercom phone button on the phone display.

A speed dial is set to the target of the intercom connection at the administrative assistant phone. If no speed dial is entered, the target intercom DN has to be dialed after pressing the intercom phone button. If a speed dial is configured, the intercom connection is immediately created after the user presses the intercom phone button. A speed dial is the preferable way to initiate an intercom call.

> **NOTE**   Instead of configuring intercom DNs from **Call Routing > Intercom > Intercom Directory Number** and then assigning the existing intercom DN to a phone intercom line, you can create the intercom DN from the Intercom Line Configuration page of a phone by entering an intercom CN that does not exist yet. In this case, all intercom DN values will be blank, and after the intercom DN has been configured, the DN-related portion is saved as a new intercom DN, and the line appearance configuration is stored at the phone intercom line. The same concept applies to phone DNs; you can create them from **Call Routing > Directory Number** or from a phone line.

Figure 16-18   *Intercom Directory Number Assignment*

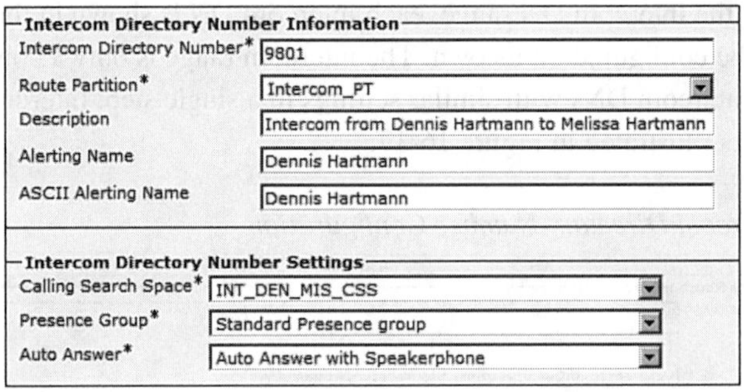

```
┌─Intercom Directory Number Information────────────────────────┐
│ Intercom Directory Number* │9801                           │
│                                                              │
│ Route Partition*           │Intercom_PT              ▼│     │
│                                                              │
│ Description                │Intercom from Dennis Hartmann to Melissa Hartmann│
│                                                              │
│ Alerting Name              │Dennis Hartmann            │     │
│                                                              │
│ ASCII Alerting Name        │Dennis Hartmann            │     │
│                                                              │
│ ┌─Intercom Directory Number Settings──────────────────────┐ │
│ │ Calling Search Space* │INT_DEN_MIS_CSS           ▼│     │ │
│ │                                                        │ │
│ │ Presence Group*       │Standard Presence group   ▼│     │ │
│ │                                                        │ │
│ │ Auto Answer*          │Auto Answer with Speakerphone ▼│ │ │
│ └────────────────────────────────────────────────────────┘ │
└──────────────────────────────────────────────────────────────┘
```

Call Back

The Cisco call back feature allows receiving of call-back notification on an IP phone when a called-party line becomes available. To receive call-back notification, a user presses the CallBack softkey upon receiving a busy or ringback tone when trying to reach a destination. Call-back notification can be activated on a line on an IP phone within the same CUCM cluster as the destination IP phone. Call-back notification cannot be activated if the called party has forwarded all calls to another extension (Call Forward All [CFA] feature). The call back feature leverages the Cisco Extended Functions service.

Example: Cisco Call Back

In Figure 16-19, IP phone user C calls IP phone user A in the same cluster. If IP phone A is busy or there is no answer, IP phone user C activates the Cisco call back feature through the CallBack softkey. When IP phone A becomes available, IP phone C receives an audible alert and visual notification that the previously dialed number has become available. CUCM remembers the dialed number, so IP phone user C can then press the Dial softkey to reach IP phone user A.

Figure 16-19 *Cisco Call Back*

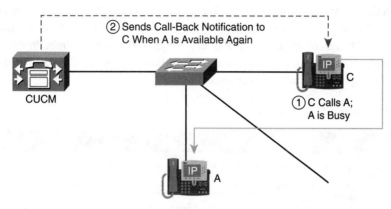

The telephone call states that support call back are busy, call forward busy, or call forward no answer. The call forward no answer state includes call forward no answer to a voice-mail system or to another extension.

To configure the call back feature, choose the softkey template (for example, the Standard User template), copy and insert the template, and name it something appropriate, such as Standard User Callback. Configure the softkey layout by choosing the On Hook call state and the Call Back option. The softkey template is shown in Figure 16-20.

Figure 16-20 *Cisco Call Back Softkey Configuration*

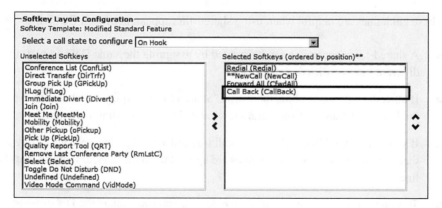

Barge and Privacy

CUCM considers a DN associated to more than one device in the same partition to be a shared-line appearance. One example of a shared-line appearance is where a DN appears on line 1 of a manager telephone and also on line 2 of an assistant telephone. Another example of a shared line is a single incoming number that is set up to appear as line 2 on every help desk telephone in an office. Figure 16-21 shows a DN that is associated with two devices. Notice that the phone name in Figure 16-21 includes an SEP prefix followed by the MAC addresses of the device. SEP is an acronym for Selsius Ethernet Phone. Selsius is the company Cisco acquired that created the CallManager product. Cisco has been involved in the development of CallManager since Version 2.0.

Figure 16-21   *Shared-Line Appearance*

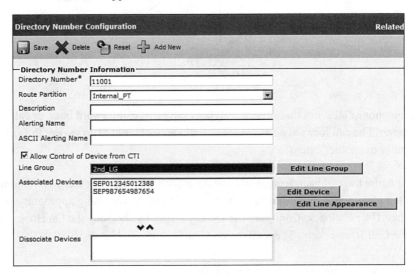

These guidelines are helpful when using shared-line appearances with CUCM:

- A shared-line appearance can be created by assigning the same DN and partition to different lines on different devices.

- If other devices share a line, the words "Shared Line" display in red next to the DN in the Directory Number Configuration window in CUCM Administration.

- If you change the CSS, call waiting, call forward, or call pickup settings on any device that uses the shared line, the changes are applied to all the devices that use that shared line.

- To stop sharing a line appearance on a device, you can change the DN or partition number for the line and update the device. (Deletion removes the DN on the current device only. The deletion does not affect the other devices.)

- Do not use shared-line appearances on any Cisco Unified IP Phone that will be used with the Attendant Console.

- Do not use shared-line appearances on any Cisco Unified IP Phone 7960 or 7961 that requires the Auto Answer capability.

The barge feature allows a manager or supervisor with the Barge softkey to enter into an existing call on a shared line. Two types of barge are available in Cisco Unified Call-Manager Release 4.0 and later:

- **Barge using built-in conference** (Barge softkey): Barge uses the built-in conference capability of the target IP phone. Barge also uses the Standard User or Standard Feature softkey template (both contain the Barge softkey). When a barge is being set up, no media interruption occurs, and the only display change to the original call is a spinning circle displayed at the right side of the Prompt Status message window at the target device. The Barge feature is supported only when the G.711 audio codec is in use. The digital signal processor (DSP) of the target phone mixes the audio conversations. When the initiator uses barge to join the call, it becomes a three-way call. When only two parties are left in the conference, they experience a brief interruption while the media streams are reconnected as a point-to-point call, releasing the shared conference resources. If the target hangs up, the caller who used barge and the other party connect in a point-to-point call. If the other party hangs up, the original call and the barged call are released.

- **Barge using shared conference** (cBarge softkey): Conference Barge (cBarge) uses a shared conference bridge. No standard softkey template includes the cBarge softkey. To enable users to access the cBarge softkey, the administrator must add it to a non-standard softkey template and then assign the softkey template to a device. When a user presses the cBarge softkey, a barge call is set up by means of the shared conference bridge, if it is available. The original call is split and then joined at the conference bridge, which causes a brief media interruption. The call information for all parties changes to barge. The barged call becomes a conference call with the barge target device as the conference controller. The conference controller can add more parties to the conference or can drop any party.

Barge configuration involves the following configuration options:

- Assign the Standard User or Standard Feature softkey template to each device that accesses barge using the built-in bridge functionality.

- To enable barge cluster-wide for all users, choose **System > Service Parameters** for the Cisco CallManager service and set the Built-In Bridge Enable cluster-wide service parameter to On. This is illustrated in Figure 16-22. Alternatively, configure the barge feature for each telephone by setting the Built-In Bridge field in the Phone Configuration window on the device.

- Set the Party Entrance Tone setting to True if you desire the target phone to hear a tone when the line is barged into.

Figure 16-22 *Cluster-Wide Barge Configuration*

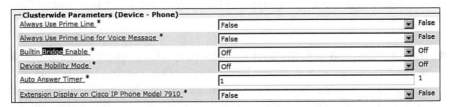

To configure the Barge feature with Shared Conference Bridge (cBarge), follow these steps:

Step 1 Assign the Standard User or Standard Feature softkey template (configure cBarge to either template) to each device that accesses barge by using the shared conference bridge.

Step 2 Set the optional cluster-wide service parameter Party Entrance Tone to True (required for tones).

Step 3 Associate the devices to the cBarge softkey template.

Step 4 Notify users that the cBarge feature is available.

The privacy feature was introduced in CUCM Release 4.0. Administrators can enable or disable the ability of users with telephones that share the same line to view call status and to barge into the call if they click the Privacy button on their phone before selecting the shared line. Administrators enable or disable privacy for each phone. The Privacy button requires a phone button template with the Privacy button to be assigned to the phone.

To configure the privacy feature, follow these steps:

Step 1 Set the optional Privacy Setting cluster-wide service parameter to True if a large number of devices will be using the privacy feature of shared lines.

Step 2 Modify one or more phone button templates to include a phone button for privacy.

Step 3 Each phone requiring privacy must have the Privacy option set to On in the Privacy drop-down menu of the Cisco Unified IP Phone Configuration window. If privacy is configured cluster-wide, the Privacy setting should be left at Default or On to enable privacy. This is illustrated in Figure 16-23. The Privacy Off setting will override the cluster-wide setting inheritance.

Figure 16-23 *Device-Level Barge Configuration*

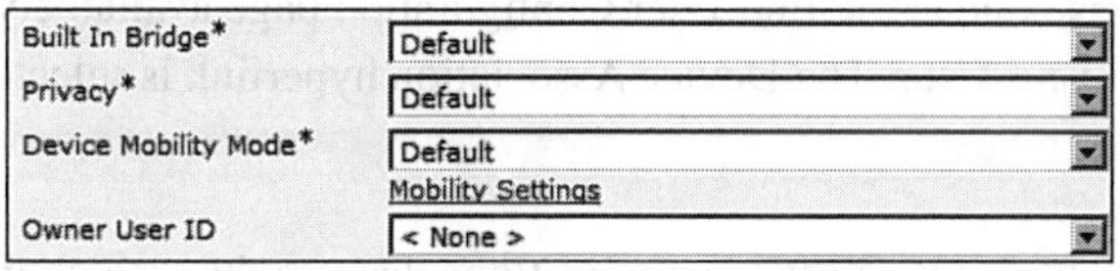

Built In Bridge*	Default
Privacy*	Default
Device Mobility Mode*	Default
	Mobility Settings
Owner User ID	< None >

Step 4 Assign the phone button template that contains the Privacy feature button to IP phones that require that feature.

When privacy is enabled, the Privacy button changes display; a black circle appears inside the Privacy field. Now, when the other user on the shared line goes off-hook on the shared line, the Barge softkey does not appear.

User Web Pages

Cisco Unified IP Phone end users can access CUCM the User Options page through their web browser to configure a variety of features on their phone.

The URL of the CUCM User Options web page is https://<CUCM IP Address>/CCMUser/.

User-definable settings include the following:

- User locale (language)

- User password

- Do Not Disturb (on/off)

- Call forward (all, busy, no answer, and no coverage)

- Message waiting indicator and ring settings

- Line text label

- Speed dials

- IP phone services and service buttons

- Personal address book

In the CUCM Enterprise Parameters pages, administrators can configure which features are made available to users by setting enterprise parameters as either True or False. For example, the administrator can set the Show Speed Dial Settings enterprise parameter to False, in which case users cannot configure speed dials on their phones.

For the phone to be self-administered, the end user account must be associated to the phone. The association is done at the End User Configuration page available via **User Management > End User**. The Device Association hyperlink is selected, and the phone is associated to the end user.

Cisco Unified IP Phone services are applications that use the web client/server and Extensible Markup Language (XML) capabilities of the Cisco Unified IP Phone. The Cisco Unified IP Phone firmware contains a micro web browser that enables limited web browsing capability. These phone service applications provide the potential for value-added services and productivity enhancement by running directly on the user's desktop phone. For purposes of this chapter, the term *phone service* refers to an application that sends and receives content to and from the Cisco Unified IP Phone.

The following phones support IP Phone services:

- Cisco Unified Wireless IP Phone 7921G

- Cisco Unified IP Phones 7940G, 7941G, and 7941G-GE

- Cisco Unified IP Phones 7960G, 7961G, and 7961G-GE

- Cisco Unified IP Phones 7970G and 7971G-GE

IP phone services can also run on the following IP phones; however, these phone models support only text-based XML applications:

- Cisco Unified IP Phone 7905G

- Cisco Unified IP Phone 7906G

- Cisco Unified IP Phone 7911G

- Cisco Unified IP Phones 7912G and 7912G-A

- Cisco Unified Wireless IP Phone 7920

All the IP phones listed here can process a limited set of Cisco-defined XML objects for enabling the user interface between the phone and the web server that contains the running phone service. Note that the phones listed here support phone services for both the Skinny Client Control Protocol (SCCP) and Session Initiation Protocol (SIP).

IP Phone Services

Typical IP phone services that might be supplied to a phone include weather information, stock quotes, and news. Deployment of Cisco Unified IP Phone services occurs using the HTTP protocol from standard web servers, such as the Apache web services.

A user can access a service from the supported phone model in two ways. The user can press the Services button, or the user can use a preconfigured phone button. When the user presses the Services button, the phone uses its HTTP client to load a specific URL that contains a service or menu of services to which the phone is subscribed. The user then chooses a service from the listing by clicking the Select softkey.

Users can subscribe only to services that are configured through CUCM Administration. The following information is configured for each service:

- URL of the server that provides the content

- Service name and description, which help end users browsing the system

- A list of parameters that are appended to the URL when it is sent to the server

These parameters personalize a service for an individual user. Examples of parameters include stock ticker symbols, city names, Zip codes, and user IDs.

From CUCM Administration, a lobby phone or other shared devices can be subscribed to a service.

After the system administrator configures the services, users can log in to the Cisco Unified IP Phone User Options and subscribe to services. From the Cisco Unified IP Phone User Options, users can subscribe to any service on their phone. (Subscriptions occur on a per-device basis.)

Guidelines and Tips

A Cisco Unified IP Phone displays graphics or text menus, depending on how the services are configured.

The Cisco Unified IP Phone 7960 supports the HTTP header that is sent with any window that includes a Refresh setting. After a fixed time, a new window can replace any XML object that displays. The user can force a reload by quickly pressing the Update softkey. If a timer parameter of 0 was sent in the header, the window moves only to the next window when you press the Update softkey. The window never automatically reloads.

The Cisco Unified IP Phone 7960 supports the following softkeys that are intended to help the data-entry process:

- **Submit**: This softkey indicates that the form is complete and that the resulting URL should be sent via HTTP.

- <<: Use the Backspace softkey to backspace within a field.

- **Cancel**: This softkey cancels the current input.

Use the vertical scroll button for field-to-field navigation.

> **NOTE**   Do not put Cisco Unified IP Phone services on any Cisco Unified CUCM server at the local site or any server that is associated with CUCM, such as the TFTP server or directory database publisher server. This precaution eliminates the possibility that errors in a Cisco Unified IP Phone service application will impact CUCM performance or interrupt call-processing services.

To configure IP phone services links in CUCM Administration, navigate to **Device > Device Settings > Phone Services**. Click the **Add New** button. The IP Phone Services Configuration window will display.

Enter the service name, description, and URL settings for the service and click **Save**. To apply changes to an existing service, update the IP Phone Services Configuration window by clicking **Update Subscriptions** to rebuild all user subscriptions. Subscriptions must be updated if the service URL was changed, a phone service parameter was removed, or a parameter name for a phone service was changed.

Chapter Summary

The following list summarizes the key points that were discussed in this chapter:

- CUCM provides several predefined user features.

- Users can also use the BLF to speed dial a directed call park number.

- The default hold-reversion timeout is defined in the CallManager Service parameters and is overruled by a setting on the line.

- Users can use an intercom line only to dial other intercom lines.

- Barge uses a built-in conference bridge; cBarge uses a shared conference bridge.

■ The User Options web page enables users to change the call forward busy and no answer for assigned phones.

■ The IP Phone Service menu is delivered by the CUCM, whereas the service itself comes from an application server.

Review Questions

Use the questions here to review what you learned in this chapter. The correct answers are found in Appendix A, "Answers to Chapter Review Questions."

1. Call park ranges are configured in which way?

   a. Per CUCM

   b. Per cluster

   c. Per device pool

   d. Per Callmanager group

2. Which function enables users in the same pickup group to pick up an incoming call?

   a. Group pickup

   b. Pickup range

   c. Call pickup

   d. Other pickup

3. Which function enables pickup groups to be associated with other pickup groups (pickup chaining)?

   a. Group pickup

   b. Pickup range

   c. Call pickup

   d. Other pickup

4. Which function enables a caller in one pickup group to pick up an incoming call in another pickup group?

   a. Group pickup

   b. Pickup range

   c. Call pickup

   d. Other pickup

5. Do Not Disturb is configurable by changing which two parameters?

   a. Softkey template

   b. Phone button template

   c. Bulk Administration tool template

   d. Phone configuration

6. Call barge is available on which of the following types of lines?

   a. Intercom directory number

   b. Directory number

   c. Shared lines

   d. Phone button template

7. The intercom feature requires which parameters?

   a. Intercom calling search space

   b. Intercom administrator

   c. Intercom partition

   d. Intercom route pattern

8. The intercom feature is available on which two phones?

   a. 7970

   b. 7961

   c. 7940

   d. 7960

   e. 7912

9. Which two parameters do you use to configure the privacy feature?

   a. User configuration

   b. Phone configuration

   c. Phone button template

   d. Softkey template

CHAPTER 17

Presence-Enabled Speed Dials and Lists

Users are more mobile than ever in the current working environment. Users work from home, the office, airport lounges, and so on. To communicate with others efficiently, it is helpful to know their current availability. How can the user be reached (phone, instant messaging [IM], or e-mail), and are they ready to communicate? Cisco Unified Communications solutions feature presence information that identifies user availability, preference, and status. This level of presence information requires a dedicated Cisco Unified Presence server.

Basic Presence is an integrated part of Cisco Unified Communications Manager (CUCM) beginning with Version 6.0. Basic Presence information includes only device status (on-hook, off-hook, and unregistered). Presence allows Unified Communications users to monitor the status of directory numbers (DN). This chapter describes how the CUCM Presence feature works and how to configure it.

Chapter Objectives

Upon completing this chapter, you will be able to describe and configure CUCM user features and be able to meet these objectives:

- Describe the CUCM Presence feature.

- Describe how CUCM natively supports the Presence feature.

- Describe how to configure the Presence feature in CUCM.

- Describe how access control for Presence subscription is supported by CUCM.

- Describe how to configure Presence access control in CUCM.

Presence

Cisco Unified Communications includes multiple options to integrate basic Presence information. The CUCM-included Presence information includes the following capabilities:

- **Presence-enabled speed dials**: Speed dial buttons that indicate the status of the target of the speed dial

- **Presence-enabled call and directory lists**: Call lists and directory entries that indicate the status of each list entry

- **Presence policy**: Tools allowing access control to Presence information

When using the Cisco Unified Presence Server product, additional features are added to those provided by the native CUCM Presence feature, including the following:

- Standards-based Session Initiation Protocol (SIP) / SIP for Instant Messaging and Presence Leveraging Extensions (SIMPLE) network interface

- User status information, not only device (line) status information

- IM capabilities, including integration with third-party servers

- Cisco Unified Personal Communicator, which is a client tool that integrates voice, video, audio conferencing, videoconferencing, and IM communications

NOTE   This lesson covers the CUCM Presence feature only.

Presence Support in CUCM

CUCM Presence is natively supported by CUCM, with no extra products or servers required. It allows an interested party (watcher) to monitor the real-time status of a DN (Presence entity).

A watcher subscribes to the status information of one or more Presence entities. The status information of a Presence entity can be viewed using Presence-enabled speed dials or Presence-enabled lists: call lists such as placed, received, or missed calls and public directory lists.

The status can be one of the following:

- Unknown (shown when the watched device is unregistered)

- On-hook

- Off-hook

In Figure 17-1, John's phone has subscribed to the status of Bryan's primary DN. The CUCM Presence feature will now keep Bryan's phone updated about the status of the subscribed Presence entity.

If Bryan goes off-hook while John is browsing the call list that includes Bryan's DN, the status information for Bryan's phone changes to indicate Bryan's availability (off-hook).

If John has a Presence-enabled speed dial for Bryan's DN, the speed dial displays the current status of Bryan's DN. John's phone also subscribes to the status of the other Presence entities (users) of the call list automatically as the call list is viewed.

Figure 17-1 *Presence Operation*

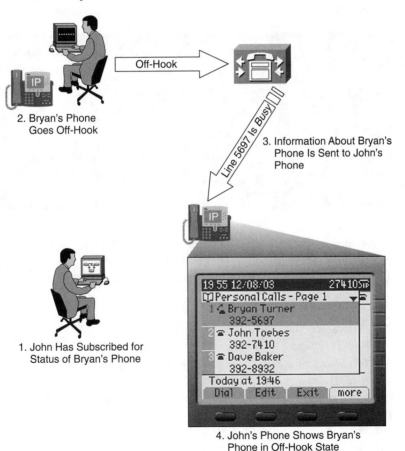

2. Bryan's Phone
Goes Off-Hook

Off-Hook

3. Information About Bryan's
Phone Is Sent to John's
Phone

Line 5697 Is Busy

1. John Has Subscribed for
Status of Bryan's Phone

19 55 12/08/03   27410📶
[📇] Personal Calls - Page 1   ▼📖
1 ⚃ Bryan Turner
      392-5697
2 ☎ John Toebes
      392-7410
3 ☎ Dave Baker
      392-8932
Today at 19:46
  Dial │ Edit │ Exit │ more

4. John's Phone Shows Bryan's
Phone in Off-Hook State

CUCM Presence allows DNs to be watched by Cisco IP Phones on the same cluster and by devices on remote clusters through a SIP trunk. Endpoints that can be reached through a SIP trunk can be watched by Cisco IP Phones, and SIP devices can watch Presence status over other trunk types in addition to SIP. Cisco IP Phones running Skinny Client Control Protocol (SCCP) and Cisco IP Phones running SIP can watch Presence entities and can be watched. If Presence subscriptions are sent over a SIP trunk, CUCM handles protocol conversion between SCCP and SIP.

Cisco IP Phones can display status information (unknown, on-hook, or off-hook) of Presence entities by using Presence-enabled speed dials or call and directory list entries, as shown in Figure 17-2.

Figure 17-2   *Presence Operation*

Presence-enabled speed dials show a symbol inside the screen of the IP phone, located at the appropriate speed dial button. Type B Cisco Unified IP Phones have an LED inside the speed dial button and indicate the Presence entity status by an illuminated button (red indicates off-hook).

The 7914 sidecar module, which adds 14 additional buttons to a Cisco Unified IP Phone, does not support Presence when running SIP. The 7940 and 7960 IP Phones also do not support Presence running SIP. These phones support Presence when using SCCP. Type B Cisco Unified IP Phone models 79x1, 79x2, 79x5, and 7970 support Presence-enabled call and directory lists and Presence-enabled speed dials regardless of the protocol used (SIP or SCCP).

Cisco IP Communicator 2.1 also supports both Presence-enabled speed dials and Presence-enabled call and directory lists. Cisco IP Communicator 2.1 added SIP support.

Presence Configuration

The CUCM Presence configuration procedure includes the following three steps:

Step 1 Enable Presence-enabled speed dials:

   a. Customize phone button templates to include Presence-enabled speed dial buttons.

   b. Apply phone button templates to phones.

   c. Configure Presence-enabled speed dial buttons.

   d. Apply subscribe calling search space to phones.

Step 2 Enable Presence-enabled call lists. Enable the BLF for Call Lists enterprise parameter

Step 3 Allow Presence subscriptions through SIP trunks. Enable CUCM Presence on SIP trunks.

Presence-enabled speed dials and call lists are independent of each other. Presence subscriptions can work between vendors or CUCM clusters through SIP trunks.

The first step for implementing Presence-enabled speed dials is to configure a phone button template that includes Presence-enabled speed dials. To configure a phone button template, go to **Device > Device Settings > Phone Button Template** and either add a new template or copy one of the default phone button templates and save it with a new name. Configure the phone button template with the desired number of Presence-enabled speed dials, as illustrated in Figure 17-3.

Figure 17-3 *Speed Dial Phone Button Template Configuration: Busy Lamp Field Speed Dial*

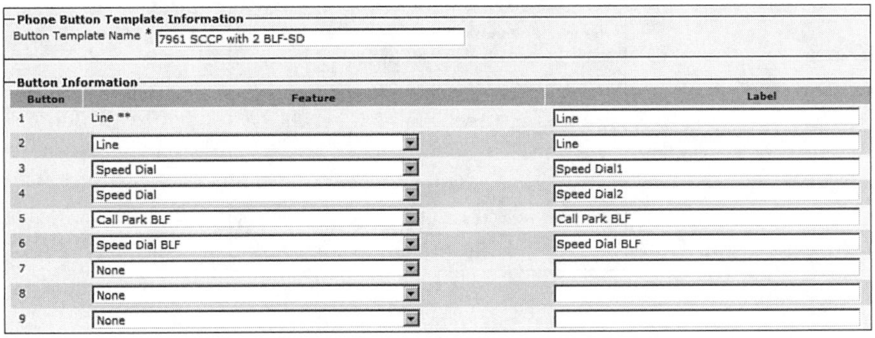

Button	Feature	Label
1	Line **	Line
2	Line	Line
3	Speed Dial	Speed Dial1
4	Speed Dial	Speed Dial2
5	Call Park BLF	Call Park BLF
6	Speed Dial BLF	Speed Dial BLF
7	None	
8	None	
9	None	

Phone Button Template Information
Button Template Name * 7961 SCCP with 2 BLF-SD

NOTE In CUCM Administration, Presence-enabled speed dials are called speed dial BLF.

Assign the previously configured phone button template to the IP phone as shown in Figure 17-4. Navigate to the Phone Configuration page from CUCM Administration (**Device > Phone > Find**) and select the appropriate template from the Phone Button Template drop-down list. Save the configuration and reset the device.

Figure 17-4   *Assign Phone Button Templates to Phone*

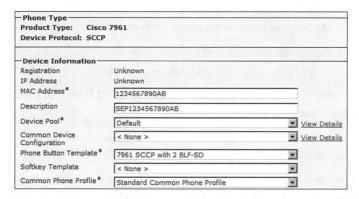

After the new phone button template has been applied, the Presence-enabled speed dials display in the Association Information area of the Phone Configuration page (left side). The phone can now use buttons for Presence-enabled speed dials. To configure the Presence-enabled speed dials, click the **Add a New BLF-SD** link shown in Figure 17-5.

Figure 17-5   *Phone Configuration: Adding Busy Lamp Field Speed Dial*

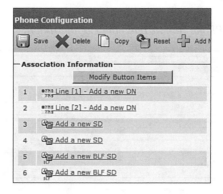

The Busy Lamp Field Speed Dial Configuration window will pop up after you click the BLF-SD link. Configure the target (Presence entity to be watched) of the Presence-enabled speed dial button, and a label will display on the phone screen next to the corresponding button. Figure 17-6 shows this configuration.

Figure 17-6 *Busy Lamp Field Speed Dial Configuration*

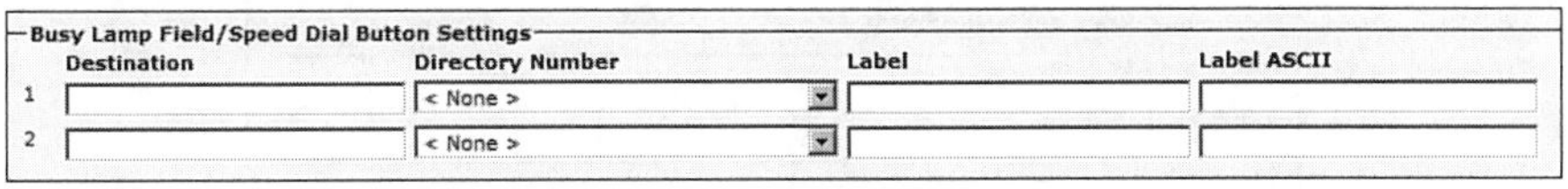

If call lists should also provide Presence information, the appropriate enterprise parameter has to be enabled, as shown in Figure 17-7. After you change this enterprise parameter, all phones that support Presence have to be reset for the change to become effective.

Figure 17-7 *Busy Lamp Field for Call Lists*

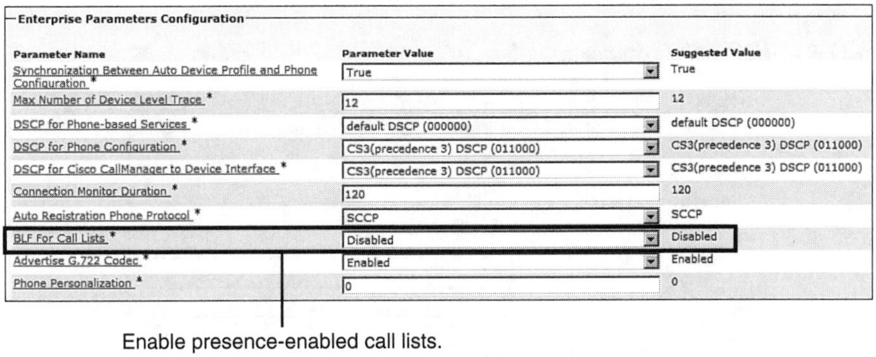

Enable presence-enabled call lists.

If Presence subscriptions will be used over a SIP trunk, Presence must be enabled on the SIP trunk. Presence is enabled through the SIP trunk security profile, not directly at the SIP trunk. Configure a SIP trunk security profile from **System > Security Profile > SIP Trunk Security Profile** configuration pages. The **Accept Presence Subscription** and **Accept Unsolicited Notification** check boxes should be checked to enable SIP Presence information, as shown in Figure 17-8.

Figure 17-8   *SIP Trunk Security Profile*

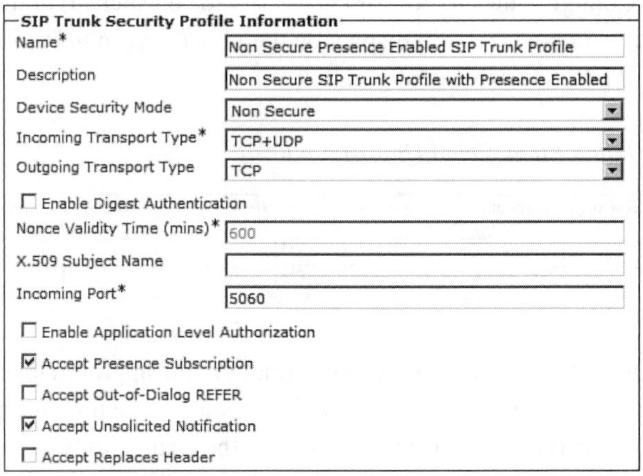

Apply the SIP trunk security profile to the SIP trunk as shown in Figure 17-9.

Figure 17-9   *SIP Trunk Presence Enablement*

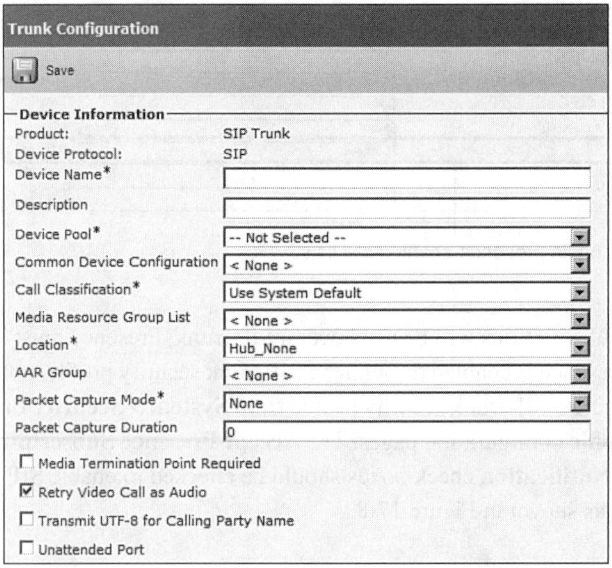

Presence Policies

CUCM Presence has multiple ways of limiting Presence information. Presence-enabled speed dials are configured statically by the CUCM administrator and cannot be configured or modified directly by a user. The administrator maintains control of the monitored

Presence entities for each watcher. Subscribe calling search spaces (CSS) also apply to Presence-enabled speed dials.

Access control for Presence-enabled call and directory lists can be provided by partitions and subscribe CSSs and by Presence groups. Each of the two methods can be used independently of each other. If both are used, both have to permit a subscription for successful watching of the Presence entity's status.

A subscribe CSS is applied to a watcher. A watcher can be a SIP trunk, an IP phone, or an end user. Subscribe CSSs do not use the concept of a device and line CSS. Watching a Presence entity is always a global function of the IP phone.

Subscribe CSSs determine which Presence entities a watcher is allowed to monitor. A subscription is permitted only if the watcher has the partition of the desired Presence entity in its subscribe CSS.

A partition can be used for both calling privileges and Presence policies. If no partition is applied to the desired Presence entity, the Presence entity is available to all watchers. Presence policies and calling privileges share a configuration element. The partitions that are applied to lines or route patterns apply to both. Therefore, implementing Presence policies impacts existing calling privileges and vice versa.

Whenever partition configuration is changed because of the implementation of one of the two features, the other one is affected. Therefore, calling privileges and Presence policies have to be designed and implemented together.

Figure 17-10 consists of three CSSs:

- CSS C-1 contains partitions P-1 and P-2.

- CSS C-2 contains partitions P-1, P-2, and P-3.

- CSS C-3 contains partition P-1 only.

Phone 1 has partition P-1 applied to its line, which is configured with DN 1001. CSS C-1 is assigned to Phone 1.

Phone 2 has partition P-2 applied to its line, which is configured with DN 1002. CSS C-2 is assigned to Phone 2.

A SIP phone with number 1003 can be reached through a SIP trunk. The corresponding route pattern 8.1003 is in partition P-3. CSS C-3 is assigned to the SIP trunk.

The effective permissions for Presence subscriptions are as follows:

■ Phone 1 is allowed to watch the status of 1002 but not of 1003.

■ Phone 2 is allowed to watch both other phones.

■ Phone 3 is allowed to subscribe to Presence information of 1001 but not of 1002.

Figure 17-10 *Subscribe CSS Example*

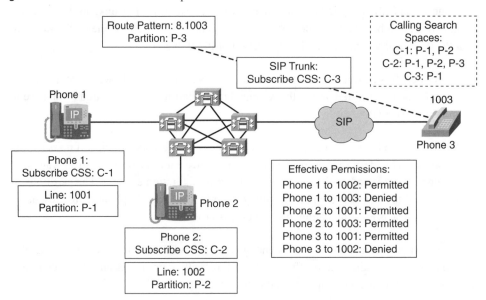

Presence policies watchers and Presence entities are put into Presence groups. Subscriptions can be allowed or denied at an intergroup level. Within a Presence group, subscriptions are always permitted (unless denied by partitions and subscribe CSS).

IP phones are configured with two or more Presence groups: One is applied to the device (in the role as a watcher), and each line can be configured with a Presence group in its role as a Presence entity.

Only one Presence group is configured on a SIP trunk. The SIP trunk can be used in both watcher and Presence entity roles. A Presence group cannot be applied to a route pattern.

Presence groups can also be assigned to end users. They are used when the end users are logging in to the phone using extension mobility or when the users are associated with a device.

> **NOTE**   Presence groups apply only to Presence-enabled call lists; they do not apply to Presence-enabled speed dials.

Figure 17-11 uses three Presence groups: G-1, G-2, and G-3. Inter-Presence group subscriptions are permitted from G-2 to G-3 and G-3 to G-1. All other inter-Presence group subscriptions are denied.

Phone 1 has Presence group G-1 applied to its line, which is configured with DN 1001. Presence group G-2 is assigned to Phone 1.

Phone 2 has Presence group G-2 applied to its line, which is configured with DN 1002. Presence group G-2 is also assigned to Phone 2.

A SIP phone with number 1003 can be reached through a SIP trunk. Presence group G-3 is assigned to the SIP trunk.

The effective permissions for Presence subscriptions are as follows:

- Phone 1 is allowed to watch the status of 1002 and 1003.

- Phone 2 is allowed to watch 1003 but not 1001.

- Phone 3 is allowed to subscribe to Presence information of 1001 but not of 1002.

Figure 17-11   *Presence Group Example*

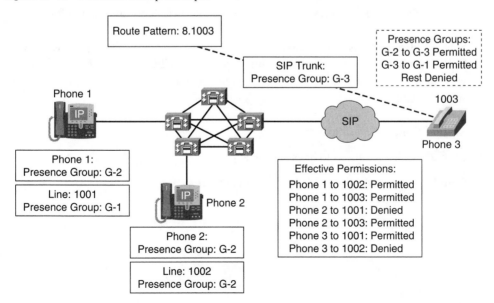

Subscribe CSSs can be used with Presence groups, or either one of them can be used alone to restrict watcher access. If both are implemented, both mechanisms have to permit the subscription to allow successful watching.

Combining both Presence policy mechanisms provides two hierarchy levels, which can prove useful in larger deployments or complex scenarios.

The following example explains how subscribe CSSs and partitions and Presence groups can be effectively combined to fulfill the given requirements:

- **Requirements**: No subscriptions are allowed between different departments. Within a department, managers can be watched only by their assistants. All other subscriptions within a department should be possible.

- **Solution**: One Presence group is configured per department. Inter-Presence group subscriptions are denied by setting the default inter-Presence group policy accordingly. One partition is configured per manager. Each of these partitions is listed only in the subscribe CSS of the respective manager's assistant.

Presence groups are used for the first level of Presence policies at the department level, and subscribe CSSs and partitions are used for additional access control within a department for the assistants to watch the managers.

Presence Policy Configuration

The CUCM Presence policy configuration is done via Presence groups, but a subscribe CSS can limit the Presence entities that the watcher can receive status information for.

Subscribe CSSs are configured the same way as traditional CSSs. The application of the CSS is focused on restricting Presence information. The CEO of the company might not want an intern to watch his phone status. The following procedure is required to implement subscribe CSSs:

Step 1 Configure partitions and CSSs.

Step 2 Assign partitions to lines and route patterns.

Step 3 Assign subscribe CSSs to phones and trunks.

Presence groups represent a straightforward mechanism to limit what Presence entities a watcher can watch. If the organizational goal includes restricting Presence information within a group, subscribe CSSs must be used. The following procedure is required to implement Presence groups:

Step 1   Configure Presence groups.

Step 2   Set the default inter-Presence group policy.

Step 3   Assign Presence groups to lines, phones, or SIP trunks.

The first two steps of implementing subscribe CSSs involve standard partitions and CSSs that will be used for Presence information. Figures 17-12 and 17-13 display subscribe CSS applications to an IP phone and SIP trunk (respectively). The subscribe CSS at the phone level limits the Presence entities that the phone can watch. The subscribe CSS at the trunk level restricts the DNs that can be watched over the SIP trunk.

Figure 17-12   *Subscribe CSS Application: Phone*

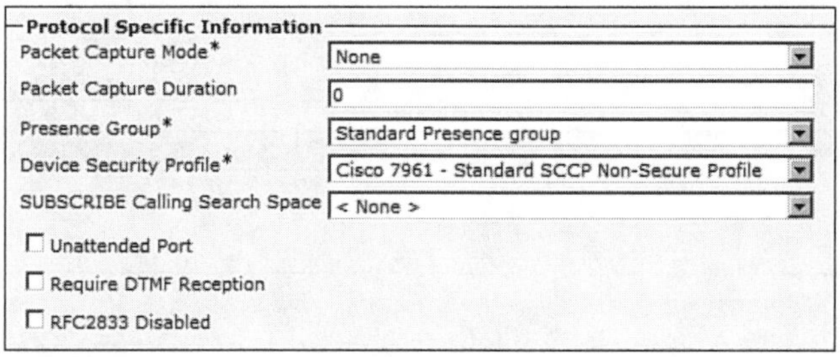

Figure 17-13   *Subscribe CSS Application: Trunk*

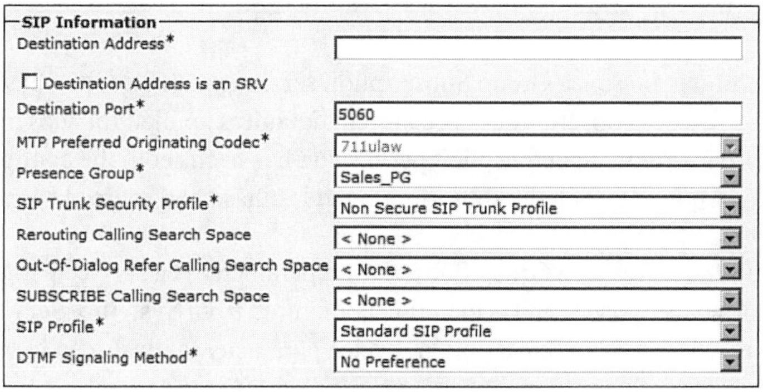

Presence groups can be configured from **System > Presence Group**. One Presence group exists by default and cannot be deleted. The default Presence group is called the Standard Presence group. All phones, lines, and SIP trunks by default are members of the Standard Presence group. The Standard Presence group can be modified in the way that the permissions to other groups can be set, but it cannot be deleted.

When adding a new Presence group, enter a name and description and configure the permission for subscriptions toward other Presence groups. The permission does not have to be entered toward all other Presence groups; the permission for subscriptions toward unconfigured Presence groups is determined by system default, which is configurable as a Cisco CallManager service parameter. Figure 17-14 shows the configuration of a Presence group.

Figure 17-14 *Presence Group Configuration*

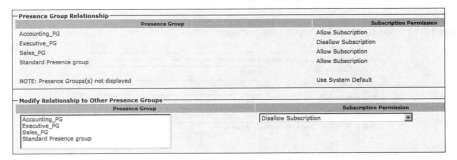

> **NOTE** Subscription permissions are configured in a *unidirectional* manner between pairs of Presence groups. It is possible to permit subscriptions from one group to another but to deny subscriptions in the opposite direction.

The Default Inter-Presence Group Subscription service parameter specifies the system default for Presence subscriptions. The system default is applied for subscriptions toward Presence groups for which no explicit permission has been set in the configuration of the Presence group from which the subscription request has been sourced.

The Default Inter-Presence Group Subscription parameter is a service parameter of the Cisco CallManager service and is therefore configured from **System > Service Parameter**. The Inter-Presence Group Subscription service parameter is illustrated in Figure 17-15.

Figure 17-15 *Inter-Presence Group Subscription Service Parameter*

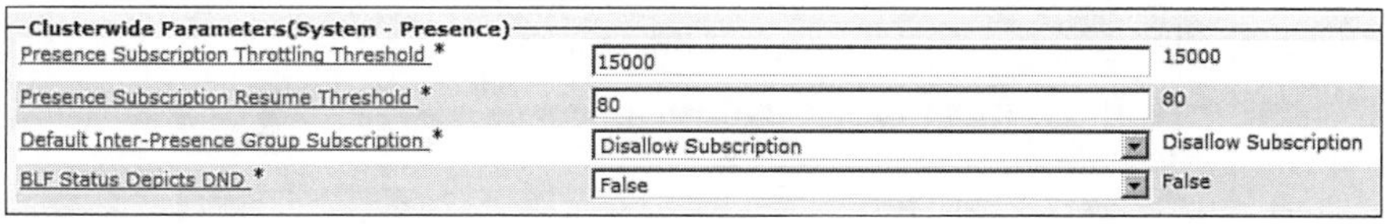

Clusterwide Parameters(System - Presence)		
Presence Subscription Throttling Threshold *	15000	15000
Presence Subscription Resume Threshold *	80	80
Default Inter-Presence Group Subscription *	Disallow Subscription	Disallow Subscription
BLF Status Depicts DND *	False	False

Figure 17-16 displays the Presence group configuration of the Cisco IP Phone.

Figure 17-16 *Cisco IP Phone Presence Group*

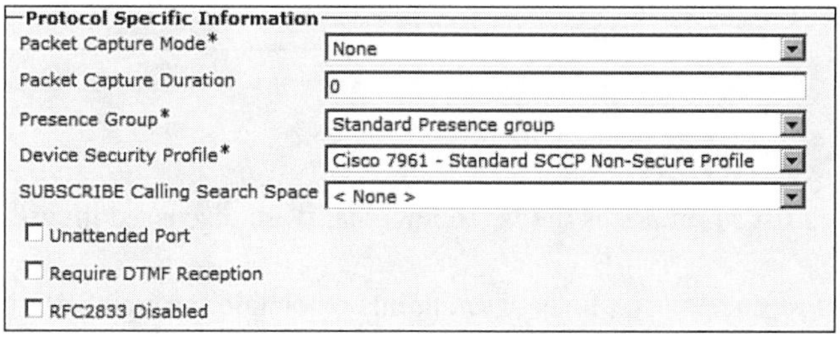

Protocol Specific Information	
Packet Capture Mode*	None
Packet Capture Duration	0
Presence Group*	Standard Presence group
Device Security Profile*	Cisco 7961 - Standard SCCP Non-Secure Profile
SUBSCRIBE Calling Search Space	< None >
☐ Unattended Port	
☐ Require DTMF Reception	
☐ RFC2833 Disabled	

IP phones are both watchers and Presence entities. An IP phone generates subscriptions when using Presence-enabled speed dials or Presence-enabled call lists. The DN of the IP phone can be watched by other subscribers. Presence groups must be applied to both the phone in the role as a subscriber and the DNs in the role as a Presence entity. Figure 17-17 displays the Presence group configuration performed at the DN.

Figure 17-17 *Directory Number Presence Group*

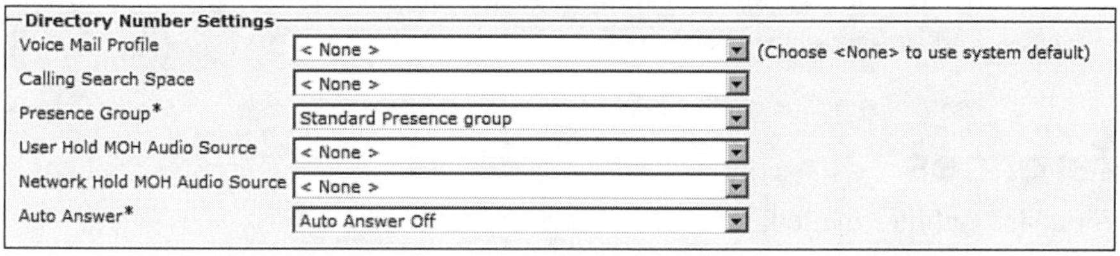

Directory Number Settings		
Voice Mail Profile	< None >	(Choose <None> to use system default)
Calling Search Space	< None >	
Presence Group*	Standard Presence group	
User Hold MOH Audio Source	< None >	
Network Hold MOH Audio Source	< None >	
Auto Answer*	Auto Answer Off	

CUCM sends subscribe messages on a SIP trunk when watching a Presence entity located on the other side of the SIP trunk. CUCM can also receive subscriptions over the SIP trunk when a DN on the cluster is being watched by a subscriber located on the other side of the trunk. The trunk can perform both subscriber and Presence entity roles. Only one Presence group can be configured on a trunk, forcing the trunk to have similar restrictions in both directions of the trunk. Figure 17-18 displays the SIP trunk Presence group configuration.

Figure 17-18 *SIP Trunk Presence Group*

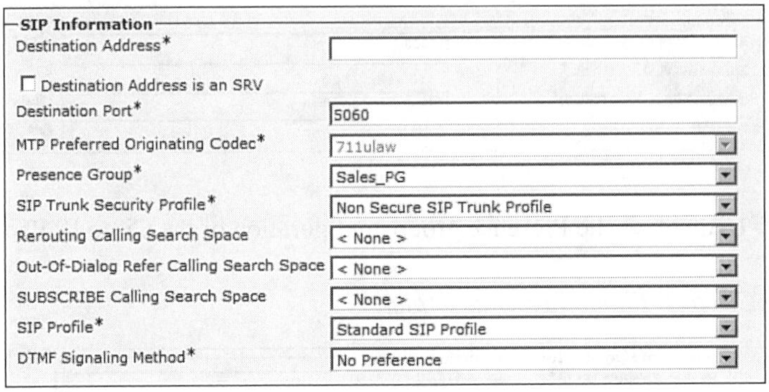

```
┌─SIP Information──────────────────────────────────────────────────┐
│ Destination Address*        [                                  ] │
│                                                                  │
│ ☐ Destination Address is an SRV                                  │
│ Destination Port*           [5060                              ] │
│ MTP Preferred Originating Codec*  [711ulaw               ▼]      │
│ Presence Group*             [Sales_PG                    ▼]      │
│ SIP Trunk Security Profile* [Non Secure SIP Trunk Profile ▼]    │
│ Rerouting Calling Search Space  [< None >                ▼]      │
│ Out-Of-Dialog Refer Calling Search Space [< None >       ▼]      │
│ SUBSCRIBE Calling Search Space  [< None >                ▼]      │
│ SIP Profile*                [Standard SIP Profile        ▼]      │
│ DTMF Signaling Method*       [No Preference               ▼]     │
└──────────────────────────────────────────────────────────────────┘
```

Chapter Summary

The following list summarizes the key points that were discussed in this chapter:

- CUCM Presence allows lines or endpoints reachable through SIP trunks to be monitored for their status (on-hook versus off-hook).

- Most IP phones support Presence-enabled speed dials; Type B Cisco IP Phones using SIP also support Presence-enabled call and directory lists.

- CUCM Presence configuration includes implementing Presence-enabled speed dials and enabling Presence-enabled call and directory lists.

- Presence policies can be applied to control Presence subscriptions.

- CUCM Presence policy configuration includes implementing partitions and subscribe CSSs and Presence groups.

References

For additional information, refer to these resources:

- **CUCM Features and Services Guide, Release 6.0(1)**: http://www.cisco.com/en/US/docs/voice_ip_comm/cucm/admin/6_0_1/ccmfeat/fsgd.pdf

- **CUCM Administration Guide, Release 6.0(1)**: http://www.cisco.com/en/US/docs/voice_ip_comm/cucm/admin/6_0_1/ccmcfg/bccm.pdf

- **Cisco Unified Communications SRND Based on CUCM 6.x**: http://www.cisco.com/en/US/products/sw/voicesw/ps556/products_implementation_design_guide_book09186a008085eb0d.html

Review Questions

Use the questions here to review what you learned in this chapter. The correct answers are found in Appendix A, "Answers to Chapter Review Questions."

1. Presence information is available over which of the following?

   a. BLF speed dials

   b. Speed dials

   c. Abbreviated dialing

   d. Fast Dial IP Phone service

2. Which component is required for Cisco Unified Personal Communicator?

   a. Cisco Unity

   b. Cisco Emergency Responder

   c. Presence Server

   d. Cisco MeetingPlace Express

3. Which technology is enabled with the Cisco Presence server?

   a. Cisco IP Phone Messenger application

   b. Call History Presence

   c. Speed Dial Presence

   d. Call Directory Presence

4. Which device is a watcher using Presence terminology?

   a. Calling party

   b. Called party

   c. Presence server

   d. Remote party

5. Which Presence message type is used for the watcher to check the status of a Presence entity?

   a. SIP subscribe

   b. SIP notify

   c. SIP refer

   d. SIP redirect

6. What are the three possible states of a watched directory number?

   a. Unregistered

   b. On-hook

   c. Off-hook

   d. Ringing

   e. Ringing: Feature

   f. Hold

7. Which of the following devices is a Presence entity?

   a. Calling party

   b. Called party

   c. Remote party

   d. Redirected number

8. Which two features restrict the watching functionality of a watcher watching a Presence entity in the same Presence group?

   a. Subscribe calling search space

   b. Calling search space

   c. Partition

   d. Class of service

9. Which three SIP features would restrict a watcher from watching a Presence group over a SIP trunk?

    a. Presence group

    b. Subscribe calling search space

    c. Route pattern

    d. Translation pattern

    e. Inter-Presence group policy

10. Presence groups apply to which of the following Presence features?

    a. BLF speed dials

    b. Call lists

    c. Speed dials

    d. Speed Dial

CHAPTER 18

Voice-Mail System Integration

This chapter covers the integration of Cisco Unity with CUCM.

Chapter Objectives

Upon completing this chapter, you will be able to integrate CUCM with voice-mail systems and set up basic voice-mail functionality. You will also be able to meet these objectives:

- Describe CUCM voice-mail integration.

- Explain Cisco Unity.

- Explain CUCM configuration for voice-mail integration.

- Explain CUCM phone configuration for voice-mail usage.

- Describe Cisco Unity configuration for CUCM integration.

- Configure Cisco Unity Subscriber.

Cisco Unity Overview

Cisco Unity is a voice messaging system that does voice mail, Unified Messaging, and fax integration. Cisco Unity also has text to speech (TTS) capabilities that allow e-mail and faxes (requires third-party fax server) to be listened to over the telephone. Voice messages can be checked over e-mail with a Unified Messaging license on Cisco Unity.

Cisco Unity integrates with IBM Lotus Notes and Microsoft Outlook e-mail clients to create a unified inbox. A unified inbox consists of e-mail, voice messaging, and fax in one e-mail inbox. Cisco Unity uses IBM Lotus Domino or Microsoft Exchange as a message store and directory services to unify system administration. The Microsoft SQL Server database is used to store all Unity configuration information (information store). Figure 18-1 illustrates the Cisco Unity integration capabilities.

Figure 18-1 *Unity Overview*

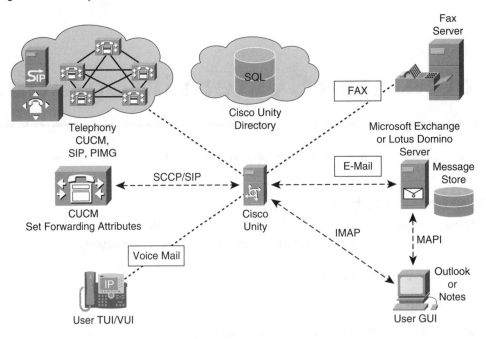

Cisco Unity runs on either a Microsoft Windows 2000 or Windows 2003 server platform. Cisco Unity is the Unified Messaging component within the Cisco family of Cisco Unified Communications system offerings. Cisco Unity integrates with CUCM natively through SCCP, but various third-party integrations are supported, too. Cisco Unity can integrate with several traditional circuit-switched phone systems. When the telephone network is ready to transition to VoIP, Cisco Unity allows migration in stages, by setting up dual-switch integration with both the circuit-switched phone system and CUCM. Cisco Unity Connection is a voice-mail and integrated messaging platform that runs on a hardened Linux appliance. Cisco Unity Express is a voice-mail-only platform that runs on a router in a network module or flash module. Neither Cisco Unity Connection nor Cisco Unity Express are covered in this book.

Cisco Unity includes the following features:

- **Intelligent Voice Mail**: The Cisco Unity voice messaging capabilities allow subscribers to listen to their messages, send voice messages to other subscribers, and customize settings such as personal greetings. Cisco Unity supports multiple automated attendants, which serve as electronic receptionists that answer and route incoming calls.

- **Cisco Unity System Administrator**: The system administrator access to Cisco Unity server occurs via a standard web browser. The Cisco Unity System Administrator (SA) is used to create, modify, or delete subscriber accounts; configure messaging options; assign classes of service; record greetings; and run reports.

- **Cisco Personal Communications Assistant**: The Cisco Personal Communications Assistant (PCA) is a website that subscribers use to access the Cisco Unity Assistant and the Cisco Unity Inbox.

- **Cisco Unity Assistant**: The Cisco Unity Assistant is a website that enables subscribers to customize mailbox settings, including recorded greetings and message-delivery options. In versions of Unity earlier than 3.1, the Cisco Unity Assistant was known as the ActiveAssistant.

- **ViewMail for Outlook**: ViewMail for Outlook (VMO) lets subscribers listen to voice messages from their Outlook inboxes by using common audio controls (play, stop, rewind, fast forward).

- **ViewMail for Notes**: ViewMail for Notes (VMN) lets subscribers listen to voice messages from their IBM Lotus Notes inbox by using common audio controls (play, stop, rewind, fast forward).

- **Cisco Unity Inbox**: The Cisco Unity Inbox is a part of Unity Assistant that lets subscribers listen to, compose, reply to, forward, and delete voice messages. Before Unity version 3.1, the Cisco Unity Inbox was known as Cisco Unity Visual Messaging Interface.

- **Multiple Languages**: With multiple languages installed, users can change the language in which Cisco Unity plays system prompts to subscribers and callers. Users can also choose one or more languages with which to display the Cisco Unity Administrator pages and the Help files.

- **Text to Speech**: The Text to Speech feature enables users to listen to their e-mail over the phone. Cisco Unity reads the text portion of e-mail messages and provides additional information such as the name of the sender (subscribers only) and the time and date that the message was sent.

- **Third-Party Fax**: Cisco Unity supports fax servers that have dedicated fax lines set up to the fax ports on the fax server. When a third-party fax server is used with Cisco Unity, the administration of the fax server is controlled by the fax server software.

  You can find a list of supported fax servers for use with Cisco Unity in Cisco Unity System Requirements, Supported Hardware and Software, available on Cisco.com at http://www.cisco.com/en/US/products/sw/voicesw/ps2237/prod_pre_installation_ guides_list.html.

- **Digital Networking**: The Digital Networking feature enables subscribers to send and receive voice messages between Cisco Unity servers at different locations.

- **AMIS Support**: Cisco Unity supports the Audio Messaging Interchange Specification (AMIS) protocol, which provides an analog mechanism for transferring voice messages between different voice messaging systems.

  You can find a list of voice messaging systems that Cisco Unity can exchange AMIS voice messages with in Cisco Unity System Requirements, Supported Hardware and Software, available on Cisco.com at http://www.cisco.com/en/US/products/sw/ voicesw/ps2237/prod_pre_installation_guides_list.html.

- **Cisco Unity Bridge**: The Cisco Unity Bridge acts as a networking gateway between Cisco Unity and an Octel system on an Octel analog network. With the Cisco Unity Bridge, subscribers can send messages to and receive messages from Octel users.

- **Enhanced Failover**: Failover is a feature that provides a simple redundancy, allowing voice messaging functions to continue if the Cisco Unity server fails or when users need to perform maintenance. To set up failover, Cisco Unity should be installed and configured on two servers: a primary server and a secondary server. If the primary server fails or if the Cisco Unity service on the primary server stops, the secondary Cisco Unity server automatically starts performing Unity operations.

- **VPIM Networking**: Cisco Unity supports the Voice Profile for Internet Mail (VPIM) protocol, which allows voice messaging systems to exchange voice, fax, and text messages over any TCP/IP network. VPIM is based on the Simple Mail Transfer Protocol (SMTP) and Multipurpose Internet Mail Extension (MIME) protocols. VPIM Networking is a licensed feature. If your organization has multiple Cisco Unity servers networked together, only one server needs to be licensed and configured for VPIM Networking. The Cisco Unity server configured for VPIM Networking is referred to as the bridgehead server.

New features in Cisco Unity 5.0 include the following:

- **Secure messaging**: Encryption of voice-mail messages increases system security, allowing system administrators to enforce voice-mail retention policies and prevent the compromise of voice messages with proprietary or confidential content forwarded to someone outside the enterprise.

- **Message Monitor**: Voice-mail messages can be screened and intercepted as they are being recorded.

- **Interrupted session recovery**: Unity can automatically return to in-progress message composition or playback if a session ends prematurely. For example, a user might hang up a phone while in the middle of listening to a long voice mail; interrupted session recovery allows the user to hear the rest of the voice mail at another time.

- **Cisco Unity Phone view**: Users can access their voice-mail inbox through the IP phone interface. They can use the message locator to view the voice-mail message queue or jump to a particular message in their inbox, view message header details, and play selected messages using softkeys on the IP phone.

- **Speech access**: Speech access allows the use of voice commands (speech recognition) to navigate menus and manage voice-mail messages.

- **Microsoft Exchange 2007 support**: Microsoft Exchange 2007 can be used with Cisco Unity as a Unified Messaging solution in Unity 5.0. Earlier versions of Unity did not support Microsoft Exchange 2007.

- **Microsoft Windows Vista support**: The ViewMail for Outlook and ViewMail for Notes clients are supported for Microsoft Windows Vista in Cisco Unity 5.0.

Voice-Mail Integration

CUCM can integrate with Cisco Unity via either Skinny Client Control Protocol (SCCP) or Session Initiation Protocol (SIP).

Cisco Unity telephony integrations are configured with the Cisco Unity Telephony Integration Manager (UTIM).

In addition to the option of adding multiple clusters by adding additional integrations for each new CUCM cluster in Cisco Unity, CUCM supports Annex M.1, Message Tunneling for Q Signaling (Q.SIG), which allows administrators to enable Q.SIG on intercluster trunks (ICT) between CUCM clusters.

The phone system sends the following information with forwarded calls to the voice-mail system:

- The extension of the called party

- The extension of the calling party (for internal calls) or the phone number of the calling party (if it is an external call and the system uses caller ID)

- The reason for the forward (the extension is busy, does not answer, or is set to forward all calls)

Cisco Unity uses this information to answer the call appropriately. A call forwarded from a subscriber phone to Cisco Unity is answered with the personal greeting of the subscriber. A call from a nonsubscriber is routed the opening greeting of the automated attendant (AA) server in Cisco Unity.

The Cisco Messaging Interface (CMI) is a CUCM service that should run on the publisher server if a Simplified Message Desk Interface (SMDI) integration to a third-party voice-mail system will be used. The CMI service is not used when integrating with Cisco Unity. Cisco Unity and CUCM support a digital IP-based integration that is much faster than using CMI integration.

The CMI service intercepts calls destined for voice mail and generates appropriate SMDI messages over RS-232 serial cables. The CMI service is compatible with any Media Gateway Control Protocol (MGCP) gateway that supports analog Foreign Exchange Station (FXS) or T1 channel associated signaling (CAS). The Cisco Catalyst 6500 WS-X6624 module and the standalone Cisco VG224 devices are two of only three gateways that support positive disconnect supervision and are therefore the only gateways currently recommended for use with the CMI service.

CUCM supports CMI integration with the following voice-mail systems:

- Octel 100, 200/300, and 250/350

- Intuity Audix

- Siemens PhoneMail

- Centigram/BayPoint (OnePoint and NuPoint Messenger)

- Lyrix ECS

- IBM Message Center

The Cisco VG248 is an SCCP gateway that supports 48 analog FXS ports through two amphenol (RJ-71) connectors and generates SMDI locally. The Cisco VG248 also supports positive disconnect supervision.

Voice-mail integration through the Cisco VG248 provides the following features and advantages:

- Multiple SMDI links per CUCM server

- SMDI failover capability

- Independence from the location of the voice-mail system

The Cisco VG248 can also support two other serial protocols that are sometimes used for voice-mail integration: NEC Message Center Interface (MCI) and Ericsson MD110 proprietary protocol.

CUCM SCCP integration with Cisco Unity provides the following features:

- Call forward to personal greeting

- Call forward to busy greeting

- Caller ID

- Easy message access. A subscriber can retrieve messages without entering an extension identifier. Cisco Unity identifies a subscriber based on the extension from which the call originated. A password is normally required, but the subscriber can be configured without a password if desired.

- Identified subscriber messaging. Cisco Unity automatically identifies a subscriber who leaves a message during a forwarded internal call. This feature is based on the extension from which the call originated (original calling party).

- Message Waiting Indication (MWI). When a message is left for a subscriber, a red light is illuminated on the Cisco IP Phone. The directory number (DN) that has a voice-mail message also displays a mail icon next to the DN on the phone.

Call Routing to Cisco Unity

The following examples describe how calls are routed through CUCM to Unity.

Outside Calls

Figure 18-2 is an example of how a call is routed from an outside caller through CUCM to a Unity system. The following list annotates the numbers that are in Figure 18-2.

1. The outside caller dials a phone number from his cell phone. The phone number dialed is a direct inward dial (DID) number that belongs to a Unity subscriber.

2. The public switched telephone network routes the caller to the gateway. The gateway router forwards the digits to CUCM for processing. The number of digits forwarded is controlled by the inbound call-routing parameters in the gateway configuration. If an internal five-digit dial plan is deployed, only the last five digits are required.

3. CUCM performs digit analysis and routes the call to the appropriate Cisco IP Phone.

4. The telephone rings four times based on the default ring no answer duration. After four rings, the Call Forward No Answer (CFNA) setting is applied and the phone is sent to the voice-mail profile of the subscriber.

5. CUCM checks the voice-mail profile of the Cisco IP Phone and forwards the call to the Unity server handling the IP phone. Unity directs the call to the subscriber greeting.

6. The caller leaves a message, and Unity directs the call to the message store. In a Unified Messaging deployment, the message store (Microsoft Exchange or IBM Lotus Domino) is external from the Cisco Unity platform.

7. The message is stored in the subscriber message store.

8. Cisco Unity sends a code to CUCM to turn on the MWI light on the phone that has a new message.

9. CUCM instructs the phone to turn on the MWI light.

10. The MWI light is illuminated on the phone.

Figure 18-2   *Outside Caller Call Flow*

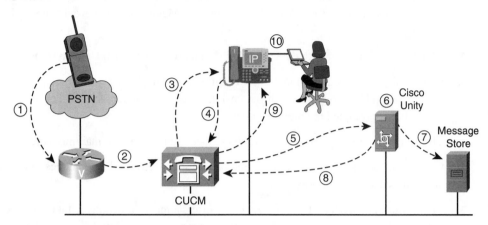

The correct calling privileges (calling search spaces [CSS]) are assigned to the voice-mail ports, gateways, phones, and MWI ports. Phone numbers are in partitions, whereas devices are assigned to CSSs.

Calling privileges (class of restriction) were covered in detail in Chapter 13, "Calling Privileges." The following calling privilege need to achieve the following:

■   The gateway should be able to reach the phones and voice-mail ports.

■   The phones should be able to reach the voice-mail ports but should not be able to dial the MWI On or MWI Off codes (extensions).

■   The voice-mail ports should be able to dial the MWI On and MWI Off extensions.

Subscriber Call Flow

A Cisco Unity subscriber is a person who has a user account on the Cisco Unity system. Each subscriber account has a Profile page that stores specific information about that subscriber, such as the extension, security code, recorded name, and the e-mail alias to send messages to. The following steps describe the call flow of a user checking a voice-mail message in Cisco Unity, as depicted in Figure 18-3:

1. The subscriber notices the MWI on his telephone and presses the Messages button on the phone to retrieve messages. CUCM receives the Messages button event from the IP phone.

2. CUCM directs the call with the caller ID information to the Cisco Unity system.

3. Cisco Unity receives the call and the extension of the telephone from the telephone system. Cisco Unity recognizes the extension from its list of subscribers. The subscriber is prompted to enter his password.

4. The user enters his password and chooses to listen to a new voice-mail message.

5. Cisco Unity accesses the subscriber's message store to retrieve the voice message when the subscriber chooses to listen to his messages.

6. The subscriber listens to the message. Unity offers a menu of actions to take with the message: save, delete, or forward. The subscriber presses the digit 3 to delete the message, and Cisco Unity verbally confirms the message is deleted. The subscriber then hangs up the phone.

7. Cisco Unity sends the subscriber's delete message command to the message store server. The message will be deleted or moved to the Deleted Items folder based on settings in the subscriber's account. Unity sends a message to CUCM to turn off the MWI code on the subscriber's IP phone.

8. CUCM sends an SCCP message to the IP phone instructing the phone to turn off the MWI.

9. The MWI light goes off on the phone.

Figure 18-3   *Subscriber Call Flow*

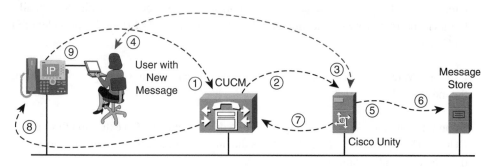

Calls Forwarded to Voice Mail

Figure 18-4 illustrates the interworking of CUCM and Cisco Unity. Incoming calls forwarded to voice mail reach the voice-mail pilot number that is also assigned to the hunt pilot of the voice-mail hunt list. The voice-mail hunt list selects the voice-mail port, which terminates the incoming call.

Figure 18-4   *Call Forward-to-Voice Mail Call Flow*

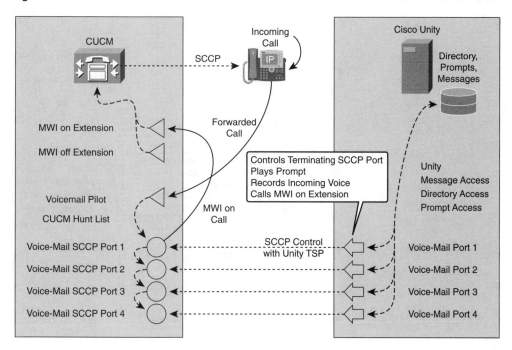

The voice-mail ports in CUCM are specialized SCCP-controlled computer telephony integration (CTI) ports. These ports are in control of the related Cisco Unity Voicemail Ports via the Telephony Application Programming Interface (TAPI) service provider (TSP) on Cisco Unity.

Using the Voicemail Ports, Cisco Unity connects the call, playing prompts and recording the messages.

Upon finishing the recording, Unity initiates a call to the MWI On extension through CUCM. The signaling of the call contains the number of the extension that has to switch the message-waiting lamp on.

CUCM then instructs the indicated phone to activate the MWI.

Accessing Messages

Figure 18-5 illustrates an internal call to the voice mail allowing a subscriber to check a voice mail.

Figure 18-5 *Message Access Call Flow*

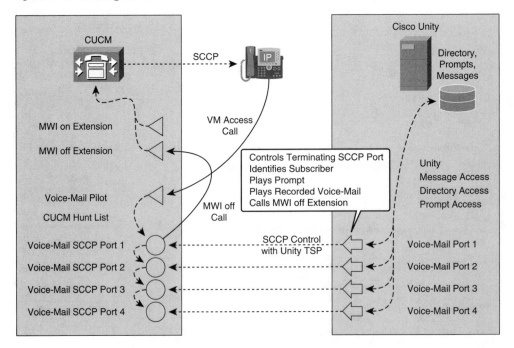

The call will be routed to the voice-mail pilot number assigned to the hunt pilot of the voice-mail hunt list.

The voice-mail hunt list selects the line group, which will use the top-down distribution algorithm to distribute the call to a voice-mail port to terminate the incoming call.

The voice-mail ports in the CUCM are specialized SCCP-controlled CTI-ports. These ports are in control of the related Cisco Unity Voicemail Ports via the Cisco Unity-CM TSP.

Using the Voicemail Ports, Cisco Unity connects the call, identifies the user, plays prompts, and plays back the messages.

When messages are deleted, Cisco Unity initiates a call to the MWI Off extension. The signaling of the call contains the number of the extension that has to switch the MWI off.

CUCM then instructs the indicated phone to deactivate MWI.

Configuration for Cisco Unity Integration

Voice-mail ports must be configured in both CUCM and Cisco Unity. The number of ports needed depends on system load and on the number of subscribers. The name of the voice-mail ports configured in CUCM must match the CallManager Device Name Prefix parameter configured on Cisco Unity.

MWI On and Off codes must be configured on both CUCM and Cisco Unity. These MWI on and off codes must be identically configured. The MWI On and Off codes are extension numbers that phones should not be able to dial. It is best practice to create a Unity_MWI partition for these numbers. The CSS applied to the Cisco Unity ports needs to have accessibility to these partitions to turn the MWI of the phone on and off (as needed).

A voice-mail profile is configured in CUCM and associated with each phone DN that will have voice mail. The voice-mail profile refers to a voice-mail pilot, which is configured with the phone number of the hunt pilot. The hunt pilot points to a hunt list, which includes a line group that consists of the DNs of the individual voice-mail ports. This is used to distribute calls among the various voice-mail ports in the system. Call coverage is covered in detail in Chapter 14, "Call Coverage."

The following CUCM and Cisco Unity configuration elements are required for Cisco Unity:

- **IP phone**: The IP phone is configured with a line CSS that can dial the voice-mail pilot point. The DN is configured with a voice-mail profile.

- **Voice-mail profile**: A voice-mail profile refers to a voice-mail pilot. The voice-mail pilot has a CSS, which allows it to dial the partition that the voice-mail ports are in. The CSS will also need to dial the MWI On and Off codes. If the Message Notification feature of Cisco Unity will be used, Cisco Unity might need to dial long-distance numbers to alert roaming users that they have a new voice mail. The CEO may want all urgent voice mails to ring their cell phone (which might have a long-distance number).

- **Voice-mail pilot**: A voice-mail pilot must be configured. The voice-mail pilot is configured the same as a hunt pilot number. The hunt pilot is leveraged so that calls to the hunt pilot can be distributed to multiple voice-mail ports.

- **Hunt pilot**: A hunt pilot is configured with the same number as the voice-mail pilot. The voice-mail pilot point is normally a DID number from the public switched telephone network (PSTN) to allow roaming users access to voice mail over the PSTN.

- **Hunt list**: A hunt list is configured with one or more line groups to distribute voice-mail calls to multiple voice-mail ports.

- **Line group**: A line group is configured to distribute voice-mail calls. The line group includes all voice-mail port DNs. Multiple line groups are used in a Cisco Unity failover model. Failover is not covered in this text.

- **Voice-mail port**: Voice-mail ports must be configured. The number of voice-mail ports configured depends on the licensed number of ports in Cisco Unity. Each voice-mail port has a unique DN associated to it. The DNs of all voice-mail ports are in partitions that only the voice-mail pilot/hunt pilot has access to. Users should dial the voice-mail pilot point, not voice-mail ports. The voice-mail ports do not need to use DID numbers because only the voice-mail pilot will be dialing the voice-mail ports.

Figure 18-6 illustrates the processing order taken when a user presses the Voice Mail button on a phone to retrieve voice mail.

Figure 18-6 *Calls to Voice Mail*

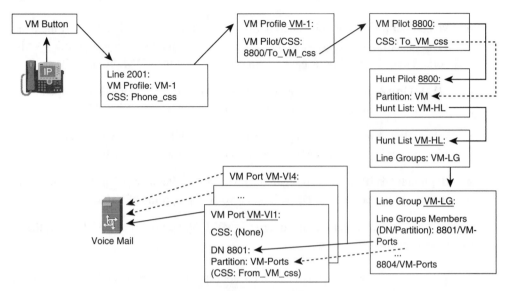

When the user of the IP phone presses the Voice Mail button of the IP phone, the following processing in CUCM occurs:

1. The voice-mail profile configured for the first line is used if the Voice Mail button is pressed without selecting a line before pressing the button. If a line was selected and then the Voice Mail button was pressed, the voice-mail profile configured at that line is used. In Figure 18-6, there is only one line. After the Voice Mail button is pressed, voice-mail profile VM-1 is used for the call to the voice-mail system.

2. Voice-mail profile VM-1 refers to voice-mail pilot 8800 with CSS To_VM_css.

3. A call to number 8800 is generated, and the CSS used for the call routing decision is To_VM_css.

4. Hunt pilot 8800 is found in the call-routing table in partition VM.

5. The hunt pilot refers to hunt list VM-HL. Line group VM-LG is the only member of hunt list VM-HL. The first available member of line group VM-LG is 8801 in partition VM-Ports.

6. The call is sent to the voice-mail system through the voice-mail port with DN 8801 in partition VM-Ports.

Calls from the voice-mail system involve the following elements:

- **Voice-mail port**: Four voice-mail ports exist: VM-VI1 to VM-VI4. Each of them has a DN (8801 through 8804), and the DNs of all voice-mail ports are in partition VM-Ports. The voice-mail ports have a CSS configured at their DN: From_VM_css.

- **MWI (On)**: A message-waiting number (8808) is configured for MWI On operations. The number is in partition MWI, and it is configured with a CSS of MWI_css.

- **MWI (Off)**: A message-waiting number (8809) is configured for MWI Off operations. The number is in partition MWI, and it is configured with CSS MWI_css.

- **IP phone**: The IP phone is configured with a line CSS Phone_css. The DN of the phone is in partition Phones. The DN refers to a voice-mail profile of *VM-1*.

When the voice-mail system wants to turn the MWI light on or off at the IP phone, the following happens:

1. The voice-mail system sends a call to the appropriate MWI number through one of the voice-mail ports (VM-VI1 in this example).

2. The device/DN CSS of the voice-mail port is used for the call-routing lookup for the dialed MWI number (8808 for MWI On).

3. In the example, CSS From_VM_css is used, and the MWI On number (8808) is found in partition MWI because partition MWI is part of the From_VM_css CSS.

4. The MWI On number 8808 now sends the on MWI to the signaled phone (2001). For this call leg, the CSS of MWI 8808, MWI_css, is used.

5. Directory number 2001 is found in partition Phones, which is a partition listed in CSS MWI_css. The MWI light is turned on.

When the voice-mail system wants to place calls to an IP phone or a route pattern to transfer a call or for message-waiting notification, the following happens:

1. The voice-mail system sends the call to the appropriate destination number through one of the voice-mail ports (VM-VI1 in this example).

2. The device/DN CSS of the voice-mail port is used for the call-routing lookup of the call.

3. In the example, CSS From_VM_css is used, and if the dialed number is in a partition that is listed in the From_VM_css CSS, the call can be transferred or the message notification can be delivered.

Figure 18-7 *Calls from Voice Mail*

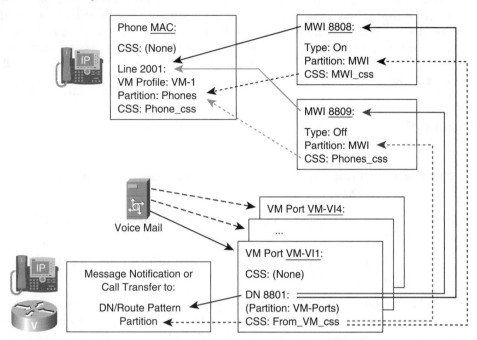

Integrating CUCM with a Cisco Unity Voice-Mail System

Seven steps are required to prepare CUCM to integrate with a Cisco Unity voice-mail system using SCCP, as follows:

Step 1   Configure MWI On and MWI Off.

Step 2   Configure the voice-mail ports.

Step 3   Configure the line group.

Step 4   Configure the hunt list.

Step 5   Configure the hunt pilot.

Step 6   Configure the voice-mail pilot.

Step 7   Configure the voice-mail profile.

> **NOTE**   Steps 2 and 3 can be performed by using the Cisco Voice Mail Port wizard. The Cisco Voice Mail Port wizard allows quick configuration of a high number of voice-mail ports by specifying the number of voice-mail ports to be created. The voice-mail ports are added and assigned to a line group. All other steps have to be performed manually. You can access the Cisco Voice Mail Port wizard from **Voice Mail > Cisco Voice Mail Port Wizard**.

Creating MWI

To add message-waiting numbers, follow these steps:

Step 1   In CUCM Administration, go to **Voice Mail > Message Waiting** and click **Add New**.

Step 2   Configure a message-waiting number and description and set the MWI to On.

Step 3   Repeat the preceding step to create a message-waiting number for MWI Off using a unique number.

The MWI On configuration is displayed in Figure 18-8. A partition at a message-waiting number specifies what devices are allowed to dial the MWI number. Voice-mail ports are the only devices that should be dialing the MWI On or MWI Off codes. The CSS at the voice-mail ports must include the partition of the MWI numbers.

Figure 18-8   *MWI On Configuration*

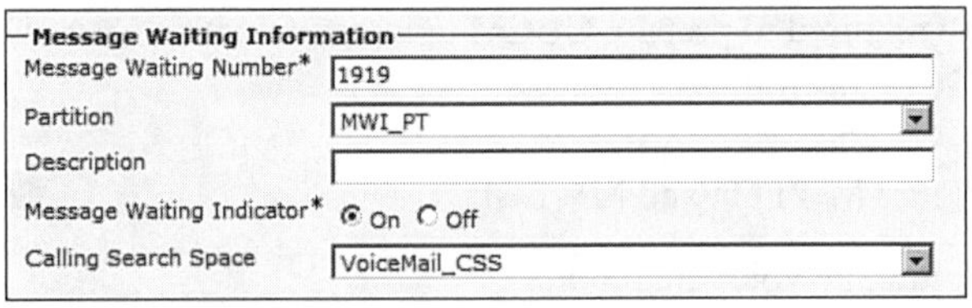

Adding Voice-Mail Ports

To add voice-mail ports, follow these steps:

Step 1   In CUCM Administration, go to **Voice Mail > Cisco Voice Mail Port**, and click **Add New**.

Step 2   Configure the voice-mail port with a port name and description and select a device pool. The port name must have a suffix of VI*x*, where *x* is a number starting with 1 for the first voice-mail port and incrementing by 1 for each additional port.

Step 3   Set the device security mode.

> **NOTE**   The device security mode is a mandatory parameter and does not have a default
> value. Therefore, it must be selected. If the CUCM cluster has not been enabled for
> security, the device security mode must be set to Non Secure Voice Mail Port for the
> voice-mail port to function correctly. To enable security in the CUCM cluster, additional
> hardware products (security tokens) have to be purchased, and the cluster has to be
> configured for secure operation. More information about how to enable security in a
> CUCM cluster is provided in *Cisco Unified Communications IP Telephony, Part 2*.

Step 4   Enter a DN for the voice-mail port.

> **NOTE**   The DN of a voice-mail port should not use a number from the DID block
> purchased from the PSTN service provider. The DNs of the voice-mail ports will not be
> dialed directly. The hunt pilot will distribute calls to various voice-mail ports after the
> ports have been placed into a line group. The hunt pilot should be in a DID range to
> enable roaming users to dial the voice-mail pilot point directly over the PSTN.

Step 5   Repeat the preceding steps to configure additional voice-mail ports.

The CSS of a voice port is composed of a device and line CSS. The combined CSS must
allow calls to subscriber phones and any other number where the voice-mail system may
perform message notification. These can be internal phone DNs, route patterns, MWI
numbers, or any dialable PSTN pattern for message notification. Figure 18-9 shows the
Voice-Mail Port Configuration window.

Adding a Line Group

To add a line group with voice-mail ports, follow these steps (as illustrated in Figure 18-10):

Step 1   In CUCM Administration, go to **Call Routing > Route/Hunt > Line
Group**, and click **Add New**.

Step 2   Enter a name for the line group, select the top-down distribution algorithm,
and add the previously configured voice-mail ports to the line group.

Figure 18-9 *Voice Mail Port Configuration*

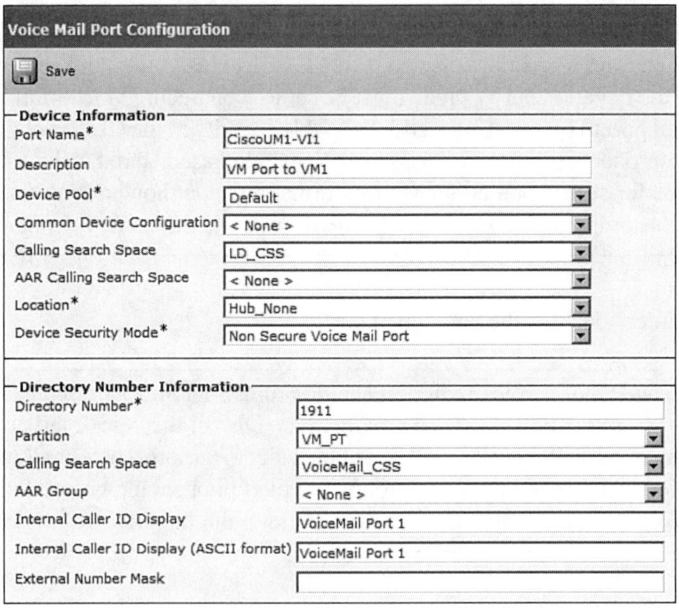

Figure 18-10 *Line Group Configuration*

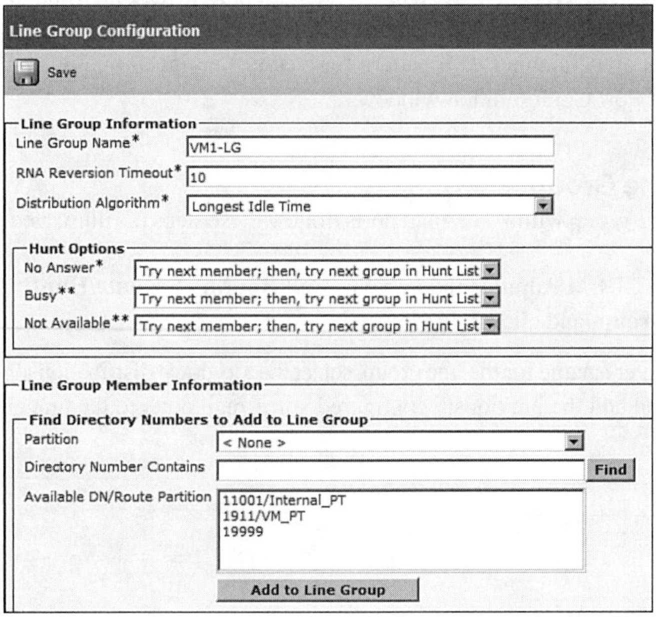

NOTE If some voice-mail ports will be used in Unity for dial out only (call transfer, message notifications, or message-waiting indication), they must not be included in the line group. The line group should contain only the voice-mail ports that are used to answer calls *to* the voice-mail system and automated-attendant system.

Adding a Hunt List

To add a hunt list using the previously configured line group, follow these steps:

Step 1 In CUCM Administration, go to **Call Routing > Route/Hunt > Hunt List**, and click **Add New**.

Step 2 Enter a name and description for the hunt list and select a CUCM group.

Step 3 Check the **Enable This Hunt List** check box and the **For Voice Mail Usage** check box.

Step 4 Add the line group that was configured in the previous step to the hunt list.

Figure 18-11 shows configuration of the hunt list.

Figure 18-11 *Hunt List Configuration*

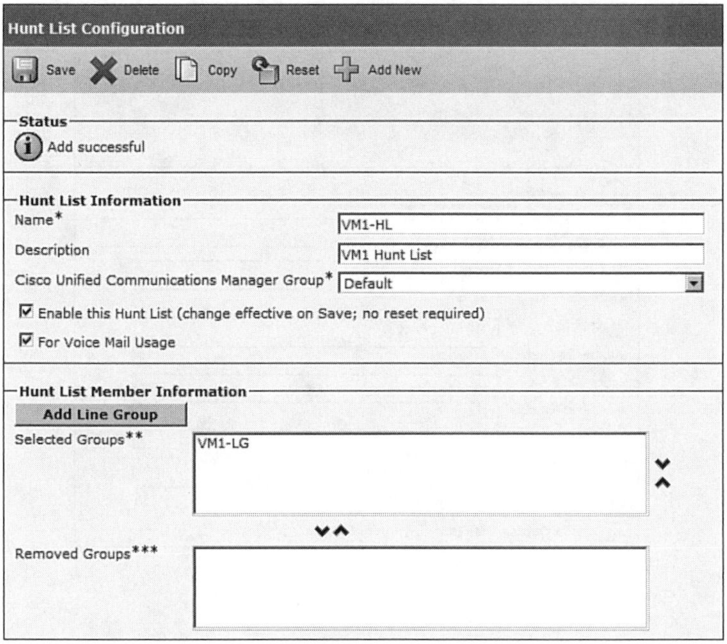

Adding a Hunt Pilot

To add a hunt pilot that refers to the previously configured hunt list, follow these steps:

Step 1   In CUCM Administration, go to **Call Routing > Route/Hunt > Hunt Pilot**, and click **Add New**.

Step 2   Enter the hunt pilot number. This is the number that the voice-mail system will reach for forwarding calls and for message retrieval.

Step 3   Enter a description for the hunt pilot.

Step 4   Select the hunt list that was configured earlier.

The partition of the hunt pilot places the hunt pilot number in a container. All devices that should be able to call the voice-mail system need to have this partition in their CSS. Users of Cisco IP Phones with a Voice Mail button will dial the hunt pilot number directly by pressing the Voice Mail button of the phone. The Voice Mail button dials the voice-mail profile's associated pilot point number. The pilot point number is the same as the hunt pilot. The phone does not need to access the hunt pilot number from its CSS because the phone will dial the DN associated with the voice-mail profile of the DN. The voice-mail profile must dial the hunt pilot. Figure 18-12 is a screen capture of the hunt pilot configuration in CUCM.

Figure 18-12   *Hunt Pilot Configuration*

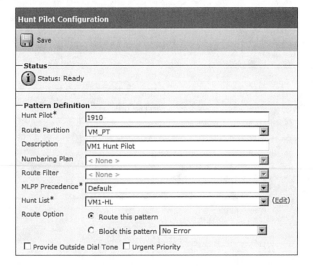

Configuring a Voice-Mail Pilot

To configure a voice-mail pilot, follow these steps:

Step 1   In CUCM Administration, go to **Voice Mail > Voice Mail Pilot**. Click **Find**, and choose the Default voice-mail pilot.

Step 1   Configure the voice mail pilot number with the same extension used on the hunt pilot. Click **Save**.

> **NOTE**   Two voice-mail pilots exist by default: the Default voice-mail pilot and the No Voice Mail voice-mail pilot. If only one voice-mail system is used, it is recommended to configure the Default voice-mail pilot. If multiple voice-mail systems are used, additional voice-mail pilots must be added. The No Voice Mail voice-mail pilot does not refer to any hunt pilot because it is only referenced from voice-mail pilots, which do not allow voice-mail integration.

The CSS of the voice-mail pilot is used for the voice-mail pilot to access the configured voice-mail pilot number (hunt pilot number associated with voice-mail profile). Figure 18-13 illustrates the voice-mail pilot configuration.

Figure 18-13   *Voice-Mail Pilot Configuration*

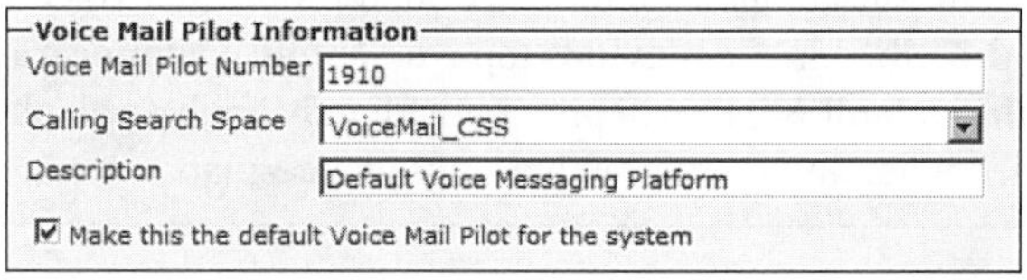

Configuring a Voice-Mail Profile

To configure a voice-mail profile, refer to the previously configured voice-mail pilot, and in CUCM Administration, go to **Voice Mail > Voice Mail Profile**. Click **Find**, and choose the Default voice-mail profile. From the Voice Mail Pilot drop-down list, select the previously configured voice-mail pilot. The voice-mail profile configuration is shown in Figure 18-14.

Voice-mail profiles are used only by Cisco IP Phones when the Voice Mail button is pressed; they are ignored when a user dials the voice-mail pilot number directly.

Figure 18-14   *Voice-Mail Profile Configuration*

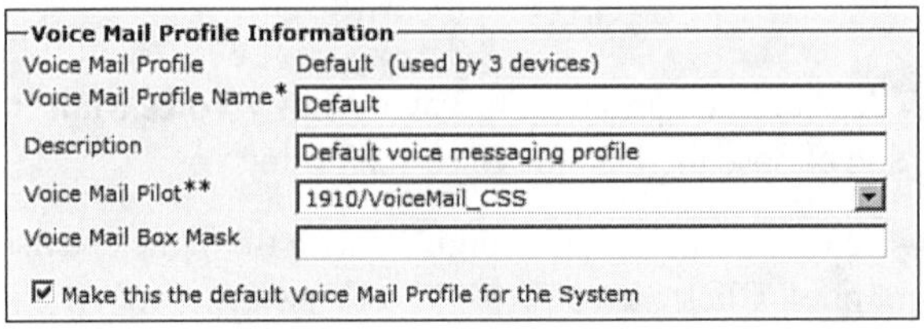

```
┌─Voice Mail Profile Information──────────────────────────────────┐
│  Voice Mail Profile        Default  (used by 3 devices)         │
│  Voice Mail Profile Name*  [Default                          ]  │
│                                                                 │
│  Description               [Default voice messaging profile  ]  │
│  Voice Mail Pilot**        [1910/VoiceMail_CSS            ][▼]  │
│  Voice Mail Box Mask       [                              ]      │
│                                                                 │
│  ☑ Make this the default Voice Mail Profile for the System      │
└─────────────────────────────────────────────────────────────────┘
```

Phone Configuration for Voice-Mail Usage

To configure phone lines to use a voice-mail system, the phone line needs to be configured with a voice-mail profile as illustrated in Figure 18-15 and described in the following steps:

Step 1   In CUCM Administration, go to **Device > Phone**, and select the IP phone that should be configured for voice-mail usage. Click the DN of the phone to be configured with the voice-mail profile.

Step 2   At each phone line, select the voice-mail profile that should be used by the DN.

NOTE   By default, all phone lines have the voice-mail profile set to Default. If only one voice-mail system is used, the Default voice-mail profile and voice-mail pilot should be configured as described in the previous topic to simplify administration. Changes performed to the Default voice-mail pilot immediately apply to all phones. This approach is recommended when integrating with a single voice-mail system.

Figure 18-15   *Voice-Mail Profile Directory Number Configuration*

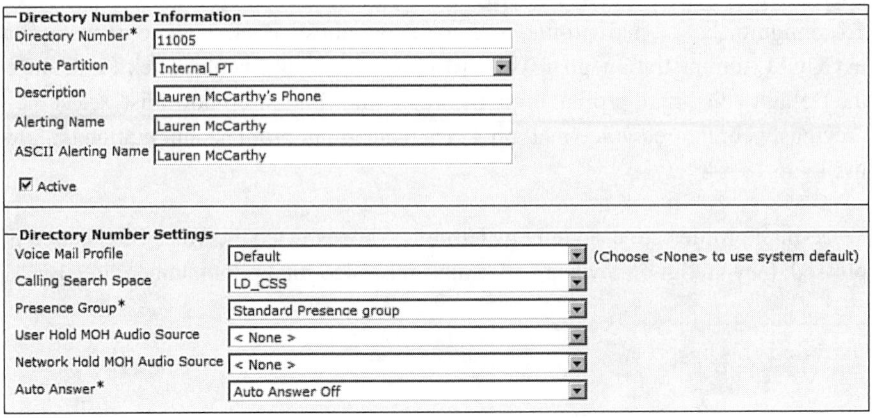

```
┌─Directory Number Information─────────────────────────────────────────┐
│  Directory Number*       [11005                                    ]  │
│  Route Partition         [Internal_PT                          ][▼]  │
│  Description             [Lauren McCarthy's Phone                 ]  │
│  Alerting Name           [Lauren McCarthy                         ]  │
│  ASCII Alerting Name     [Lauren McCarthy                         ]  │
│  ☑ Active                                                            │
│                                                                      │
│─Directory Number Settings───────────────────────────────────────────│
│  Voice Mail Profile           [Default                  ][▼]  (Choose <None> to use system default) │
│  Calling Search Space         [LD_CSS                   ][▼]         │
│  Presence Group*              [Standard Presence group  ][▼]         │
│  User Hold MOH Audio Source   [< None >                 ][▼]         │
│  Network Hold MOH Audio Source[< None >                 ][▼]         │
│  Auto Answer*                 [Auto Answer Off           ][▼]        │
└──────────────────────────────────────────────────────────────────────┘
```

The phone lines have to be configured to forward calls to the voice-mail system. This is configured from the DN configuration, but it can also be configured at the user web pages.

If Call Forward All (CFA) is selected, all other call-forward settings are ignored. If CFA is not enabled, the other call-forward settings are used based on the event (Call Forward Busy [CFB], Call Forward No Answer [CFNA], Call Forward Unregistered [CFUR]). CFNC applies only to lines that forwarded calls to a hunt list where hunting is exhausted and the hunt pilot is configured to perform final forwarding based on the personal preference. Figure 18-16 shows configuration of call forwarding.

Figure 18-16 *Call-Forward Configuration*

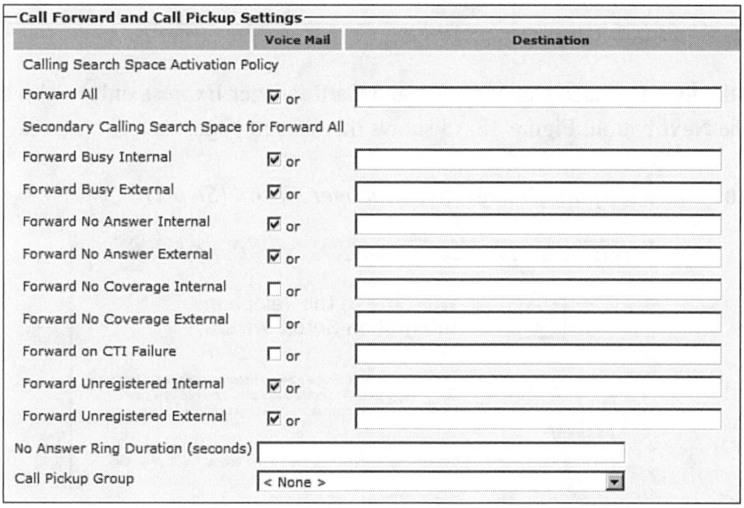

Cisco Unity Configuration

Cisco Unity SCCP integration requires the following tasks:

Step 1 Launch the Integration tool.

Step 2 Start the Integration wizard.

Step 3 Create a new SCCP CUCM integration.

Step 4 Update the Unity-CM TSP.

Locate and start the Cisco Unity Telephony Integration Manager (UTIM) on the Cisco Unity server. This program is part of the Cisco Unified Integration and Configuration Assistant (CUICA) wizard, but the program can also be launched by clicking the Manage Integrations icon in the Unity program group. CUICA is shown in Figure 18-17. Click the **Create Integration** icon in CUICA to start the Integration wizard.

Figure 18-17   *Unity Telephony Integration Manager Wizard (Step 1)*

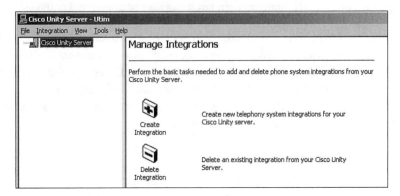

Select the **SCCP** (Cisco CallManager and CallManager Express only) radio button and click the **Next** button. Figure 18-18 shows this wizard page.

Figure 18-18   *Unity Telephony Integration Manager Wizard (Step 2)*

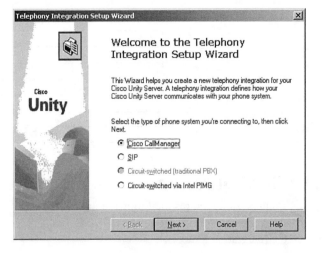

The integration name can be called CUCM or a descriptive integration name of your choosing, as illustrated in Figure 18-19. The cluster name needs to be entered, too. These settings have only local relevance on the Unity server.

Figure 18-19   *Unity Telephony Integration Manager Wizard (Step 3)*

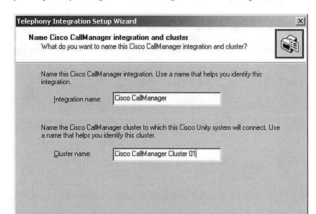

Define the IP address and the SCCP port of the CUCM. This setting has to be identical to the settings in CUCM. The SCCP default port is 2000. This is displayed in Figure 18-20.

Figure 18-20   *Unity Telephony Integration Manager Wizard (Step 4)*

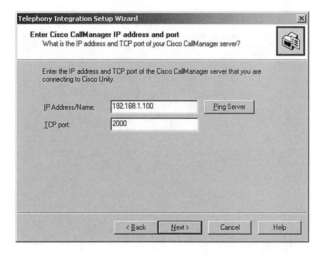

Define the IP address and the port number of a secondary CUCM for redundancy. This is displayed in Figure 18-21.

Figure 18-21   *Unity Telephony Integration Manager Wizard (Step 5)*

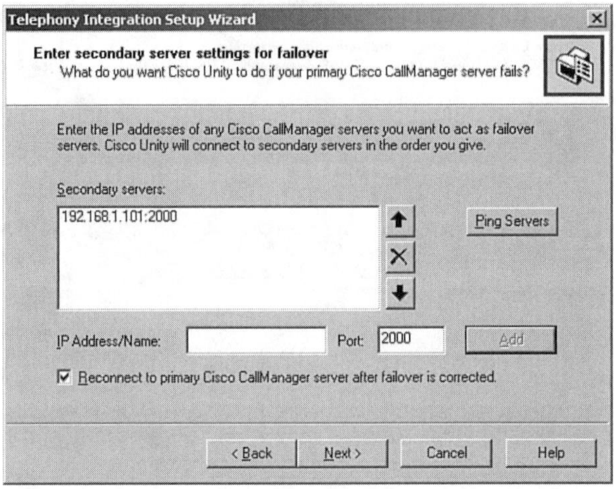

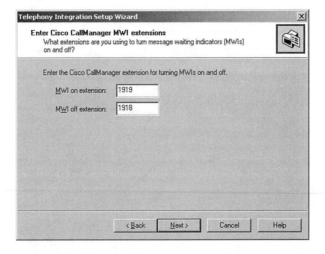

Configure the same MWI Off and MWI On codes that were previously configured in CUCM. This is displayed in Figure 18-22.

Figure 18-22   *Unity Telephony Integration Manager Wizard (Step 6)*

Configure the number of ports that have been licensed for the Cisco Unity server. Configure the CallManager device name prefix that is configured identically in CUCM. Click the Verify button to test the ports between the two systems. Do not proceed until the test completes successfully. If the test fails, troubleshoot the integration configuration parameters. If the test completes successfully, click **OK** in the Test window, and then click **Next**. This is displayed in Figure 18-23.

Figure 18-23 *Unity Telephony Integration Manager Wizard (Step 7)*

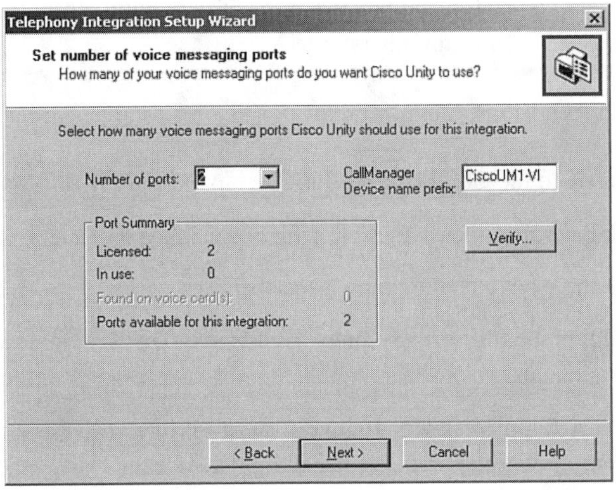

Verify that the information configuration information is correct. Click **Finish** to complete the integration tasks.

The Integration Manager now prompts you to restart the Cisco Unity services. Click **Yes** to restart the Cisco Unity services. This is displayed in Figure 18-24. The task tray icon is a good indicator of the Cisco Unity services state. A red X indicates the services are down.

Figure 18-24 *Unity Telephony Integration Manager Wizard (Step 8)*

A compatibility matrix called the Cisco Unity SCCP Compatibility Matrix is available at Cisco.com (http://www.cisco.com/en/US/docs/voice_ip_comm/unity/compatibility/matrix/cutspmtx.html). Refer to most recent information to figure out whether the Cisco Unity-CM TSP and the CUCM versions are compatible. This information is crucial for planning an upgrade.

The compatibility matrix provides information about the version of the Cisco Unity-CM TSP that is required for a specific version of CUCM. Download the appropriate version to your Cisco Unity system and then start the installation of the Cisco Unity-CM TSP.

NOTE   Do not use the CUCM-provided TSP for Cisco Unity.

Cisco Unity Subscriber Configuration

Each phone user who needs a mailbox in Cisco Unity requires a subscriber account created in the Cisco Unity System Administrator (SA).

To add a subscriber, follow these steps:

Step 1 Navigate to the Cisco Unity Admin web page and log in.

Step 2 Click the Subscriber hyperlink, which is displayed in Figure 18-25.

Step 3 Click the + sign to add a new subscriber.

Step 4 Configure the following settings: Last Name, Display Name and Extension, and so on.

Step 5 Click the floppy disk icon to save. The subscriber will be configured for self-enrollment the first time he attempts to use the Unity voice-mail system. Figure 18-26 shows the Add Subscriber page.

> **NOTE** Additional Unity information is available in *Cisco Unity Deployment and Solutions Guide* (Cisco Press, 2004).

Figure 18-25 *Unity Subscriber Profile Configuration Page*

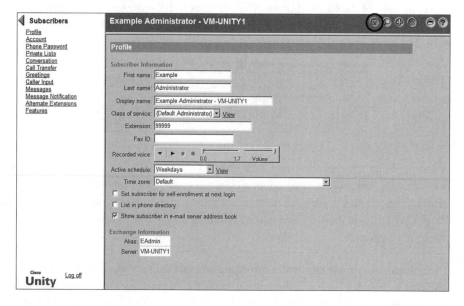

Figure 18-26   *Unity Add New Subscriber Configuration Page*

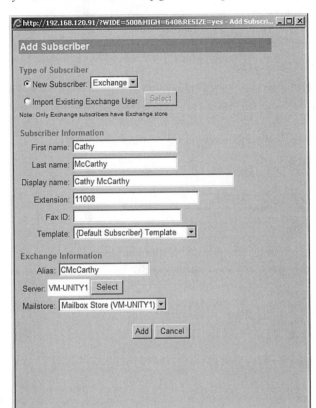

Chapter Summary

The following list summarizes the key points that were discussed in this chapter:

- Cisco Unity can integrate with multiple CUCM clusters if they are connected via Q.SIG trunks.

- Cisco Unity has an auto-attendant function integrated.

- The voice-mail ports have to be added manually to the hunt list.

- The voice-mail settings are assigned to the line by selecting a voice-mail profile.

- The voice-mail port names configured in CUCM must match the CallManager device name prefix on the Unity side.

References

For additional information, refer to http://www.ciscounitytools.com.

Review Questions

Use the questions here to review what you learned in this chapter. The correct answers are found in Appendix A, "Answers to Chapter Review Questions."

1. Which voice-mail integration protocol uses an RS-233 link?

   a. SMDI

   b. SCCP

   c. AMIS

   d. SIP

2. Where are Cisco Unity voice mails stored?

   a. Information store

   b. SQL server database

   c. Message store

   d. Active Directory

3. Where is the configuration information of a subscriber account stored in Cisco Unity?

   a. Information store

   b. SQL server database

   c. Message store

   d. Active Directory

4. Which component requires a calling search space that allows access to the MWI On and Off codes?

   a. Voice-mail port

   b. Voice-mail pilot

   c. Voice-mail profile

   d. Hunt pilot

5. Which call-distribution component is configured with a directory number that matches the voice-mail pilot?

    a. Voice-mail port

    b. Hunt pilot

    c. Hunt list

    d. Voice-mail profile

    e. Line group

6. Pressing the Messages button on the Cisco IP Phone dials which element?

    a. Voice-mail port

    b. Voice-mail pilot

    c. Voice-mail profile

    d. Hunt pilot

7. Which component on Cisco Unity converts SCCP to message calls that can be used by the message and information store?

    a. TAPI

    b. MAPI

    c. JTAPI

    d. TSP

8. Where is a voice-mail profile assigned?

    a. Phone

    b. Directory number

    c. Call-routing database

    d. Translation pattern

CHAPTER 19

Cisco Unified Video Advantage

Cisco Unified Video Advantage (CUVA) is a video telephony solution comprising the CUVA software and Cisco Video Telephony (VT) Camera, a USB camera. With the Cisco VT Camera attached to a PC co-located with a Cisco IP Phone, users can place and receive video calls on the enterprise IP telephony network. Video to the desktop represents a paradigm shift in business communications.

Chapter Objectives

Upon completing this chapter, you will be able to configure CUVA and Cisco Unified Communications Manager (CUCM) to make video telephony calls. You will also be able to meet these objectives:

■ Describe CUVA.

■ Describe the protocols used between the components of CUVA.

■ Describe how to configure CUCM to support CUVA.

■ Describe how to install CUVA on a PC.

■ Describe how to verify and diagnose CUVA operation on a PC.

CUVA Overview

CUVA brings video telephony functionality to all the Cisco Unified IP Phone Type B phone models and the higher-end Type A models (7940 and 7960). The software is coupled with a USB camera that allows a PC connected to a Cisco IP Phone to add video to telephone calls without requiring any extra button pushing or mouse clicking. Versions of the Video Advantage software later than 2.0 allow any USB-based video device to be used with the CUVA software. A Cisco IP Phone enabled with CUVA has the features and functionality of a full-featured IP video phone. Supplementary services, such as call forward, transfer, hold, and mute, are available for video calls. CUVA is intended for desktop-to-desktop IP video telephony environments, not as a general-purpose videoconferencing solution for use in conference rooms.

CUCM Release 4.0(1) with Service Release 2 or later is required to run CUVA.

NOTE   When you are using Cisco IP Communicator 2.0 or later and CUVA 2.0 or later, CUVA can interact with Cisco IP Communicator and a Cisco IP Phone. CUVA and Cisco IP Communicator have to run on the same PC in this case.

CUVA software provides the user with an easy-to-use graphical interface, including these options:

- **Camera On**: Users can turn the camera on and off.

- **Video Check**: Users can check their video before calls are placed or received.

- **Mute Video on Audio Mute**: When users mute the audio on the IP phone, video is automatically paused until the audio on the IP phone is restored.

- **Video Signal Indicators**: The quality of the incoming and outgoing video is graphically displayed.

- **Connectivity Indicator**: Graphics are used to indicate the state of the connection from the PC to its associated Cisco IP Phone or Cisco IP Communicator.

The CUVA software must be running on a computer connected directly to the PC access port on the back of the Cisco IP Phone for the video client and phone to associate to each other. The Cisco IP Phone registers its video capabilities with CUCM after it associates with CUVA.

If a call is placed between two video-capable IP Phones, the call is transparently set up as a video call where the audio channel is on the IP phone and the video channel is on the PC.

The mid-call feature allows the video stream to be brought up at any time during an audio call as soon as CUVA is started on the PC. The association between the phone and computer is illustrated in Figure 19-1.

Figure 19-1 *Phone and CUVA Association*

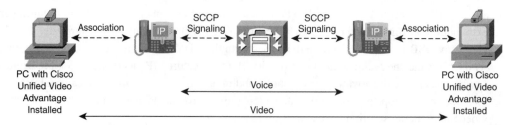

CUVA supports three types of video codecs: H.263, H.264, and the Cisco wideband video codec. The Cisco wideband video codec places the least demand on the PC because there is little to no compression of the video stream. The uncompressed video stream will require 7 Mbps of bandwidth resources.

More CPU power is needed to run the H.263 and H.264 compressed video codecs, but they require far less bandwidth resources on the network. Ensure that your PCs have enough CPU and memory resources available before running the H.263 or H.264 video codecs. The CUVA H.263 and H.264 codecs support a bandwidth range from 50 kbps to 1.5 Mbps.

CUVA Communication Flows

CUVA leverages several communications protocols, as detailed in Table 19-1.

Table 19-1   *CUVA Communication Protocols*

Networking Protocol	Description	Usage Notes
Cisco Audio Session Tunnel (CAST)	Allows communication between the Cisco IP Phone and associated software, such as CUVA. TCP source and destination port 4224. Cisco proprietary protocol.	CAST is used between CUVA and the IP phone to build an association. The PC discovers the IP phone, using Cisco Discovery Protocol (CDP). CAST is also used to send signaling information for video streams from the IP phone to CUVA. CAST signaling features include call video stream start and stop, hold, and resume.
Cisco Discovery Protocol (CDP)	Layer 2 Cisco proprietary device discovery protocol that runs on Cisco manufactured equipment. Works only between directly connected equipment.	CUVA uses CDP to communicate its capabilities to the Cisco IP Phone, and the Cisco IP Phone uses CDP to communicate information, such as its IP address, to CUVA.
Real-Time Transport Protocol (RTP)	A standard for using User Datagram Protocol (UDP) to transport real-time data, such as interactive voice and video, over data networks.	RTP is used to encapsulate and stream the audio (between Cisco IP Phones) and video (between CUVA endpoints).
Skinny Client Control Protocol (SCCP)	A Cisco protocol using low-bandwidth messages that allows the exchange of signaling messages between IP devices and the CUCM. Uses TCP port 2000.	CUVA does not use SCCP itself. It uses CAST to send signaling messages to the Cisco IP Phone, which acts as a proxy and passes the signaling messages to CUCM using SCCP.

When a Windows PC runs CUVA using a hardware-based Cisco IP Phone, the PC should be connected to the PC port of the Cisco Unified IP Phone. In most configurations, the PC will be in a different VLAN from the Cisco IP Phone. All IP-based communication between CUVA and the Cisco IP Phone needs to be routed. Only CDP is exchanged directly.

CDP exchange between the IP phone and Video Advantage application takes place so that CUVA and the Cisco IP Phone can discover one another. A CDP driver is installed and bound to the TCP/IP stack on the PC during the installation of CUVA. This driver allows the CUVA application to dynamically learn the IP address of the Cisco IP Phone during the CDP exchange and associate with it. This feature allows mobility of the application between different IP phones on the network. The user may connect a PC to the PC port of any video-enabled Cisco IP Phone on the network and begin making video telephony calls. CDP also provides a measure of security in that the IP Phone responds only to association messages from a CUVA client that matches the IP address of the device that is connected to its PC port, minimizing the risk of someone else associating with your Cisco IP Phone over the network and receiving video when calls are placed on your IP phone. The Cisco IP Phone begins listening for CAST messages on TCP port 4224.

CUVA and the IP phone then exchange CAST protocol messages over TCP/IP. CUVA sends a CAST message to the IP phone, which is normally in a different IP subnet (VLAN). The packet first travels through the PC VLAN to the default gateway, where it is routed toward the IP phone. The CAST protocol allows CUVA to associate with the IP phone and receive event messages from the IP phone when calls are placed or received. After this association process occurs between the CUVA client and the IP phone, the IP phone updates its registration status with CUCM, advising CUCM of its video capabilities.

The Cisco IP Phone acts as a proxy toward CUVA for the setup of video streams. Only the signaling is proxied through the phone. The IP phone specifies the IP address of the PC for the video stream and its own IP address for the audio stream. CUCM communicates only with the Cisco IP Phone to set up video calls. The IP phone then communicates the video setup to CUVA using the CAST protocol. The CAST messages between the IP phone and CUVA have to be routed between the voice and the PC VLAN again.

Figure 19-2 illustrates the following video call process:

Step 1   CDP runs on both the Cisco IP Phone and the CUVA application on the desktop PC. The CDP announcement from the Cisco IP Phone includes the IP address of the Cisco IP Phone.

Step 2   The PC initiates a CAST association to the Cisco IP Phone. Because the Cisco IP Phone is in a different IP subnet (VLAN), the PC sends the association to the Layer 2 destination MAC address of the router to be routed to the Cisco IP Phone's IP subnet (VLAN). The PC and Cisco IP Phone create an association to each other.

Step 3   A user picks up the Cisco IP Phone and dials an extension that is video enabled and running CUVA. CUCM sends SCCP signaling to the Cisco IP Phone indicating that it should open a video call. The Cisco IP Phone contacts the desktop PC to indicate.

Step 4   The Cisco IP Phone opens an RTP bearer audio channel with the destination phone, and the PC opens an RTP bearer video channel with the destination PC's CUVA application.

Figure 19-2   *Video Call Setup*

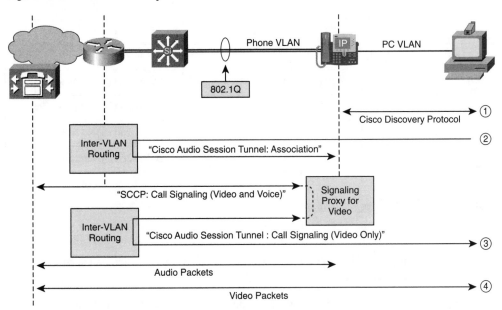

The audio channel of a video stream consists of the audio codecs used by CUCM. The G.711 audio codec bit rate is 64 kbps, and the G.729 audio codec is 8 kbps.

The bit rate available for the video channel depends on the audio codec and the video call speed. The video channel bit rate is the speed of the video call minus the bit rate of the audio codec. A 384-kbps video call with G.711 audio will create a video channel of 320 kbps (384 kbps minus 64 kbps). A G.729 audio codec with the same video speed (384 kbps) would result in a 376 kbps video channel (384 kbps minus 8 kbps).

Table 19-2 lists video call speeds with different audio codecs and the resulting video channel bit rates.

Table 19-2 *Video Bit Rates*

Video Call Speed	Audio Code / Rate	Video Codec / Rate
128 kbps	G.711 (64 kbps)	H.263/H.264 (64 kbps)
128 kbps	G.729 (8 kbps)	H.263/H.264 (120 kbps)
128 kbps	G.728 (16 kbps)	H.263/H.264 (112 kbps)
384 kbps	G.711 (64 kbps)	H.263/H.264 (376 kbps)
384 kbps	G.729 (8 kbps)	H.263/H.264 (320 kbps)
768 kbps	G.729 (8 kbps)	H.263/H.264 (760 kbps)
768 kbps	G.711 (64 kbps)	H.263/H.264 (704 kbps)
1.472 Mbps	G.729 (8 kbps)	H.263/H.264 (1.464 Mbps)
1.472 Mbps	G.711 (64 kbps)	H.263/H.264 (1.408 Mbps)
7 Mbps	G.729 (8 kbps)	H.263/H.264 (6.992 Mbps)
7 Mbps	G.711 (64 kbps)	H.263/H.264 (6.936 Mbps)

CUCM Configuration

CUCM CUVA configuration includes the following steps:

Step 1   Configure regions with the maximum audio codec and video call speed to be used per video call.

Step 2   Configure the maximum allowed bandwidth used by video calls within or between locations.

Step 3   Configure the IP phone in CUCM to support CUVA.

Step 4   Verify CUVA support on the IP phone.

The CUCM region configuration specifies the audio codec type to use between regions, and the video setting specifies the bandwidth to use between regions. The audio codec and video call bandwidth fields perform similar functions. The audio codec value defines the maximum bit rate allowed for the audio channel in both audio only and video calls, and the video call bandwidth value defines the maximum bit rate for both the audio and video channel in a video call.

A video bandwidth value of none would pass audio-only calls, if the calling device has the Retry Video Call as Audio option enabled. The region settings are configured under **System > Region**. Each region must be configured to set the relationship to the other regions. The region configuration is illustrated in Figure 19-3.

Figure 19-3   *Region Configuration*

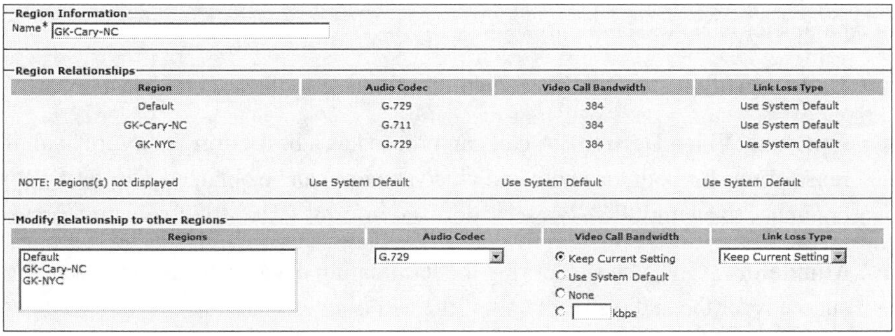

The locations configuration in CUCM applies call admission control (CAC) to limit the number of audio and video calls that can be placed between locations. Locations typically represent geographical sites that are separated over an IP WAN.

Both the Audio Bandwidth and the Video Bandwidth fields offer the options of Unlimited and a numeric bandwidth value. Video bandwidth can be set to None to disallow video calls over the IP WAN (between locations). If numeric values are configured, they use two different calculation models:

- **Audio Bandwidth field**: The value entered has to include the Layer 3 (IP) and Layer 4 (UDP/RTP) overhead required for the call. G.729 calls require 24 kbps because the audio codec operates at 8kbps, and the overhead operates at 16kbps. G.711 calls require 80 kbps because the audio codec operates at 64 kbps, and the overhead operates at 16kbps.

- **Video Bandwidth field**: The value in the Video Bandwidth field is entered without overhead factoring. The video bandwidth is dynamically configured by subtracting the audio codec bandwidth from the full video bandwidth allowed.

Resource Reservation Protocol (RSVP) is the only topology-aware CAC mechanism. The H.323 gatekeeper and locations CAC mechanisms are not topology aware. H.323 gatekeepers and locations work on a hub-and-spoke physical topology premise. Most WANs today are partial-mesh or full-mesh environments using Multiprotocol Label Switching

(MPLS) virtual private networks (VPN). H.323 gatekeepers and locations can still be used in these environments with branch-to-branch connectivity, but the CAC mechanisms would not be able to make full use of the topologies' bandwidth capabilities. RSVP settings include the following:

- **Use System Default**: The RSVP policy to the selected location matches the CUCM Default Interlocation RSVP Policy service parameter. The default value for this service parameter is No Reservation.

- **No Reservation**: No RSVP reservations are made to the selected location.

- **Optional (Video Desired)**: A call can proceed as a best-effort audio-only call if no reservations for both the audio and video streams can be obtained. Cisco RSVP Agent continues to attempt RSVP reservation and informs CUCM if reservation succeeds.

- **Mandatory**: CUCM does not ring the terminating device until RSVP reservation succeeds for the audio stream and, if the call is a video call, for the video stream as well.

- **Mandatory (Video Desired)**: A video call can proceed as an audio-only call if a reservation for the video stream cannot be obtained.

Most CUCM administrators use the RSVP system default.

> **NOTE** More information about CAC using locations and RSVP-enabled locations is provided in the *Cisco Unified Communications IP Telephony, Part 2*.

To configure locations, navigate to **System > Locations** via CUCM Administration. Location configuration is illustrated in Figure 19-4.

Figure 19-4 *Location Configuration*

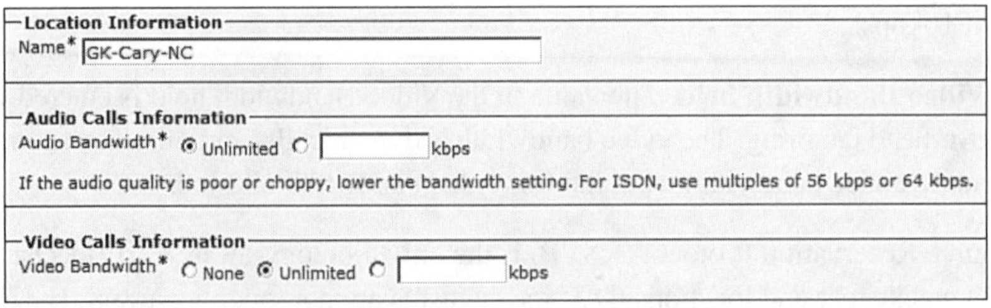

You can find the IP phone configuration settings that are required for video support in the IP Phone Configuration window of CUCM Administration. The following configurations are necessary:

■ The PC that has CUVA installed needs to be physically connected to a PC port of the IP phone. Ensure that the PC port of the IP phone is not disabled under the CUCM IP phone configuration. The PC port is enabled by default.

■ The Video Capabilities field needs to be set to Enabled to allow the phone to participate in video calls. The video capabilities are disabled by default.

The Retry Video Call as Audio check box is located in the Phone Configuration window and is activated by default. If you uncheck this check box, a video call that fails to connect is not attempted as an audio-only call instead. Figure 19-5 shows the video-related settings of the IP phone.

Figure 19-5 *Phone Video Settings*

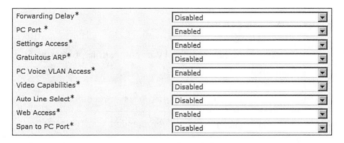

An IP phone or IP Communicator enabled for video displays a video camera icon in the lower-right corner of its LCD screen. Figure 19-6 shows this icon in IP Communicator.

Figure 19-6 *IP Phone Video Verification*

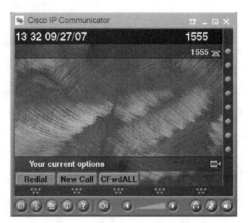

CUVA Installation

CUVA installation includes the following steps:

Step 1   Verify hardware requirements.

Step 2   Verify software requirements.

Step 3   Install CUVA software and hardware.

Table 19-3 displays the recommended installation requirements to install CUVA.

Table 19-3   *CUVA Installation Requirements*

PC Feature	Minimum Requirements
CPU	CUVA using H.263: 1.9 GHz or higher Pentium IV or compatible processor (Streaming SIMD Extensions support required) CUVA using H.264: 2.4 GHz or higher Pentium IV or compatible processor (Streaming SIMD Extensions support required) 2.8 GHz or higher compatible processor recommended
System memory	512 MB minimum, 1 GB recommended
Free disk space	At least 100 MB, 200 MB when being used with Cisco IP Communicator
USB port	At least 1 free USB (1.1 or 2.0 compliant) port, Version 2.0 recommended
Video display	Minimum: DirectX 9.0-compatible graphics card with 32 MB of video RAM; for dual-headed configurations, 64 MB Recommended: DirectX 9.0-compatible graphics card with 64 MB of video RAM; for dual-headed configurations, 128 MB
Network	Minimum: 10/100 network interface card (NIC)

The minimum requirement for the operating system of the PC is either Microsoft Windows 2000 Professional with Service Pack 4 or later or Microsoft Windows XP Professional with Service Pack 2 or later. CUVA 2.1 supports the Microsoft Windows Vista operating system.

NOTE   Ensure CAST connectivity between the Cisco IP Telephony device and CUVA application. A host-based intrusion prevention system or personal firewall might block this communication by default.

Launch the installation file and complete these steps (illustrated in Figure 19-7):

Step 1   Make sure that the Cisco VT Camera is *not* connected to the PC.

Step 2   Follow the instructions in the dialog boxes that appear to complete the installation of CUVA:

- In the Welcome window, click **Next** to start the Installation wizard.

- In the License Agreement window, click **I Accept the Terms in the License Agreement**, and then click **Next**.

- In the Destination Folder window, accept the default installation folder or click **Change** to enter a different installation folder. When you have finished, click **Next**.

- In the Ready to Install the Program window, click **Install** and wait until you see the Shortcut Options window. Depending on the setup of your PC and the operating system that you use, there might be additional windows or messages that require your attention before you get to the Shortcut Options window.

- In the Shortcut Options window, make your choices about icons to be added to the Quick Launch bar or to the desktop. You can also choose whether you want CUVA to be started automatically at system startup. Click **Next** when you have made your selection.

- A window appears indicating that the installation has been completed. Confirm the message by clicking **Finish**.

- If you are prompted to restart the PC, click **Yes** to restart the PC.

Step 3   When prompted by the installation, plug in the camera. All necessary drivers are installed to the system.

Step 4   After the new hardware has been added, the PC needs to be rebooted. CUVA is ready to be used.

Figure 19-7 *CUVA Installation*

① Install Cisco Unified Video Advantage with Installation Wizard.

② Plug in camera.

③ Camera will be found automatically.

④ Installation is complete.

CUVA Verification Tools

Verify the association of CUVA and the IP phone or Cisco IP Communicator from the status displayed on the CUVA application window.

When the CUVA application is started, it will show icons for the Cisco VT Camera in the middle, Cisco IP Communicator on the left, and an IP phone on the right. A successful CAST association is indicated by a green line, and an unsuccessful connection is indicated by a broken red line. Figure 19-8 shows an example of a successful and unsuccessful connection.

Figure 19-8 *CUVA Verification*

The video-check verification of CUVA enables the end user to verify the send and receive configuration of the video client. Choose **Video** > **Start Video Check** from the CUVA client or click the button in the lower-right corner of the CUVA application window. While the video check is being performed, two popup windows appear. One popup window displays the Local view, and the other popup window display the Remote view. The lower right of each window displays green bars if they are successful transmitting or receiving data. During the video check, the same image appears in both windows, as shown in Figure 19-9.

Figure 19-9 *CUVA Video Check*

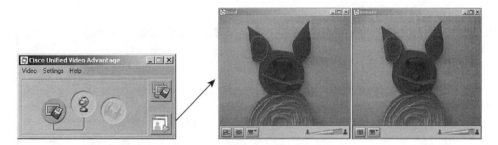

During an active call, the Diagnostics tool can be launched to obtain valuable troubleshooting information. The Diagnostics tool provides some technical details about the current state of the CUVA software that is running on the PC and some indications about the Cisco VT Camera frame rates and errors.

To use the Diagnostics tool, open the CUVA main window and double right-click the application window. The Diagnostics window appears. Do not double left-click (double-click). Only a double right-click will bring up the video diagnostics window.

The Diagnostics tool allows monitoring of CDP messages, CAST packets, and active call statistics. Figure 19-10 shows the Diagnostics tool.

Figure 19-10   *CUVA Diagnostics Tool*

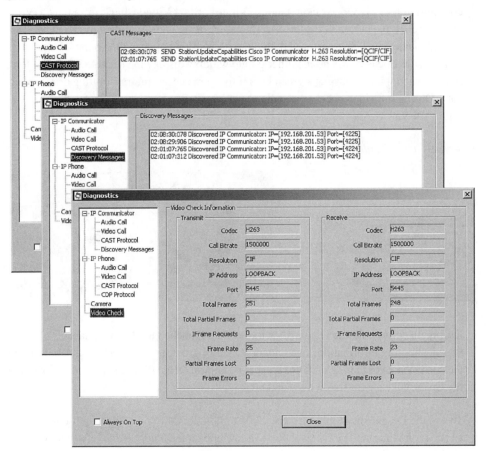

Chapter Summary

The following list summarizes the key points that were discussed in this chapter:

- CUVA adds video capabilities to Cisco IP Phones by using software and a camera on a PC attached to the IP phone.

- CUVA discovers the IP phone by listening to CDP messages and uses the CAST protocol to associate with the IP phone and to send and receive signaling messages.

- To enable CUVA, IP phones have to be video enabled, and regions and locations have to be configured to permit video calls.

- Before installing CUVA on the PC, verify hardware and software requirements.

- CUVA includes tools to verify the association with the IP phone, check the camera, and perform diagnostics.

References

For additional information, refer to these resources:

- **Installation and Troubleshooting Guide for Cisco Unified Video Advantage Release 2.0**: http://www.cisco.com/en/US/docs/video/cuva/2_0/english/adminstration/guide/admin2_0.html

- **CUCM Administration Guide, Release 6.0(1)**: http://www.cisco.com/en/US/docs/voice_ip_comm/cucm/admin/6_0_1/ccmcfg/bccm.pdf

- **Cisco Unified Communications SRND Based on CUCM 6.x**: http://www.cisco.com/go/srnd

Review Questions

Use the questions here to review what you learned in this chapter. The correct answers are found in Appendix A, "Answers to Chapter Review Questions."

1. Which Cisco IP Phone does not support Cisco Unified Video Advantage?

   a. 7940

   b. 7960

   c. 7911

   d. 7912

2. How many RTP bearer channels are used for a video call?

   a. One

   b. Two

   c. None

   d. Three

3. Which two video codecs support a compression rate of 384 kbps?

   a. H.260

   b. H.261

   c. H.263

   d. H.264

4. Which protocol is used by the Cisco IP Phone to discover the Cisco Unified Video Advantage client?

   a. CDP

   b. CAST

   c. SCCP

   d. RTP

5. Which protocol is used to proxy SCCP signaling from the Cisco IP Phone to the Cisco Unified Video Advantage client?

   a. CDP

   b. CAST

   c. SCCP

   d. RTP

6. Which protocol is used for signaling with CUCM?

   a. SIP

   b. SCCP

   c. H.323

   d. MGCP

7. What speed will a video channel use if 384 kbps is configured with the G.729 audio codec?

   a. 384 kbps

   b. 376 kbps

   c. 320 kbps

   d. 256 kbps

8. What call admission control mechanism is used with video in centralized call-processing architectures?

    a. Gatekeeper

    b. Regions

    c. Device pool

    d. Locations

Answers to Chapter Review Questions

Chapter 1

1. C
2. D
3. C
4. B
5. C
6. A
7. E
8. D
9. D
10. C

Chapter 2

1. C
2. D
3. A
4. B
5. B
6. C
7. C
8. A
9. C

Chapter 3
1. B
2. A, C, and D
3. A, C, and D

Chapter 4
1. D
2. C
3. A
4. E
5. F
6. A
7. D
8. B and D
9. C

Chapter 5
1. C
2. B and C
3. C
4. B
5. B
6. A
7. B
8. B
9. A
10. C

Chapter 6

1. A

2. D

3. D

4. C

5. A

6. C

7. A

8. C

9. B

Chapter 7

1. A, B, and C

2. A

3. A

4. A and B

5. A

6. B

7. B

8. D

9. A

10. C

Chapter 8

1. B
2. D
3. D
4. C
5. A
6. A
7. A
8. C
9. C
10. B

Chapter 9

1. A
2. D
3. D
4. A
5. A
6. B
7. D
8. A
9. A and D
10. A

Chapter 10

1. B
2. C
3. C
4. A
5. A
6. A and E
7. D

Chapter 11

1. A
2. A
3. B
4. A
5. B
6. E
7. C and D

Chapter 12

1. A
2. B
3. C
4. A
5. B
6. D
7. C
8. C
9. D
10. C

Chapter 13

1. A
2. B
3. A
4. B and C
5. D
6. C
7. E
8. C
9. D
10. C

Chapter 14

1. A
2. C
3. A and B
4. B
5. D
6. C
7. D
8. A
9. D
10. C

Chapter 15

1. A

2. C

3. A

4. B and D

5. D

6. A and C

7. B and D

8. A

9. B

10. C

Chapter 16

1. A

2. C

3. D

4. A

5. A and D

6. C

7. A

8. A and B

9. B and C

Chapter 17

1. A
2. C
3. A
4. A
5. A
6. A, B, and C
7. B
8. A
9. A, B, and E
10. B

Chapter 18

1. A
2. C
3. A
4. A
5. B
6. B
7. D
8. B

Chapter 19

1. D

2. B

3. C and D

4. A

5. A

6. B

7. B

8. D

Index

Symbols

? command, 81

Numerics

1 call-processing redundancy, 46–48
802.1q trunk ports, 175–175
911 emergency, 331

A

AAR (automated alternate routing), 287
abbreviated dialing, 252
access control, Cisco UC database, 17
activating feature services on CUCM, 99
adding IP phones to CUCM, 186, 208–216
    via auto registration, 202–205
    via BAT, 206–207
Administration interface (CUCM), 75–76
alerts available for hold reversion, 414
annunciators, 369, 373
application users
    LDAPv3 synchronization, 128
    user accounts, 114
        managing, 119–121, 124–125
        privileges, 115–116
applications layer (Cisco UC), 6
assigning privileges to end users, 117
associating end user accounts with phones, 428
attributes of end users, 114
authentication
    LDAPv3 authentication, 126, 134
        configuring, 137
    SIP third-party IP phones, 159-161

B

auto registration
    adding IP phones to CUCM, 202–203
    configuring, 204–205
automating call pickup, 412

bandwidth configuration (CUVA), 495
Barge feature
    cBarge, configuring, 426
    configuring, 425
basic installation (CUCM), 61–63
BAT (Bulk Administration Tool), 118
    adding IP phones to CUCM, 206–210, 212–213
        TAPS phone insertion process, 207
BLF Speed Dial, configuring, 441
boot sequence of Cisco IP Phones, 151–152, 154
BPS (Bulk Provisioning Service), 209
broadcast distribution algorithm, 347

C

calculating required phone licences, 25
Call Back feature, configuring, 422–423
call classification, 278
call control layer (Cisco UC), 5
call coverage, 340
call forwarding, 340
    examples, 356, 359–361
call hunting, 340–342, 348
    call forwarding options, examples, 356, 359–361
    configuring, 350–352
    hunt forward settings, 354–356
    hunt lists, 345
        adding, 352

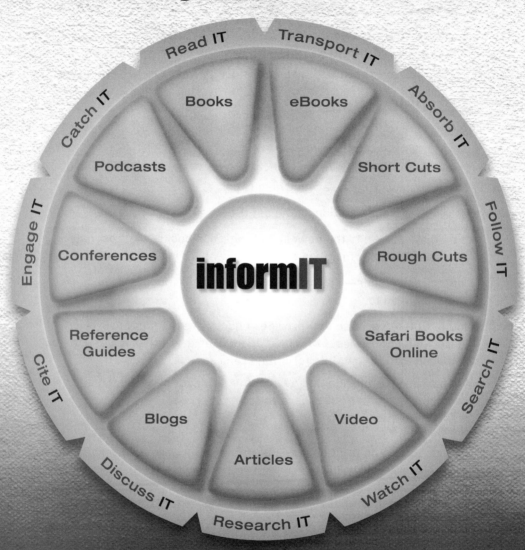

Go Beyond the Book

inform**IT**

Read IT
- Books
- eBooks

Transport IT

Absorb IT
- Short Cuts

Catch IT
- Podcasts

Engage IT
- Conferences

Follow IT
- Rough Cuts

Cite IT
- Reference Guides

Search IT
- Safari Books Online

Discuss IT
- Blogs

Watch IT
- Video

Research IT
- Articles

11 WAYS TO LEARN IT at **www.informIT.com/learn**

The digital network for the publishing imprints of Pearson Education

 Addison Cisco Press EXAM/CRAM **IBM** QUE   SAMS

34861630R10342

Made in the USA
Middletown, DE
30 January 2019